507 Taste of Home Recipes in One Big Book Make for a Year of Terrific Eating!

TASTE OF HOME magazine features the best food shared by fantastic cooks from across the country—that's what makes it America's #1 cooking magazine...and what makes our annual cookbooks a yearly "must-have" as well.

This *2006 Taste of Home Annual Recipes* cookbook contains every single delicious recipe published during 2005, plus 19 "bonus" recipes—507 recipes in all—so you have a year's worth of terrific eating in one convenient recipe collection!

Whether you're fixing dinner for your family, cooking for a holiday crowd or simply whipping up something for yourself, you'll have plenty of fitting recipes from which to choose. To get you started, take a peek at the winners of our six national recipes contests held last year.

• Candy Creations. At Christmastime, even those who don't normally crave candy are tempted by festive trays full of the treats. Cookie Dough Truffles (p. 120) appealed the most to our judges' sweet tooths, taking first place. Adorable Coconut Snowmen (p. 123) rolled away with a close second.

• Choice Chicken. Versatile and lip-smacking good, chicken has long been a favorite for summer picnics and Sunday dinners. The taste panel eagerly filled their plates with contest-winner Spinach Crab Chicken (p. 75) and second-place finisher Grilled Raspberry Chicken (p. 75).

• Best-Ever Brownies. Need a lunch box goodie or an after-school snack? A potluck pleaser or dressed-up dessert? Scrumptious brownies fill the bill, as grand-prize winner Blond Brownies a la Mode (p. 110) and runner-up Coffee 'n' Cream Brownies (p. 108) deliciously prove. Yum!

• Sensational Strawberries. Sweet and juicy, fresh strawberries are the stars of early summer menus. Strawberry Cream Crepes (p. 154) put that seasonal berry to wonderful use, winning top honors. In second place, Strawberry Tartlets (p. 155) are ripe for the picking, too.

• Carrot Call-Out. Cooks know that carrots are good for you and also add flavor and color to meals. Party Carrots (p. 48) were so popular with our judges that the dish was picked the best of

the bunch. Layered Carrot Cake (p. 130) was rooted out from the entries and awarded second place.

• Crisps & Cobblers. The mixture of sweet baked fruit, a crunchy topping and a cool dollop of whipped cream or ice cream is not only yummy but comforting, too. Apple Crumble (p. 148) topped our judges' list of favorites, while Blueberry Cornmeal Cobbler (p. 149) came in second.

With 507 recipes in this big colorful cookbook, you won't run out of dishes to prepare for your family any time soon. You're sure to find something for everyone and every occasion.

OH-SO-COMFORTING. Apple Crumble (p. 148) won the grand prize and Blueberry Cornmeal Cobbler (p. 149) took second place in our national "Crisps & Cobblers" contest.

2006 Taste of Home Annual Recipes

Editor: Jean Steiner
Art Director: Lori Arndt
Executive Editor/Books: Heidi Reuter Lloyd
Senior Editor/Books: Julie Schnittka
Graphic Art Associates:
Ellen Lloyd, Catherine Fletcher
Proofreader: Julie Blume
Editorial Assistant: Barb Czysz

Taste of Home®

Executive Editor: Kathy Pohl
Food Editor: Janaan Cunningham
Associate Food Editors:
Diane Werner RD, Coleen Martin
Managing Editor: Ann Kaiser
Assistant Managing Editor: Barbara Schuetz
Art Director: Emma Acevedo
Copy Editor: S.K. Enk
Senior Recipe Editor: Sue A. Jurack
Recipe Editors: Janet Briggs, Mary King
Test Kitchen Director: Mark Morgan RD
Assistant Food Editor: Karen Wright
Senior Home Economist: Patricia Schmeling
Test Kitchen Home Economists:
Nancy Fridirici, Peggy Fleming RD,
Tina Johnson, Ann Liebergen,
Wendy Stenman, Amy Welk-Thieding
Test Kitchen Assistants: Suzanne Kern,
Rita Krajcir, Kris Lehman, Sue Megonigle,
Megan Taylor
Editorial Assistants: Barb Czysz,
Mary Ann Koebernik
Set Stylists: Julie Ferron,
Stephanie Marchese, Sue Myers,
Jennifer Bradley Vent
Food Photographers: Rob Hagen,
Dan Roberts, Jim Wieland
Food Stylists: Kristin Arnett,
Sarah Thompson, Joylyn Trickel
Photographers' Assistant: Lori Foy
Senior Vice President, Editor in Chief:
Catherine Cassidy
President: Barbara Newton
Chairman and Founder: Roy Reiman

Taste of Home Books
©2005 Reiman Media Group, Inc.
5400 S. 60th St., Greendale WI 53129

International Standard Book Number:
0-89821-457-2
International Standard Serial Number:
1094-3463

PICTURED AT RIGHT: Clockwise from upper left: Banana Split Brownie Pie (p. 128), Santa Fe Cheesecake (p. 6), Brisket with Cranberry Gravy (p. 63), Sensational Slush (p. 7) and Peachy Chicken, Bacon Onion Asparagus and Golden Garlic Bread (p. 257).

Taste of Home 2006 Annual Recipes

PICTURED ON FRONT COVER. Clockwise from upper left: Chocolate Torte (p. 211), Triple-Cheese Macaroni (p. 236) and Ribs with a Kick (p. 76).

PICTURED ON BACK COVER. Clockwise from upper left: Lattice Blackberry Bars (p. 102), Fluffy Raspberry Torte (p. 150) and Chocolate Berry Cheesecake (p. 153).

For additional copies of this book, write *Taste of Home* Books, P.O. Box 908, Greendale WI 53129.

To order by credit card, call toll-free 1-800/344-2560 or visit our Web site at www.reimanpub.com.

Snacks & Beverages

Whether you're relaxing with family watching TV or hosting a party with friends, the evening won't be complete without some fun snacks and beverages.

GRAB SOME SNACKS. Clockwise from upper left: Garlic-Herb Potato Nests (p. 23), Cheddar Shrimp Nachos (p. 12), Warm Savory Cheese Spread (p. 8), Spiced Citrus Cider (p. 8) and Roasted Pepper Tart (p. 10).

minutes or until center is almost set.

Place pan on a wire rack. Spread sour cream over cheesecake. Carefully run a knife around the edge of the pan to loosen; cool for 1 hour. Refrigerate overnight. Remove sides of pan just before serving. Garnish with yellow pepper, onions and tomato. Refrigerate leftovers. **Yield:** 16-20 servings.

Passover Meatballs

Prep: 30 min.   **Cook:** 50 min.

These moist and slightly sweet meatballs are popular with family and friends during the spring holiday season. They're bound to become a tradition at your house.
—*Julie Sollinger, Chicago, Illinois*

      2 eggs, lightly beaten
      1 cup water, *divided*
1-1/2 cups finely chopped onion, *divided*
    1/2 cup matzo meal
      1 teaspoon salt
    1/4 teaspoon pepper
      2 pounds ground beef
      1 can (8 ounces) tomato sauce
      1 cup sugar
    1/2 cup lemon juice

In a large bowl, combine the eggs, 1/2 cup water, 1/2 cup onion, matzo meal, salt and pepper. Crumble beef over mixture and mix well. Shape into 1-in. balls.

In a Dutch oven, combine the tomato sauce, sugar, lemon juice, and remaining water and onion. Add meatballs; bring to a boil. Reduce heat; cover and simmer for 45 minutes or until meat is no longer pink. Serve with a slotted spoon. **Yield:** 6 dozen.

Editor's Note: Matzo meal can be found in the kosher or ethnic section of your grocery store.

Santa Fe Cheesecake

(Pictured above)

Prep: 25 min.   **Bake:** 30 min. + chilling

All of my favorite Southwestern ingredients are combined in this savory cheesecake. It looks and tastes fantastic!
—*Jean Ecos, Hartland, Wisconsin*

    1 cup crushed tortilla chips
    3 tablespoons butter, melted
    2 packages (8 ounces *each*) cream cheese, softened
    2 eggs, lightly beaten
    2 cups (8 ounces) shredded Monterey Jack cheese
    1 can (4 ounces) chopped green chilies, drained
    1 cup (8 ounces) sour cream
    1 cup chopped sweet yellow pepper
  1/2 cup chopped green onions
  1/3 cup chopped tomato

Combine tortilla chips and butter; press onto bottom of a greased 9-in. springform pan. Place on a baking sheet. Bake at 325° for 15 minutes.

In a large mixing bowl, beat cream cheese and eggs on low speed just until combined. Stir in Monterey Jack cheese and chilies; pour over crust. Bake for 30-35

Chutney Dip

Prep: 5 min. + chilling

When you're looking for a dip with a difference, try this tangy blend. Made with yogurt and a healthy dash of curry, this dip goes great with all kinds of veggies.
—*Zelda De Hoedt, Cedar Rapids, Iowa*

☑ **Uses less fat, sugar or salt. Includes Nutritional Analysis and Diabetic Exchanges.**

    1 cup (8 ounces) reduced-fat plain yogurt
    3 tablespoons chutney
    2 tablespoons chopped green onions
    1 teaspoon curry powder
    1 medium green pepper
Assorted fresh vegetables

In a small bowl, combine the yogurt, chutney, onions and curry powder. Cover and refrigerate for 2 hours. Cut top off green pepper; remove seeds and membrane. Fill with dip. Serve with vegetables. **Yield:** about 1 cup.

Nutritional Analysis: 3 tablespoons dip equals 37 calories, 1 g fat (trace saturated fat), 3 mg cholesterol, 27 mg sodium, 6 g carbohydrate, trace fiber, 2 g protein. **Diabetic Exchange:** 1/2 low-fat milk.

Sensational Slush

(Pictured below)

Prep: 25 min. + freezing

Colorful and refreshing, this sweet-tart slush has become a family favorite. I freeze the mix in 2- and 4-cup containers so it can be served in small portions for individuals or the whole family. I also freeze crushed strawberries to make preparation simpler.   —Connie Friesen, Altona, Manitoba

  1/2 **cup sugar**
    1 **package (3 ounces) strawberry gelatin**
    2 **cups boiling water**
    2 **cups sliced fresh strawberries**
    1 **cup unsweetened pineapple juice**
    1 **can (12 ounces) frozen lemonade**
      concentrate, thawed
    1 **can (12 ounces) frozen limeade**
      concentrate, thawed
    2 **cups cold water**
    2 **liters lemon-lime soda, chilled**

In a large bowl, dissolve sugar and gelatin in boiling water. Place the strawberries and pineapple juice in a blender or food processor; cover and process until smooth. Add to the gelatin mixture. Stir in concentrates and cold water. Cover and freeze for 8 hours or overnight.

Remove from the freezer 45 minutes before serving. For each serving, combine 1/2 cup slush mixture with 1/2 cup lemon-lime soda; stir well. **Yield:** 20 servings.

Shrimp Jalapeno Boats

(Pictured above)

Prep/Total Time: 30 min.

These appealing "boats" make an attractive addition to any appetizer tray. We love jalapenos and so do a lot of our friends.   —Peggy Wolfgang, Canby, Oregon

  18 **medium jalapeno peppers**
    2 **cartons (8 ounces *each*) spreadable chive**
      and onion cream cheese
  1/2 **cup shredded sharp cheddar cheese**
  1/2 **cup sliced green onions**
  1/2 **pound frozen small cooked shrimp,**
      thawed

Cut jalapenos in half and remove seeds. Place in two ungreased 15-in. x 10-in. x 1-in. baking pans. In a small mixing bowl, combine the cream cheese, cheddar cheese and onions; spoon into the jalapeno halves. Top with shrimp. Bake at 400° for 18-22 minutes or until the jalapenos are tender. **Yield:** 3 dozen.

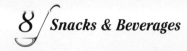

Clam-Stuffed Mushrooms

(Pictured above)

Prep: 20 min.   **Bake:** 20 min.

Seafood lovers will savor these yummy bites. I stuff mushroom caps with a pleasing combination of minced clams, cheese and seasonings.
—Maria Regakis
Somerville, Massachusetts

  24 **large fresh mushrooms**
   2 **cans (6-1/2 ounces** *each***) minced clams, drained**
 3/4 **cup dry bread crumbs**
 1/2 **cup grated Parmesan cheese**
 1/2 **cup finely chopped green pepper**
   1 **small onion, finely chopped**
   2 **garlic cloves, minced**
   2 **tablespoons Italian seasoning**
   2 **tablespoons dried parsley flakes**
 1/8 **teaspoon pepper**
1-1/2 **cups butter, melted,** *divided*
 1/2 **cup shredded mozzarella cheese**

Remove mushroom stems (discard or save for another use); set caps aside. In a large bowl, combine the clams, bread crumbs, Parmesan cheese, green pepper, onion, garlic, Italian seasoning, parsley and pepper. Stir in 3/4 cup butter. Fill each mushroom cap with about 1 tablespoon clam mixture.

Place in an ungreased 15-in. x 10-in. x 1-in. baking pan. Sprinkle with mozzarella; drizzle with remaining butter. Bake, uncovered, at 350° for 20-25 minutes or until lightly browned. Serve warm. **Yield:** 2 dozen.

Spiced Citrus Cider

(Pictured on page 4)

Prep: 10 min.   **Cook:** 1 hour

What could be better than sipping a tangy cup of this hot cider on a cold winter day? It sure warms the spirits!
—Harriet Stichter, Milford, Indiana

✓ **Uses less fat, sugar or salt. Includes Nutritional Analysis and Diabetic Exchanges.**

   5 **cups water**
   4 **medium lemons, sliced**
   4 **medium oranges, sliced**
   2 **cinnamon sticks (3 inches)**
   2 **teaspoons whole allspice**
   3 **quarts apple cider**
   1 **cup sugar**

In a large saucepan, bring the water, lemons, oranges and spices to a boil. Reduce heat; cover and simmer for 1 hour. Strain and discard fruit and spices. Transfer citrus mixture to a large soup kettle. Stir in the cider and sugar; heat through. **Yield:** 20 servings (1 gallon).

Nutritional Analysis: 3/4 cup (prepared with sugar substitute) equals 94 calories, 0 fat (0 saturated fat), 0 cholesterol, 16 mg sodium, 24 g carbohydrate, 2 g fiber, trace protein. **Diabetic Exchange:** 1-1/2 fruit.

Warm Savory Cheese Spread

(Pictured on page 4)

Prep: 15 min.   **Bake:** 1 hour

Served in a bread bowl, this colorful cheese dip gets added flavor from bacon and veggies. It's perfect for parties any time of the year.
—Marilu Hynes
McLeod Hill, New Brunswick

   2 **cups mayonnaise**
   2 **cups (8 ounces) shredded cheddar cheese**
   1 **large onion, finely chopped**
   8 **bacon strips, cooked and crumbled**
 1/2 **cup finely chopped sweet red pepper**
 1/2 **cup finely chopped green pepper**
   1 **teaspoon dried oregano**
 1/2 **teaspoon garlic powder**
   1 **round loaf (1 pound) sourdough bread**
Assorted crackers

In a large bowl, combine the first eight ingredients. Cut the top fourth off the loaf of bread; carefully hollow out bottom, leaving a 1-in. shell (save removed bread for another use). Spoon cheese mixture into bread shell. Wrap in a piece of heavy-duty foil (about 24 in. x 18 in.). Bake at 350° for 1 hour or until heated through.

Serve with crackers. **Yield:** 4 cups.

Editor's Note: Reduced-fat or fat-free mayonnaise is not recommended for this recipe.

Fried Shoestring Carrots

Prep/Total Time: 25 min.

I came up with these fun snacks myself. We like to serve them hot with ranch-style dressing as a dipping sauce.
— *Kim Gammill, Raymondville, Texas*

    2 cups self-rising flour
1-1/2 cups water
    1 teaspoon salt, *divided*
  3/4 teaspoon cayenne pepper, *divided*
  1/2 teaspoon pepper, divided
   10 cups shredded carrots
Oil for deep-fat frying

In a large bowl, whisk flour, water, 1/2 teaspoon salt, 1/4 teaspoon cayenne and 1/4 teaspoon pepper until smooth. Stir in carrots. In a small bowl, combine the remaining salt, cayenne and pepper; set aside.

In an electric skillet or deep-fat fryer, heat oil to 375°. Drop spoonfuls of carrot mixture, a few at a time, into oil; cook for 3-4 minutes or until golden brown, stirring frequently. Drain on paper towels; sprinkle with reserved seasoning mixture. **Yield:** 10 servings.

Editor's Note: As a substitute for each cup of self-rising flour, place 1-1/2 teaspoons baking powder and 1/2 teaspoon salt in a measuring cup. Add all-purpose flour to measure 1 cup.

Chicken Satay

(Pictured at right)

Prep: 15 min. + marinating **Grill:** 5 min.

These golden skewered chicken snacks are marinated and grilled, then served with a zesty Thai-style peanut butter sauce. — *Sue Gronholz, Beaver Dam, Wisconsin*

☑ **Uses less fat, sugar or salt. Includes Nutritional Analysis and Diabetic Exchanges.**

    2 pounds boneless skinless chicken breasts
  1/2 cup milk
    6 garlic cloves, minced
    1 tablespoon brown sugar
    1 tablespoon *each* ground coriander, ground turmeric and ground cumin
    1 teaspoon salt
    1 teaspoon white pepper
  1/8 teaspoon coconut extract
PEANUT BUTTER SAUCE:
  1/3 cup peanut butter

  1/3 cup milk
    2 green onions, chopped
    1 small jalapeno pepper, seeded and finely chopped
    2 to 3 tablespoons lime juice
    2 tablespoons soy sauce
    1 garlic clove, minced
    1 teaspoon sugar
    1 teaspoon minced fresh cilantro
    1 teaspoon minced fresh gingerroot
  1/8 teaspoon coconut extract

Flatten chicken to 1/4-in. thickness; cut lengthwise into 1-in.-wide strips. In a large resealable plastic bag, combine the milk, garlic, brown sugar, seasonings and extract. Add chicken; seal bag and turn to coat. Refrigerate for 8 hours or overnight.

In a bowl, whisk the sauce ingredients until blended. Cover and refrigerate until serving. Drain and discard marinade. Thread two chicken strips each onto metal or soaked wooden skewers.

Grill, uncovered, over medium-hot heat for 2-3 minutes on each side or until chicken juices run clear. Serve with sauce. **Yield:** 8 servings (1 cup sauce).

Nutritional Analysis: 2 skewers with 2 tablespoons sauce (prepared with reduced-fat peanut butter, fat-free milk and reduced-sodium soy sauce) equals 202 calories, 6 g fat (1 g saturated fat), 63 mg cholesterol, 428 mg sodium, 8 g carbohydrate, 1 g fiber, 27 g protein. **Diabetic Exchanges:** 3 lean meat, 1/2 starch.

Editor's Note: When cutting or seeding hot peppers, use rubber or plastic gloves to protect your hands. Avoid touching your face.

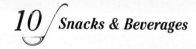
Roasted Pepper Tart

(Pictured on page 4)

Prep: 20 min. + chilling
Bake: 40 min. + cooling

For picnics, I whisk this tart out of the oven, wrap it in foil and head out! —Marian Platt, Sequim, Washington

1-1/2 cups all-purpose flour
1/8 teaspoon salt
1/2 cup cold butter
3 to 4 tablespoons water
3 medium sweet red peppers, halved and seeded
2 medium green peppers, halved and seeded
1/3 cup olive oil
2 garlic cloves, minced
4-1/2 teaspoons minced fresh oregano
2 cups (8 ounces) shredded Monterey Jack cheese, *divided*
1 can (2-1/4 ounces) sliced ripe olives, drained

In a large bowl, combine flour and salt; cut in butter until crumbly. Gradually add water, tossing with a fork until dough forms a ball. Cover; refrigerate for 1 hour.

Broil peppers 4 in. from the heat until the skins are blistered and blackened, about 10 minutes. Immediately place peppers in a bowl; cover and let stand for 15-20 minutes. Peel off and discard charred skin. Coarsely chop peppers; place in a bowl. Add the oil, garlic and oregano; toss to coat. Set aside.

Roll out dough to fit a 12-in. pizza pan. Transfer to pan. Prick dough thoroughly with a fork. Bake at 350° for 30-35 minutes or until lightly browned and crust begins pulling away from edges of pan. Cool completely.

Sprinkle 1 cup cheese over crust. Sprinkle with pepper mixture and remaining cheese. Arrange olives around edge. Bake at 350° for 10-15 minutes or until cheese is melted. Serve immediately. **Yield:** 12 servings.

Nacho Snack Mix

Prep: 10 min.　**Bake:** 2 hours + cooling

This colorful mixture of bite-sized snack foods, cereal and crackers gets its south-of-the-border accent from taco seasoning. —Liz Loder, Fox Point, Wisconsin

4 cups Crispix cereal
1 can (4-1/2 ounces) crisp cheese ball snacks
3 cups corn chips
2 cups pretzel sticks
1 cup cheese-flavored snack crackers
2 tablespoons taco seasoning
1/2 cup vegetable oil
1/2 cup butter, melted

In a bowl, combine first five ingredients. Spread in two ungreased 15-in. x 10-in. x 1-in. baking pans. Combine taco seasoning, oil and butter; pour over cereal mixture and toss to coat. Bake at 200° for 2 hours, stirring every 30 minutes. Cool. Store in airtight containers. **Yield:** 4 quarts.

Editor's Note: This recipe was prepared with Planters' Cheeze Balls.

Corn 'n' Squash Quesadillas

(Pictured at right)

Prep: 40 min.　**Cook:** 10 min.

Grilled vegetables give these quesadillas their distinctive flair, while cumin and jalapeno peppers add a little zip. —Mildred Sherrer, Bay City, Texas

2 medium ears sweet corn, husks removed
2 medium yellow summer squash, halved lengthwise
1/2 small sweet onion, cut into 1/4-inch slices
1 to 2 jalapeno peppers
1 tablespoon minced fresh basil
1-1/2 teaspoons minced fresh oregano
1 garlic clove, minced
1/4 teaspoon salt
1/4 teaspoon ground cumin
6 flour tortillas (8 inches)
1 cup (4 ounces) shredded Monterey Jack cheese
1 tablespoon canola oil

Grill corn, covered, over medium heat for 10 minutes; turn. Place the squash, onion and jalapenos on grill; cover and cook for 10 minutes, turning once. When vegetables are cool enough to handle, remove corn from the cobs, chop the squash and onion, and seed and chop the jalapenos. Place in a large bowl.

Stir in the basil, oregano, garlic, salt and cumin. Place 1/2 cup filling on one side of each tortilla; sprinkle with the cheese. Fold tortillas over filling. On a griddle or large skillet, cook quesadillas in oil over medium heat for 1-2 minutes on each side or until heated through. Cut into wedges. **Yield:** 6 servings.

Editor's Note: When cutting or seeding hot peppers, use rubber or plastic gloves to protect your hands. Avoid touching your face.

Chicken and Pork Egg Rolls

(Pictured above right)

Prep: 2-1/2 hours　**Cook:** 30 min.

I developed this recipe a number of years ago after watching my neighbor's wife make crispy egg rolls many times

FUN FINGER FOODS like Corn 'n' Squash Quesadillas and Chicken and Pork Egg Rolls (shown above) add appeal to any party.

while I was stationed in Hawaii. I think mine are just as good as hers! —Bruce Beaver, Florissant, Missouri

   1 medium head cabbage, shredded
   3 celery ribs, chopped
   1 can (8 ounces) bamboo shoots, drained and chopped
   1 can (8 ounces) sliced water chestnuts, drained and chopped
   5 green onions, chopped
   1 to 2 garlic cloves, minced
   2 tablespoons vegetable oil
2-1/4 cups diced cooked chicken breasts
   2 cups diced cooked pork
 1/4 cup chicken broth
 1/4 cup soy sauce
 1/4 teaspoon salt
 1/4 teaspoon pepper
   2 packages (16 ounces *each*) egg roll wrappers
   1 egg, beaten
Additional oil for deep-fat frying
SAUCE:
1-1/2 cups unsweetened pineapple juice
 3/4 cup cider vinegar
 1/2 cup packed brown sugar
   1 tablespoon soy sauce
 1/8 to 1/4 teaspoon white pepper
   3 tablespoons cornstarch
   2 tablespoons cold water

In a large nonstick wok, stir-fry the cabbage, celery, bamboo shoots, water chestnuts, onions and garlic in oil until crisp-tender. Stir in the chicken, pork, broth, soy sauce, salt and pepper. Cook and stir for 1 minute or until heated through.

Position an egg roll wrapper with one point toward you. Place about 1/4 cup meat mixture in the center. Fold bottom corner over filling; fold sides toward center over filling. Roll toward the remaining point. Moisten top corner with beaten egg; press to seal. Repeat with remaining wrappers and filling.

In an electric skillet or deep-fat fryer, heat the oil to 375°. Fry egg rolls, a few at a time, for 1-2 minutes on each side or until golden brown. Drain on paper towels.

In a saucepan, combine first five sauce ingredients. Bring to a boil. Combine cornstarch and cold water until smooth; stir into boiling mixture. Cook and stir for 2 minutes or until thickened. Serve warm with egg rolls. **Yield:** about 3 dozen.

Zippy Cranberry Appetizer

(Pictured above)

Prep: 20 min. + chilling

Tart cranberry flavor blends nicely with mustard and horseradish in this out-of-the-ordinary cracker spread. It's quick to fix, too. —*Maria Hattrup, The Dalles, Oregon*

- 1/2 cup sugar
- 1/2 cup packed brown sugar
- 1 cup water
- 1 package (12 ounces) fresh *or* frozen cranberries
- 1 to 3 tablespoons prepared horseradish
- 1 tablespoon Dijon mustard
- 1 package (8 ounces) cream cheese, softened
- Assorted crackers

In a large saucepan, bring sugars and water to a boil over medium heat. Stir in cranberries; return to a boil. Cook for 10 minutes or until thickened, stirring occasionally. Cool.

Stir in horseradish and mustard. Transfer to a bowl; refrigerate until chilled. Just before serving, spread cream cheese over crackers; top with cranberry mixture. **Yield:** 2-1/2 cups.

Olive-Rice Cheese Spread

Prep: 20 min. + chilling

My daughter, Amy, won a blue ribbon for this recipe at our town's Wild Rice Festival. —*Sandy Tichy Kelliher, Minnesota*

- 1 package (8 ounces) cream cheese, softened
- 1/4 cup grated Parmesan cheese
- 2 tablespoons prepared Italian salad dressing
- 1 teaspoon dried basil
- 1/4 teaspoon pepper
- 1 cup cooked wild rice
- 2 tablespoons diced carrot
- 2 tablespoons snipped fresh chives
- 1 tablespoon sliced stuffed green olives
- 1 tablespoon sliced ripe olives
- 1/4 to 1/2 cup slivered almonds, toasted

In a small mixing bowl, beat cream cheese, Parmesan cheese, salad dressing, basil and pepper until smooth. Stir in the rice, carrot, chives and olives. Transfer to a serving bowl. Cover and refrigerate for at least 1 hour. Just before serving, top with almonds. **Yield:** 2 cups.

Citrus Iced Tea

Prep: 20 min. + cooling

I think I have finally hit on a from-scratch recipe for iced tea that doesn't have that artificial sweetener aftertaste. —*Dawn Lowenstein, Hatboro, Pennsylvania*

✓ **Uses less fat, sugar or salt. Includes Nutritional Analysis and Diabetic Exchanges.**

- 2 quarts water, *divided*
- 6 individual tea bags
- 1 to 2 mint sprigs
- 1/2 ounce sugar-free lemonade soft drink mix
- 2 cups orange juice

In a Dutch oven, bring 1 qt. of water to a boil. Add tea bags and mint. Cover and steep for 10 minutes. Strain; discard tea bags and mint. In a large container, combine lemonade mix and remaining water. Stir in the tea and orange juice. Cool. Serve over ice. **Yield:** 8 servings.

Nutritional Analysis: 1 cup equals 32 calories, trace fat (0 saturated fat), 0 cholesterol, 1 mg sodium, 7 g carbohydrate, trace fiber, trace protein. **Diabetic Exchange:** 1/2 fruit.

Editor's Note: This recipe was tested with one 1/2-oz. tub of Crystal Light lemonade soft drink mix.

Cheddar Shrimp Nachos

(Pictured on page 4)

Prep/Total Time: 20 min.

These fun finger foods in tortilla chip scoops are just the thing for get-togethers. —*Lisa Feld, Grafton, Wisconsin*

- 3/4 pound deveined peeled cooked shrimp, chopped

1-1/2 cups (6 ounces) shredded cheddar cheese
1 can (4 ounces) chopped green chilies, drained
1/3 cup chopped green onions
1/4 cup sliced ripe olives, drained
1/2 cup mayonnaise
1/4 teaspoon ground cumin
48 tortilla chip scoops

In a large bowl, combine the shrimp, cheese, chilies, onions and olives. Combine the mayonnaise and cumin; add to shrimp mixture and toss to coat. Drop by tablespoonfuls into tortilla scoops. Place on ungreased baking sheets. Bake at 350° for 5-10 minutes or until cheese is melted. Serve warm. **Yield:** 4 dozen.

Brie with Artichokes

(Pictured below)

Prep/Total Time: 20 min.

If you're looking for something special for your holiday hors d'oeuvres table, this tangy elegant appetizer will fill the bill. It is so popular with my friends that I try to keep Brie cheese and artichoke hearts on hand at all times.
—Lucy Banks, Jackson, Mississippi

1 round (4-1/2 ounces) Brie *or* Camembert cheese
1/3 cup chopped canned water-packed artichoke hearts
2 teaspoons minced fresh basil
1 teaspoon olive oil
1 garlic clove, minced
Salt and cayenne pepper to taste
Assorted crackers

Slice Brie in half horizontally. Place the bottom half in a small round baking dish or pie plate. Combine the artichokes, basil, oil, garlic, salt and cayenne; spread over Brie. Replace top. Bake, uncovered, at 350° for 10-15 minutes or until heated through. Serve with crackers. **Yield:** 4 servings.

Garden-Fresh Bruschetta

(Pictured above)

Prep/Total Time: 30 min.

This easy-to-fix bruschetta is so easy! Serve it as an appetizer or as a colorful side dish.   —Rachel Garcia
Honolulu, Hawaii

1 garlic clove, peeled and halved
14 slices French bread (3/4 inch thick)
4 medium tomatoes, seeded and diced
1/4 cup chopped red onion
2 tablespoons olive oil
1 tablespoon minced fresh basil
1/4 teaspoon salt
1/8 teaspoon pepper
14 fresh basil leaves

Rub cut side of garlic over one side of each slice of bread. Place bread, garlic side down, on an ungreased baking sheet. Bake at 350° for 5 minutes on each side or until lightly browned. In a bowl, combine the tomatoes, onion, oil, minced basil, salt and pepper; spoon about 2 tablespoons onto each piece of toast. Top each with a basil leaf. **Yield:** 14 servings.

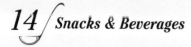

Mark's Marinated Mushrooms

(Pictured below)

Prep: 15 min. + marinating

This appetizer is equally delicious served hot or cold. It's a real crowd-pleaser.
—*Mark Curry*
Buena Vista, Colorado

   1 pound small fresh mushrooms
   1 small onion, thinly sliced
1/3 cup white wine vinegar
1/3 cup vegetable oil
   1 teaspoon salt
   1 teaspoon ground mustard

In a large saucepan, combine all ingredients. Bring to a boil over medium-high heat. Cook, uncovered, for 6 minutes, stirring once. Cool to room temperature. Transfer to a bowl; cover and refrigerate overnight. **Yield:** 3 cups.

Nuggets with Dill Sauce

Prep: 30 min.   **Cook:** 15 min.

A creamy sauce, seasoned with dill and relish, enhances these fun-to-eat fried chicken bites. —*Carol Crooks*
Jonesboro, Georgia

1/2 cup all-purpose flour
   2 teaspoons sesame seeds
1/2 teaspoon salt
   1 egg, lightly beaten
1/2 cup water

Oil for frying
   1 pound boneless skinless chicken breasts, cut into 1-inch cubes
DILL SAUCE:
1/2 cup sour cream
   2 tablespoons dill pickle relish
   1 teaspoon dill weed

In a bowl, combine the flour, sesame seeds and salt. Combine the egg and water; stir into the dry ingredients just until moistened. In an electric skillet, heat 1 in. of oil to 375°.

Dip chicken into batter. Fry chicken, a few pieces at a time, for 1 to 1-1/2 minutes on each side or until golden brown. Drain on paper towels; keep warm. In a small bowl, combine sauce ingredients. Serve with chicken nuggets. **Yield:** 2 dozen.

Enchilada Meatballs

(Pictured at right)

Prep: 20 min.   **Bake:** 20 min.

I've had this recipe so long that I don't remember who gave it to me. Before I retired, these tasty little treats were popular during snack time at work. They're a good way to use up leftover corn bread. —*Mearl Harris*
West Plains, Missouri

   2 cups crumbled corn bread
   1 can (10 ounces) enchilada sauce, *divided*
1/2 teaspoon salt
1-1/2 pounds ground beef
   1 can (8 ounces) tomato sauce
1/2 cup shredded Mexican cheese blend

In a large bowl, combine the corn bread, 1/2 cup enchilada sauce and salt. Crumble beef over mixture; mix well. Shape into 1-in. balls. Place in a greased 15-in. x 10-in. x 1-in. baking pan. Bake, uncovered, at 350° for 18-22 minutes or until meat is no longer pink.

Meanwhile, in a small saucepan, heat tomato sauce and remaining enchilada sauce. Drain meatballs; place in a serving dish. Top with sauce and sprinkle with cheese. Serve with toothpicks. **Yield:** about 4-1/2 dozen.

Festive Crab Cups

(Pictured above right)

Prep/Total Time: 25 min.

Stir up excitement at parties with these picture-perfect tarts filled with a pleasant combination of cream cheese, crabmeat and cranberry sauce. —*Barbara Nowakowski*
North Tonawanda, New York

MAKE GUESTS MERRY at your holiday gathering with tasty Enchilada Meatballs, Festive Crab Cups and Seasoned Fish Crackers (shown above).

1/3 cup cream cheese, softened
1/4 cup canned crabmeat, drained, flaked and cartilage removed
2 tablespoons chopped green onions
1 package (2.1 ounces) frozen miniature phyllo tart shells
1/3 cup whole-berry cranberry sauce

In a small bowl, combine cream cheese, crab and onions until blended. Place tart shells on an ungreased baking sheet. Drop 1 tablespoon of the crab mixture into each shell. Top each with 1 teaspoon cranberry sauce. Bake at 375° for 12-15 minutes or until heated through. **Yield:** 15 appetizers.

Seasoned Fish Crackers

(Pictured above)

Prep: 10 min. **Bake:** 15 min. + cooling

These zesty little bites are easy to fix and irresistible to eat. Once you start snacking on them, you'll have a difficult time stopping. For parties, I double the recipe. Even then, I never have enough! —Deanne Causey, Midland, Texas

3 packages (6 ounces *each*) bite-size cheddar cheese fish crackers
1 envelope ranch salad dressing mix
3 teaspoons dill weed
1/2 teaspoon garlic powder
1/2 teaspoon lemon-pepper seasoning
1/4 teaspoon cayenne pepper
2/3 cup vegetable oil

Place the crackers in a large bowl. Combine the remaining ingredients; drizzle over crackers and toss to coat evenly. Transfer to two ungreased 15-in. x 10-in. x 1-in. baking pans. Bake at 250° for 15-20 minutes, stirring occasionally. Cool completely. Store in an airtight container. **Yield:** about 2-1/2 quarts.

Go Ahead—Play with Your Food

KIDS WILL RUN to the kitchen to help you make any of the fun foods featured here...and be so proud when you serve them, too!

Graham Cracker Santas

(Pictured below)

Prep/Total Time: 20 min.

A co-worker made these cute treats for our potluck Christmas party, and I got the recipe from her. It's easy to double if you want more. They are so eye-catching, everyone loves them!
—Ray Taylor, Memphis, Tennessee

  1-1/4 cups vanilla frosting, *divided*
Red liquid and paste food coloring
  12 graham cracker squares
  36 miniature marshmallows, halved
  24 red-hot candies
   6 small red gumdrops, halved

Tint 1 cup frosting light pink with liquid food coloring. Spread over the graham crackers. Tint remaining frosting with paste food coloring. Pipe onto one corner of each cracker for hat; add a marshmallow half for pom-pom.

   For each Santa, arrange remaining marshmallow halves for beard, red-hots for eyes and a gumdrop half for nose. **Yield:** 1 dozen.

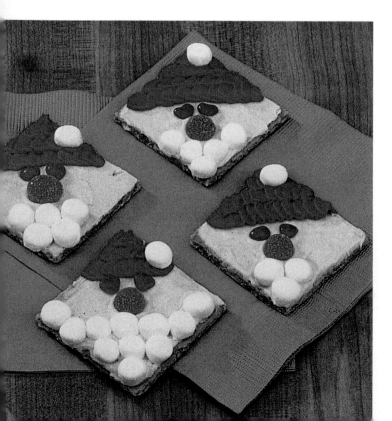

Jingle Bell Shrimp Spread

(Pictured above)

Prep/Total Time: 15 min.

Ring in the holidays with this easy and appealing shrimp spread shaped like a bell. It takes only a few ingredients and whips up in no time at all, but folks seem to absolutely love it! I receive so many compliments whenever I bring it to a party.
—Janet Thomas
McKees Rocks, Pennsylvania

  12 ounces cream cheese, softened
   1 cup chopped onion
   1 cup chopped celery
   1 can (6 ounces) small shrimp, rinsed and drained
Paprika
Stuffed olives
Assorted crackers

In a small mixing bowl, beat cream cheese until smooth. Stir in the onion, celery and shrimp. Spread onto a platter in the shape of a bell. Sprinkle with paprika. Place one olive at base of bell for clapper. Cut remaining olives in half; outline the bell. Serve with crackers. **Yield:** 10-12 servings.

Disappearing Fruit Dip

Prep/Total Time: 10 min.

This tangy dip never lasts long at our house because every-one is always reaching for just a little more. For variety, try substituting orange juice and orange peel for the lime.
—Camille Langford, Branson, Missouri

- 1 **package (8 ounces) cream cheese, softened**
- 1 **jar (7 ounces) marshmallow creme**
- 1 **tablespoon lime juice**
- 1 **teaspoon grated lime peel**
Dash ground ginger
Assorted fresh fruit

In a mixing bowl, beat the cream cheese, marshmal-low creme, lime juice, lime peel and ginger until smooth. Serve with fruit. Refrigerate leftovers. **Yield:** 2 cups.

Easter Bunny Cheese Spread

(Pictured at right)

Prep: 20 min. + chilling

For an Easter party, I created this rabbit centerpiece from a cheese ball recipe. My children enjoyed decorating it using carrots and jelly beans! Why not hop to it and en-joy making and serving the colorful appetizer yourself?
—Beth Paulson, De Pere, Wisconsin

- 3 **packages (8 ounces *each*) cream cheese, softened**
- 2 **packages (2-1/2 ounces *each*) thinly sliced deli beef, finely chopped**
- 12 **stuffed olives, chopped**
- 2 **teaspoons dill weed**
- 1 **teaspoon prepared horseradish**
- 1 **teaspoon Worcestershire sauce**
- 3 **green onions**
- 6 **miniature jelly beans**
- 1 **small carrot**
Fresh vegetables *and/or* crackers

In a mixing bowl, combine the cream cheese, beef, olives, dill, horseradish and Worcestershire sauce. Finely chop two green onions; add to cream cheese mixture. On a large platter, form cheese mixture into a bunny shape. Cover and refrigerate for 8 hours or overnight.

Insert jelly beans for bunny's eyes, nose and but-tons. Cut carrot in half lengthwise; place cut side up above head for ears. Cut green portion of remaining onion into six 2-in.-long pieces; place next to nose for whiskers. Serve with vegetables and/or crackers. **Yield:** 4 cups.

Strawberry Spiders

Enlist your kids or grandkids to help make these not-so-scary Strawberry Spiders from Ray Tay-lor of Memphis, Tennessee. They are fun and tasty snacks!

To make two dozen, round up 96 pretzel sticks; 12 fresh strawberries; 1/2 cup chocolate chips, melted; and 48 miniature semisweet chips.

For each spider, set four pretzels parallel. Re-move berry stems and cut each berry in half length-wise. Dip cut side in melted chocolate; press onto pretzel sticks to make the spider's body and eight legs. Attach two mini chip eyes with a little melted chocolate.

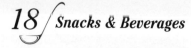

Chicken Salad Cups

(Pictured below)

Prep: 30 min. + chilling   **Bake:** 10 min. + cooling

Pineapple and almonds enhance the creamy chicken salad in these cute tartlets made with convenient refrigerated pie pastry.   —Lois Holdson, Millersville, Maryland

- 1 package (15 ounces) refrigerated pie pastry
- 2 cups diced cooked chicken
- 1 can (8 ounces) unsweetened crushed pineapple, drained
- 1/2 cup slivered almonds
- 1/2 cup chopped celery
- 1/2 cup shredded cheddar cheese
- 1/2 cup mayonnaise
- 1/2 teaspoon salt
- 1/2 teaspoon paprika

TOPPING:
- 1/2 cup sour cream
- 1/4 cup mayonnaise
- 1/2 cup shredded cheddar cheese

Cut each sheet of pie pastry into 4-1/2-in. rounds; reroll scraps and cut out additional circles. Press pastry onto the bottom and up the sides of 14 ungreased muffin cups. Bake at 450° for 6-7 minutes or until golden brown. Cool on a wire rack.

In a bowl, combine the chicken, pineapple, almonds, celery, cheese, mayonnaise, salt and paprika; refrigerate until chilled.

Just before serving, spoon two rounded tablespoonfuls of chicken salad into each pastry cup. Combine sour cream and mayonnaise; spoon over filling. Sprinkle with cheese. **Yield:** 14 servings.

Caramel Fruit Dip

Prep/Total Time: 15 min.

This creamy, melt-in-your-mouth dip, served with assorted fruits, makes a refreshing accompaniment to a holiday cheese tray.   —Trish Gehlhar, Ypsilanti, North Dakota

- 2 packages (8 ounces *each*) cream cheese, softened
- 1 cup packed brown sugar
- 1/2 cup caramel ice cream topping

Assorted fresh fruit

In a small mixing bowl, beat cream cheese and brown sugar until smooth. Add caramel topping; beat until blended. Serve with fruit. Refrigerate leftovers. **Yield:** 3 cups.

Onion Brie Pizza

Prep: 30 min.   **Bake:** 20 min. + standing

Serve this unique pizza for a family supper or an elegant buffet.   —Cindy Bedell, West Lafayette, Indiana

- 6 medium sweet onions, thinly sliced
- 1/4 cup butter
- 1 package (16 ounces) hot roll mix
- 1-1/4 cups warm water (120° to 130°)
- 2 tablespoons olive oil
- 8 ounces Brie, rind removed and cut into small pieces
- 1/3 cup sliced almonds

In a large skillet, cook onions in butter over medium-low heat for 25 minutes or until golden brown, stirring occasionally. Meanwhile, prepare hot roll mix according to package directions, using the warm water and oil. Place dough in a greased bowl, turning once to grease top. Cover and let stand for 5 minutes.

Roll out dough to a 14-in. circle; transfer to a greased 14-in. pizza pan. Top with onions, Brie and almonds. Bake at 400° for 18-20 minutes or until golden brown. Let stand for 10 minutes before cutting. **Yield:** 8 servings.

Apricot Kielbasa Slices

Prep/Total Time: 15 min.

These easy-to-fix sausage bites are coated in a thick, zesty sauce with just the right amount of sweetness.   —Barbara McCalley, Allison Park, Pennsylvania

- 1 pound fully cooked kielbasa *or* Polish sausage, cut into 1/4-inch slices
- 1 jar (12 ounces) apricot preserves

2 tablespoons lemon juice
2 teaspoons Dijon mustard
1/4 teaspoon ground ginger

In a large skillet, brown sausage; drain and set aside. Add the remaining ingredients to the skillet; cook over low heat for 2-3 minutes or until heated through, stirring occasionally. Return sausage to the pan; cook for 5-6 minutes or until heated through. Serve warm. **Yield:** 4 dozen.

Herbed Deviled Eggs

Prep/Total Time: 25 min.

Wondering what to do with hard-cooked eggs when Easter has passed? I make deviled eggs with a twist, adding a mix of herbs to the filling. —Sue Seymour
Valatie, New York

6 hard-cooked eggs
2 tablespoons minced chives
2 tablespoons plain yogurt
2 tablespoons mayonnaise
1 tablespoon chopped fresh tarragon
1 tablespoon minced fresh parsley
2-1/2 teaspoons prepared mustard
1 teaspoon snipped fresh dill
Salt and pepper to taste

Cut eggs in half lengthwise; remove yolks and set whites aside. In a small bowl, mash yolks. Stir in the remaining ingredients. Pipe or stuff into egg whites. Refrigerate until serving. **Yield:** 1 dozen.

Peppy Provolone Slices

Prep/Total Time: 30 min.

I make this timeless treat using frozen bread dough. For added flavor, try dipping the slices in either pizza or spaghetti sauce. —Lois Clay, Belle Vernon, Pennsylvania

1 loaf (1 pound) frozen bread dough, thawed
8 ounces sliced pepperoni
8 ounces sliced provolone cheese
1 cup sliced jalapeno pepper rings

On a greased baking sheet, roll out dough into a 15-in. x 12-in. rectangle. Place half of the pepperoni lengthwise in two rows down center third of rectangle. Top with half of the cheese and peppers. Fold one side of dough over filling. Top with the remaining pepperoni, cheese and peppers.

Fold remaining dough over filling; pinch edges and ends to seal. Bake at 350° for 20-25 minutes or until golden brown. Slice and serve warm. **Yield:** 4-6 servings.

Creamy Black Bean Salsa

(Pictured above)

Prep/Total Time: 20 min.

I love sour cream on Mexican dishes, so I decided to add it to a salsa recipe. It always goes fast, so you may want to double the recipe. —Darlene Brenden, Salem, Oregon

1 can (15 ounces) black beans, rinsed and drained
1-1/2 cups frozen corn, thawed
1 cup finely chopped sweet red pepper
3/4 cup finely chopped green pepper
1/2 cup finely chopped red onion
1 tablespoon minced fresh parsley
1/2 cup sour cream
1/4 cup mayonnaise
2 tablespoons red wine vinegar
1 teaspoon ground cumin
1 teaspoon chili powder
1/2 teaspoon salt
1/4 teaspoon garlic powder
1/8 teaspoon pepper
Tortilla chips

In a large bowl, combine the beans, corn, peppers, onion and parsley. Combine the sour cream, mayonnaise, vinegar and seasonings; pour over corn mixture and toss gently to coat. Serve with tortilla chips. Refrigerate leftovers. **Yield:** 4 cups.

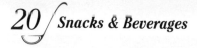

Put Some Punch in the Season

YOU'LL QUENCH their thirst in a festive way when you serve guests these refreshing beverages at a holiday party or open house! Adding to the merry atmosphere is a pretty ice ring our Test Kitchen staff created to decorate your punch bowl.

Cranberry Fruit Punch

(Pictured at right)

Prep/Total Time: 10 min.

I tried different combinations of juices until I came up with this pleasant punch that's not too sweet. It's perfect when you're serving a lot of holiday sweets. —Jean Ann Herritt
Canton, Ohio

6 cups grapefruit juice, chilled
1 can (46 ounces) pineapple juice, chilled
4 cups cranberry-raspberry juice, chilled
4 cups cranberry-apple juice, chilled
1 can (12 ounces) frozen cranberry juice concentrate, thawed
1 can (12 ounces) frozen grape juice concentrate, thawed
1 can (12 ounces) frozen lemonade concentrate, thawed
4 cups raspberry *or* cherry soda, chilled

In a large container, combine the first seven ingredients. Stir in soda. Serve immediately over ice if desired. **Yield:** about 36 servings (7 quarts).

Open House Punch

(Pictured at right)

Prep: 10 min. + chilling

This sunny punch is great for parties and weddings. I use tea bags rather than instant tea when brewing the tea for a stronger flavor. —Janice Wilson, Mansfield, Pennsylvania

6 quarts water
10 cups brewed tea
5 cups sugar
4 cans (12 ounces *each*) frozen orange juice concentrate, thawed
4 cans (12 ounces *each*) frozen lemonade concentrate, thawed
1 can (12 ounces) frozen pineapple juice concentrate, thawed
4 liters ginger ale, chilled

In a large container, combine the first six ingredients; stir until sugar is dissolved. Cover and refrigerate until chilled. Just before serving, transfer to a punch bowl. Stir in ginger ale. **Yield:** 85 servings (4 gallons).

Fruity Slush

(Pictured at right)

Prep: 10 min. + freezing

"Refreshing and different" is the response I usually get when I serve this frosty combination. —Carrie Bonikowske
Stevens Point, Wisconsin

☑ **Uses less fat, sugar or salt. Includes Nutritional Analysis and Diabetic Exchanges.**

1 package (3 ounces) raspberry gelatin
1 cup boiling water
2 cups cold water
2 cups cranberry juice
1 can (12 ounces) frozen pink lemonade concentrate, thawed
1 can (12 ounces) frozen orange juice concentrate, thawed
1 liter lemon-lime soda, chilled

In a large bowl, dissolve gelatin in boiling water; stir in the cold water, cranberry juice and concentrates. Pour into a 2-1/2-qt. freezer container; cover and freeze overnight.

Remove container from the freezer 2 hours before serving. Fill glasses two-thirds full with slush; stir about 1 cup soda into each glass. **Yield:** 13 servings (about 2 quarts).

Nutritional Analysis: 1 cup (prepared with sugar-free gelatin, reduced-calorie cranberry juice and diet lemon-lime soda) equals 102 calories, trace fat (trace saturated fat), 0 cholesterol, 14 mg sodium, 26 g carbohydrate, trace fiber, 1 g protein. **Diabetic Exchange:** 1-1/2 fruit.

Ice Ring Wreath

(Pictured above right)

Here's a cool way to keep your party beverage frosty while giving it an eye-catching look, too. The festive ice ring from our Test Kitchen staff is easy and can be made days ahead.

4 cups cold distilled water, *divided*
3 large limes
1 package (12 ounces) fresh cranberries

SPARKLING SIPPERS. Cool Cranberry Fruit Punch (in pitcher), Open House Punch with Ice Ring Wreath (in bowl) and Fruity Slush (in glasses) are delightful for gatherings.

Pour 1 cup of distilled water into a 4-1/2- cup ring mold lightly coated with nonstick cooking spray. Peel limes, keeping peel in large pieces. Using miniature tree cookie cutters, cut trees from the peel. Place shapes upside down in top of ring mold. Save lime pulp for another use. Place cranberries between tree shapes. Rearrange if necessary before freezing. Freeze until solid.

Gently add remaining water; freeze. To use, wrap bottom of solidly frozen mold in a warm towel until loosened or dip mold in pan of warm water. Float ice ring, fruit side up, in cold punch. **Yield:** 1 ice ring.

More Punch Trims

- Freeze strawberries, pitted cherries, raspberries, grapes or mint in ice cube trays using some of the punch or fruit drink as the liquid. Float these in the punch or in individual cups.
- Tie bows or knots from thin strips of lemon, lime and orange peel to float in punch cups.

or until lightly browned. Serve with spread. **Yield:** 4 cups (4 dozen pita triangles).

Editor's Note: This recipe was tested in a 1,100-watt microwave.

Roasted Carrot Dip

Prep: 15 min.   **Bake:** 45 min.

Once you start eating this delicious dip, it's difficult to stop. The smooth texture and sweet carrot flavor go great with the crisp pita wedges. —Alana Rowley, Calgary, Alberta

 10 **medium carrots**
  5 **garlic cloves, peeled**
  2 **tablespoons olive oil**
  6 to 8 **tablespoons water**
  2 **teaspoons white wine vinegar**
 1/2 **cup mayonnaise**
 1/4 **cup sour cream**
 1/8 **teaspoon sugar**
 1/8 **teaspoon salt**
 1/8 **teaspoon pepper**
  4 to 6 **pita breads (6 inches)**
  2 to 3 **tablespoons butter, melted**

Cut carrots in half widthwise; cut lengthwise into 1/2-in.-thick slices. In a bowl, combine the carrots, garlic and oil; toss to coat. Transfer to a greased 15-in. x 10-in. x 1-in. baking pan. Bake, uncovered, at 425° for 20 minutes. Stir; bake 15-20 minutes longer or until carrots are tender. Cool slightly.

In a blender, combine 6 tablespoons water, vinegar, mayonnaise, sour cream, sugar, salt, pepper and carrot mixture; cover and process until smooth. Add additional water if needed to achieve desired consistency. Transfer to a bowl; refrigerate until serving.

Brush both sides of pita breads with butter. Cut in half; cut each half into six wedges. Place on ungreased baking sheets. Bake at 350° for 4 minutes on each side or until lightly browned. Serve with carrot dip. **Yield:** 8-10 servings.

A Touch of Greek Dip

Prep/Total Time: 10 min.

Serve this pleasing dip with chips or raw vegetables, or try a spoonful on top of a baked potato. —Emily Chaney Blue Hill, Maine

✓ **Uses less fat, sugar or salt. Includes Nutritional Analysis and Diabetic Exchanges.**

 1/2 **cup fat-free milk**
 1/2 **cup 1% cottage cheese**
 1/2 **cup crumbled feta cheese**

Tomato Spinach Spread

(Pictured above)

Prep/Total Time: 20 min.

Everyone at our get-togethers raves about this festive-looking zippy dip. —Eleonora Marinelli Hagerstown, Maryland

  1 **package (8 ounces) cream cheese, softened**
 1/3 **cup milk**
 1/4 **teaspoon salt**
 1/4 **teaspoon cayenne pepper**
  2 **medium tomatoes, seeded and chopped**
  1 **package (10 ounces) frozen chopped spinach, thawed and squeezed dry**
  1 **small onion, finely chopped**
PITA TRIANGLES:
  1 **tablespoon butter, melted**
  1 **tablespoon olive oil**
  6 **whole pita breads**
  1 **teaspoon ground cumin**
  1 **teaspoon lemon-pepper seasoning**

In a small mixing bowl, beat the cream cheese, milk, salt and cayenne until smooth. Stir in the tomatoes, spinach and onion. Spoon into an ungreased microwave-safe 9-in. pie plate. Microwave, uncovered, on high for 5 minutes or until heated through, stirring once.

Meanwhile, combine butter and oil; brush over both sides of pitas. Cut each pita into eight wedges; place on ungreased baking sheets. Combine cumin and lemon-pepper; sprinkle over both sides of wedges. Broil 4 in. from the heat for 2-3 minutes on each side

1 teaspoon dried oregano
1/4 teaspoon grated lemon peel
Pepper to taste
Assorted raw vegetables

In a blender, combine the milk, cottage cheese, feta cheese, oregano, lemon peel and pepper; cover and process until smooth. Transfer to a small bowl. Serve with vegetables. **Yield:** 1-1/4 cups.

Nutritional Analysis: 1 serving (1/4 cup) equals 54 calories, 2 g fat (1 g saturated fat), 7 mg cholesterol, 213 mg sodium, 2 g carbohydrate, 1 g fiber, 6 g protein. **Diabetic Exchange:** 1/2 milk.

Crunchy Cucumber Rounds

Prep/Total Time: 30 min.

I found the recipe for these cute crisp appetizers in an old cookbook several years ago. They're fun to serve because people inevitably ask, "What's in this?" Make sure your cucumber slices are dry so the fruit mixture will stick to the tops. —Phyllis Pollock, Erie, Pennsylvania

1 cup finely chopped red apple
1 can (8 ounces) unsweetened crushed
   pineapple, drained
1/4 cup finely chopped pecans, toasted
1/4 cup sour cream
1/8 teaspoon salt
3 medium cucumbers

In a small bowl, combine the apple, pineapple, pecans, sour cream and salt. Cover and refrigerate until chilled. To score cucumbers, cut lengthwise strips through peel. Cut each cucumber into 16 slices. Blot with paper towels to remove moisture. Spoon 1 teaspoon apple mixture onto each slice. **Yield:** 4 dozen.

Garlic-Herb Potato Nests

(Pictured on page 4)

Prep: 25 min.   **Bake:** 20 min. + cooling

These elegant-looking little appetizers are quite simple to prepare. The crunchy nests filled with herb cheese "eggs" are a real eye-catcher, too. —Donna Cline
Pensacola, Florida

2 cups grated peeled potatoes, drained and
   squeezed dry
1 egg white, lightly beaten
1/4 teaspoon salt
1/8 teaspoon pepper
1/3 cup garlic-herb cheese spread
Fresh dill sprigs

In a bowl, combine the potatoes, egg white, salt and pepper. Place 1 tablespoonful in each of 24 greased miniature muffin cups, lining the bottom and sides of cups. Bake at 375° for 20-25 minutes or until golden brown. Cool for 2 minutes before removing from pans to wire racks to cool completely.

Shape 1/2 teaspoonfuls of cheese into ovals; place in potato nests. Garnish with dill. Serve at room temperature. **Yield:** 2 dozen.

Chicken Poppers

(Pictured below)

Prep: 15 min.   **Cook:** 20 min.

Wrapped in bacon, these cute chicken bites can be served with your favorite dipping sauce. —Charlene Crump
Montgomery, Alabama

3 pounds boneless skinless chicken breasts
1 cup ground fully cooked ham
25 to 30 cubes cheddar cheese (1/2-inch cubes)
1 pound sliced bacon
2 to 3 tablespoons olive oil
1 cup chicken broth
1/2 teaspoon salt
1/2 teaspoon pepper

Flatten chicken to 1/4-in. thickness; cut into 1-1/2-in. strips. Spread each with 1 teaspoon ham. Place a cheese cube on the end of each strip; roll up. Cut each slice of bacon in half widthwise. Wrap each around a chicken roll-up; secure each with a toothpick.

In a large skillet, cook roll-ups in oil until bacon is crispy, about 10 minutes. Add the broth, salt and pepper; bring to a boil. Reduce heat; cover and simmer for 10-15 minutes or until chicken juices run clear. Serve warm. Refrigerate leftovers. **Yield:** 25-30 appetizers.

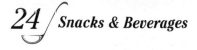

Deviled Eggs

Prep/Total Time: 20 min.

French onion dip adds flavor to the creamy filling in these popular appetizers. —*Joyce Turley Slaughters, Kentucky*

  6 hard-cooked eggs
1/4 cup mayonnaise
  2 teaspoons French onion dip
  1 teaspoon evaporated milk
1/2 teaspoon prepared mustard
Paprika, optional

Slice eggs in half lengthwise; remove yolks and set whites aside. In a small bowl, mash the yolks. Stir in the mayonnaise, onion dip, milk and mustard. Pipe or stuff into egg whites. Sprinkle with paprika if desired. Refrigerate until serving. **Yield:** 1 dozen.

Breaded Chicken Wings

(Pictured at far right)

Prep: 15 min.   **Bake:** 30 min.

No one can pass up seconds of these golden-brown goodies. Basil, garlic and onion flavor the crumb coating that covers the wings. —*Nancy Schmidt, Center, Colorado*

2/3 cup dry bread crumbs
  1 teaspoon onion powder
  1 teaspoon dried basil
1/2 teaspoon garlic salt
1/2 teaspoon paprika
  1 egg
  1 tablespoon water
 10 whole chicken wings

In a large resealable plastic bag, combine the bread crumbs, onion powder, basil, garlic salt and paprika. In a small bowl, whisk egg and water. Cut chicken wings into three sections; discard wing tips. Dip wings in egg, then place in bag and shake to coat. Place in a greased 15-in. x 10-in. x 1-in. baking pan. Bake at 425° for 30-35 minutes or until juices run clear, turning once. **Yield:** 6-8 servings.

Warm Asparagus-Crab Spread

(Pictured at far right)

Prep/Total Time: 30 min.

When my children entertain, I like to help them with the cooking, and this dip is always a hit. Cashew nuts give this creamy mixture a nice crunch. —*Camille Wisniewski Jackson, New Jersey*

  1 medium sweet red pepper, chopped
  3 green onions, sliced
  2 medium jalapeno peppers, seeded and
     finely chopped
  2 teaspoons vegetable oil
  1 can (15 ounces) asparagus spears,
     drained and chopped
  2 cans (6 ounces *each*) crabmeat, drained,
     flaked and cartilage removed
  1 cup mayonnaise
1/2 cup grated *or* shredded Parmesan cheese
1/2 cup chopped cashews
Assorted crackers

In a large skillet, saute the red pepper, onions and jalapenos in oil until tender. Add the asparagus, crab, mayonnaise and Parmesan cheese; mix well.

Transfer to a greased 1-qt. baking dish. Sprinkle with cashews. Bake, uncovered, at 375° for 20-25 minutes or until bubbly. Serve with crackers. **Yield:** 3 cups.

Editor's Note: Reduced-fat or fat-free mayonnaise is not recommended for this recipe. When seeding hot peppers, use rubber or plastic gloves to protect your hands. Avoid touching your face.

Mushroom Quesadillas

(Pictured at right)

Prep/Total Time: 20 min.

Crisp and cheesy, these Mexican-style snacks are fun and flavorful. We hosted a family reunion one spring and made a fiesta dinner. Everyone loved these quesadillas. —*Jeri Dobrowski, Beach, North Dakota*

  1 pound fresh mushrooms, chopped
  2 to 3 jalapeno peppers, seeded and
     chopped
  2 tablespoons olive oil
1/4 cup minced fresh cilantro
Vegetable oil
  8 flour tortillas (7 inches)
  2 cups (8 ounces) shredded Monterey Jack
     cheese
Salsa and guacamole, optional

In a large skillet, saute mushrooms and jalapenos in olive oil until tender and liquid is nearly evaporated. Add cilantro; cook and stir for 1 minute. Remove from the heat.

Heat 1 tablespoon vegetable oil in a large skillet; add one tortilla. Top with 1/2 cup cheese, 1/3 cup mushroom mixture and another tortilla. Cook for 2-3 minutes on each side or until lightly browned.

Repeat with the remaining tortillas, cheese and mushroom mixture, adding more oil as needed. Serve with salsa and guacamole if desired. **Yield:** 4 servings.

White Chocolate Party Mix

(Pictured below)

Prep: 10 min. + standing

I get rave reviews every time I prepare this crispy combination of cereal, popcorn, pretzels, nuts and candies. Coated in white chocolate, this mix is great for meetings, parties and gift giving. —Rose Wentzel, St. Louis, Missouri

 16 **cups popped popcorn**
  3 **cups Frosted Cheerios**
1-1/2 **cups pecan halves**
  1 **package (14 ounces) milk chocolate M&M's**

  1 **package (10 ounces) pretzel sticks**
  1 **package English toffee bits (10 ounces)** *or* **almond brickle bits (7-1/2 ounces)**
  2 **packages (10 to 12 ounces** *each***) vanilla** *or* **white chips**
  2 **tablespoons vegetable oil**

In a large bowl, combine the first six ingredients. In a microwave or heavy saucepan, melt chips and oil; stir until smooth. Pour over popcorn mixture and toss to coat.

Immediately spread onto two baking sheets; let stand until dry, about 2 hours. Store in an airtight container. **Yield:** 9-1/2 quarts.

GOODIES like Breaded Chicken Wings, Warm Asparagus-Crab Spread, Mushroom Quesadillas and White Chocolate Party Mix (shown above) will spice up any occasion.

Salads & Dressings

Looking to toss together a lighter lunch or dinner? You're sure to find a refreshingly different salad here to suit your taste buds.

TOSS ONE TOGETHER. Clockwise from upper left: Triple-Cranberry Salad Mold (p. 28), Campfire Taco Salad (p. 30), Asparagus Berry Salad (p. 30), Jalapeno Potato Salad (p. 28) and Mint Dressing for Fruit (p. 29).

Jalapeno Potato Salad

(Pictured on page 26)

Prep: 30 min. + chilling

This is a zippy spin on traditional potato salad that's perfect for a picnic! —*Sarah Woodruff, Watertown, South Dakota*

 6 medium red potatoes, peeled and cubed
 2 celery ribs, chopped
 2 hard-cooked eggs, chopped
 1/4 cup chopped onion
 2 small jalapeno peppers, seeded and chopped
 1/4 cup mayonnaise
 3 tablespoons spicy brown mustard
 3 teaspoons hot pepper sauce
 1/4 teaspoon ground cumin
 1/4 teaspoon pepper

Place the potatoes in a large saucepan and cover with water. Bring to a boil. Reduce heat; cover and cook for 10-15 minutes or until tender. Drain; cool to room temperature.

In a large serving bowl, combine potatoes, celery, eggs, onion and jalapenos. In a small bowl, combine the mayonnaise, mustard, hot pepper sauce, cumin and pepper. Pour over potato mixture and toss gently to coat. Cover and refrigerate overnight. **Yield:** 5 servings.

Editor's Note: When cutting or seeding hot peppers, use rubber or plastic gloves to protect your hands. Avoid touching your face.

Apple-Walnut Tossed Salad

(Pictured above)

Prep/Total Time: 25 min.

The pretty, flavorful cranberry dressing for this fall salad is also good for gift-giving. —*Mary Walton Kelso, Washington*

 1/4 cup red wine vinegar
 1/4 cup fresh cranberries
 2 tablespoons honey
 1 tablespoon sugar
 1 tablespoon chopped red onion
 1/4 teaspoon salt
 1/4 teaspoon pepper
 3/4 cup vegetable oil
 2 packages (5 ounces *each*) spring mix salad greens
 3 medium Red Delicious apples, thinly sliced
 1 cup chopped walnuts, toasted

For cranberry vinaigrette, combine the first seven ingredients in a blender; cover and process until blended. While processing, gradually add oil in a steady stream. Transfer to a serving dish. In a large bowl, toss the salad greens, apples and walnuts. Serve with vinaigrette. **Yield:** 8 servings.

Triple-Cranberry Salad Mold

(Pictured on page 26)

Prep: 20 min. + chilling

What's a holiday meal without at least one jolly gelatin salad chock-full of fruit and nuts? My mother made this one for every holiday, and now my husband says he can't imagine Christmas without it! —*Kristi Jo Chiles Portsmouth, Rhode Island*

 2 packages (3 ounces *each*) cranberry gelatin
 3 cups boiling water
 1 cup cranberry juice
 2 packages (3 ounces *each*) cream cheese, softened
 1 carton (8 ounces) frozen whipped topping, thawed
 1 cup chopped walnuts
 1 cup chopped celery
 1 cup chopped fresh *or* frozen cranberries

In a large bowl, dissolve the gelatin in boiling water; stir in cranberry juice. Refrigerate until slightly thickened. In a small mixing bowl, beat the cream cheese until smooth. Add the whipped topping until blended. Fold into the gelatin mixture. Fold in walnuts, celery and cranberries.

Pour into a 3-qt. ring mold coated with nonstick cooking spray. Refrigerate until set. Unmold onto a serving plate. **Yield:** 8-10 servings.

Mint Dressing for Fruit

(Pictured on page 26)

Prep/Total Time: 10 min.

This mild minty dressing nicely complements fresh fruits such as melon, strawberries, blueberries and peaches.
—Diane Thompson, Nutrioso, Arizona

✓ **Uses less fat, sugar or salt. Includes Nutritional Analysis and Diabetic Exchanges.**

- 1/2 cup sour cream
- 2 tablespoons minced fresh mint
- 2 tablespoons minced fresh cilantro
- 2 tablespoons olive oil
- 2 tablespoons cider vinegar
- 1 teaspoon sugar
- 1 teaspoon lemon juice
- 1/2 teaspoon ground cumin

Assorted fresh fruit

In a small bowl, combine sour cream, mint, cilantro, oil, vinegar, sugar, lemon juice and cumin. Serve with fruit. **Yield:** about 1 cup.

Nutritional Analysis: 1/4 cup dressing (prepared with reduced-fat sour cream) equals 107 calories, 9 g fat (3 g saturated fat), 10 mg cholesterol, 21 mg sodium, 4 g carbohydrate, trace fiber, 2 g protein. **Diabetic Exchange:** 2 fat.

Crispy Chicken Strip Salad

(Pictured at right)

Prep: 40 min.   **Cook:** 10 min.

Serve this attractive main-dish salad for a luncheon with friends, and you're sure to win raves. Well-seasoned chicken strips, raspberries and candied pecans top a bed of fresh greens flavored with a fruity vinaigrette.
—Lillian Julow, Gainesville, Florida

- 1 tablespoon butter
- 1/2 cup pecan halves
- 2 tablespoons sugar
- 3/4 cup all-purpose flour
- 2 tablespoons minced fresh tarragon *or* 2 teaspoons dried tarragon
- 1 tablespoon grated lemon peel
- 2 eggs
- 1 pound boneless skinless chicken breasts, cut into 1-inch strips
- 2 tablespoons vegetable oil
- 4 cups spring mix salad greens
- 1 cup torn Bibb *or* Boston lettuce
- 1/2 cup raspberry vinaigrette
- 2 cups fresh *or* frozen unsweetened raspberries

In a small skillet, melt butter. Add pecans and cook over medium heat until nuts are toasted, about 4 minutes. Sprinkle with sugar. Cook and stir for 2-4 minutes or until sugar is melted. Transfer to a greased foil-lined baking sheet; cool completely.

In a large resealable bag, combine the flour, tarragon and lemon peel. In a shallow bowl, beat the eggs. Add chicken strips to flour mixture in batches; seal and shake to coat. Dip in eggs, then return to bag and coat again. In a large skillet over medium heat, cook chicken in oil for 6-8 minutes or until no longer pink, turning once.

Break the pecans apart. Toss the greens and lettuce with vinaigrette; arrange on individual plates. Top with raspberries, chicken strips and pecans. **Yield:** 4 servings.

Sunny Carrot Salad

(Pictured below)

Prep/Total Time: 10 min.

Almonds and sunflower kernels give a pleasing crunch to this speedy variation on traditional carrot-raisin salad.
—*Barb Hunter, Ponder, Texas*

- 3 **cups shredded carrots**
- 2 **cups unsweetened crushed pineapple, drained**
- 1/2 **cup golden raisins**
- 1/3 **cup mayonnaise**
- 1/2 **cup sliced almonds**
- 1/3 **cup unsalted sunflower kernels**

In a large serving bowl, combine the carrots, pineapple and raisins. Stir in mayonnaise. Cover and refrigerate until serving. Just before serving, add almonds and sunflower kernels; toss to coat. **Yield:** 5 servings.

Asparagus Berry Salad

(Pictured on page 27)

Prep/Total Time: 30 min.

When strawberries and asparagus are at their peak, this salad is sensational! Sometimes I add grilled chicken or salmon to create a refreshing but filling main-dish salad.
—*Trisha Kruse, Eagle, Idaho*

- 1 **pound fresh asparagus, trimmed and cut into 1-inch pieces**
- 3 **tablespoons olive oil, *divided***
- 1/4 **teaspoon salt**
- 1/4 **teaspoon coarsely ground pepper**
- 8 **cups spring mix salad greens**

- 3 **cups sliced fresh strawberries**
- 1/2 **small red onion, thinly sliced**
- 1/2 **cup chopped walnuts, toasted**
- 2 **tablespoons balsamic vinegar**
- 2 **teaspoons sugar**

In a bowl, toss the asparagus with 1 tablespoon oil. Spread in a single layer in a greased 15-in. x 10-in. x 1-in. baking pan. Sprinkle with salt and pepper. Bake at 400° for 15-20 minutes or until tender.

In a large salad bowl, toss greens, strawberries, onion, walnuts and asparagus. In a small bowl, whisk the vinegar, sugar and remaining oil. Drizzle over the salad and toss to coat. **Yield:** 6-8 servings.

Campfire Taco Salad

(Pictured on page 27)

Prep/Total Time: 25 min.

Served in a corn chip bag, this easy outdoor meal is flavorful and fun. My neighbor entertained Girl Scouts with this clever recipe. —*Jean Komlos, Plymouth, Michigan*

- 6 **snack-size bags (1 ounce *each*) corn chips**
- 1 **can (15 ounces) chili without beans**
- 3 **cups (12 ounces) shredded cheddar cheese**
- 3/4 **cup sour cream**
- 1 **jar (8 ounces) mild salsa**
- 1/2 **medium head iceberg lettuce, shredded**

Cut the top off each bag of chips; set aside. Place chili in a saucepan; cook on a grill over medium heat for 10 minutes or until heated through, stirring occasionally. Spoon about 2 tablespoons of chili into each bag of chips. Top with cheese, sour cream, salsa and lettuce. **Yield:** 6 servings.

Black Bean Avocado Salad

Prep: 20 min. + chilling

You can taste the essence of summer in this refreshing salad I serve with grilled chicken. —*Sue Kauffman Columbia City, Indiana*

- 1 **can (15 ounces) black beans, rinsed and drained**
- 1 **can (11 ounces) Mexicorn, drained**
- 1-1/3 **cups chopped peeled avocados**
- 1 **cup chopped seeded cucumber**
- 1 **cup chopped seeded tomatoes**
- 1/2 **cup thinly sliced green onions**
- 1 **small jalapeno pepper, seeded and chopped**
- 1 **teaspoon lime juice**

DRESSING:
- 2 tablespoons cider vinegar
- 1 tablespoon olive oil
- 1 teaspoon ground cumin
- 1/2 teaspoon dried oregano
- 1/4 teaspoon salt
- 1/8 teaspoon pepper

In a large bowl, combine the first eight ingredients. In a small bowl, whisk the dressing ingredients. Pour over salad and toss to coat. Cover and refrigerate for at least 1 hour before serving. **Yield:** 8 servings.

Editor's Note: When cutting or seeding hot peppers, use rubber or plastic gloves to protect your hands. Avoid touching your face.

Waldorf Tuna Salad

Prep/Total Time: 20 min.

I dress up tuna salad deliciously with apple, raisins, dates and walnuts...then drizzle it all with a tangy yogurt dressing. —*Shirley Glaab, Hattiesburg, Mississippi*

✓ Uses less fat, sugar or salt. Includes Nutritional Analysis and Diabetic Exchanges.

- 2 cans (6 ounces *each*) light water-packed tuna, drained and flaked
- 1 large red apple, chopped
- 1/3 cup chopped celery
- 1/3 cup raisins
- 1/3 cup chopped dates
- 1/4 cup chopped walnuts
- 1/2 cup fat-free plain yogurt
- 1/4 cup reduced-fat mayonnaise
- 4 lettuce leaves
- 1/4 cup shredded reduced-fat Monterey Jack cheese

In a large bowl, combine tuna, apple, celery, raisins, dates and walnuts. Combine yogurt and mayonnaise; add to tuna mixture and toss to coat. Serve on lettuce-lined plates; sprinkle with cheese. **Yield:** 4 servings.

Nutritional Analysis: 3/4 cup equals 340 calories, 12 g fat (2 g saturated fat), 36 mg cholesterol, 495 mg sodium, 34 g carbohydrate, 4 g fiber, 28 g protein. **Diabetic Exchanges:** 2-1/2 lean meat, 1-1/2 fruit, 1 starch, 1 fat.

Basil Chicken Over Greens

(Pictured above right)

Prep: 40 min. + marinating   **Cook:** 15 min.

This eye-catching salad entree pairs basil-stuffed chicken breasts with sliced fennel and salad greens.
—*Marie Rizzo, Interlochen, Michigan*

- 4 boneless skinless chicken breast halves (6 ounces *each*)
- 1/2 cup plus 1/3 cup Italian salad dressing, *divided*
- 1 package (10 ounces) Italian-blend salad greens
- 1 medium fennel bulb, sliced
- 1/4 cup minced fresh basil
- 2 plum tomatoes, chopped
- 1 egg
- 1 tablespoon water
- 2/3 cup seasoned bread crumbs
- 1/2 cup grated Parmesan cheese
- 2 tablespoons olive oil

Chopped fennel fronds, optional

Flatten chicken to 1/4-in. thickness; place in a large resealable plastic bag. Add 1/2 cup salad dressing; seal bag and turn to coat. Refrigerate for 30 minutes. Arrange salad greens and fennel slices on a serving platter; drizzle with remaining dressing. Cover and refrigerate.

Drain and discard marinade. Place 1 tablespoon of basil on each piece of chicken; top with tomatoes. Roll up jelly-roll style, starting with a short side; tie with kitchen string. In a shallow bowl, beat egg and water. In another shallow bowl, combine bread crumbs and Parmesan cheese. Dip chicken in egg mixture, then roll in crumb mixture.

In a large nonstick skillet over medium heat, cook chicken in oil on all sides for 15-20 minutes or until juices run clear. Slice and arrange over greens. Garnish with fennel fronds if desired. **Yield:** 4 servings.

In a bowl, combine the rice, lentils, tomato, onions and parsley. In a small bowl, combine the remaining ingredients. Pour over rice mixture; toss to coat. Cover and refrigerate for at least 1 hour. **Yield:** 7 servings.

Nutritional Analysis: 1/2 cup equals 111 calories, 3 g fat (trace saturated fat), trace cholesterol, 369 mg sodium, 18 g carbohydrate, 4 g fiber, 4 g protein. **Diabetic Exchanges:** 1 starch, 1/2 lean meat.

Mandarin Vegetable Medley

Prep: 20 min. + chilling

This crisp and refreshing salad is loaded with good-for-you ingredients and coated with a from-scratch light honey-lemon dressing. I serve it whenever I prepare grilled turkey or chicken.
—*Sandy D'Agostino*
Murphys, California

✓ **Uses less fat, sugar or salt. Includes Nutritional Analysis and Diabetic Exchanges.**

   1 pound fresh asparagus, trimmed and cut into 2-inch pieces
   1 can (14-1/2 ounces) reduced-sodium chicken broth
   2 cups fresh snow peas
   1 can (15 ounces) whole baby corn, rinsed and drained
   1 can (11 ounces) mandarin oranges, drained
   1 can (8 ounces) sliced water chestnuts, drained
   2 celery ribs, thinly sliced
1/2 cup finely chopped red onion
   1 green onion, thinly sliced
DRESSING:
   5 tablespoons lemon juice
   2 tablespoons olive oil
   2 tablespoons reduced-sodium soy sauce
   1 tablespoon honey
   1 teaspoon Dijon mustard
   2 garlic cloves, minced
   1 teaspoon pepper
1/2 teaspoon salt
   2 teaspoons sesame seeds, toasted

In a large skillet, bring asparagus and broth to a boil. Reduce heat; cover and simmer for 3 minutes or until crisp-tender. Drain; immediately place the asparagus in ice water. Drain and pat dry.

In a large bowl, combine the peas, corn, oranges, water chestnuts, celery, onions and asparagus. In a small bowl, whisk the lemon juice, oil, soy sauce, honey, mustard, garlic, pepper and salt. Pour over vegetables. Cover and refrigerate for at least 1 hour. Sprinkle with sesame seeds. **Yield:** 8 servings.

Brown Rice Lentil Salad

(Pictured above)

Prep: 10 min.   **Cook:** 45 min. + chilling

My family isn't always crazy about trying new recipes. The first time I served this salad, they took tiny helpings just to appease me. But the unanimous verdict was "It tastes great!" —*DeAnn Howard, Grinnell, Iowa*

✓ **Uses less fat, sugar or salt. Includes Nutritional Analysis and Diabetic Exchanges.**

1/2 cup uncooked brown rice
   1 cup water
   1 teaspoon chicken bouillon granules
   1 cup cooked lentils
   1 medium tomato, seeded and diced
1/3 cup thinly sliced green onions
   1 tablespoon minced fresh parsley
   2 tablespoons red wine vinegar
   1 tablespoon olive oil
   2 garlic cloves, minced
   2 teaspoons lime juice
   2 teaspoons Dijon mustard
1/2 teaspoon salt
1/4 teaspoon pepper

In a saucepan over medium heat, bring the rice, water and bouillon to a boil. Reduce heat; cover and simmer for 40 minutes or until rice is tender. Cool.

Nutritional Analysis: 1 cup equals 106 calories, 4 g fat (trace saturated fat), 0 cholesterol, 432 mg sodium, 15 g carbohydrate, 4 g fiber, 3 g protein. **Diabetic Exchanges:** 1 vegetable, 1/2 starch, 1/2 fat.

Springtime Spinach Salad

Prep/Total Time: 25 min.

I came up with this recipe as a way to use early spring produce. The toasted walnuts give the salad a rich earthy flavor that ties it all together. —*Trisha Kruse Boise, Idaho*

  1 **pound fresh asparagus, trimmed and cut into 1-inch pieces**
  1 **tablespoon olive oil**
  1 **package (10 ounces) fresh spinach, torn**
  2 **cups fresh strawberries, sliced**
1/2 **cup chopped walnuts, toasted**
1/3 **cup vegetable oil**
  3 **tablespoons raspberry vinegar**
  1 **teaspoon sugar**
1/2 **teaspoon salt**

Place asparagus in a foil-lined 15-in. x 10-in. x 1-in. baking pan; sprinkle with olive oil and toss to coat. Bake, uncovered, at 400° for 15 minutes or until crisp-tender, turning occasionally. Cool.

In a large bowl, combine the spinach, strawberries, walnuts and asparagus. In a jar with a tight-fitting lid, combine the vegetable oil, vinegar, sugar and salt; shake well. Drizzle over salad and toss to coat. Serve immediately. **Yield:** 10 servings.

Summer Chicken Salad

(Pictured at right)

Prep: 10 min. **Cook:** 25 min. + chilling

I found this recipe many years ago in a church cookbook and have made it many times since. It's special enough for a fancy dinner but easy enough to fix for a light lunch. There's a kick to the tangy citrus dressing, which even my picky son enjoys. —*Nancy Whitford, Edwards, New York*

  4 **boneless skinless chicken breast halves (4 ounces *each*)**
  1 **can (14-1/2 ounces) chicken broth**
  6 **cups torn mixed salad greens**
  2 **cups halved fresh strawberries**
CITRUS DRESSING:
1/2 **cup fresh strawberries, hulled**
1/3 **cup orange juice**
  2 **tablespoons vegetable oil**
  1 **tablespoon lemon juice**

  2 **teaspoons grated lemon peel**
  1 **teaspoon sugar**
1/2 **teaspoon chili powder**
1/4 **teaspoon salt**
1/4 **teaspoon pepper**
1/4 **cup chopped walnuts, toasted**

Place chicken in a large skillet; add broth. Bring to a boil. Reduce heat; cover and simmer for 20-25 minutes or until the juices run clear. Drain; cover and refrigerate. In a large bowl, combine the greens and the halved strawberries; refrigerate.

In a blender, combine the hulled strawberries, orange juice, oil, lemon juice, lemon peel, sugar, chili powder, salt and pepper. Cover and process until smooth. Pour into a small saucepan. Bring to a boil. Reduce heat; simmer for 5-6 minutes until slightly thickened. Cool slightly.

Drizzle half of the dressing over greens and berries; toss to coat. Divide among four plates. Cut chicken into 1/8-in. slices; arrange over salads. Drizzle remaining dressing over chicken; sprinkle with nuts. **Yield:** 4 servings.

Cheesy Beef Taco Salad

(Pictured below)

Prep/Total Time: 30 min.

I often double this recipe just so there are leftovers for lunch the next day! —Arlene Ghent, St. Joseph, Michigan

 1-1/2 pounds ground beef
 1-1/2 cups chopped onion
  1 cup diced celery
  1 cup diced green pepper
  2 garlic cloves, minced
  1 pound process cheese (Velveeta), cubed
  1 can (10 ounces) diced tomatoes and green chilies, undrained
  2 teaspoons chili powder
  2 teaspoons ground cumin
 1-1/2 cups crushed corn chips
Shredded lettuce
Chopped green onions
  2 large tomatoes, cut into wedges

In a large skillet, cook the beef, onion, celery, green pepper and garlic over medium heat until meat is no longer pink and vegetables are tender; drain. Stir in the cheese, tomatoes, chili powder and cumin. Cook and stir over low heat until cheese is melted. Stir in corn chips.

Line six salad plates with lettuce; sprinkle with green onions. Top each with 1 cup beef mixture. Garnish with tomato wedges. **Yield:** 6 servings.

Apple-Cheddar Tossed Salad

Prep/Total Time: 15 min.

My mother makes this colorful salad for all sorts of special occasions. —Amy Osborne-Schebler, Davenport, Iowa

 10 cups torn mixed salad greens
  1 cup chopped red apple
  1 cup cubed cheddar cheese
  1 cup chopped walnuts, toasted
HONEY DRESSING:
 2/3 cup honey
  2 tablespoons cider vinegar
  1 teaspoon celery seed
  1 teaspoon ground mustard
  1 teaspoon paprika
  1 teaspoon lemon juice
  1 teaspoon grated onion
 1/4 teaspoon salt
  1 cup vegetable oil

In a large salad bowl, combine the greens, apple, cheese and walnuts. In a blender or food processor, combine the first eight dressing ingredients. While processing, gradually add the oil in a steady stream. Serve with salad. **Yield:** 10 servings.

Crunchy Pea Salad

Prep/Total Time: 15 min.

Radishes and water chestnuts put the crunch in this appealing salad draped in a light mayonnaise dressing. —Barbara Kopfmann, West Bend, Wisconsin

✓ **Uses less fat, sugar or salt. Includes Nutritional Analysis and Diabetic Exchanges.**

  1 package (16 ounces) frozen peas, thawed
  1 can (8 ounces) sliced water chestnuts, drained
 1/2 cup diced radishes
 1/2 cup diced sweet red pepper
 1/3 cup diced red onion
 1/3 cup reduced-fat mayonnaise
  1 teaspoon dill weed
 1/2 teaspoon garlic salt
 1/2 teaspoon poppy seeds

In a large serving bowl, combine peas, water chestnuts, radishes, red pepper and onion. In a small bowl, combine the remaining ingredients. Pour over vegetables and toss gently to coat. Cover and refrigerate until serving. **Yield:** 6 servings.

Nutritional Analysis: 2/3 cup equals 120 calories, 3 g fat (trace saturated fat), 4 mg cholesterol, 358 mg sodium, 19 g carbohydrate, 5 g fiber, 5 g protein. **Diabetic Exchanges:** 1 starch, 1 vegetable, 1/2 fat.

Anise Fruit Bowl

Prep: 30 min. + chilling

Toss together your favorite fruits for this delightful medley dressed with a pleasant anise-laced syrup. This dish always goes over well. —*Alberta McKay, Bartlesville, Oklahoma*

   2 **cups water**
1-1/4 **cups sugar**
   3 **tablespoons lemon juice**
   2 **tablespoons aniseed**
1/2 **teaspoon salt**
 12 **cups assorted fresh fruit**

In a small saucepan, combine the water, sugar, lemon juice, aniseed and salt. Bring to a boil. Reduce heat; simmer, uncovered, for 15 minutes. Remove from the heat. Cover and refrigerate until chilled.

   Strain syrup; discard aniseed. Place fruit in a large bowl. Add syrup; toss to coat. Cover; refrigerate until serving. Serve with a slotted spoon. **Yield:** 16 servings.

Special Pepper Salad

Prep: 15 min. + chilling

Strips of ham and Swiss cheese enhance the sweet pepper mix in this refreshing salad. —*Cheryl Maczko Arthurdale, West Virginia*

✓ **Uses less fat, sugar or salt. Includes Nutritional Analysis and Diabetic Exchanges.**

 1 *each* **small green, sweet red and yellow pepper, julienned**
 1 **banana pepper, seeded and cut into rings**
1/4 **pound fully cooked lean ham, cut into 2-inch strips**
 2 **ounces Swiss cheese, cut into 2-inch strips**
 1 **small red onion, julienned**
1/4 **cup canned chopped green chilies, drained**
DRESSING:
 3 **tablespoons cider vinegar**
 3 **tablespoons olive oil**
 1 **teaspoon ground mustard**
 1 **teaspoon pepper**
 1 **teaspoon minced fresh dill**
1/4 **teaspoon sugar**
 2 **to 5 drops hot pepper sauce, optional**

In a large salad bowl, combine peppers, ham, cheese, onion and chilies. In a blender, combine dressing ingredients; cover and process until blended. Drizzle over salad; toss to coat. Cover and refrigerate for at least 1 hour. Serve with a slotted spoon. **Yield:** 6 servings.

   Nutritional Analysis: 3/4 cup equals 149 calories, 11 g fat (3 g saturated fat), 16 mg cholesterol, 262 mg sodium, 6 g carbohydrate, 2 g fiber, 7 g protein. **Diabetic Exchanges:** 2 fat, 1 vegetable, 1/2 lean meat.

   Editor's Note: When cutting or seeding hot peppers, use rubber or plastic gloves to protect your hands. Avoid touching your face.

Blueberry Chicken Salad

(Pictured above)

Prep: 15 min. + chilling

This excellent combination goes together quickly in the morning to take for lunch or makes a nice light salad for a summer supper. —*Kari Caven, Post Falls, Idaho*

 2 **cups fresh blueberries**
 2 **cups cubed cooked chicken breast**
3/4 **cup chopped celery**
1/2 **cup diced sweet red pepper**
1/2 **cup thinly sliced green onions**
 1 **carton (6 ounces) lemon yogurt**
 3 **tablespoons mayonnaise**
1/2 **teaspoon salt**
Bibb lettuce leaves, optional

Set aside a few blueberries for garnish. In a large bowl, gently combine the chicken, celery, red pepper, onions and remaining blueberries. Combine the yogurt, mayonnaise and salt; drizzle over chicken mixture and gently toss to coat.

   Cover and refrigerate for at least 30 minutes. Serve on lettuce-lined plates if desired. Top with reserved blueberries. **Yield:** 4 servings.

Soups & Sandwiches

Served alone or together
as a meal, these soups and
sandwiches will soon become
mainstays in your home.

PLEASING PAIRS. Clockwise from upper left: Turkey Meatball Subs (p. 42), Hearty Goose Soup (p. 43), Buffalo Chicken Wraps (p. 40), Venison Chili Con Carne (p. 42) and Beef Brisket on Buns (p. 39).

Warm Ham 'n' Swiss Wraps

(Pictured above)

Prep/Total Time: 30 min.

I love to make these wraps when we have a busy week. They're easy to put together…and my family gobbles them up. You can adapt the filling to use ingredients you have on hand or to suit your own tastes. —Cheryl Schut
Jenison, Michigan

- 6 **flour tortillas (10 inches)**
- 1 **pound thinly sliced deli ham**
- 2 **cups (8 ounces) shredded Swiss cheese**
- 3 **cups chopped lettuce**
- 1 **medium tomato, seeded and diced**
- 1/2 **cup diced cucumber**
- 2 **tablespoons chopped green pepper**
- 2 **green onions, chopped**

DRESSING:
- 3/4 **cup mayonnaise**
- 3 **tablespoons milk**
- 2 **teaspoons sugar**
- 1 **teaspoon prepared mustard**
- 1/2 **teaspoon celery seed**

On each tortilla, layer four slices of ham and 1/3 cup cheese; roll up and secure with toothpicks. Place in an ungreased 11-in. x 7-in. x 2-in. baking pan. Cover and bake at 350° for 14-16 minutes or until cheese is melted.

Meanwhile, combine the lettuce, tomato, cucumber, green pepper and onions. In a small bowl, whisk all of the dressing ingredients. Unroll the tortillas halfway; top each with 1/3 cup lettuce mixture and 1 table-

spoon dressing. Roll up again and serve immediately. **Yield:** 6 servings.

Firehouse Chili

Prep: 20 min.   **Cook:** 1-1/2 hours

As one of the cooks at the firehouse, I used to prepare meals for 10 men. This chili was among their favorites.
—Richard Clements, San Dimas, California

✓ **Uses less fat, sugar or salt. Includes Nutritional Analysis and Diabetic Exchanges.**

- 4 **pounds ground beef**
- 2 **medium onions, chopped**
- 1 **medium green pepper, chopped**
- 3 **cans (28 ounces *each*) stewed tomatoes, cut up**
- 4 **cans (16 ounces *each*) kidney beans, rinsed and drained**
- 1 **can (14-1/2 ounces) beef broth**
- 3 **tablespoons chili powder**
- 2 **tablespoons ground coriander**
- 2 **tablespoons ground cumin**
- 4 **garlic cloves, minced**
- 1 **teaspoon dried oregano**

In a Dutch oven, cook the beef, onions and green pepper over medium heat until meat is no longer pink; drain. Stir in the remaining ingredients. Bring to a boil. Reduce heat; cover and simmer for 1-1/2 hours or until flavors are blended. **Yield:** 11 servings.

Nutritional Analysis: 1-1/2 cups (prepared with lean ground beef and reduced-sodium broth) equals 485 calories, 13 g fat (5 g saturated fat), 82 mg cholesterol, 856 mg sodium, 48 g carbohydrate, 12 g fiber, 45 g protein.

Southwestern Chicken Soup

Prep: 10 min.   **Cook:** 25 min.

This hearty soup is chock-full of chicken, corn, black beans and diced tomatoes seasoned with zippy Southwestern flavor. Mexican corn bread makes a delicious accompaniment. —Terri Stevens, Ardmore, Oklahoma

- 1/2 **pound boneless skinless chicken breasts, cut into 1/2-inch cubes**
- 1/4 **cup finely chopped onion**
- 2 **garlic cloves, minced**
- 2 **tablespoons olive oil**
- 1 **can (15-1/4 ounces) whole kernel corn, drained**
- 1 **can (15 ounces) black beans, rinsed and drained**

1 can (14-1/2 ounces) chicken broth
1 can (10 ounces) diced tomatoes and green chilies, undrained
1 teaspoon ground cumin
1/2 teaspoon salt
1/2 teaspoon chili powder
1/8 teaspoon cayenne pepper
Plain yogurt and minced fresh cilantro

In a large skillet over medium heat, cook the chicken, onion and garlic in oil until chicken is lightly browned and onion is tender.

Stir in the corn, beans, broth, tomatoes, cumin, salt, chili powder and cayenne. Bring to a boil. Reduce heat; cover and simmer for 10-15 minutes. Garnish with yogurt and cilantro. **Yield:** 4 servings.

Beef Brisket on Buns

(Pictured on page 36)

Prep: 25 min. + standing   **Bake:** 5 hours

This beef brisket turns out so tender and delicious every time! —*Deb Waggoner, Grand Island, Nebraska*

1/2 teaspoon ground ginger
1/2 teaspoon ground mustard
1 fresh beef brisket (4 to 5 pounds)
2 cups water
1 cup ketchup
1/2 cup Worcestershire sauce
2 tablespoons brown sugar
2 teaspoons Liquid Smoke, optional
1 teaspoon chili powder
16 to 20 sandwich buns, split, optional

Combine the ginger and mustard; rub over brisket. Place on a rack in a shallow roasting pan. Bake, uncovered, at 325° for 2 hours.

Let stand for 20 minutes. Thinly slice meat across grain. Place in a foil-lined 13-in. x 9-in. x 2-in. baking dish. In a bowl, combine water, ketchup, Worcestershire sauce, brown sugar, Liquid Smoke if desired and chili powder; pour over meat. Cover tightly with foil; bake 3 hours longer or until tender. Serve on buns if desired. **Yield:** 16-20 servings.

Turkey Vegetable Soup

(Pictured at right)

Prep: 15 min.   **Cook:** 1 hour

Low-sodium ingredients don't diminish the full flavor of this brothy soup. The ground turkey gives the soup a heartiness everyone will welcome on a cold blustery evening.
—*Bonnie LeBarron, Forestville, New York*

✓ Uses less fat, sugar or salt. Includes Nutritional Analysis and Diabetic Exchanges.

1 pound lean ground turkey
1 cup chopped celery
1/2 cup chopped onion
2 to 3 garlic cloves, minced
2 cans (14-1/2 ounces *each*) reduced-sodium beef broth
2-1/2 cups reduced-sodium tomato juice
1 can (14-1/2 ounces) diced tomatoes, drained
1 cup sliced fresh mushrooms
3/4 cup frozen French-style green beans
1/2 cup sliced carrots
1-1/2 teaspoons Worcestershire sauce
1 teaspoon dried parsley flakes
1 teaspoon dried thyme
1/2 teaspoon sugar
1/2 teaspoon dried basil
1/4 teaspoon pepper
1 bay leaf

In a Dutch oven coated with nonstick cooking spray, saute turkey, celery, onion and garlic until meat is no longer pink and vegetables are tender; drain. Stir in remaining ingredients. Bring to a boil.

Reduce heat; cover and simmer for 1 hour or until vegetables are tender. Discard bay leaf. **Yield:** 4 servings.

Nutritional Analysis: 1-1/2 cups equals 272 calories, 10 g fat (3 g saturated fat), 94 mg cholesterol, 783 mg sodium, 20 g carbohydrate, 5 g fiber, 25 g protein. **Diabetic Exchanges:** 2-1/2 lean meat, 1 starch, 1 vegetable, 1/2 fat.

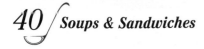
Sweet Onion BBQ Burgers

(Pictured below)

Prep: 30 min. + marinating   **Grill:** 15 min.

Smoked cheese, sauteed onions and a special sauce make these moist burgers out of the ordinary!
—Christie Gardiner, Eagle Mountain, Utah

- 1/2 cup dry bread crumbs
- 2 teaspoons onion salt
- 2 teaspoons brown sugar
- 1 egg, beaten
- 1 pound ground beef
- 1-1/4 cups barbecue sauce

SAUCE:
- 1/2 cup mayonnaise
- 1/2 cup barbecue sauce
- 1 teaspoon brown sugar

ONION TOPPING:
- 2 tablespoons butter
- 1/4 cup honey
- 2 large sweet onions, thinly sliced
- 4 slices smoked cheddar cheese
- 4 hamburger buns, split

In a bowl, combine the bread crumbs, onion salt and brown sugar. Add egg. Crumble beef over mixture and mix well. Shape into four patties. Place in a shallow dish; pour barbecue sauce over patties. Cover and refrigerate for 2-4 hours.

In a small bowl, combine the sauce ingredients; cover and refrigerate until serving. For topping, melt the butter in a large skillet. Stir in honey until blended. Add onions; saute for 15-20 minutes or until tender and lightly browned. Keep warm.

Drain and discard barbecue sauce. Grill patties, uncovered, over medium-hot heat for 5-7 minutes on each side or until juices run clear. Top each with a cheese slice; grill 1 minute longer or until cheese is melted. Serve on buns with sauce and onion topping. **Yield:** 4 servings.

Buffalo Chicken Wraps

(Pictured on page 37)

Prep/Total Time: 25 min.

Blue cheese dressing and hot pepper sauce enhance these tortilla wraps filled with chicken, cheese, lettuce and tomatoes.   —Athena Russell, Florence, South Carolina

- 1 cup all-purpose flour
- 1 teaspoon salt
- 1/4 teaspoon pepper
- 1/2 cup buttermilk
- 4 boneless skinless chicken breast halves
- 1 cup vegetable oil
- 1/2 cup hot pepper sauce
- 1/4 cup butter, melted
- 4 spinach tortillas (10 inches)
- 1 cup shredded lettuce
- 1 cup (4 ounces) shredded cheddar cheese
- 2/3 cup chopped tomatoes
- 1/2 cup blue cheese salad dressing

In a shallow bowl, combine the flour, salt and pepper. Place buttermilk in another shallow bowl. Dip chicken in buttermilk, then roll in flour mixture. In a large skillet, cook chicken in oil for 8-10 minutes or until juices run clear. Drain on paper towels; cut into strips.

In a bowl, combine the hot pepper sauce and butter. Dip chicken strips into mixture, coating both sides. Place chicken in the center of each tortilla. Layer with lettuce, cheese and tomatoes; drizzle with salad dressing. Bring up sides of tortillas; secure with toothpicks if desired. **Yield:** 4 servings.

Coney Island Sauce

You can get that hot dog stand taste right at home with this recipe!   —Shirley Heston, Pickerington, Ohio

- 1/2 pound ground beef
- 1/4 cup chopped onion
- 2 tablespoons chopped celery
- 1 can (8 ounces) tomato sauce
- 2 tablespoons brown sugar
- 1 tablespoon lemon juice
- 2-1/4 teaspoons Worcestershire sauce
- 3/4 teaspoon chili powder
- 1/2 teaspoon prepared mustard
- 1/4 teaspoon salt
- 8 hot dogs
- 8 hot dog buns, split

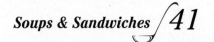

In a large skillet, cook beef, onion and celery over medium heat until meat is no longer pink; drain. Stir in tomato sauce, brown sugar, lemon juice, Worcestershire sauce, chili powder, mustard and salt. Bring to a boil. Reduce heat; simmer, uncovered, for 15-20 minutes or until sauce is thickened, stirring occasionally.

Grill or cook hot dogs according to package directions. Place hot dogs in buns; top with sauce. **Yield:** 8 servings with sauce.

Zesty Chicken Soup

Prep: 25 min. **Cook:** 40 min.

This spicy soup, chock-full of chicken and vegetables, freezes well. —Gwen Nelson, Castro Valley, California

✓ **Uses less fat, sugar or salt. Includes Nutritional Analysis and Diabetic Exchanges.**

1-1/4 **pounds boneless skinless chicken breasts**
    4 **cups water**
    1 **medium onion, chopped**
    2 **celery ribs, chopped**
    4 **garlic cloves, minced**
    1 **tablespoon canola oil**
    1 **can (14-1/2 ounces) Mexican diced tomatoes**
    1 **can (14-1/2 ounces) diced tomatoes**
    1 **can (8 ounces) tomato sauce**
    1 **cup medium salsa**
    3 **medium zucchini, halved and sliced**
    2 **medium carrots, sliced**
    1 **cup frozen white corn**
    1 **can (4 ounces) chopped green chilies**
    3 **teaspoons ground cumin**
    2 **teaspoons chili powder**
    1 **teaspoon dried basil**
Shredded cheddar cheese and tortilla chips, optional

Place chicken in a Dutch oven or soup kettle; add water. Bring to a boil; reduce heat. Cover and simmer for 10-15 minutes or until chicken juices run clear. Remove chicken; cut into 1/2-in. cubes. Return to cooking liquid.

In a large skillet, saute onion, celery and garlic in oil until tender; add to the Dutch oven. Stir in the tomatoes, tomato sauce, salsa, zucchini, carrots, corn, chilies, cumin, chili powder and basil. Bring to a boil. Reduce heat; cover and simmer for 20-25 minutes or until vegetables are tender.

Garnish with cheese and tortilla chips if desired. Soup may be frozen for up to 3 months. **Yield:** 10 servings (3-3/4 quarts).

Nutritional Analysis: 1-1/2 cups (calculated without cheese and tortilla chips) equals 152 calories, 3 g fat (1 g saturated fat), 31 mg cholesterol, 523 mg sodium,

18 g carbohydrate, 6 g fiber, 16 g protein. **Diabetic Exchanges:** 2 vegetable, 1 lean meat, 1/2 starch.

Chicken Veggie Fajitas

(Pictured above)

Prep/Total Time: 20 min.

Our family absolutely loves these fajitas, which are so quick to prepare. —Eleanor Martens, Rosenort, Manitoba

    3 **tablespoons lemon juice**
    1 **tablespoon soy sauce**
    1 **tablespoon Worcestershire sauce**
    2 **teaspoons vegetable oil**
    1 **garlic clove, minced**
1/2 **teaspoon ground cumin**
1/2 **teaspoon dried oregano**
3/4 **pound boneless skinless chicken breasts, cut into 1/2-inch strips**
    1 **small onion, sliced and separated into rings**
1/2 ***each* medium green, sweet red and yellow pepper, julienned**
    4 **flour tortillas (6 inches), warmed**
Shredded cheddar cheese, optional

In a small bowl, combine the first seven ingredients. Place chicken and vegetables in a single layer in a greased 15-in. x 10-in. x 1-in. baking pan; drizzle with 1/4 cup lemon juice mixture. Broil 4-6 in. from the heat for 4 minutes.

Turn chicken and vegetables; drizzle with remaining lemon juice mixture. Broil 4 minutes longer or until chicken juices run clear. Serve on tortillas with cheese if desired. **Yield:** 4 servings.

Turkey Meatball Subs

(Pictured on page 36)

Prep/Total Time: 30 min.

Here's an easy and nutritious way to make meatballs without all the mess of frying. Slather them with spaghetti sauce and tuck them in a sub sandwich roll—and you have a hearty lunch in hand that folks of all ages simply gobble up. —Cheryl Maczko, Arthurdale, West Virginia

>   1 medium onion, finely chopped
>   1 medium green pepper, finely chopped
>   2 garlic cloves, minced
>   1/2 teaspoon dried parsley flakes
>   1/4 teaspoon *each* dried basil, thyme and
>   rosemary, crushed
>   1/4 teaspoon salt
>   1/4 teaspoon pepper
>   1 jar (26 ounces) meatless spaghetti sauce,
>   *divided*
>   1 pound ground turkey
>   4 to 6 submarine *or* hoagie buns, split
>   1/2 to 3/4 cup shredded mozzarella cheese

In a bowl, combine the onion, green pepper, garlic, parsley and seasonings. Stir in 1/2 cup spaghetti sauce. Crumble turkey over mixture and mix well.

Shape into 1-in. balls. Place on a greased broiler pan. Broil 4-6 in. from the heat for 8 minutes. Turn and broil 3-5 minutes longer or until meat is no longer pink.

Transfer meatballs to a large saucepan; add remaining spaghetti sauce. Bring to a boil. Reduce heat; cover and simmer for 5 minutes. Serve meatballs and sauce on buns. Sprinkle with cheese. **Yield:** 4-6 servings.

Corn and Squash Soup

(Pictured above)

Prep/Total Time: 25 min.

This hearty soup pairs squash and cream-style corn. My family says it's their favorite squash dish, and friends always comment on its wonderful flavor. —Janice Zook
White River Junction, Vermont

>   12 bacon strips, diced
>   1 medium onion, chopped
>   1 celery rib, chopped
>   2 tablespoons all-purpose flour
>   1 can (14-1/2 ounces) chicken broth
>   6 cups mashed cooked butternut squash
>   2 cans (8-3/4 ounces *each*) cream-style corn
>   2 cups half-and-half cream
>   1 tablespoon minced fresh parsley
> 1-1/2 teaspoons salt
>   1/2 teaspoon pepper
> Sour cream, optional

In a large saucepan, cook bacon over medium heat until crisp. Remove to paper towels; drain, reserving 2 tablespoons drippings. In the drippings, saute onion and celery until tender. Stir in flour until blended. Gradually stir in broth. Bring to a boil; cook and stir for 2 minutes or until slightly thickened.

Reduce heat to medium. Stir in the squash, corn, cream, parsley, salt, pepper and bacon. Cook and stir until heated through. Garnish with sour cream if desired. **Yield:** 8 servings (2-1/2 quarts).

Venison Chili Con Carne

(Pictured on page 36)

Prep: 20 min.   **Cook:** 1 hour

I like to serve this thick, spicy chili over rice. The venison is tender, and the blend of spices, tomatoes and Italian hot sausage gives it plenty of zip. —Kim Vaughn
Hampton, Virginia

>   1 pound bulk hot Italian sausage
>   1 large onion, diced
>   1 medium sweet red pepper, diced
>   2 pounds venison steak, cut into 1-1/2-inch
>   cubes
>   2 tablespoons olive oil
>   1 can (28 ounces) crushed tomatoes
>   1 can (14-1/2 ounces) beef broth
>   1/4 cup tomato paste
>   1 tablespoon brown sugar
>   2 teaspoons ground cumin

2 teaspoons chili powder
1 teaspoon dried oregano
1/2 teaspoon crushed red pepper flakes
Salt and pepper to taste
1/4 cup minced fresh parsley
Hot cooked rice

In a Dutch oven, cook the sausage, onion and red pepper over medium heat until meat is no longer pink; drain and set aside.

In the same pan, brown venison in oil; drain. Add the tomatoes, broth, tomato paste, brown sugar, cumin, chili powder, oregano, pepper flakes, salt, pepper and sausage mixture. Simmer, uncovered, for 1 to 1-1/2 hours or until venison is tender. Stir in parsley. Serve over rice. **Yield:** 6 servings.

Hearty Goose Soup

(Pictured on page 37)

Prep: 15 min.   **Cook:** 5 hours

After my son went goose hunting, I had to cook what he brought home. So I got ingredients together and came up with this chunky soup chock-full of pasta and vegetables.
—Loretta Fenrich, Bonney Lake, Washington

2-1/4 cups cubed uncooked goose
1 pound red potatoes, cubed
1 large onion, chopped
1 *each* medium green, sweet yellow and red pepper, chopped
2 medium carrots, cut into 1/2-inch slices
1 cup water
3 garlic cloves, minced
2 teaspoons dried basil
Salt and pepper to taste
1 can (15 ounces) tomato sauce
1 can (14-1/2 ounces) Italian stewed tomatoes
2 cups uncooked elbow macaroni

In a 5-qt. slow cooker, combine goose, potatoes, onion, peppers, carrots, water, garlic, basil, salt and pepper. Cover and cook on high for 4 hours or until meat juices run clear and vegetables are tender.

Stir in tomato sauce and tomatoes; cook 1 hour longer. Just before serving, cook macaroni according to package directions; drain. Stir into the soup. **Yield:** 13 servings (about 3 quarts).

Shredded Pork Sandwiches

(Pictured at right)

Prep: 25 min.   **Cook:** 25 min. + cooling

The country ribs used for these sandwiches get tender quickly under pressure. Mom's pressure cooker makes things easy for our family of three.   *—Anna Minegar*
Zollo Springs, Florida

3 to 4 pounds bone-in country-style pork ribs
5 cups water, *divided*
1 cup finely chopped onion
3/4 cup ketchup
1-1/2 teaspoons Worcestershire sauce
1 teaspoon salt
1/8 teaspoon pepper
1 tablespoon all-purpose flour
8 kaiser rolls, split

Place the ribs in a pressure cooker; add 4 cups water. Close cover securely; place pressure regulator on vent pipe. Bring cooker to full pressure over high heat. Reduce heat to medium-high and cook for 25 minutes. (Pressure regulator should maintain a slow steady rocking motion; adjust heat if needed.)

Meanwhile, in a large saucepan, combine the onion, ketchup, Worcestershire sauce, salt and pepper. Combine the flour and remaining water until smooth; stir into onion mixture. Bring to a boil. Reduce heat; cover and simmer for 15 minutes.

Remove pressure cooker from the heat; allow pressure to drop on its own. Remove ribs with a slotted spoon; cool slightly. When cool enough to handle, remove and discard bones. Shred pork with two forks; add to the sauce. Cook for 10 minutes or until heated through. Serve on rolls. **Yield:** 8 servings.

Editor's Note: This recipe was tested at 13 pounds of pressure (psi).

Side Dishes & Condiments

Put away those canned veggies! Instead, reach for these from-scratch side dishes and condiments to complement your main dishes.

ROUND OUT A MEAL. Clockwise from upper left: Grilled Summer Veggies (p. 46), Sausage Corn Bread Dressing (p. 50), Sweet Pickled Asparagus (p. 52), Baked Cranberry Sauce (p. 48) and Habanero Apricot Jam (p. 46).

Habanero Apricot Jam

(Pictured on page 44)

Prep: 15 min.   **Cook:** 15 min. + processing

This zippy and versatile jam was a blue-ribbon winner at our county fair. I mix it with applesauce as a condiment for pork, with cranberry sauce for poultry and with cream cheese as a spread on celery sticks. It's a beautiful color…and in "hot" demand as a gift item!
—*Janet Eckhoff, Woodland, California*

    3-1/2 **pounds fresh apricots**
        6 **tablespoons lemon juice**
        2 **to 4 habanero peppers, seeded**
        1 **package (1-3/4 ounces) powdered fruit pectin**
        7 **cups sugar**

Pit and chop apricots; place in a Dutch oven or soup kettle. Stir in lemon juice. Place habaneros in a blender; add a small amount of apricot mixture. Cover and process until smooth. Return to the pan. Stir in pectin. Bring to a full rolling boil. Quickly stir in sugar. Return to a full rolling boil; boil and stir for 1 minute.

Pour hot mixture into hot sterilized jars, leaving 1/4-in. headspace. Adjust caps. Process for 10 minutes in a boiling-water bath. For best results, let processed jam stand at room temperature for 2 weeks to set up. **Yield:** 11 half-pints.

Editor's Note: When cutting or seeding hot peppers, use rubber or plastic gloves to protect your hands. Avoid touching your face.

Pickled Baby Carrots

(Pictured above)

Prep: 20 min. + chilling

With their mild herb flavor, these baby carrots make a delightful addition to a casual meal. Plan ahead because they need to chill for several hours. —*Audrey Cremer Harmony, Minnesota*

    2 **pounds fresh baby carrots**
    2/3 **cup white wine vinegar**
    1/2 **cup honey**
    2 **tablespoons mustard seed**
    2 **tablespoons dill weed**
    1 **teaspoon salt**

Place 1 in. of water in a large saucepan; add carrots. Bring to a boil. Reduce heat; cover and simmer for 5-6 minutes or until crisp-tender. Drain.

In a large bowl, combine the remaining ingredients. Stir in carrots. Cover and refrigerate for 8 hours or overnight, stirring several times. Serve with a slotted spoon. **Yield:** 8-10 servings.

Grilled Summer Veggies

(Pictured on page 44)

Prep: 10 min. + marinating   **Grill:** 20 min.

After tasting a delicious mix of vegetables that a friend grilled, I went home and came up with a similar medley that I really like. You can adjust the ingredients to your taste. —*Sherri Hetrick, Maryville, Missouri*

✓ Uses less fat, sugar or salt. Includes Nutritional Analysis and Diabetic Exchanges.

    3/4 **cup Italian salad dressing**
      2 **tablespoons balsamic vinegar**
      1 **tablespoon dried parsley flakes**
  1-1/2 **teaspoons lemon-pepper seasoning**
      1 **teaspoon Cajun seasoning**
      1 **medium zucchini, cut into 1/4-inch slices**
      1 **medium yellow summer squash, cut into 1/4-inch slices**
      1 **small onion, julienned**
    1/2 **medium green pepper, julienned**
      1 **large carrot, cut into 1/4-inch slices**

1 celery rib, cut into 3/4-inch slices
4 whole fresh mushrooms, quartered

In a large resealable plastic bag, combine salad dressing, vinegar, parsley, lemon-pepper and Cajun seasoning. Add vegetables; seal bag and turn to coat. Let stand for 15 minutes; drain. Arrange vegetables on a grill rack. Grill, covered, over medium heat for 20-25 minutes or until tender, turning frequently. **Yield:** 4 servings.

Nutritional Analysis: 3/4 cup (prepared with fat-free Italian dressing) equals 61 calories, 1 g fat (trace saturated fat), 1 mg cholesterol, 512 mg sodium, 13 g carbohydrate, 3 g fiber, 3 g protein. **Diabetic Exchange:** 2 vegetable.

Glazed Carrot Coins

Prep/Total Time: 25 min.

These glossy carrots, flavored with orange juice, cinnamon and ginger, are pretty enough for a special meal. To save time, you could substitute two 15-ounce cans of carrots for the fresh ones. —*Helen Bethel, Maysville, North Carolina*

✓ **Uses less fat, sugar or salt. Includes Nutritional Analysis and Diabetic Exchanges.**

2 tablespoons butter
2 tablespoons brown sugar
2 tablespoons orange juice
1/4 teaspoon salt
1/4 teaspoon ground ginger
1/8 teaspoon ground cinnamon
6 medium carrots, cut into 1/2-inch slices

In a small saucepan, melt butter over medium heat. Stir in the brown sugar, orange juice, salt, ginger and cinnamon. Add the carrots and cover and cook for 20-25 minutes or until tender, stirring occasionally. **Yield:** 4 servings.

Nutritional Analysis: 3/4 cup (prepared with reduced-fat butter) equals 94 calories, 3 g fat (2 g saturated fat), 10 mg cholesterol, 217 mg sodium, 17 g carbohydrate, 3 g fiber, 1 g protein. **Diabetic Exchanges:** 2 vegetable, 1/2 fruit.

Pearl Onion Broccoli Bake

(Pictured at right)

Prep: 20 min.   **Bake:** 25 min.

With its creamy white cheese sauce and buttery crumb topping, this dish is great comfort food. If you're looking for a mild way to dress up broccoli, this is it.
—*Charles Keating, Manchester, Maryland*

4 packages (8 ounces *each*) frozen
broccoli cuts

4 cups frozen pearl onions
1/2 cup butter, *divided*
1/4 cup all-purpose flour
3/4 teaspoon salt
1/8 teaspoon pepper
2 cups milk
2 packages (3 ounces *each*) cream cheese, cubed
2 cups soft bread crumbs
1 cup (4 ounces) shredded cheddar cheese

In a large saucepan, cook broccoli in 1 in. of water until almost tender; drain. Cook pearl onions in 1 in. of water until almost tender; drain.

In a large saucepan, melt 1/4 cup butter; stir in flour, salt and pepper until smooth. Gradually add milk. Bring to a boil; cook and stir for 1-2 minutes or until thickened. Reduce heat; stir in cream cheese until smooth and blended.

Place broccoli and onions in a greased 13-in. x 9-in. x 2-in. baking dish. Add sauce and gently stir to coat. Melt the remaining butter; toss with bread crumbs. Sprinkle crumbs and cheddar cheese over vegetables. Bake, uncovered, at 350° for 25-30 minutes or until topping is golden brown. **Yield:** 12-15 servings.

Colorful Roasted Veggies

(Pictured below)

Prep/Total Time: 30 min.

My mom often serves this delicious vegetable dish pleasantly flavored with rosemary. It's my favorite.
—*Adrian Martin, Mechanicsburg, Pennsylvania*

☑ **Uses less fat, sugar or salt. Includes Nutritional Analysis and Diabetic Exchanges.**

    4 medium carrots, julienned
1-1/2 pounds fresh asparagus, trimmed and
        halved
    1 large green pepper, julienned
    1 medium sweet red pepper, julienned
    1 medium red onion, sliced and separated
        into rings
    5 cups fresh cauliflowerets
    5 cups fresh broccoli florets
  1/4 to 1/2 cup olive oil
    3 tablespoons lemon juice
    3 garlic cloves, minced
    1 tablespoon dried rosemary, crushed
    1 teaspoon salt
    1 teaspoon pepper

In a large bowl, combine the vegetables. In a small bowl, whisk the oil, lemon juice, garlic, rosemary, salt and pepper until blended. Drizzle over vegetables and toss to coat.

Transfer to two greased 15-in. x 10-in. x 1-in. baking pans. Bake, uncovered, at 400° for 20-25 minutes or until tender, stirring occasionally. **Yield:** 12 servings.

Nutritional Analysis: 3/4 cup (calculated with 1/4 cup olive oil) equals 88 calories, 5 g fat (1 g saturated fat), 0 cholesterol, 228 mg sodium, 10 g carbohydrate, 4 g fiber, 3 g protein. **Diabetic Exchanges:** 2 vegetable, 1 fat.

Baked Cranberry Sauce

(Pictured on page 44)

Prep/Total Time: 30 min.

We live in cranberry country and are always looking for good recipes to use them. This dish is perfect for Thanksgiving Day. —*Kathy Olsen, Provincetown, Massachusetts*

    1 pound fresh *or* frozen cranberries,
        thawed
1-1/2 cups chopped pecans
    1 cup flaked coconut
    1 cup orange marmalade
  3/4 cup sugar
  1/2 cup water

In a large bowl, combine all ingredients. Pour into a greased 11-in. x 7-in. x 2-in. baking dish. Bake, uncovered, at 350° for 25-30 minutes or until cranberries are tender. Serve warm or cold. Refrigerate leftovers. **Yield:** 10 servings.

Party Carrots

Prep: 15 min. **Bake:** 20 min.

Even people who don't like carrots change their minds after tasting this easy-to-fix dish. It's nice for potlucks because you can prepare it ahead of time. —*Bertha Johnson Indianapolis, Indiana*

    2 pounds carrots, sliced
    2 teaspoons chicken bouillon granules
    8 ounces process cheese (Velveeta), cubed
    2 tablespoons butter
    1 package (8 ounces) cream cheese, cubed
    4 green onions, sliced
  1/4 teaspoon salt
  1/4 teaspoon pepper

Place 1 in. of water in a large saucepan; add carrots and bouillon. Bring to a boil. Reduce heat. Cover and simmer for 7-9 minutes or until crisp-tender.

Meanwhile, in another large saucepan, combine process cheese and butter. Cook and stir over low heat until melted. Add the cream cheese, onions, salt and pepper. Cook and stir until cream cheese is melted.

Drain carrots; stir into cheese sauce. Transfer to a greased shallow 2-qt. baking dish. Cover and bake at 350° for 20-25 minutes or until bubbly. **Yield:** 8 servings.

Sweet Corn 'n' Peppers

(Pictured below)

Prep/Total Time: 30 min.

Peppers add a nice punch to this mouth-watering grilled sweet corn. —*Grace Camp, Owingsville, Kentucky*

> 1 medium sweet red pepper, julienned
> 1 medium green pepper, julienned
> 1 medium jalapeno pepper, seeded and julienned
> 1 medium sweet onion, cut into thin wedges
> 1/2 teaspoon salt
> 1/2 teaspoon pepper
> 1/8 teaspoon cayenne pepper
> Dash paprika
> 6 large ears sweet corn, husks removed and halved

In a bowl, combine the peppers and onion. Combine the salt, pepper, cayenne and paprika; sprinkle half over the vegetables and set aside. Sprinkle remaining seasoning mixture over corn.

Place the corn on a vegetable grilling rack coated with nonstick cooking spray or in a perforated disposable aluminum pan. Grill, covered, over medium heat for 10 minutes. Add reserved vegetables. Grill, covered, 5-10 minutes longer or until vegetables are tender, stirring occasionally and rotating corn. **Yield:** 6 servings.

Editor's Note: When cutting or seeding hot peppers, use rubber or plastic gloves to protect your hands. Avoid touching your face.

Asparagus with Cream Sauce

(Pictured above)

Prep/Total Time: 15 min.

This lovely side dish has been a favorite in our family for many years—especially for Easter dinners. Fresh green beans can be substituted for the asparagus.
—*Arletta Slocum, Venice, Florida*

> 2 cups water
> 2 pounds fresh asparagus, trimmed
> 1/2 cup chopped onion
> 2 tablespoons butter
> 2 tablespoons all-purpose flour
> 1 teaspoon garlic powder
> 1 teaspoon lemon-pepper seasoning
> 1/2 teaspoon salt
> 1 cup chicken broth
> 1/4 cup minced fresh parsley
> 2 tablespoons cider vinegar
> 1 teaspoon dill weed
> 1 cup (8 ounces) sour cream

In a large skillet, bring water to a boil. Add asparagus; cover and boil for 3 minutes. Meanwhile, in a small skillet, saute onion in butter until tender. Stir in the flour, garlic powder, lemon-pepper and salt until blended. Gradually stir in broth. Add the parsley, vinegar and dill.

Bring to a boil; cook and stir 2 minutes or until thickened. Reduce heat to low; whisk in sour cream. Drain asparagus; arrange on a serving platter. Top with cream sauce. **Yield:** 8-10 servings.

Wild Rice Medley

(Pictured above)

Prep/Total Time: 30 min.

I'm always looking for new ways to dress up rice. This recipe pairs nicely with chicken or pork chops.
— *Shirley Glaab, Hattiesburg, Mississippi*

✓ Uses less fat, sugar or salt. Includes Nutritional Analysis and Diabetic Exchanges.

- 1 **medium onion, finely chopped**
- 1 **garlic clove, minced**
- 1 **tablespoon olive oil**
- 1/2 **cup uncooked long grain rice**
- 1 **cup chicken broth**
- 3 **medium tomatoes, peeled and chopped**
- 1-1/2 **cups cooked wild rice**
- 1 **teaspoon** *each* **minced fresh rosemary, thyme, oregano and marjoram**

In a small saucepan, saute the onion and garlic in oil until tender. Add the long grain rice; cook and stir for 2 minutes. Stir in the broth; bring to a boil. Reduce heat; cover and simmer for 20 minutes or until liquid is absorbed and rice is tender. Stir in tomatoes, wild rice and seasonings; heat through. **Yield:** 6 servings.

Nutritional Analysis: 1/2 cup (prepared with reduced-sodium broth) equals 147 calories, 3 g fat (trace saturated fat), 0 cholesterol, 113 mg sodium, 27 g carbohydrate, 2 g fiber, 4 g protein. **Diabetic Exchange:** 2 starch.

Sausage Corn Bread Dressing

(Pictured on page 45)

Prep: 30 min.   **Bake:** 50 min.

Made with turkey sausage, herbs, fruit and veggies, this corn bread stuffing lets you enjoy all the trimmings without the guilt. — *Rebecca Baird, Salt Lake City, Utah*

✓ Uses less fat, sugar or salt. Includes Nutritional Analysis and Diabetic Exchanges.

- 1 **cup all-purpose flour**
- 1 **cup cornmeal**
- 1/4 **cup sugar**
- 3 **teaspoons baking powder**
- 1 **teaspoon salt**
- 1 **cup 1% buttermilk**
- 1/4 **cup unsweetened applesauce**
- 2 **egg whites**

DRESSING:

- 1 **pound turkey Italian sausage links, casings removed**
- 4 **celery ribs, chopped**
- 1 **medium onion, chopped**
- 1 **medium sweet red pepper, chopped**
- 2 **medium tart apples, chopped**
- 1 **cup chopped roasted** *or* **canned sweet chestnuts**
- 3 **tablespoons minced fresh parsley**
- 2 **garlic cloves, minced**
- 1/2 **teaspoon dried thyme**
- 1/2 **teaspoon pepper**
- 1 **cup reduced-sodium chicken broth**
- 1 **egg white**

For corn bread, combine the first five ingredients in a large bowl. Combine the buttermilk, applesauce and egg whites; stir into dry ingredients just until moistened. Pour into an 8-in. square baking dish coated with nonstick cooking spray. Bake at 400° for 20-25 minutes or until a toothpick inserted near the center comes out clean. Cool on a wire rack.

In a large nonstick skillet, cook the sausage, celery, onion and red pepper over medium heat until meat is no longer pink; drain. Transfer to a large bowl. Crumble corn bread over mixture. Add apples, chestnuts, parsley, garlic, thyme and pepper. Stir in broth and egg white.

Transfer to a 13-in. x 9-in. x 2-in. baking dish coated with nonstick cooking spray. Cover and bake at 325° for 40 minutes. Uncover; bake 10 minutes longer or until lightly browned. **Yield:** 16 servings.

Nutritional Analysis: 3/4 cup equals 164 calories, 3 g fat (1 g saturated fat), 16 mg cholesterol, 473 mg sodium, 25 g carbohydrate, 2 g fiber, 8 g protein. **Diabetic Exchanges:** 1-1/2 starch, 1 vegetable.

Editor's Note: Dressing can be prepared as directed and used to stuff a 10- to 12-pound turkey.

Onion-Bacon Baby Carrots

(Pictured at right)

Prep: 35 min. **Bake:** 45 min.

I came up with this side dish for Thanksgiving, and it was a big hit. Now it has a place at our holiday table as well as impromptu get-togethers with family and friends.
—Diana Morrison Poole, Rock Hill, South Carolina

- 2 large sweet onions, sliced
- 1 tablespoon olive oil
- 2 pounds fresh baby carrots, halved lengthwise
- 1 teaspoon salt
- 1/4 teaspoon coarsely ground pepper
- 1/4 cup maple syrup
- 2 tablespoons butter
- 1/2 cup french-fried onions
- 8 bacon strips, cooked and crumbled
- 1/4 cup chopped green onions

In a large skillet, cook onions in oil over medium heat for 15-20 minutes or until golden brown, stirring frequently.

In a large bowl, combine the onions, carrots, salt and pepper; toss to combine. Transfer to a greased shallow 3-qt. baking dish. Cover and bake at 400° for 40-45 minutes or until tender.

Stir in the syrup and butter. Sprinkle with french-fried onions and bacon. Bake, uncovered, 5 minutes longer or until fried onions are browned. Sprinkle with green onions. Serve with a slotted spoon. **Yield:** 8 servings.

Spaghetti Squash Supreme

(Pictured below)

Prep/Total Time: 30 min.

I often use the empty squash shells as serving dishes for this unique side dish. The bacon complements the squash and Swiss cheese combination nicely. It's attractive and fun to eat!
—Jean Williams, Stillwater, Oklahoma

- 1 large spaghetti squash (about 3-1/2 pounds)
- 4 bacon strips, diced
- 3 tablespoons butter
- 1 tablespoon brown sugar
- 1/2 teaspoon salt
- 1/4 teaspoon pepper
- 1/2 cup shredded Swiss cheese

Cut squash in half lengthwise; discard seeds. Place one squash half cut side down on a microwave-safe plate. Cover and microwave on high for 8 minutes or until easily pierced with a fork, turning once. Repeat with second squash half. When cool enough to handle, scoop out squash, separating strands with a fork; set aside.

In a skillet, cook bacon over medium heat until crisp. Using a slotted spoon, remove to paper towels; drain, reserving drippings. Add the butter, brown sugar, salt and pepper to the drippings. Stir in squash and bacon; heat through. Remove from the heat; stir in cheese just until blended. Serve immediately. **Yield:** 4 servings.

Editor's Note: This recipe was tested in a 1,100-watt microwave.

Sweet Pickled Asparagus

(Pictured on page 45)

Prep: 15 min.   **Process:** 20 min.

We enjoy lots of fresh asparagus in the spring. This is how my grandmother used to pickle it.
—*Valerie Giesbrecht, Othello, Washington*

- 10 pounds fresh asparagus
- 5 tablespoons dill seed
- 5 teaspoons mixed pickling spices
- 2 quarts water
- 3 cups cider vinegar
- 2/3 cup sugar
- 1/4 cup canning salt

Wash, drain and trim asparagus; cut into 5-3/4-in. spears (discard ends or save for another use). Pack asparagus into five 1-qt. jars to within 1/2 in. of top. Place 1 tablespoon dill seed and 1 teaspoon pickling spices in each jar.

In a Dutch oven, bring water, vinegar, sugar and salt to a boil. Ladle boiling liquid over asparagus, leaving 1/4-in. headspace. Adjust caps. Process 20 minutes in a boiling-water bath. **Yield:** 5 quarts.

Guilt-Free Mac 'n' Cheese

(Pictured below)

Prep: 10 min.   **Bake:** 35 min.

I wanted to make macaroni and cheese that tasted good but didn't add on pounds. I think I've done it!
—*Ruth Ann Stoy, Newport, Michigan*

✓ Uses less fat, sugar or salt. Includes Nutritional Analysis and Diabetic Exchanges.

- 1/2 cup fat-free milk
- 1 cup 1% cottage cheese
- 1/4 cup finely chopped onion
- 2 tablespoons grated Parmesan cheese
- 1/4 teaspoon salt
- Pepper to taste
- 3 cups cooked elbow macaroni
- 1/2 cup shredded reduced-fat cheddar cheese, *divided*

In a blender, combine the milk, cottage cheese, onion, Parmesan cheese, salt and pepper; cover and process until smooth. Pour into a bowl; stir in the macaroni and 1/4 cup cheese.

Transfer to a 1-qt. baking dish coated with nonstick cooking spray. Sprinkle with remaining cheese. Cover and bake at 350° for 30 minutes. Uncover; bake 5-10 minutes longer or until edges are bubbly. **Yield:** 4 servings.

Nutritional Analysis: 3/4 cup equals 268 calories, 5 g fat (3 g saturated fat), 15 mg cholesterol, 515 mg sodium, 35 g carbohydrate, 2 g fiber, 18 g protein. **Diabetic Exchanges:** 2 starch, 2 lean meat.

Wilted Garlic Spinach

Prep/Total Time: 20 min.

I give my energy-packed side dish an Oriental twist with soy sauce. I sometimes serve it over rice. Try garnishing it with toasted sesame seeds.
—*Dotty Egge*
Pelican Rapids, Minnesota

✓ Uses less fat, sugar or salt. Includes Nutritional Analysis and Diabetic Exchanges.

- 1 teaspoon cornstarch
- 1 teaspoon sugar
- 2 tablespoons chicken broth
- 1 tablespoon reduced-sodium soy sauce
- 1/2 teaspoon sesame oil
- 6 garlic cloves, minced
- 1 tablespoon canola oil
- 3/4 pound fresh spinach, trimmed

In a small bowl, combine the cornstarch, sugar, broth, soy sauce and sesame oil until smooth; set aside.

In a small skillet, saute the garlic in canola oil for 1 minute. Stir broth mixture and add to skillet. Cook and stir over medium heat until slightly thickened. Add spinach; cook and stir for 2 minutes or just until spinach is wilted and coated with sauce. Serve with a slotted spoon. **Yield:** 4 servings.

Nutritional Analysis: 1/2 cup equals 66 calories, 4 g fat (1 g saturated fat), 0 cholesterol, 248 mg sodium, 6 g carbohydrate, 2 g fiber, 3 g protein. **Diabetic Exchanges:** 1 vegetable, 1 fat.

Caramelized Onion Jam

(Pictured above)

Prep: 1 hour 20 min. + cooling   **Process:** 10 min.

This savory jam is very good served with meats—we especially like it with venison. People who enjoy garlic and onions think it's terrific. —Vanessa Lambert
Sioux Falls, South Dakota

  4 whole garlic bulbs
  1 teaspoon vegetable oil
  5 cups chopped sweet onions (1-1/2 pounds)
1/4 cup butter, cubed
3/4 cup cider vinegar
1/2 cup lemon juice
1/4 cup balsamic vinegar
1-1/2 teaspoons ground mustard
  1 teaspoon salt
3/4 teaspoon white pepper
1/2 teaspoon ground ginger
1/4 teaspoon ground cloves
  6 cups sugar
  1 pouch (3 ounces) liquid fruit pectin

Remove papery outer skin from garlic (do not peel or separate cloves). Cut the tops off garlic bulbs; brush with oil. Wrap each bulb in heavy-duty foil. Bake at 425° for 30-35 minutes or until softened. Cool for 10-15 minutes.

In a Dutch oven, saute onions in butter for 30-40 minutes or until lightly browned. Squeeze softened garlic into pan. Stir in cider vinegar, lemon juice, balsamic vinegar, mustard, salt, pepper, ginger and cloves. Bring to a rolling boil. Gradually add sugar, stirring constantly. Return to a boil for 3 minutes.

Add pectin; bring to a full rolling boil. Boil for 1 minute, stirring constantly. Remove from the heat; let

stand for 3 minutes. Skim off foam. Pour hot mixture into hot jars, leaving 1/2-in. headspace. Adjust caps. Process for 10 minutes in a boiling-water bath. **Yield:** about 3-1/2 pints.

Horseradish Creamed Carrots

(Pictured below)

Prep: 30 min.   **Bake:** 20 min.

My family enjoys this flavorful side dish with just about any meat. Carrots never tasted so good! —Meredith Sayre
Burlington, Kentucky

  2 pounds carrots, cut into 1/2-inch slices
3/4 cup mayonnaise
1/3 cup half-and-half cream
1/4 cup prepared horseradish
  2 tablespoons finely chopped onion
  1 teaspoon salt
1/4 teaspoon pepper
1/2 cup crushed cornflakes
  2 tablespoons butter, melted

Place 1 in. of water in a saucepan; add carrots. Bring to a boil; reduce heat. Cover and simmer for 8-10 minutes or until crisp-tender; drain.

In a large bowl, combine the mayonnaise, cream, horseradish, onion, salt and pepper; add the carrots and toss to coat.

Transfer to a greased 1-1/2-qt. baking dish. Combine cornflake crumbs and butter; sprinkle over carrots. Bake, uncovered, at 350° for 20-25 minutes or until bubbly. **Yield:** 6 servings.

Main Dishes

If you've run out of answers to the nightly
"what's for dinner?" question, here are 62 delicious
solutions that are guaranteed to please your family!

MEALTIME SOLUTIONS. Clockwise from upper left: Brisket with Cranberry Gravy (p. 63), Kielbasa Cabbage Skillet (p. 60), Louisiana Shrimp (p. 56), Peach-Glazed Salmon (p. 58) and Oriental Chicken Thighs (p. 56).

This is a Lenten favorite at our home. I serve it right out of the roaster with corn on the cob and boiled potatoes.
—*Sundra Hauck, Bogalusa, Louisiana*

 1 pound butter, cubed
 3 medium lemons, sliced
 2 tablespoons plus 1-1/2 teaspoons coarsely ground pepper
 2 tablespoons Worcestershire sauce
 2 garlic cloves, minced
 1/2 teaspoon salt
 1/2 teaspoon hot pepper sauce
 2-1/2 pounds uncooked shell-on medium shrimp

In a large saucepan, combine the first seven ingredients. Bring to a boil. Reduce heat; cover and simmer for 30 minutes, stirring occasionally.

Place shrimp in a large roasting pan; pour butter mixture over top. Bake, uncovered, at 375° for 20-25 minutes or until shrimp turn pink. Serve warm with a slotted spoon. **Yield:** 10 servings.

Baked Barbecued Brisket

(Pictured above)

Prep: 20 min.   **Bake:** 3-1/2 hours

This simple recipe never fails me. I always hope that there are leftovers for some sandwiches the next day.
—*Joan Hallford, North Richland Hills, Texas*

 1 tablespoon all-purpose flour
 1 fresh beef brisket (5 pounds)
 2 to 4 teaspoons Liquid Smoke, optional
 1/2 teaspoon celery seed
 1/4 teaspoon pepper
 1 cup chili sauce
 1/4 cup barbecue sauce

Place flour in a large oven roasting bag; shake to coat bag. Rub brisket with Liquid Smoke if desired, celery seed and pepper; place in bag. Place in a roasting pan. Combine chili sauce and barbecue sauce; pour over brisket. Seal bag.

With a knife, cut six 1/2-in. slits in top of bag. Bake at 325° for 3-1/2 to 4 hours or until meat is tender. Let stand for 5 minutes. Carefully remove brisket from bag. Thinly slice meat across the grain. **Yield:** 16-20 servings.

Louisiana Shrimp

(Pictured on page 54)
Prep: 40 min.   **Bake:** 20 min.

Oriental Chicken Thighs

(Pictured on page 54)

Prep: 15 min.   **Cook:** 50 min.

A thick tangy sauce coats the golden chicken pieces in this savory skillet recipe. I like to serve them over long grain rice or with a helping of ramen noodle slaw.
—*Dave Farrington, Midwest City, Oklahoma*

 5 bone-in chicken thighs, skin removed
 5 teaspoons olive oil
 1/3 cup warm water
 1/4 cup packed brown sugar
 2 tablespoons orange juice
 2 tablespoons soy sauce
 2 tablespoons ketchup
 1 tablespoon white vinegar
 4 garlic cloves, minced
 1/2 teaspoon crushed red pepper flakes
 1/4 teaspoon Chinese five-spice powder
 2 teaspoons cornstarch
 2 tablespoons cold water
Hot cooked rice
Sliced green onions

In a large skillet over medium heat, brown chicken in oil for 18-20 minutes or until juices run clear. Meanwhile, in a jar with a tight-fitting lid, combine the warm water, brown sugar, orange juice, soy sauce, ketchup, vinegar, garlic, pepper flakes and five-spice powder; shake until the sugar is dissolved. Pour over the chicken.

Bring to a boil. Reduce heat; simmer, uncovered, for 30-35 minutes or until chicken is tender, turning occasionally. Combine cornstarch and cold water until smooth; gradually stir into skillet. Bring to a boil; cook and stir for 2 minutes or until thickened. Serve with rice. Garnish with green onions. **Yield:** 5 servings.

Pork Loin with Potatoes

Prep: 25 min. + marinating
Bake: 2-3/4 hours + standing

I love to cook and to have friends and family for dinner. Onions, garlic, potatoes and herbs from my garden go into this tasty oven meal. —*Phyl Broich-Wessling*
Garner, Iowa

 1 bone-in pork loin roast (5 pounds)
 3 garlic cloves, sliced
 3 tablespoons olive oil
 1/4 teaspoon paprika
 1/4 teaspoon pepper
 1/8 teaspoon dried thyme
 6 medium potatoes, peeled
 1/2 teaspoon salt
ONION MUSHROOM GRAVY:
 1 cup water
 1 cup beef broth
 2 medium onions, sliced
 1-1/4 cups chopped fresh mushrooms
 1 tablespoon butter
 1 tablespoon vegetable oil
 1/4 cup all-purpose flour
 2 tablespoons minced fresh parsley
 1/4 teaspoon pepper

Cut slits in top of roast; insert garlic slices. Combine the oil, paprika, pepper and thyme; rub over roast. Place in a large resealable plastic bag; seal and refrigerate the roast overnight.

Transfer roast to a shallow roasting pan. Bake, uncovered, at 350° for 1-3/4 hours. Meanwhile, place potatoes and salt in a saucepan and cover with water. Bring to a boil. Reduce heat; simmer, uncovered, for 15 minutes or until almost tender. Drain; cool slightly. Cut potatoes into quarters; arrange around roast.

Bake 45 minutes longer or until a meat thermometer reads 160° and potatoes are tender, basting potatoes with drippings occasionally. Remove potatoes; keep warm. Cover roast and let stand for 15 minutes before carving.

For gravy, pour drippings and loosened browned bits into a measuring cup. Skim fat, reserving 2 tablespoons drippings. Add water and broth to reserved drippings; set aside. In a large saucepan, saute onions and mushrooms in butter and oil until tender.

Stir in flour until blended. Gradually stir in broth mixture. Bring to a boil; cook and stir for 2 minutes or until thickened. Stir in parsley and pepper. Serve with roast and potatoes. **Yield:** 8-10 servings.

Pineapple Chicken Fajitas

(Pictured below)

Prep: 25 min.   **Cook:** 10 min.

Honey and pineapple add a sweet twist to these fajitas that my family loves. Coleslaw and baked or fried potatoes are great accompaniments. —*Raymonde Bourgeois*
Swastika, Ontario

 2 pounds boneless skinless chicken
   breasts, cut into strips
 1 tablespoon olive oil
 1 *each* medium green, sweet red and yellow
   pepper, julienned
 1 medium onion, cut into thin wedges
 2 tablespoons fajita seasoning mix
 1/4 cup water
 2 tablespoons honey
 1 tablespoon dried parsley flakes
 1 teaspoon garlic powder
 1/2 teaspoon salt
 1/2 cup unsweetened pineapple chunks,
   drained
 8 flour tortillas (10 inches), warmed

In a large nonstick skillet, cook chicken in oil for 4-5 minutes. Add peppers and onion; cook and stir 4-5 minutes longer. In a bowl, combine the seasoning mix and water; stir in the honey, parsley, garlic powder and salt. Stir into skillet.

Add pineapple. Cook and stir for 1-2 minutes or until chicken juices run clear and vegetables are tender. Place chicken mixture on one side of each tortilla; fold tortillas over filling. **Yield:** 8 fajitas.

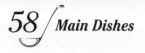

Sweet Salsa Chicken

(Pictured below)

Prep: 20 min. + marinating **Bake:** 20 min.

My family loves this saucy Southwestern-style chicken, and it fits well within my sensible meal plan. Add fresh pasta and a tossed salad for a satisfying dinner.
—*Joanne Watters, Cobourg, Ontario*

✓ **Uses less fat, sugar or salt. Includes Nutritional Analysis and Diabetic Exchanges.**

- 1-1/2 cups salsa
- 2/3 cup honey
- 1/2 cup orange juice
- 1/2 cup reduced-sodium soy sauce
- 1/4 cup Dijon mustard
- 4 teaspoons olive oil
- 1/2 teaspoon ground ginger
- 6 boneless skinless chicken breast halves (4 ounces *each*)
- 1-1/2 teaspoons cornstarch
- 2 tablespoons cold water

In a bowl, combine the first seven ingredients. Pour 1-1/2 cups into a large resealable plastic bag; add the chicken. Seal bag and turn to coat; refrigerate for 2 hours. Cover and refrigerate remaining marinade.

Drain and discard marinade from chicken. Place the chicken in an 11-in. x 7-in. x 2-in. baking dish coated with nonstick cooking spray; top with reserved marinade. Bake, uncovered, at 375° for 20-25 minutes or until juices run clear. Remove chicken and keep warm.

In a small saucepan, combine cornstarch and cold water until smooth; stir in pan juices. Bring to a boil; cook and stir for 2 minutes or until thickened. Pour over chicken. **Yield:** 6 servings.

Nutritional Analysis: 1 chicken breast half with 1/4 cup sauce equals 251 calories, 5 g fat (1 g saturated fat), 63 mg cholesterol, 1,039 mg sodium, 28 g carbohydrate, 3 g fiber, 27 g protein. **Diabetic Exchanges:** 3 lean meat, 2 fruit.

Venison Taco Pie

Prep: 10 min. **Bake:** 25 min.

The whole family is sure to enjoy this savory casserole. A refrigerated biscuit crust and packaged taco seasoning make preparation easy.
—*Karen Witman*
North Irwin, Pennsylvania

- 1 pound ground venison
- 1 can (11 ounces) Mexicorn, drained
- 1 can (8 ounces) tomato sauce
- 1 envelope taco seasoning
- 1 tube (7-1/2 ounces) refrigerated buttermilk biscuits
- 1 cup (4 ounces) shredded cheddar cheese

In a large skillet, cook venison over medium heat until no longer pink; drain. Stir in the corn, tomato sauce and taco seasoning; keep warm.

For crust, press biscuits onto the bottom and up the sides of an ungreased 9-in. pie plate. Bake at 350° for 5 minutes. Spoon venison mixture into crust. Sprinkle with cheese. Bake for 20-25 minutes or until filling is bubbly and biscuits are golden brown. Let stand for 5 minutes before serving. **Yield:** 6 servings.

Peach-Glazed Salmon

(Pictured on page 54)

Prep: 10 min. + marinating **Grill:** 15 min.

A local restaurant used fresh peaches to garnish a salmon dish, which gave me this idea for grilling the fish we catch. It's a beautiful presentation and quick to prepare.
—*Valerie Homer, Juneau, Alaska*

- 1 cup butter, cubed
- 1 cup peach preserves
- 1 tablespoon lime juice
- 1 garlic clove, minced
- 1/2 teaspoon prepared mustard
- 2 salmon fillets (1 pound *each*)
- 1/2 cup fresh *or* frozen sliced peaches

In a microwave-safe bowl, combine butter and preserves. Cover and microwave on high for 45-60 seconds. Stir in the lime juice, garlic and mustard until blended. Cool. Set aside 1 cup for basting and serving.

Place the salmon fillets in a large resealable plastic

bag; add remaining peach mixture. Seal bag and turn to coat. Marinate for 20 minutes.

Drain and discard marinade. Coat grill rack with non-stick cooking spray before starting the grill. Place salmon skin side down on grill rack. Grill, covered, over medium heat for 5 minutes. Spoon half of reserved peach mixture over salmon. Grill 10-15 minutes longer or until fish flakes easily with a fork, basting frequently. Serve with sliced peaches and remaining peach mixture. **Yield:** 8 servings.

Editor's Note: This recipe was tested in a 1,100-watt microwave.

Peppered Chicken Breasts

Prep: 25 min.   **Bake:** 15 min.

Black pepper is prominent in this succulent baked entree, yet it doesn't overpower the tender chicken flavor or the creamy mustard sauce. It's easy to make and elegant.
—Jill Morzillo, Louisville, Kentucky

   4 **boneless skinless chicken breast halves**
     (4 ounces *each***)**
   2 **teaspoons olive oil**
   2 **teaspoons pepper**
 1/4 **teaspoon salt**
MUSTARD SAUCE:
   2 **teaspoons cornstarch**
 1/3 **cup sour cream**
   1 **cup chicken broth**
 1/4 **cup white grape juice**
 1/4 **cup chopped green onions**
   2 **teaspoons Dijon mustard**
Snipped chives

Rub chicken with oil; sprinkle with pepper and salt. Place in a greased 11-in. x 7-in. x 2-in. baking dish. Bake, uncovered, at 425° for 15-20 minutes or until juices run clear.

Meanwhile, in a small bowl, combine cornstarch and sour cream until smooth; set aside. In a small saucepan, combine broth, grape juice and onions. Bring to a boil; cook for 4-5 minutes or until liquid is reduced to 1 cup. Gradually whisk in sour cream mixture.

Bring to a boil; cook and stir for 2 minutes or until thickened. Stir in mustard until blended. Serve over chicken. Sprinkle with chives. **Yield:** 4 servings.

Pot Roast with Vegetables

(Pictured above right)

Prep: 20 min.   **Cook:** 40 min. + cooling

My mother used this recipe at least once a week when I was a child. It's conveniently made in a pressure cooker,

so it's quicker than most stovetop pot roasts and always turns out tender.   *—Cheryl Rihn, Bloomer, Wisconsin*

   1 **boneless beef sirloin tip roast (3 pounds)**
   2 **tablespoons vegetable oil**
   4 **large potatoes, peeled and quartered**
   4 **large carrots, cut into 2-inch pieces**
   1 **large onion, cut into wedges**
   2 **cups water**
   1 **teaspoon beef bouillon granules**
 1/2 **teaspoon salt**
 1/4 **teaspoon pepper**
   3 **tablespoons cornstarch**
   3 **tablespoons cold water**

In a pressure cooker, brown roast in oil on all sides. Add potatoes, carrots, onion and water. Close cover securely; place pressure regulator on vent pipe. Bring cooker to full pressure over high heat. Reduce heat to medium-high; cook for 40 minutes. (Pressure regulator should maintain a slow steady rocking motion; adjust heat if needed.)

Remove from the heat; allow pressure to drop on its own. Remove meat and vegetables; keep warm. Bring cooking juices in pressure cooker to a boil. Add bouillon, salt and pepper. Combine cornstarch and cold water until smooth; stir into juices. Bring to a boil; cook and stir for 2 minutes or until thickened. Serve with roast and vegetables. **Yield:** 6-8 servings.

Editor's Note: This recipe was tested at 13 pounds of pressure (psi).

Kielbasa Cabbage Skillet

(Pictured on page 54)

Prep: 10 min. **Cook:** 1 hour

*Spicy kielbasa sausage and plentiful cabbage and pota-
toes give this dish a satisfying Old World flair. My husband never liked cabbage before I made this, but now he
does!* —Romaine Wetzel, Ronks, Pennsylvania

> 1 **pound fully cooked kielbasa *or* Polish
>   sausage, cut into 1/2-inch slices**
> 4 **tablespoons butter, *divided***
> 1 **large head cabbage (4 pounds), coarsely
>   chopped**
> 2 **medium onions, chopped**
> 3 **cans (8 ounces *each*) tomato sauce**
> 1/2 **cup sugar**
> 1 **tablespoon paprika**
> 3 **to 4 large potatoes, peeled and cubed**

In a large deep skillet or Dutch oven, brown the
sausage in 2 tablespoons butter; remove and set
aside. In the same pan, saute the cabbage and onions
in remaining butter until onions are tender.

Combine the tomato sauce, sugar and paprika;
pour over cabbage mixture. Bring to a boil. Reduce
heat; cover and simmer for 20 minutes. Add the potatoes and reserved sausage. Cover and simmer for
30 minutes or until potatoes are tender. **Yield:** 8-10
servings.

Rosemary Pork Chops

(Pictured at far right)

Prep: 10 min. + marinating **Bake:** 30 min.

*I like to grill these chops in summer. When I'm entertaining,
I often serve them with Parmesan-roasted potatoes and
candied carrots.* —Lisa Morman, Minot, North Dakota

☑ **Uses less fat, sugar or salt. Includes Nutritional
Analysis and Diabetic Exchanges.**

> 1/2 **cup soy sauce**
> 1/4 **cup water**
> 3 **tablespoons brown sugar**
> 1 **tablespoon dried rosemary, crushed**
> 4 **boneless pork loin chops (7 ounces *each*)**

In a large resealable plastic bag, combine the soy
sauce, water, brown sugar and rosemary; add pork
chops. Seal bag and turn to coat; refrigerate for 3 hours.

Drain and discard marinade. Place the chops in a
greased 11-in. x 7-in. x 2-in. baking dish. Bake, uncovered, at 350° for 30-35 minutes or until juices run
clear. **Yield:** 4 servings.

Nutritional Analysis: 1 pork chop (prepared with

reduced-sodium soy sauce) equals 281 calories, 11 g
fat (4 g saturated fat), 96 mg cholesterol, 359 mg
sodium, 3 g carbohydrate, trace fiber, 39 g protein.
Diabetic Exchange: 5 lean meat.

Sweet-and-Sour Chops

(Pictured at right)

Prep: 20 min. **Bake:** 40 min.

*Pineapple chunks and pepper rings accent this sweet-and-
sour entree.* —Shirley Heston, Pickerington, Ohio

> 1/2 **cup all-purpose flour**
> 1/2 **teaspoon salt**
> 4 **bone-in pork loin chops (7 ounces *each*)**
> 2 **tablespoons vegetable oil**
> 1 **can (20 ounces) unsweetened pineapple
>   chunks, drained**
> 1 **small green pepper, cut into rings**
> 1 **cup sugar**
> 2 **tablespoons cornstarch**
> 1 **cup chicken broth**
> 1 **cup cider vinegar**
> 1/3 **cup ketchup**
> 1/4 **cup cold water**
> **Hot cooked rice**

In a large resealable plastic bag, combine the flour and
salt. Add pork chops, one at a time, and shake to
coat. In a large skillet, brown chops in oil on both sides.
Transfer to a greased 13-in. x 9-in. x 2-in. baking dish.
Top with pineapple and green pepper; set aside.

In a small saucepan, combine sugar, cornstarch,
broth, vinegar, ketchup and water until smooth. Bring to
a boil over medium heat; cook and stir for 2 minutes or
until thickened. Pour over chops. Bake, uncovered, at
325° for 40-45 minutes or until a meat thermometer
reads 160°. Serve over rice. **Yield:** 4 servings.

Swiss-Stuffed Chops

(Pictured at right)

Prep: 25 min. **Cook:** 45 min.

*These delectable chops are easy, yet they taste like you've
fussed.* —Joan Hallford, North Richland Hills, Texas

> 1 **cup (4 ounces) shredded Swiss cheese**
> 1 **jar (4-1/2 ounces) sliced mushrooms,
>   drained**
> 1/4 **cup minced fresh parsley**
> 4 **bone-in pork loin chops (7 ounces *each*)**
> 1 **egg**
> 6 **tablespoons dry bread crumbs**
> **Dash pepper**

2 tablespoons vegetable oil
1/3 cup water
1 tablespoon all-purpose flour
1/4 cup cold water

In a bowl, combine the cheese, mushrooms and parsley. Cut a pocket in each pork chop by slicing almost to the bone. Stuff each with 1/2 cup cheese mixture; secure with toothpicks. In a shallow bowl, beat the egg. In another shallow bowl, combine the bread crumbs and pepper. Dip the chops in egg, then coat with crumbs.

In a large skillet, brown the chops in oil on both sides. Add water. Cover and simmer for 40-45 minutes or until juices run clear. Remove chops and keep warm; discard toothpicks.

Combine flour and cold water until smooth; stir into pan juices. Cook and stir for 2 minutes or until thickened. Spoon over pork chops. **Yield:** 4 servings.

TAKE YOUR PICK from Rosemary Pork Chops, Sweet-and-Sour Chops or Swiss-Stuffed Chops (shown above) for dinner—each one is delicious.

Chicken Pepper Stir-Fry

(Pictured below)

Prep/Total Time: 30 min.

I challenged myself one day to create a sweet and spicy stir-fry using only the ingredients I had on hand. It had to be sweet yet tangy for our liking. I think I have finally mastered this dish. —Kelly Baumgardt, Seymour, Wisconsin

- 1 *each* small green, sweet red and yellow pepper, julienned
- 1 medium onion, quartered
- 2 garlic cloves, minced
- 4 tablespoons olive oil, *divided*
- 3/4 pound boneless skinless chicken breasts, cubed
- 3/4 teaspoon Cajun seasoning
- 1/3 cup packed brown sugar
- 2 teaspoons cornstarch
- 1 tablespoon water
- 1 tablespoon lemon juice
- 1 tablespoon honey mustard
- 1 teaspoon soy sauce
- 1 teaspoon Worcestershire sauce

Hot cooked rice, optional

In a large skillet, stir-fry the peppers, onion and garlic in 2 tablespoons oil until crisp-tender. Remove and keep warm. In the same skillet, stir-fry the chicken and Cajun seasoning in remaining oil until juices run clear.

In a small bowl, combine the brown sugar, corn-starch, water, lemon juice, mustard, soy sauce and Worcestershire sauce; pour over chicken. Return pepper mixture to the pan; cook and stir for 1 minute. Serve with rice if desired. **Yield:** 3-4 servings.

Christmas Meat Pie

Prep: 1-1/4 hours   **Bake:** 50 min.

Because my husband hunts, I'm always trying new ways to use venison. When I incorporated it into my meat pie recipe—a traditional French-Canadian dish—it was a smash hit! We make dozens of these pies as Christmas gifts. —Jan Stahl, Flin Flon, Manitoba

- 1 pound ground pork
- 1 pound ground venison
- 3 cups water
- 2 medium onions, chopped
- 1 medium carrot, chopped
- 2 tablespoons beef gravy mix
- 2 teaspoons dried thyme
- 2 teaspoons ground mustard
- 3 garlic cloves, minced
- 1 teaspoon rubbed sage
- 1 teaspoon pepper
- 1/2 teaspoon salt
- 3 cups hot mashed potatoes (prepared without butter *or* milk)

Pastry for double-crust pie (9 inches)
Milk

In a large skillet, cook pork and venison over medium heat until no longer pink; drain. Stir in water, onions, carrot, gravy mix, thyme, mustard, garlic, sage, pepper and salt. Bring to a boil. Reduce heat; simmer, uncovered, for 1 hour or until vegetables are tender, stirring occasionally. Drain. Stir in potatoes.

Line a 9-in. deep-dish pie plate with bottom pastry; trim even with edge. Add meat mixture. Roll out remaining pastry to fit top of pie. Make decorative cutouts or cut slits in pastry; place over filling. Trim, seal and flute edges.

Brush pastry and cutouts with milk; place cutouts on the pie. Bake at 400° for 15 minutes. Reduce heat to 350°; bake 35-40 minutes longer or until golden brown. **Yield:** 6-8 servings.

Dijon Leg of Lamb

Prep: 10 min. + marinating   **Grill:** 50 min. + standing

This special entree is always on our Easter table, and I serve it for other events throughout the year. I first tasted this delicious lamb at a dinner party given by a friend. —Christy Porter, Centennial, Colorado

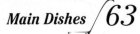

- 1 cup Dijon mustard
- 1/2 cup soy sauce
- 2 tablespoons olive oil
- 1 tablespoon chopped fresh rosemary *or* 1 teaspoon dried rosemary, crushed
- 1 teaspoon ground ginger
- 1 garlic clove, minced
- 1 boneless leg of lamb (4 to 5 pounds)

In a bowl, whisk the first six ingredients. Remove 2/3 cup; cover and refrigerate for serving. Cut leg of lamb horizontally from the long side to within 1 in. of opposite side. Open meat so it lies flat; trim and discard fat. Place lamb in a large resealable plastic bag; add remaining mustard sauce. Seal bag and turn to coat. Refrigerate overnight.

Drain and discard marinade. Coat grill rack with nonstick cooking spray before starting the grill. Prepare grill for indirect medium heat, using a drip pan.

Place lamb over drip pan. Grill, covered, for 50-70 minutes or until meat reaches desired doneness (for medium-rare, a meat thermometer should read 145°; medium, 160°; well-done, 170°). Let stand for 10 minutes before slicing. Warm reserved mustard sauce; serve with lamb. **Yield:** 8-10 servings.

Brisket with Cranberry Gravy

(Pictured on page 54)

Prep: 25 min. **Cook:** 8 hours

Cranberry sauce adds a pleasant sweetness to this slow-cooked brisket. Use jellied sauce instead of whole-berry sauce if you like. —Nina Hall, Citrus Heights, California

- 1 fresh beef brisket (2-1/2 pounds)
- 1/2 teaspoon salt
- 1/4 teaspoon pepper
- 1 can (16 ounces) whole-berry cranberry sauce
- 1 can (8 ounces) tomato sauce
- 1/2 cup chopped onion
- 1 tablespoon prepared mustard

Rub brisket with salt and pepper; place in a 5-qt. slow cooker. Combine the remaining ingredients; pour over brisket. Cover and cook on low for 8-10 hours or until meat is tender. Remove brisket; thinly slice across the grain. Skim fat from cooking juices; serve with brisket. **Yield:** 6-8 servings.

Spinach Shrimp Fettuccine

(Pictured above right)

Prep/Total Time: 20 min.

I experimented for a couple of years before perfecting this colorful dish, and everyone raves about it. It's easy and light and fits into my busy schedule. —Kirstin Walker Chesapeake, Virginia

✓ Uses less fat, sugar or salt. Includes Nutritional Analysis and Diabetic Exchanges.

- 1 pound uncooked fettuccine
- 1 package (6 ounces) baby spinach
- 4 garlic cloves, minced
- 2 tablespoons olive oil
- 1 pound uncooked medium shrimp, peeled and deveined
- 2 medium plum tomatoes, seeded and chopped
- 1/2 teaspoon Italian seasoning
- 1/4 teaspoon salt
- 1/4 cup shredded Parmesan cheese

Cook fettuccine according to package directions. Meanwhile, in a large skillet, saute the spinach and garlic in oil for 2 minutes or until spinach begins to wilt.

Add the shrimp, tomatoes, Italian seasoning and salt; saute for 2-3 minutes or until shrimp turn pink. Drain the fettuccine and add to skillet; toss to coat. Sprinkle with Parmesan cheese. **Yield:** 8 servings.

Nutritional Analysis: 1-1/4 cups equals 283 calories, 5 g fat (1 g saturated fat), 85 mg cholesterol, 209 mg sodium, 41 g carbohydrate, 3 g fiber, 17 g protein. **Diabetic Exchanges:** 2 starch, 2 vegetable, 1-1/2 lean meat.

in. baking dish.

In the same skillet, saute the mushrooms in butter until tender. Spoon reserved marinade over chicken. Top with cheeses and mushrooms. Place bacon strips in a crisscross pattern over chicken. Bake, uncovered, at 375° for 20-25 minutes or until a meat thermometer reads 160°. Sprinkle with parsley. **Yield:** 4 servings.

Poached Salmon

Prep/Total Time: 15 min.

This salmon recipe is so easy, and people often tell me it's the best-tasting salmon they've ever had. The fish is moist and tender, and the dill sauce is a delightful complement. —Kathleen Jones, Newberg, Oregon

✓ Uses less fat, sugar or salt. Includes Nutritional Analysis and Diabetic Exchanges.

```
1/4  cup fat-free mayonnaise
1/4  cup reduced-fat plain yogurt
  2 to 3 tablespoons minced fresh dill
  1  green onion, chopped
1-1/2 teaspoons minced fresh basil
  4  whole peppercorns
  1  bay leaf
  1  salmon fillet (1 pound), cut into 4 pieces
```

For dill sauce, combine the mayonnaise, yogurt, dill, onion and basil in a blender; cover and process until smooth. Cover and refrigerate until serving.

Place 2 in. of water, peppercorns and bay leaf in a large skillet. Bring to a boil. Reduce heat; add salmon. Cook, uncovered, for 4-8 minutes or until fish flakes easily with a fork. Remove with a slotted spoon. Discard bay leaf. Serve fish with dill sauce. **Yield:** 4 servings.

Nutritional Analysis: 1 portion of salmon with 2 tablespoons dill sauce equals 230 calories, 13 g fat (3 g saturated fat), 69 mg cholesterol, 198 mg sodium, 3 g carbohydrate, trace fiber, 23 g protein. **Diabetic Exchanges:** 3 lean meat, 2 fat.

Bacon-Cheese Topped Chicken

(Pictured above)

Prep: 40 min. + marinating   **Bake:** 20 min.

Mushrooms, bacon strips and Monterey Jack cheese top these tender marinated chicken breasts that provide a flavorful dining experience with just a little fuss. —Melanie Kennedy, Battle Ground, Washington

```
1/2  cup Dijon mustard
1/2  cup honey
4-1/2 teaspoons vegetable oil, divided
1/2  teaspoon lemon juice
  4  boneless skinless chicken breast halves
1/4  teaspoon salt
1/8  teaspoon pepper
Dash paprika
  2  cups sliced fresh mushrooms
  2  tablespoons butter
  1  cup (4 ounces) shredded Monterey Jack
     cheese
  1  cup (4 ounces) shredded cheddar cheese
  8  bacon strips, partially cooked
  2  teaspoons minced fresh parsley
```

In a bowl, combine the mustard, honey, 1-1/2 teaspoons oil and lemon juice. Pour 1/2 cup into a large resealable plastic bag; add the chicken. Seal the bag and turn to coat; refrigerate for 2 hours. Cover and refrigerate the remaining marinade.

Drain and discard the marinade from chicken. In a large skillet over medium heat, brown the chicken in remaining oil on all sides. Sprinkle with salt, pepper and paprika. Transfer to a greased 11-in. x 7-in. x 2-

Stuffed Zucchini Boats

Prep: 25 min.   **Bake:** 40 min.

Here's a great way to put that zucchini crop to good use. I stuff the "boats" with a tasty ground beef filling. —Isabel Fowler, Fairbanks, Alaska

✓ Uses less fat, sugar or salt. Includes Nutritional Analysis and Diabetic Exchanges.

```
  1  pound lean ground beef
  1  large onion, chopped
  3  cups cubed French bread
```

1 package (10 ounces) frozen chopped
   spinach, thawed and squeezed dry
1/2 cup minced fresh parsley
1/2 cup tomato sauce
1/4 cup shredded Parmesan cheese
1 egg, beaten
1 teaspoon salt
1/2 teaspoon dried thyme
6 medium zucchini (6 to 8 inches)
1 cup water

In a large skillet, cook beef and onion over medium heat until meat is no longer pink; drain. Stir in bread cubes, spinach, parsley, tomato sauce, Parmesan cheese, egg, salt and thyme; set aside.

Cut each zucchini in half lengthwise. Scoop out seeds, leaving 1/4-in. shells. Spoon about 6 tablespoons beef mixture into each zucchini half. Place in two ungreased 13-in. x 9-in. x 2-in. baking dishes. Pour 1/2 cup water into each dish. Cover and bake at 350° for 30 minutes. Uncover; bake 10 minutes longer or until zucchini is tender. **Yield:** 6 servings.

Nutritional Analysis: 2 stuffed zucchini halves equals 242 calories, 8 g fat (3 g saturated fat), 75 mg cholesterol, 857 mg sodium, 21 g carbohydrate, 5 g fiber, 22 g protein. **Diabetic Exchanges:** 2 lean meat, 1 starch, 1 vegetable, 1 fat.

Grilled T-Bone Steaks

(Pictured at right)

Prep: 10 min. + marinating   **Grill:** 20 min.

Grilling brings out the robust flavor of this steak marinade. Enjoy it while camping or at home.   —*Beth Wenger*
                                         Dayton, Virginia

1/2 cup water
1/2 cup soy sauce
2 tablespoons brown sugar
2 tablespoons lemon juice
2 tablespoons red wine vinegar
2 tablespoons vegetable oil
1 tablespoon Montreal steak seasoning
1/2 teaspoon garlic powder
1/2 teaspoon hot pepper sauce
1/4 teaspoon pepper
4 beef T-bone steaks (1 inch thick)

In a large resealable plastic bag, combine the first 10 ingredients. Add steaks; seal the bag and turn to coat. Refrigerate overnight.

Drain and discard marinade. Grill steaks, covered, over medium heat for 8-12 minutes on each side or until meat reaches desired doneness (for medium-rare, a meat thermometer should read 145°; medium, 160°; well-done, 170°). **Yield:** 4 servings.

Camper's Breakfast Hash

(Pictured below)

Prep/Total Time: 25 min.

When we go camping with family and friends, I'm always asked to make this hearty breakfast.
            —*Linda Krivanek, Oak Creek, Wisconsin*

1/4 cup butter, cubed
2 packages (20 ounces *each*) refrigerated
   shredded hash brown potatoes
1 package (7 ounces) brown-and-serve
   sausage links, cut into 1/2-inch pieces
1/4 cup chopped onion
1/4 cup chopped green pepper
12 eggs, lightly beaten
Salt and pepper to taste
1 cup (4 ounces) shredded cheddar cheese

In a large skillet, melt butter. Add the potatoes, sausage, onion and green pepper. Cook, uncovered, over medium heat for 10-15 minutes or until potatoes are lightly browned, turning once.

Push potato mixture to the sides of pan. Pour eggs into center of pan. Cook and stir over medium heat until eggs are completely set. Season with salt and pepper. Reduce heat; stir eggs into potato mixture. Top with cheese; cover and cook for 1-2 minutes or until cheese is melted. **Yield:** 8 servings.

Asparagus Chicken Crepes

(Pictured above)

Prep: 40 min. + chilling   **Cook:** 30 min.

With a saucy ham and asparagus filling, these savory crepes make a lovely dinner. They're a wonderful change of pace from everyday fare.
—Angela Leinenbach
Mechanicsville, Virginia

　　2　**eggs**
　3/4　**cup milk**
　1/2　**cup all-purpose flour**
　3/4　**teaspoon sugar**
　1/2　**cup condensed cream of chicken soup, undiluted**
　　1　**teaspoon Worcestershire sauce**
Dash ground nutmeg
　　1　**cup chopped cooked chicken**
　　1　**cup cut fresh *or* frozen asparagus, thawed**
　1/3　**cup chopped fully cooked ham**
　1/2　**cup grated Parmesan cheese, *divided***
　1/2　**cup heavy whipping cream, whipped**
　1/3　**cup mayonnaise**

For crepe batter, beat eggs and milk in a small mixing bowl. Combine flour and sugar; add to egg mixture and mix well. Cover and refrigerate for 1 hour.

Heat a lightly greased 8-in. nonstick skillet; pour 3 tablespoons batter into the center of skillet. Lift and tilt pan to coat bottom evenly. Cook until top appears dry; turn and cook 15-20 seconds longer. Remove to a wire rack. Repeat with remaining batter, greasing skillet as needed. When cool, stack crepes with waxed paper between.

In a small bowl, combine soup, Worcestershire sauce and nutmeg. Set aside 1/4 cup. Add the chicken, asparagus and ham to remaining soup mixture. Spoon 2 tablespoonfuls over each crepe; roll up tightly. Place seam side down in a greased 9-in. square baking pan. Spoon reserved soup mixture over crepes. Sprinkle with 1/4 cup Parmesan cheese.

Cover and bake at 375° for 20-25 minutes. Gradually fold cream into mayonnaise. Spread over crepes. Sprinkle with remaining Parmesan. Broil 6 in. from the heat for 3-5 minutes or until bubbly and golden brown. **Yield:** 4 servings.

Cabbage Roll Casserole

Prep: 20 min.   **Bake:** 55 min.

I layer cabbage and a ground beef filling lasagna-style in this hearty casserole that cabbage-roll lovers will savor.
—Doreen Martin, Kitimat, British Columbia

✓ **Uses less fat, sugar or salt. Includes Nutritional Analysis and Diabetic Exchanges.**

　　2　**pounds ground beef**
　　1　**large onion, chopped**
　　3　**garlic cloves, minced**
　　2　**cans (15 ounces *each*) tomato sauce, *divided***
　　1　**teaspoon dried thyme**
　1/2　**teaspoon dill weed**
　1/2　**teaspoon rubbed sage**
　1/4　**teaspoon salt**
　1/4　**teaspoon pepper**
　1/4　**teaspoon cayenne pepper**
　　2　**cups cooked rice**
　　4　**bacon strips, cooked and crumbled**
　　1　**medium head cabbage (2 pounds), shredded**
　　1　**cup (4 ounces) shredded mozzarella cheese**

In a large skillet, cook beef, onion and garlic over medium heat until meat is no longer pink; drain. Stir in one can of tomato sauce and seasonings. Bring to a boil. Reduce heat: cover and simmer for 5 minutes. Stir in rice and bacon; heat through. Remove from the heat.

Layer a third of the cabbage in a greased 13-in. x 9-in. x 2-in. baking dish. Top with half of the meat mixture. Repeat layers; top with remaining cabbage. Pour remaining tomato sauce over top.

Cover and bake at 375° for 45 minutes. Uncover; sprinkle with cheese. Bake 10 minutes longer or until cheese is melted. Let stand for 5 minutes before serving. **Yield:** 12 servings.

Nutritional Analysis: 1 serving equals 230 calories, 8 g fat (4 g saturated fat), 44 mg cholesterol, 620 mg sodium, 18 g carbohydrate, 3 g fiber, 20 g protein. **Diabetic Exchanges:** 3 vegetable, 2-1/2 lean meat, 1/2 fat.

Pork Chops 'n' Pierogies

(Pictured below)

Prep/Total Time: 25 min.

This meal-in-one pork chop dinner is a different way to use pierogies. —*Greta Igl, Menomonee Falls, Wisconsin*

- 8 frozen potato and onion pierogies
- 2 bone-in pork loin chops (3/4 inch thick)
- 1/2 teaspoon salt, *divided*
- 1/2 teaspoon pepper, *divided*
- 4 tablespoons butter, *divided*
- 1 medium sweet onion, sliced and separated into rings
- 1 medium Golden Delicious apple, cut into 1/4-inch slices
- 1/4 cup sugar
- 1/4 cup cider vinegar

Cook pierogies according to package directions. Meanwhile, sprinkle pork chops with 1/4 teaspoon salt and 1/4 teaspoon pepper. In a large skillet, cook chops in 2 tablespoons butter over medium heat until juices run clear; remove and keep warm.

In the same skillet, saute the onion in remaining butter for 3 minutes. Add apple; saute until almost tender. Stir in the sugar, vinegar, and remaining salt and pepper. Bring to a boil. Reduce the heat; simmer, uncovered, for 5 minutes. Drain pierogies. Add the pork chops and pierogies to skillet; stir to coat. **Yield:** 2 servings.

Marinated Flank Steak

(Pictured above)

Prep: 5 min. + marinating   **Broil:** 15 min.

Add a salad and crusty rolls to this full-flavored steak, and you have a simple but excellent meal for family or guests. This steak is also great cooked on the grill.
—*Jean Metcalf, Blaine, Minnesota*

✓ Uses less fat, sugar or salt. Includes Nutritional Analysis and Diabetic Exchanges.

- 1/4 cup soy sauce
- 2 tablespoons vegetable oil
- 2 tablespoons tomato paste
- 1 garlic clove, minced
- 3/4 teaspoon dried oregano
- 3/4 teaspoon pepper
- 1 pound beef flank steak

In a large resealable plastic bag, combine the first six ingredients. Cut a 1/8-in.-deep diamond pattern into both sides of steak. Place in the bag; seal and turn to coat. Refrigerate overnight.

Drain and discard marinade. Place steak on a broiler pan. Broil 4 in. from the heat for 7-8 minutes on each side or until meat reaches desired doneness (for medium-rare, a meat thermometer should read 145°; medium, 160°; well-done, 170°). **Yield:** 4 servings.

Nutritional Analysis: 3 ounces cooked meat equals 208 calories, 12 g fat (4 g saturated fat), 54 mg cholesterol, 531 mg sodium, 1 g carbohydrate, trace fiber, 23 g protein. **Diabetic Exchanges:** 3 lean meat, 1 fat.

Corn Bread Pork Casserole

(Pictured above)

Prep: 15 min.   **Bake:** 35 min.

Satisfying stuffing and moist chops make this dish special enough for company. The recipe can easily be doubled or tripled. —LaDonna Reed, Ponca City, Oklahoma

    2 boneless pork loin chops (4 ounces *each*)
1/2 pound sliced fresh mushrooms
    2 tablespoons all-purpose flour
1/2 cup chicken broth
1/2 cup sour cream
    1 tablespoon shredded Parmesan cheese
    2 garlic cloves, minced
Pepper to taste
1/2 cup corn bread stuffing

In a skillet coated with nonstick cooking spray, brown chops on both sides; set aside. In same skillet, saute mushrooms until tender. Transfer mushrooms to a 1-1/2-qt. baking dish coated with nonstick cooking spray.

In a small bowl, combine flour and broth until smooth. Stir in sour cream, Parmesan cheese, garlic and pepper; pour over mushrooms. Top with pork chops. Cover and bake at 350° for 25 minutes. Sprinkle with stuffing. Bake 10 minutes longer or until meat juices run clear. **Yield:** 2 servings.

Chicken Cacciatore

Prep: 35 min.   **Bake:** 1 hour

This is probably one of my favorite recipes. Olives and pearl onions make it a little different from the traditional dish. —Robert Richardson, Indianapolis, Indiana

1/4 cup all-purpose flour
    4 bone-in chicken breast halves
    2 tablespoons olive oil
1/4 pound sliced fresh mushrooms
    1 medium onion, thinly sliced
    1 garlic clove, minced
    1 can (14-1/2 ounces) diced tomatoes, undrained
3/4 cup frozen pearl onions, thawed
1/2 cup chicken broth
    3 tablespoons tomato paste
1/2 teaspoon dried basil
1/4 teaspoon salt
1/4 teaspoon dried oregano
1/4 teaspoon dried thyme
1/8 teaspoon pepper
    1 bay leaf
1/2 cup whole pitted ripe olives
Hot cooked pasta

Place flour in a large resealable plastic bag; add chicken and shake to coat. In a large skillet, brown chicken in oil on both sides. Remove chicken to a greased 13-in. x 9-in. x 2-in. baking dish.

In the same skillet, saute the mushrooms, onion and garlic until tender. Add the tomatoes, pearl onions, broth, tomato paste and seasonings. Bring to a boil; pour over chicken. Cover and bake at 350° for 45-50 minutes or until chicken juices run clear. Add olives; bake 15 minutes longer. Discard bay leaf. Serve with pasta. **Yield:** 4 servings.

Thanksgiving Stuffed Turkey

Prep: 1-1/2 hours   **Bake:** 4 hours + standing

I've tried fancy stuffing recipes for our Thanksgiving bird, but none hits the spot like my mother's simple mixture of bread, eggs and caramelized vegetables. —Lillian Julow Gainesville, Florida

    2 large onions, chopped
    3 celery ribs, chopped
    2 medium carrots, finely chopped
3/4 cup butter, *divided*
    2 loaves (1 pound *each*) day-old egg bread, cubed
    1 cup chicken broth
    1 cup minced fresh parsley
1/4 cup egg substitute
    1 turkey (16 to 18 pounds) with giblets and neck
1/2 teaspoon garlic salt
1/2 teaspoon paprika
GRAVY:
4-1/2 cups water, *divided*
    1 medium carrot, halved

1 celery rib, halved
1 small onion, quartered
1 bay leaf
6 whole peppercorns
6 tablespoons all-purpose flour
1/4 teaspoon salt

In a large skillet, saute onions, celery and carrots in 1/2 cup butter until tender. In a bowl, combine bread cubes, onion mixture, broth, parsley and egg substitute.

Remove giblets and neck from turkey; cover and refrigerate. Just before baking, loosely stuff turkey with stuffing. Place remaining stuffing in a greased 2-qt. baking dish; refrigerate. Skewer turkey openings; tie drumsticks with kitchen string. Place breast side up on a rack in a shallow roasting pan. Melt remaining butter; brush over turkey. Sprinkle with garlic salt and paprika.

Bake, uncovered, at 325° for 4 to 4-1/2 hours or until a meat thermometer reads 180° for turkey and 160° for stuffing, basting every 30 minutes after the first hour. (Cover loosely with foil if turkey browns too quickly.)

For gravy, in a saucepan, combine 4 cups water, carrot, celery, onion, giblets, neck, bay leaf and peppercorns. Bring to a boil; reduce heat. Cover and simmer 1 hour until giblets are tender; strain broth. Set aside.

Bake additional stuffing, covered, for 25-30 minutes. Uncover; bake 10 minutes longer. Remove turkey; cover and let stand for 20 minutes before carving.

Pour turkey drippings and loosened browned bits into a measuring cup; skim fat. In the saucepan used for the gravy, combine flour, salt and remaining water until smooth. Stir in the drippings and reserved broth. Bring to a boil; cook and stir for 2 minutes or until thickened. Serve with turkey and stuffing. **Yield:** 16-18 servings (3 cups gravy, 16 cups stuffing).

One-Pot Pork and Rice

Prep: 20 min.   **Bake:** 1 hour

Green pepper and onion enhance the Spanish-style rice and tender chops, which are covered with diced tomatoes and gravy.   *—Duna Stephens, Palisade, Colorado*

6 boneless pork loin chops (5 ounces *each*)
2 teaspoons canola oil
1 cup uncooked long grain rice
1 large onion, sliced
1 large green pepper, sliced
1 envelope pork gravy mix
1 can (28 ounces) diced tomatoes, undrained
1-1/2 cups water

In a Dutch oven, brown pork chops in oil on both sides; drain. Remove chops. Layer rice, onion and green pepper in Dutch oven; top with pork chops. Combine the gravy mix, tomatoes and water; pour over chops.

Cover; bake at 350° for 1 hour or until meat juices run clear and rice is tender. **Yield:** 6 servings.

Stir-Fried Basil Chicken

(Pictured below)

Prep: 15 min. + marinating   **Cook:** 10 min.

Fresh basil is a standout in this easy-to-make chicken entree.   *—Mildred Sherrer, Fort Worth, Texas*

1 tablespoon water
1 tablespoon soy sauce
2 teaspoons sugar
1-3/4 pounds boneless skinless chicken breasts, cut into strips
3 green onions, sliced
6 teaspoons canola oil, *divided*
3 garlic cloves, minced
1/4 teaspoon crushed red pepper flakes
6 cups sliced bok choy
1 cup loosely packed fresh basil leaves, thinly sliced

In a large resealable bag, combine the water, soy sauce and sugar; add chicken. Seal bag and turn to coat. Refrigerate for 30 minutes.

In a wok or skillet, stir-fry the onions in 1 teaspoon oil until crisp-tender. Stir in the garlic and pepper flakes; cook and stir for 1 minute. Remove and keep warm.

Drain and discard any marinade from chicken. In the same wok, stir-fry chicken in 3 teaspoons oil for 4-5 minutes or until juices run clear. Meanwhile, in another skillet, saute bok choy in remaining oil until crisp-tender. Add onion mixture to chicken. Stir in basil; heat through. Serve over the bok choy. **Yield:** 4 servings.

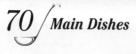

Put the Freeze on Easy Entrees

DON'T be left out in the cold on busy nights when you don't have time to cook! These easy-to-fix dishes are perfect for making ahead and freezing. They'll be ready when you need them!

Beef Taco Lasagna

(Pictured at far right)

Prep: 30 min.   **Bake:** 35 min. + standing

This recipe makes two big pans. Freeze one or both to enjoy later. —Stacey Compton, Toledo, Ohio

24 lasagna noodles
2 pounds lean ground beef
2 envelopes taco seasoning
4 egg whites
2 cartons (15 ounces *each*) ricotta cheese
8 cups (2 pounds) shredded cheddar cheese
2 jars (24 ounces *each*) chunky salsa

Cook noodles according to package directions. Meanwhile, in a large skillet, cook beef over medium heat until no longer pink; drain. Stir in taco seasoning. In a small bowl, combine egg whites and ricotta cheese. Drain noodles.

In each of two 13-in. x 9-in. x 2-in. baking dishes, layer four noodles, 3/4 cup ricotta mixture, half of the beef mixture and 1-1/3 cups cheddar cheese. Top each with four noodles, 3/4 cup ricotta mixture, 1-1/2 cups salsa and 1-1/3 cups cheese. Repeat.

Cover and freeze one casserole for up to 3 months. Bake the second casserole, uncovered, at 350° for 35-40 minutes or until heated through. Let stand for 10 minutes before cutting. **Yield:** 2 casseroles (8 servings each).

To use frozen casserole: Thaw in the refrigerator for 8 hours. Bake as directed.

Hearty Jambalaya

(Pictured at far right)

Prep: 25 min.   **Cook:** 10 min.

This meaty and satisfying jambalaya is a favorite I make often. —Mel Miller, Perkins, Oklahoma

1 pound fully cooked kielbasa *or* Polish sausage, cut into 1/2-inch slices
1 pound boneless skinless chicken breasts, cubed
1 large onion, chopped
1/2 cup chopped celery
1/2 cup chopped green pepper
4 garlic cloves, minced
2 tablespoons butter
1 can (14-1/2 ounces) diced tomatoes, undrained
1 can (6 ounces) tomato paste
1/2 teaspoon hot pepper sauce
1/4 to 1/2 teaspoon cayenne pepper
1/8 teaspoon garlic powder
1/8 teaspoon white pepper
1/8 teaspoon pepper
1/2 pound uncooked medium shrimp, peeled and deveined
Hot cooked rice, optional

In a Dutch oven or large saucepan, saute the sausage, chicken, onion, celery, green pepper and garlic in butter until chicken is no longer pink. Stir in the tomatoes, tomato paste and seasonings. Bring to a boil. Reduce heat; cover and simmer for 6-8 minutes or until chicken is no longer pink.

Stir in the shrimp. Cover and simmer for 4 minutes or until shrimp turn pink. Serve over the rice if desired; or cool, cover and freeze up to 2 months. **Yield:** 8 servings.

Two-Meat Spaghetti Sauce

(Pictured at right)

Prep: 20 min.   **Cook:** 45 min.

This robust home-style pasta sauce tastes just as good after it's been frozen. —Candi Johnsen West Plains, Missouri

1 pound ground beef
1 pound Italian sausage links, cut into 3/4-inch slices
1 large onion, chopped
2 cans (15 ounces each) tomato sauce
1 can (16 ounces) stewed tomatoes
1 can (6 ounces) tomato paste
3/4 cup water
1 can (4 ounces) mushroom stems and pieces, drained
1/2 cup sliced stuffed olives, optional
2 teaspoons Italian seasoning
1-1/2 teaspoons Worcestershire sauce
1 teaspoon garlic powder
1 teaspoon sugar

1/2 teaspoon chili powder
1/4 teaspoon dried oregano
1/4 teaspoon celery salt
1 bay leaf
Hot cooked spaghetti

In a Dutch oven, cook the beef, sausage and onion over medium heat until the meat is no longer pink; drain. Add the tomato sauce, tomatoes, tomato paste, water, mushrooms, olives if desired and seasonings. Bring to a boil. Reduce the heat; simmer, uncovered, for 45-60 minutes or until sauce reaches desired thickness.

Discard bay leaf. Serve over spaghetti; or cool, cover and freeze for up to 2 months. **Yield:** 9 servings.

FIT FOR FREEZING are Beef Taco Lasagna, Hearty Jambalaya and Two-Meat Spaghetti Sauce (shown above).

Manicotti with Spicy Sausage

(Pictured below)

Prep: 30 min.   **Bake:** 1 hour

It's easy to fill the uncooked manicotti shells for this zesty pasta bake. I receive compliments on this hearty entree every time I serve it. —Jeaune Hadl, Lexington, Kentucky

- 1 **pound bulk spicy Italian sausage**
- 1 **can (28 ounces) crushed tomatoes**
- 1 **jar (26 ounces) marinara sauce**
- 2 **eggs, beaten**
- 3 **cups ricotta cheese**
- 3/4 **cup grated Parmesan cheese**
- 1 **can (4 ounces) chopped green chilies**
- 3 **tablespoons minced fresh parsley**
- 1 **teaspoon Italian seasoning**
- 1/2 **teaspoon salt**
- 1/2 **teaspoon garlic powder**
- 1/2 **teaspoon pepper**
- 18 **uncooked manicotti shells**
- 1/2 **cup shredded mozzarella cheese**

In a large skillet, cook sausage over medium heat until no longer pink; drain and set aside. In the same skillet, bring tomatoes and marinara sauce to a boil. Reduce heat; cover and simmer for 10 minutes. In a large bowl, combine the eggs, ricotta, Parmesan cheese, chilies, parsley, Italian seasoning, salt, garlic powder and pepper.

Divide 2 cups of sauce between two greased 13-in. x 9-in. x 2-in. baking dishes. Stuff uncooked manicotti shells with cheese mixture. Place in prepared pans. Sprinkle with sausage; top with remaining sauce.

Cover and bake at 375° for 50 minutes. Uncover; sprinkle with mozzarella cheese. Bake 10 minutes longer or until cheese is melted and manicotti is tender. Let stand for 5 minutes before serving. **Yield:** 8-10 servings.

Spiced Beef Roast

Prep: 25 min. + marinating
Bake: 2-1/4 hours + standing

In the South, this tangy roast is traditionally served cold or at room temperature, but we like it piping hot. It's great for special occasions, and the leftovers are fantastic.
—Barb Bredthauer, Omaha, Nebraska

✓ **Uses less fat, sugar or salt. Includes Nutritional Analysis and Diabetic Exchanges.**

- 1 **medium onion, thinly sliced**
- 1 **cup white vinegar**
- 1/2 **cup beef broth**
- 1/2 **cup packed brown sugar**
- 1 **bay leaf**
- 1 **teaspoon ground ginger**
- 3/4 **teaspoon salt**
- 1/2 **teaspoon *each* ground allspice, cinnamon and nutmeg**
- 1/2 **teaspoon pepper**
- 1/8 **teaspoon cayenne pepper**
- 1 **boneless beef sirloin tip roast *or* round roast (2 pounds)**
- 3/4 **cup *each* chopped dried plums and apricots**
- 1/4 **cup golden raisins**
- 1 **teaspoon cornstarch**
- 2 **tablespoons cold water**

For marinade, combine the onion, vinegar, broth, brown sugar, bay leaf and seasonings in a small saucepan. Cook and stir over medium heat until sugar is dissolved. Cool to room temperature.

Pierce roast several times with a meat fork; place in a large resealable plastic bag. Add cooled marinade. Seal bag and turn to coat; refrigerate for 8 hours or overnight.

Place the meat and the marinade in an ungreased 11-in. x 7-in. x 2-in. baking dish. Bake, uncovered, at 325° for 1-1/2 hours. Stir in the dried fruit and raisins. Bake 45-55 minutes longer or until the meat and fruit

are tender. Discard the bay leaf.

Remove roast to a platter; let stand for 10 minutes before slicing. For gravy, combine cornstarch and water until smooth. Pour the pan juices into a saucepan; gradually stir in cornstarch mixture. Bring to a boil; cook and stir for 2 minutes or until thickened. Serve with beef. **Yield:** 8 servings.

Nutritional Analysis: 3 ounces cooked beef with 2 tablespoons gravy equals 317 calories, 6 g fat (2 g saturated fat), 71 mg cholesterol, 285 mg sodium, 38 g carbohydrate, 4 g fiber, 26 g protein. **Diabetic Exchanges:** 3 lean meat, 1-1/2 fruit, 1 starch.

Old-Fashioned Chicken Potpie

Prep: 1 hour   **Bake:** 15 min.

I always have leftover chicken broth on hand and use it for many things, including this comforting entree. You can bake your own biscuits, like I do, or buy them at the store. I like to bake extra biscuits to eat with butter and jam.
—Liliane Jahnke, Cypress, Texas

1-1/2 cups sliced fresh mushrooms
    1 cup sliced fresh carrots
  1/2 cup chopped onion
  1/3 cup butter
  1/3 cup all-purpose flour
1-1/2 cups chicken broth
1-1/2 cups milk
    4 cups cubed cooked chicken breast
    1 cup frozen peas
    1 jar (2 ounces) diced pimientos, drained
    1 teaspoon salt
BISCUIT TOPPING:
    2 cups all-purpose flour
    4 teaspoons baking powder
    2 teaspoons sugar
  1/2 teaspoon salt
  1/2 teaspoon cream of tartar
  1/2 cup cold butter
  2/3 cup milk

In a large saucepan, saute the mushrooms, carrots and onion in butter until tender; sprinkle with flour. Gradually stir in broth and milk until blended. Bring to a boil; cook and stir for 2 minutes or until thickened. Add the chicken, peas, pimientos and salt; heat through. Pour into a greased shallow 2-1/2-qt. baking dish; set aside.

In a large bowl, combine the flour, baking powder, sugar, salt and cream of tartar. Cut in butter until mixture resembles coarse crumbs; stir in milk just until moistened. Turn onto a lightly floured surface; knead 8-10 times. Pat or roll out to 1/2-in. thickness; cut with a floured 2-1/2-in. biscuit cutter.

Place biscuits over chicken mixture. Bake, uncov-

ered, at 400° for 15-20 minutes or until biscuits are golden brown. **Yield:** 6-8 servings.

Dinner in a Packet

(Pictured above)

Prep: 10 min.   **Grill:** 30 min.

Kids enjoy making this simple dinner as much as eating it. I got the recipe years ago at Guide Camp.
—Louise Graybiel, Toronto, Ontario

✓ Uses less fat, sugar or salt. Includes Nutritional Analysis and Diabetic Exchanges.

    1 boneless pork loin chop (4 ounces)
    1 medium potato, sliced
    1 large carrot, sliced
  1/4 cup frozen peas
    1 tablespoon onion soup mix

Place the pork chop on a double thickness of heavy-duty foil (about 18 in. x 14 in.). Top with potato, carrot and peas. Sprinkle with soup mix. Seal foil tightly. Grill, covered, over medium heat for 30-35 minutes or until the meat juices run clear, turning occasionally. **Yield:** 1 serving.

Nutritional Analysis: 1 packet (prepared with reduced-sodium onion soup mix) equals 481 calories, 9 g fat (3 g saturated fat), 91 mg cholesterol, 474 mg sodium, 55 g carbohydrate, 8 g fiber, 43 g protein.

with plastic wrap. Flatten to 1/4-in. thickness. Remove plastic; sprinkle steak with 1/8 teaspoon salt and pepper. Set aside. In a skillet, cook bacon until crisp. Remove to paper towels. Drain, reserving 2 tablespoons drippings.

In the drippings, saute leeks, yellow peppers and 1 cup celery until tender. Stir in spinach, thyme, basil and bacon. Spoon over meat to within 1/2 in. of edges. Roll up tightly jelly-roll style, starting with a long side. Tie with kitchen string.

Rub steak with garlic and remaining salt. In a large skillet, brown meat in oil on all sides. Place in a greased shallow roasting pan. Add onion and remaining celery. Combine remaining ingredients; pour over steak. Cover loosely with foil.

Bake at 350° for 1 hour. Baste with drippings. Bake, uncovered, 15 minutes longer or until meat reaches desired doneness (for medium-rare, a meat thermometer should read 145°; medium, 160°; well-done, 170°). Let stand 10-15 minutes. Remove string and slice. Discard bay leaf; thicken juices if desired. **Yield:** 6 servings.

Stuffed Flank Steak

(Pictured above)

Prep: 30 min. **Bake:** 1-1/4 hours + standing

This colorful beef dish was always a favorite request for birthday dinners while I was growing up. Savory and stuffed full of vegetables, it's as tender as the memories it still brings back every time I make it. —Julie Etzel
Tualatin, Oregon

   1 **beef flank steak (about 1-1/2 pounds)**
1/8 **teaspoon plus 1/2 teaspoon salt, *divided***
1/8 **teaspoon pepper**
   4 **bacon strips, diced**
   3 **leeks, sliced**
1-1/2 **cups chopped sweet yellow peppers**
1-1/2 **cups chopped celery, *divided***
1/2 **pound baby spinach, torn**
   1 **teaspoon dried thyme**
   1 **teaspoon dried basil**
   2 **garlic cloves, minced**
   3 **tablespoons olive oil**
   1 **medium onion, cut into wedges**
   1 **cup water**
1/2 **cup beef broth**
   2 **teaspoons tomato paste**
   1 **bay leaf**

Cut steak horizontally from a long side to within 1/2 in. of opposite side. Open steak so it lies flat; cover

Thai-Style Brisket

Prep: 1 hour **Cook:** 8-1/2 hours

I let my slow cooker do most of the work when preparing this brisket. —Teri Rasey-Bolf, Cadillac, Michigan

   1 **fresh beef brisket (3 to 4 pounds), cut in half**
   3 **tablespoons olive oil, *divided***
   1 **cup chunky peanut butter**
2/3 **cup soy sauce**
   4 **teaspoons sesame oil**
   1 **tablespoon minced fresh cilantro**
   1 **tablespoon lemon juice**
   1 **teaspoon garlic powder**
   1 **teaspoon crushed red pepper flakes**
   1 **teaspoon pepper**
   1 **tablespoon cornstarch**
   1 **cup water**
1-1/4 **cups julienned carrots**
   1 **medium sweet red pepper, sliced**
   1 **medium green pepper, sliced**
1/2 **cup chopped green onions**
   1 **cup unsalted peanuts, optional**
Hot cooked rice

In a large skillet over medium-high heat, brown brisket on both sides in 2 tablespoons olive oil. Transfer meat and drippings to a 5-qt. slow cooker. Combine the next eight ingredients; pour over brisket. Cover and cook on low for 8-9 hours or until meat is tender.

Remove meat; keep warm. Combine cornstarch and water until smooth; stir into cooking juices. Cover; cook on high for 30 minutes or until thickened. Meanwhile, in a skillet or wok, stir-fry vegetables in remaining oil until crisp-tender. Add peanuts if desired. Stir cooking juices and stir into vegetable mixture.

Thinly slice meat across the grain. Place rice on a large serving platter; top with meat and vegetable mixture. **Yield:** 6-8 servings.

Grilled Raspberry Chicken

(Pictured below right)

Prep: 15 min. + marinating   **Grill:** 30 min.

Raspberry vinaigrette and raspberry jam lend a lovely fruit flavor to this moist chicken dish I created. Because the recipe uses thighs and drumsticks, it's also economical. I make it often.   —Gloria Warczak, Cedarburg, Wisconsin

- 1 cup plus 4-1/2 teaspoons raspberry vinaigrette, *divided*
- 2 tablespoons minced fresh rosemary *or* 2 teaspoons dried rosemary, crushed, *divided*
- 6 chicken thighs
- 6 chicken drumsticks
- 1/2 cup seedless raspberry jam
- 1-1/2 teaspoons lime juice
- 1/2 teaspoon soy sauce
- 1/8 teaspoon garlic powder

In a large resealable plastic bag, combine 1 cup vinaigrette and half of the rosemary. Add chicken. Seal bag and turn to coat; refrigerate for 1 hour. In a bowl, combine the jam, lime juice, soy sauce, garlic powder, and remaining vinaigrette and rosemary; set aside.

Drain and discard marinade. Place chicken skin side down on grill rack. Grill, covered, over indirect medium heat for 20 minutes. Turn; grill 10-20 minutes longer or until juices run clear, basting occasionally with raspberry sauce. **Yield:** 6 servings.

Spinach Crab Chicken

(Pictured at right)

Prep: 45 min.   **Cook:** 40 min.

I altered a friend's recipe for crab-stuffed chicken to include one of my favorite vegetables—spinach. Now my husband requests this elegant entree all the time. Served over rice, it's special enough for company, too.   —Vicki Melie Glenwood, Iowa

- 1/2 cup finely chopped onion
- 1/4 cup chopped fresh mushrooms
- 1/4 cup finely chopped celery
- 3 tablespoons butter
- 3 tablespoons all-purpose flour

- 1/2 teaspoon salt, *divided*
- 1 cup chicken broth
- 1/2 cup milk
- 4 boneless skinless chicken breast halves (6 ounces *each*)
- 1/8 teaspoon white pepper
- 1/2 cup dry bread crumbs
- 1 can (6 ounces) crabmeat, drained, flaked and cartilage removed
- 12 fresh spinach leaves, chopped
- 1 tablespoon minced fresh parsley
- 1 cup (4 ounces) shredded Swiss cheese

Hot cooked rice

For sauce, in a skillet, saute the onion, mushrooms and celery in butter until tender. Stir in flour and 1/4 teaspoon salt until blended. Gradually add broth and milk. Bring to a boil; cook and stir for 1-2 minutes or until thickened. Remove from the heat.

Flatten chicken to 1/4-in. thickness; sprinkle with pepper and remaining salt. In a bowl, combine the bread crumbs, crab, spinach and parsley; stir in 1/2 cup sauce. Spoon 1/4 cup down the center of each chicken breast half. Roll up; secure with toothpicks. Place seam side down in a greased 13-in. x 9-in. x 2-in. baking dish. Top with remaining sauce.

Cover and bake at 375° for 35-45 minutes or until juices run clear. Sprinkle with cheese. Broil 4-6 in. from the heat for 5 minutes or until lightly browned. Discard the toothpicks. Serve with the rice. **Yield:** 4 servings.

Spinach Chicken Manicotti

(Pictured below)

Prep: 1 hour   **Bake:** 35 min.

Pepper and nutmeg spice up the rich sauce in this hearty pasta dish. I made this for my husband on our first Valentine's Day when we were dating. It was a big success.
—Amy Luce, Mansfield, Texas

✓ **Uses less fat, sugar or salt. Includes Nutritional Analysis and Diabetic Exchanges.**

    1 large onion, chopped
    1 garlic clove, minced
    1 teaspoon olive oil
2-1/2 cups diced cooked chicken breast
    1 package (10 ounces) frozen chopped spinach, thawed and squeezed dry
  3/4 cup diced fully cooked lean ham
  1/4 cup grated Parmesan cheese
    2 egg whites
  1/2 teaspoon dried basil
  1/8 teaspoon pepper
Dash ground nutmeg
  12 uncooked manicotti shells
SAUCE:
  3/4 cup all-purpose flour
    3 cups reduced-sodium chicken broth
    1 cup fat-free milk
  1/4 teaspoon salt
  1/8 teaspoon ground nutmeg
  1/8 teaspoon pepper
Dash cayenne pepper
  1/4 cup grated Parmesan cheese

In a small skillet, saute onion and garlic in oil until tender. In a large bowl, combine the onion mixture with the next eight ingredients; set aside.

Cook manicotti shells according to package directions. Meanwhile, for sauce, combine flour and broth in a large saucepan until smooth. Stir in the milk, salt, nutmeg, pepper and cayenne.

Bring to a boil over medium heat; cook and stir for 2 minutes or until thickened. Spoon 1 cup into the chicken mixture. Add Parmesan cheese to remaining sauce.

Spread 1 cup sauce into a 13-in. x 9-in. x 2-in. baking dish coated with nonstick cooking spray. Drain shells; stuff with the chicken mixture. Arrange over sauce. Drizzle with remaining sauce. Cover and bake at 375° for 35-40 minutes or until bubbly and heated through. **Yield:** 6 servings.

Nutritional Analysis: 1 serving equals 372 calories, 7 g fat (2 g saturated fat), 58 mg cholesterol, 866 mg sodium, 43 g carbohydrate, 4 g fiber, 35 g protein. **Diabetic Exchanges:** 4 very lean meat, 2 starch, 2 vegetable, 1/2 fat.

Ribs with a Kick

(Pictured on front cover)

Prep: 30 min.   **Grill:** 2 hours 5 min.

The meat just falls off the bones of these slowly grilled spareribs. My mom created the delicious sauce, tweaking it until it suited my dad's taste. I have to agree with him that these ribs are the best I've ever had.
—Desiree Whittaker, Rathdrum, Idaho

    2 medium onions, chopped
    2 garlic cloves, minced
    2 tablespoons butter
    1 cup packed brown sugar
    1 cup water
    1 cup spicy ketchup
    3 tablespoons white vinegar
    3 tablespoons Worcestershire sauce
    1 tablespoon Liquid Smoke, optional
    2 teaspoons ground mustard
    2 teaspoons chili powder
    1 teaspoon paprika
  1/2 teaspoon cayenne pepper
    1 teaspoon salt
  1/2 teaspoon onion salt
  1/2 teaspoon garlic salt
  1/2 teaspoon pepper
    5 to 6 pounds baby back ribs, cut into serving-size pieces

In a large saucepan, saute onions and garlic in butter until tender. Stir in the brown sugar, water, ketchup, vinegar, Worcestershire sauce, Liquid Smoke if desired, mustard, chili powder, paprika and cayenne.

Bring to a boil. Reduce heat; simmer and stir until thickened, about 10 minutes. Remove from the heat.

Combine the salt, onion salt, garlic salt and pepper; sprinkle over ribs. Grill ribs, covered, over indirect medium heat for 1-3/4 hours or until meat is very tender. Set aside 1 cup barbecue sauce for serving.

Brush some of remaining sauce over ribs; cook 20 minutes longer, turning ribs and basting with sauce. Serve with reserved sauce. **Yield:** 5-6 servings.

Editor's Note: This recipe was tested with Heinz Hot & Spicy Kick'rs ketchup.

Spaghetti Casserole

Prep: 20 min.   **Bake:** 40 min.

I always get asked for a copy of this family-pleasing recipe. The hearty meatless main dish—a combination of spaghetti and lasagna ingredients—is cheesy and well seasoned with a creamy tomato sauce.   —Kathy Bence
Edmonds, Washington

✓ **Uses less fat, sugar or salt. Includes Nutritional Analysis and Diabetic Exchanges.**

- 6 ounces uncooked spaghetti
- 1 tablespoon butter
- 1/3 cup shredded Parmesan cheese
- 1 jar (26 ounces) meatless spaghetti sauce
- 2 cups chopped green pepper
- 1 can (14-1/2 ounces) diced tomatoes, drained
- 1 carton (8 ounces) part-skim ricotta cheese
- 1 can (8 ounces) mushroom stems and pieces, drained
- 1 small onion, chopped
- 3 garlic cloves, minced
- 12 fresh basil leaves, thinly sliced
- 1/2 teaspoon dried oregano
- 3 cups (12 ounces) shredded part-skim mozzarella cheese, *divided*

Cook spaghetti according to package directions; drain. Add butter and Parmesan cheese; toss to coat. In a large bowl, combine the spaghetti sauce, green pepper and tomatoes. In a blender, process the ricotta cheese until pureed. Add to the spaghetti sauce mixture. Stir in the mushrooms, onion, garlic, basil, oregano and 1-1/2 cups mozzarella cheese. Add the spaghetti; toss to coat.

Transfer to a 13-in. x 9-in. x 2-in. baking dish coated with nonstick cooking spray. Sprinkle with the remaining mozzarella. Cover; bake at 350° for 40-45 minutes or until heated through. **Yield:** 9 servings.

Nutritional Analysis: 1 serving equals 301 calories, 12 g fat (7 g saturated fat), 41 mg cholesterol, 774

mg sodium, 31 g carbohydrate, 4 g fiber, 18 g protein. **Diabetic Exchanges:** 2 starch, 2 fat, 1 lean meat.

Pesto Shrimp Pasta

(Pictured above)

Prep/Total Time: 30 min.

A dash of red pepper puts zip in this lively seafood main dish.   —Gloria Jones Grenga, Newnan, Georgia

- 8 ounces uncooked spaghetti
- 1 cup loosely packed fresh basil leaves
- 1/4 cup lemon juice
- 2 garlic cloves, peeled
- 3 tablespoons olive oil, *divided*
- 1/2 teaspoon salt
- 1 pound fresh asparagus, trimmed and cut into 2-inch pieces
- 3/4 pound uncooked medium shrimp, peeled and deveined
- 1/8 teaspoon crushed red pepper flakes

Cook spaghetti according to package directions. Meanwhile, in a blender or food processor, combine the basil, lemon juice, garlic, 1 tablespoon oil and salt; cover and process until smooth.

In a large skillet, saute the asparagus in remaining oil until crisp-tender. Add the shrimp and pepper flakes. Cook and stir until shrimp turn pink. Drain the spaghetti; place in a large bowl. Add basil mixture; toss to coat. Add shrimp mixture and mix well. **Yield:** 4 servings.

Grilled Fish in a Flash!

IT DOESN'T get much easier. After no more than 20 minutes on the grill, any of these fish or shrimp entrees is ready to enjoy! They're highly recommended by several of our *Taste of Home* readers.

Halibut with Bacon

Prep: 25 min. + marinating   **Grill:** 10 min.

This can be an easy weeknight meal or part of an elegant dinner.   —*Pat Hockett, Wrangell, Alaska*

  1/2 **cup lime juice**
  1/2 **cup chopped green onions**
    2 **tablespoons vegetable oil**
    2 **tablespoons minced fresh cilantro**
    2 **tablespoons chopped seeded jalapeno peppers**
    1 **teaspoon salt**
  1/2 **teaspoon pepper**
    4 **halibut steaks (6 ounces** *each***)**
    8 **bacon strips**

In a large resealable plastic bag, combine the first seven ingredients. Add halibut; seal bag and turn to coat. Refrigerate for 10-15 minutes, turning once.

In a large skillet, cook bacon over medium heat until cooked but not crisp. Drain on paper towels. Drain and discard marinade from halibut. Wrap two slices of bacon over the top and sides of each steak; secure with soaked wooden toothpicks.

Coat grill rack with nonstick cooking spray before starting the grill. Place halibut, bacon side down, on grill rack. Grill, covered, over medium heat for 4-6 minutes on each side or until fish flakes easily with a fork. Discard toothpicks. **Yield:** 4 servings.

Editor's Note: When cutting or seeding hot peppers, use rubber or plastic gloves to protect your hands. Avoid touching your face.

Tuna Steaks with Salsa

(Pictured at far right)

Prep/Total Time: 25 min.

Fish is often served with salsa in restaurants. Why not try it at home? Mango and carrots make this salsa unique.
   —*Harriet Stichter, Milford, Indiana*

    1 **cup shredded carrots**
  3/4 **cup chopped peeled mango**
    2 **tablespoons lime juice**

    1 **tablespoon minced chives**
  1/4 **teaspoon salt,** *divided*
  1/4 **teaspoon pepper,** *divided*
  1/8 **teaspoon ground coriander**
  1/8 **teaspoon ground cumin**
    4 **tuna steaks (6 ounces** *each***)**

For salsa, in a bowl, combine the carrots, mango, lime juice, chives, 1/8 teaspoon salt, 1/8 teaspoon pepper, coriander and cumin; set aside. Sprinkle tuna steaks with the remaining salt and pepper.

Coat grill rack with nonstick cooking spray before starting the grill. Grill tuna, covered, over medium heat for 5-7 minutes on each side or until fish flakes easily with a fork. Top with salsa. **Yield:** 4 servings.

Skillet-Grilled Catfish

(Pictured at right)

Prep/Total Time: 25 min.

You can use this recipe with any thick fish fillet, but I suggest catfish or haddock. The Cajun flavor is great!
   —*Traci Krick, Bear, Delaware*

  1/4 **cup all-purpose flour**
  1/4 **cup cornmeal**
    1 **teaspoon onion powder**
    1 **teaspoon dried basil**
  1/2 **teaspoon garlic salt**
  1/2 **teaspoon dried thyme**
  1/4 to 1/2 **teaspoon white pepper**
  1/4 to 1/2 **teaspoon cayenne pepper**
  1/4 to 1/2 **teaspoon pepper**
    4 **catfish fillets (6 to 8 ounces** *each***)**
  1/4 **cup butter**

In a large resealable bag, combine the first nine ingredients. Add catfish, one fillet at a time, and shake to coat. Place a large cast-iron skillet on a grill rack over medium-hot heat. Melt butter in skillet; add catfish. Grill, covered, for 6-8 minutes on each side or until fish flakes easily with a fork. **Yield:** 4 servings.

Shrimp Kabobs

(Pictured at right)

Prep: 35 min. + marinating   **Grill:** 10 min.

Marinating the shrimp in Italian dressing adds wonderful flavor to these colorful kabobs.   —*Sharon Aweau,
Kapolei, Hawaii*

☑ **Uses less fat, sugar or salt. Includes Nutritional Analysis and Diabetic Exchanges.**

> 1 cup Italian salad dressing, *divided*
> 2 pounds uncooked jumbo shrimp, peeled and deveined
> 2 large onions
> 16 large fresh mushrooms
> 2 large green peppers, cut into 1-1/2-inch pieces
> 16 cherry tomatoes

In a large resealable plastic bag, combine 1/2 cup salad dressing and shrimp. Cut each onion into eight wedges. In another large resealable plastic bag, combine the vegetables and remaining salad dressing. Seal bags; turn to coat. Refrigerate for 2 hours, turning occasionally.

Drain and discard marinade. On eight metal or soaked wooden skewers, alternately thread the shrimp and vegetables. Grill the kabobs, covered, over medium heat for 3 minutes on each side or until the shrimp turn pink. **Yield:** 8 servings.

Nutritional Analysis: 1 kabob (prepared with fat-free dressing) equals 150 calories, 2 g fat (trace saturated fat), 169 mg cholesterol, 630 mg sodium, 13 g carbohydrate, 3 g fiber, 21 g protein. **Diabetic Exchanges:** 2-1/2 very lean meat, 2 vegetable.

SAVORY CATCH. Tuna Steaks with Salsa, Skillet-Grilled Catfish and Shrimp Kabobs (shown above) are sizzling with great flavor.

Glazed Meat Loaf

(Pictured above)

Prep: 15 min.   **Bake:** 1 hour + standing

Grated carrots and cheese add a hint of color and good taste to this nourishing, homey loaf. My family always looks forward to meat loaf sandwiches the next day.
—*Sandy Etelamaki, Ishpeming, Michigan*

- 2 eggs, beaten
- 2/3 cup milk
- 1-1/2 cups (6 ounces) shredded cheddar cheese
- 1 cup crushed saltines (about 30 crackers)
- 1 cup finely shredded carrots
- 1/2 cup finely chopped onion
- 1/2 teaspoon salt
- 1/4 teaspoon garlic powder
- 1/4 teaspoon pepper
- 2 pounds lean ground beef
- 1/2 cup packed brown sugar
- 1/2 cup ketchup
- 2 tablespoons Dijon mustard

In a large bowl, combine the eggs, milk, cheese, saltines, carrots, onion, salt, garlic powder and pepper. Crumble beef over mixture and mix well. Shape into a loaf. Place in a greased 13-in. x 9-in. x 2-in. baking dish. Bake, uncovered, at 350° for 50 minutes.

For glaze, in a small saucepan, bring the brown sugar, ketchup and mustard to a boil. Reduce heat; simmer, uncovered, for 3-5 minutes or until heated through. Spoon over meat loaf. Bake 10-15 minutes longer or until meat is no longer pink and a meat thermometer reads 160°. Drain; let stand for 10 minutes before slicing. **Yield:** 12 servings.

Primavera Chicken

Prep: 15 min.   **Cook:** 25 min.

You'll love the way the nutmeg in this pretty pasta dish blends with the cayenne pepper. I usually double the recipe because I like the leftovers even better! This entree is especially good served with homemade pesto bread.
—*Vicky Root, Greenville, Ohio*

- 1-1/3 pounds boneless skinless chicken breasts, cut into strips
- 1 teaspoon salt, *divided*
- 1/2 teaspoon pepper, *divided*
- 2 tablespoons olive oil
- 1 medium sweet red pepper, julienned
- 1 cup sliced fresh mushrooms
- 2 green onions, chopped
- 1/8 teaspoon ground nutmeg
- 1/8 teaspoon cayenne pepper
- 2/3 cup heavy whipping cream
- 1/2 cup chicken broth
- 8 ounces uncooked linguine
- 2/3 cup pine nuts, toasted
- 1/2 cup frozen peas, thawed
- Shredded Parmesan cheese, optional

Sprinkle chicken with 1/2 teaspoon salt and 1/4 teaspoon pepper. In a large skillet, cook chicken in oil over medium-high heat for 8-10 minutes or until juices run clear. Remove and keep warm.

In the same skillet, saute the red pepper, mushrooms, onions, nutmeg and cayenne just until vegetables are tender. Add cream and broth. Bring to a boil; cook until sauce is reduced by a third.

Cook the linguine according to package directions; drain. Add the chicken, linguine, pine nuts, peas, and remaining salt and pepper to sauce; heat through. Garnish with Parmesan cheese if desired. **Yield:** 4 servings.

Sesame Beef Tenderloin

Prep: 10 min. + marinating
Bake: 55 min. + standing

A sesame seed and honey glaze makes this roast so elegant and moist. —*Sara Dakin, Longmont, Colorado*

- 1/4 cup soy sauce
- 1 green onion, chopped
- 1 teaspoon ground ginger
- 1 teaspoon Dijon mustard
- 2 garlic cloves, minced
- 1 beef tenderloin (3 pounds)
- 1/4 cup honey
- 2 tablespoons sesame seeds, toasted

In a large resealable bag, combine the first five ingredients. Add the tenderloin; seal bag and turn to coat.

Refrigerate for 2 hours, turning several times.

Drain and discard marinade. Brush beef with honey; sprinkle with sesame seeds. Place in a shallow roasting pan. Bake at 400° for 25 minutes. Cover with foil. Bake 30-35 minutes longer or until meat reaches desired doneness (for medium-rare, a meat thermometer should read 145°; medium, 160°; well-done, 170°). Let stand for 10 minutes before slicing. **Yield:** 10-12 servings.

Brined Roasting Chicken

Prep: 30 min. + marinating **Bake:** 1 hour 20 min.

I discovered the art of brining turkey a few years ago and transferred the technique to roasting a whole chicken. I guarantee you will have a moist bird and rich flavorful gravy from the pan drippings. —Julie Noyes, Louisville, Kentucky

      8 cups warm water
  1/2 cup kosher salt
  1/4 cup packed brown sugar
      3 tablespoons molasses
      1 tablespoon whole peppercorns, crushed
      1 tablespoon whole allspice, crushed
      2 teaspoons ground ginger
      1 roasting chicken (4 pounds)
      4 cups cold water
      1 teaspoon vegetable oil
  3/4 to 1 cup chicken broth
      1 tablespoon all-purpose flour

For brine, combine first seven ingredients in a large kettle. Bring to a boil; cook and stir until salt is dissolved. Remove from heat. Cool to room temperature.

Remove giblets from chicken; discard. Place cold water in a 2-gal. resealable plastic bag; add chicken. Place in a roasting pan. Carefully pour cooled brine into bag. Squeeze out as much air as possible; seal bag and turn to coat. Refrigerate for 3-4 hours, turning several times.

Discard brine. Rinse chicken with water; pat dry. Skewer chicken openings; tie drumsticks together. Brush with oil. Place chicken in a roasting pan. Bake, uncovered, at 350° for 80-90 minutes or until a meat thermometer reads 180°, basting occasionally with pan drippings (cover loosely with foil if chicken browns too quickly).

Remove chicken to a serving platter and keep warm. Pour drippings and loosened browned bits into a measuring cup; skim fat and discard. Add enough broth to measure 1 cup. In a small saucepan, combine flour and broth mixture until smooth. Bring to a boil; cook and stir for 2 minutes or until thickened. Serve with the chicken. **Yield:** 4-6 servings.

Editor's Note: For best results, do not use a prebasted chicken for this recipe. However, if you do, omit the salt in the brine.

Perch with Cucumber Relish

(Pictured below)

Prep/Total Time: 25 min.

I give fish a healthy flavor lift with homemade relish. Tangy vinegar and tarragon lend zest, and chopped cucumber and radishes add garden-fresh color.   —Mildred Sherrer Fort Worth, Texas

✓ **Uses less fat, sugar or salt. Includes Nutritional Analysis and Diabetic Exchanges.**

  2/3 cup chopped seeded cucumber
  1/2 cup chopped radishes
      2 tablespoons white vinegar
      1 teaspoon canola oil
  1/4 teaspoon sugar
  1/4 teaspoon dried tarragon
  1/8 teaspoon salt
      2 tablespoons butter
      4 perch *or* tilapia fillets (6 ounces *each*)

For relish, in a bowl, combine the cucumber, radishes, vinegar, oil, sugar, tarragon and salt; set aside. In a large skillet, melt butter over medium-high heat. Cook fillets for 3-4 minutes on each side or until fish flakes easily with a fork. Serve with relish. **Yield:** 4 servings.

Nutritional Analysis: 1 fillet with 3 tablespoons relish equals 222 calories, 9 g fat (4 g saturated fat), 168 mg cholesterol, 241 mg sodium, 1 g carbohydrate, trace fiber, 33 g protein. **Diabetic Exchanges:** 4 very lean meat, 2 fat.

Spaghetti Squash Primavera

(Pictured below)

Prep: 25 min.   **Cook:** 20 min.

Sunny-colored squash shells make attractive bowls for this satisfying meatless main dish, perfect for a summertime supper. The recipe showcases a medley of vegetables.
—*CoraLee Collis, Ankeny, Iowa*

   1 **large spaghetti squash (3-1/2 pounds)**
1/4 **cup sliced carrot**
1/4 **cup chopped red onion**
1/4 **cup diced sweet red pepper**
1/4 **cup diced green pepper**
   1 **garlic clove, minced**
   2 **teaspoons vegetable oil**
   1 **cup thinly sliced yellow summer squash**
   1 **cup thinly sliced zucchini**
   1 **can (14-1/2 ounces) Italian stewed tomatoes**
1/2 **cup frozen corn, thawed**
1/2 **teaspoon salt**
1/2 **teaspoon dried oregano**
1/8 **teaspoon dried thyme**
   4 **teaspoons grated Parmesan cheese**
   2 **tablespoons minced fresh parsley**

Cut spaghetti squash in half lengthwise; discard seeds. Place cut side up on a microwave-safe plate; cover with waxed paper. Microwave on high for 9 minutes or until tender.

Meanwhile, in a large skillet, saute the carrot, onion, peppers and garlic in oil for 3 minutes. Add yellow squash and zucchini; saute 2-3 minutes longer or until squash is tender.

Reduce heat; add tomatoes, corn, salt, oregano and thyme. Cook 5 minutes longer or until heated through, stirring occasionally.

Separate spaghetti squash strands with a fork. Spoon vegetable mixture into squash; sprinkle with Parmesan cheese and parsley. **Yield:** 4 servings.

Editor's Note: This recipe was tested in a 1,100-watt microwave.

Pecan-Crusted Chicken

Prep/Total Time: 25 min.

With its crispy pecan coating and creamy mustard sauce, this easy-to-prepare chicken can sure perk up a meal. Cayenne pepper puts a little zip into each bite, but I think my husband likes this dish just for the sauce.
—*Marjorie MacDonald, Huntsville, Ontario*

3/4 **cup finely chopped pecans**
   2 **tablespoons cornstarch**
   2 **tablespoons minced fresh parsley**
3/4 **teaspoon dried thyme**
1/2 **teaspoon salt**
1/4 **teaspoon ground mustard**
1/4 **teaspoon cayenne pepper**
   1 **egg**
   4 **boneless skinless chicken breast halves**
   2 **tablespoons vegetable oil**
MUSTARD SAUCE:
1/2 **cup sour cream**
   2 **tablespoons Dijon mustard**
1/2 **teaspoon sugar**
Pinch salt

In a shallow bowl, combine the first seven ingredients. In another shallow bowl, beat the egg. Dip chicken in egg, then roll in pecan mixture. In a large skillet, cook chicken in oil for 15-20 minutes or until juices run clear. In a small bowl, whisk the sauce ingredients. Serve with chicken. **Yield:** 4 servings.

Open-Faced Turkey Tacos

Prep/Total Time: 20 min.

I like to serve this filling open-faced tortilla with a side of cold applesauce. If you like things spicy, simply add more salsa.
—*Alice Jenne, Marengo, Illinois*

✓ **Uses less fat, sugar or salt. Includes Nutritional Analysis and Diabetic Exchanges.**

   1 **pound lean ground turkey**
   1 **medium onion, chopped**
   1 **can (16 ounces) fat-free refried beans**
   1 **jar (16 ounces) salsa**
 10 **flour tortillas (6 inches), warmed**
   2 **cups shredded lettuce**
   2 **medium tomatoes, chopped**

mer for 12-15 minutes or until meat juices run clear.

Remove the chops and keep warm. Combine cornstarch and water until smooth; stir into skillet. Bring to a boil; cook and stir for 1-2 minutes or until thickened. Spoon over the pork chops. **Yield:** 4 servings.

Tender Barbecued Chicken

(Pictured below)

Prep: 20 min.   **Cook:** 10 min. + cooling

When we can't barbecue on the grill, I bring out my pressure cooker for this fall-off-the-bone BBQ chicken. The jazzed-up BBQ sauce adds good flavor.   —Diane Hixon
Niceville, Florida

  1 **broiler/fryer chicken (3 to 4 pounds),**
     cut up
  2 **tablespoons vegetable oil**
  2 **cups barbecue sauce**
1-1/2 **cups coarsely chopped onions**
  1 **large green pepper, chopped**

In a pressure cooker, brown chicken in oil in batches over medium heat. Combine the barbecue sauce, onions and green pepper in pressure cooker. Return chicken to the pan; stir to coat.

Close cover securely; place pressure regulator on vent pipe. Bring cooker to full pressure over high heat. Reduce heat to medium-high and cook for 10 minutes. (Pressure regulator should maintain a slow steady rocking motion; adjust heat if needed.) Remove from the heat; allow pressure to drop on its own. **Yield:** 4 servings.

Editor's Note: This recipe was tested at 13 pounds of pressure (psi).

---

  2 **medium green peppers, chopped**
  2 **medium sweet red peppers, chopped**
10 **tablespoons fat-free sour cream**

In a large skillet, cook turkey and onion over medium heat until the meat is no longer pink; drain. Add beans and salsa; cook and stir until heated through. Spread 1/2 cup turkey mixture over each tortilla. Top with lettuce, tomatoes, peppers and sour cream. **Yield:** 10 servings.

Nutritional Analysis: 1 serving equals 264 calories, 6 g fat (2 g saturated fat), 38 mg cholesterol, 588 mg sodium, 36 g carbohydrate, 6 g fiber, 15 g protein. **Diabetic Exchanges:** 2 starch, 2 lean meat, 1 vegetable.

Onion-Apricot Pork Chops

(Pictured above)

Prep/Total Time: 30 min.

Dressed up with a glossy sauce, these tender chops are ready in a half hour!   *—Phyllis Schmalz*
Kansas City, Kansas

  4 **boneless pork loin chops (1/2 inch thick)**
  1 **tablespoon butter**
  1 **large onion, sliced and separated into rings**
1/2 **cup chopped dried apricots**
1-1/2 **cups beef broth**
1/4 **cup orange marmalade**
  1 **teaspoon minced fresh gingerroot**
  1 **garlic clove, minced**
Dash ground nutmeg
  1 **tablespoon cornstarch**
4-1/2 **teaspoons cold water**

In a large skillet, brown pork chops in butter over medium-high heat. Add the onion and apricots. Combine the broth, marmalade, ginger, garlic and nutmeg; pour into skillet. Bring to a boil. Reduce heat; cover and sim-

Breads, Rolls & Muffins

Bread has long been a staple in homes across the world...but it's far from ordinary as these recipes deliciously prove.

MOUTH-WATERING MAINSTAYS. Clockwise from upper left: Cornmeal Pan Rolls (p. 93), Sunshine Sweet Rolls (p. 88), Almond Berry Muffins (p. 88) and Spiced Pear Bread (p. 86).

In an electric skillet, heat oil to 375°. Drop tablespoonfuls of dough, a few at a time, into hot oil. Fry for 1-1/2 to 2 minutes on each side or until deep golden brown. Drain on paper towels. Roll warm doughnuts in sugar or serve with syrup. **Yield:** about 4-1/2 dozen.

Spiced Pear Bread

(Pictured on page 84)

Prep: 15 min.   **Bake:** 50 min. + cooling

My mom and I put up our own pears, so I always have plenty on hand when I want to make this wonderful bread. —Rachael Barefoot, Linden, Michigan

✓ Uses less fat, sugar or salt. Includes Nutritional Analysis and Diabetic Exchanges.

   3 cans (15-1/4 ounces *each*) sliced pears, drained and mashed
   1 cup sugar
   1/4 cup unsweetened applesauce
   1/4 cup canola oil
   3 eggs
 3-1/4 cups all-purpose flour
   3 teaspoons ground cinnamon
   1 teaspoon baking soda
   1 teaspoon baking powder
   1 teaspoon ground cloves
   1/2 teaspoon salt

In a large mixing bowl, combine the first five ingredients. Combine the remaining ingredients; gradually add to pear mixture and mix well. Pour into four 5-3/4-in. x 3-in. x 2-in. loaf pans coated with nonstick cooking spray.

Bake at 350° for 50-60 minutes or until a toothpick inserted near the center comes out clean. Cool 10 minutes before removing from pans to wire racks. **Yield:** 4 mini loaves (6 slices each).

Nutritional Analysis: 1 slice equals 160 calories, 3 g fat (trace saturated fat), 27 mg cholesterol, 131 mg sodium, 30 g carbohydrate, 1 g fiber, 3 g protein. **Diabetic Exchange:** 2 starch.

Portuguese Doughnuts

(Pictured above)

Prep: 25 min. + rising   **Cook:** 30 min.

Fresh warm doughnuts are a tradition in my Portuguese heritage, especially during the Easter season. Some people like to roll these doughnuts without holes in sugar. Others prefer eating these sweets with maple syrup. Either way, they're wonderful! —Isabella Castro
Atwater, California

   2 packages (1/4 ounce *each*) active dry yeast
   1/2 cup warm water (110° to 115°)
 1-1/2 cups warm milk (110° to 115°)
   5 eggs, beaten
   5 tablespoons sugar
   1/4 cup butter, softened
   1/2 teaspoon salt
   5 to 5-1/2 cups all-purpose flour
Oil for deep-fat frying
Granulated sugar *or* maple syrup

In a large mixing bowl, dissolve yeast in warm water. Add the milk, eggs, sugar, butter and salt; beat until smooth. Stir in enough flour to form a soft dough (do not knead). Place in a greased bowl, turning once to grease top. Cover and let rise in a warm place until doubled, about 1 hour.

Fennel Breadsticks

Prep: 40 min. + rising   **Bake:** 25 min.

Great with salad or soup, these Italian-style breadsticks have a mild fennel taste. I also like to serve them with spaghetti or lasagna. —Joan Hallford
North Richland Hills, Texas

   1 package (1/4 ounce) active dry yeast
   3/4 cup warm water (110° to 115°)
   3/4 cup vegetable oil

3/4 cup milk
1 tablespoon fennel seed, crushed
1-1/2 teaspoons salt
4-1/2 cups all-purpose flour, *divided*
1 egg
1 tablespoon water

In a large mixing bowl, dissolve yeast in warm water. Add the oil, milk, fennel seed and salt. Beat in 3-1/2 cups flour. Stir in enough remaining flour to form a soft dough. Turn onto a floured surface; knead until smooth and elastic, about 6-8 minutes. Place in a greased bowl, turning once to grease top. Cover and let rise in a warm place until doubled, about 1 hour.

Punch dough down. Let rest for 10 minutes. Turn onto a lightly floured surface; divide into fourths. Work with one portion of dough at a time, keeping remaining dough covered with plastic wrap. Cut each portion into 17 pieces; roll each into a 7-in. rope.

Place 1 in. apart on greased baking sheets. Beat egg and water; brush over dough. Bake at 325° for 25-30 minutes or until golden brown. Remove to wire racks. **Yield:** 68 breadsticks.

Polish Poppy Seed Loaves

(Pictured below right)

Prep: 50 min. + rising   **Bake:** 35 min. + cooling

Traditionally, these loaves were eaten after sundown on Christmas Eve as part of a 12-course meal. At our house, we never can wait that long to bite into the pretty spiral slices of this tender, coffee cake-like treat.
                    —Linda Gronewaller, Hutchinson, Kansas

2 packages (1/4 ounce *each*) active dry yeast
1/2 cup warm water (110° to 115°)
4-1/2 cups all-purpose flour
3/4 cup sugar
1/2 teaspoon salt
1/2 cup cold butter
2 eggs
2 egg yolks
1/2 cup sour cream
1 teaspoon vanilla extract
FILLING:
3 tablespoons poppy seeds
2 tablespoons butter
1/4 cup raisins
2 tablespoons honey
2 teaspoons lemon juice
1/4 cup finely chopped candied orange peel
2 teaspoons grated lemon peel
2 egg whites
1/2 cup sugar

ICING:
1 cup confectioners' sugar
2 tablespoons lemon juice

In a small bowl, dissolve yeast in warm water. In a large mixing bowl, combine the flour, sugar and salt; cut in butter until mixture resembles fine crumbs. Combine eggs, yolks and yeast mixture; add to crumb mixture and mix well. Beat in sour cream and vanilla until smooth. Turn onto a floured surface; knead until smooth and elastic, about 6-8 minutes. Do not let rise. Divide in half. Roll out into two 12-in. squares; cover with plastic wrap.

In a small skillet, cook and stir poppy seeds and butter over medium heat for 3 minutes. Stir in the raisins, honey and lemon juice. Transfer to a bowl; cool for 10 minutes. Stir in candied orange peel and lemon peel.

In a small mixing bowl, beat egg whites until foamy. Gradually beat in sugar, 1 tablespoon at a time, on high just until stiff peaks form and sugar is dissolved. Fold into poppy seed mixture. Spread over each square to within 1/2 in. of edges. Roll up each square jelly-roll style; pinch seams to seal.

Place on a greased baking sheet. Cover and let rise until nearly doubled, about 45 minutes. Bake at 350° for 35-40 minutes or until golden brown. Remove from pan to wire racks to cool. Combine icing ingredients; drizzle over cooled loaves. **Yield:** 2 loaves.

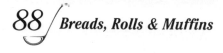

Aniseed Yeast Rolls

(Pictured below)

Prep: 30 min. + rising   **Bake:** 20 min.

These hard-crusted golden-brown gems have a mild anise flavor and a soft pillowy texture with a sprinkling of aniseed on top.   —*Amy Short, Lesage, West Virginia*

5-1/4 to 5-3/4 cups all-purpose flour
3/4 cup packed brown sugar
1-1/2 teaspoons salt
   2 packages (1/4 ounce *each*) active dry yeast
   4 teaspoons aniseed, *divided*
3/4 cup water
1/2 cup butter, cubed
   6 eggs

In a large mixing bowl, combine 2 cups flour, brown sugar, salt, yeast and 3 teaspoons aniseed. In a saucepan, heat water and butter to 120°-130°. Add to dry ingredients; beat just until moistened. Add five eggs; beat until smooth. Stir in enough remaining flour to form a soft dough.

Turn onto a floured surface; knead until smooth and elastic, about 6-8 minutes. Place in a greased bowl, turning once to grease top. Cover and let rise in a warm place until nearly doubled, about 1 hour.

Punch dough down. Turn onto a lightly floured surface; divide into 22 pieces. Shape each into a ball. Place 2 in. apart on greased baking sheets. Cover and let rise until nearly doubled, about 30 minutes. Beat remaining egg; brush over dough. Sprinkle with

remaining aniseed. Bake at 350° for 20-22 minutes or until golden brown. Remove from pans to wire racks. **Yield:** 22 rolls.

Almond Berry Muffins

(Pictured on page 85)

Prep: 20 min.   **Bake:** 20 min.

I made these moist muffins to take to the office, and they were a hit. Sugared almonds give them a crunchy topping. When strawberries aren't in season, I use individually frozen cut strawberries directly from the freezer.
—*Deborah Feinberg, East Setauket, New York*

1-1/4 cups sliced almonds, *divided*
   1 egg white, lightly beaten
1-1/2 cups sugar, *divided*
   1/4 cup shortening
   1/4 cup butter, softened
   2 eggs
   1 teaspoon vanilla extract
1/2 teaspoon almond extract
   2 cups all-purpose flour
   1 teaspoon baking powder
1/2 teaspoon salt
1/4 teaspoon baking soda
3/4 cup buttermilk
1-1/4 cups fresh strawberries, chopped

In a bowl, combine 1 cup almonds and egg white. Add 1/2 cup sugar; toss to coat. Spoon into a greased 15-in. x 10-in. x 1-in. baking pan. Bake at 350° for 9-11 minutes or until golden brown, stirring occasionally.

In a large mixing bowl, cream shortening, butter and remaining sugar until light and fluffy. Add eggs, one at a time, beating well after each. Beat in extracts. Combine flour, baking powder, salt and baking soda; add to creamed mixture alternately with buttermilk. Fold in strawberries and remaining almonds.

Fill greased or paper-lined muffin cups two-thirds full. Sprinkle with sugared almonds. Bake at 350° for 20-25 minutes or until a toothpick comes out clean. Cool for 5 minutes before removing from the pans to wire racks. **Yield:** 1-1/2 dozen.

Sunshine Sweet Rolls

(Pictured on page 85)

Prep: 30 min. + rising   **Bake:** 25 min.

This bread machine recipe is my new favorite. The cream cheese filling and drizzled glaze make these golden-brown rolls a special treat for breakfast or snacking.
—*Alice Shepherd, Maryville, Tennessee*

1-1/2 cups warm water (110° to 115°)
1/4 cup vegetable oil
1/4 cup shredded carrot
4-1/2 cups all-purpose flour
1/4 cup sugar
1-1/2 teaspoons salt
2 teaspoons active dry yeast
FILLING:
1 package (8 ounces) cream cheese, softened
1/4 cup sugar
1 teaspoon vanilla extract
1 package (3 ounces) cook-and-serve vanilla pudding mix
1 jar (6 ounces) carrot baby food
1 teaspoon ground cinnamon
GLAZE:
1/2 cup confectioners' sugar
2 to 3 teaspoons orange juice
1/2 teaspoon grated orange peel
1/4 teaspoon vanilla extract

In bread machine pan, place the first seven ingredients in order suggested by manufacturer. Select dough setting (check dough after 5 minutes of mixing; add 1 to 2 tablespoons of water or flour if needed).

Meanwhile, in a small mixing bowl, beat cream cheese, sugar and vanilla; set aside. In a microwave-safe bowl, combine pudding mix, baby food and cinnamon until smooth. Cover; microwave on high for 2 minutes. Stir.

When cycle is completed, turn dough onto a lightly floured surface. Divide in half; shape each portion into a ball. Roll each into a 9-in. x 8-in. rectangle. Spread the cream cheese mixture to within 1/2 in. of edges; top with carrot mixture. Roll up jelly-roll style, starting with long sides; pinch seams to seal.

Cut each into six rolls. Place cut side up in two greased 9-in. square baking pans. Cover and let rise in a warm place until doubled, about 30 minutes. Bake at 350° for 25-30 minutes or until golden brown. Cool on wire racks for 5 minutes. Combine glaze ingredients; drizzle over warm rolls. **Yield:** 1 dozen.

Editor's Note: This recipe was tested in a 1,100-watt microwave.

Cappuccino Muffins

(Pictured above right)

Prep: 20 min. **Bake:** 25 min.

I found this recipe while thumbing through some old cookbooks. The muffins are great with a cup of coffee, but my kids like them with milk. —Leslie Rosengarten
Minster, Ohio

2 cups all-purpose flour
1/2 cup sugar

1/2 cup packed brown sugar
2 teaspoons baking powder
2 teaspoons instant coffee granules
1 teaspoon ground cinnamon
1/4 teaspoon salt
1 egg
1 cup milk
1/2 cup butter, melted
1 teaspoon vanilla extract
1 cup miniature semisweet chocolate chips
TOPPING:
6 tablespoons all-purpose flour
1/4 cup packed brown sugar
1/2 teaspoon ground cinnamon
1/4 cup cold butter

In a large mixing bowl, combine the flour, sugars, baking powder, coffee granules, cinnamon and salt. Whisk the egg, milk, butter and vanilla; stir into dry ingredients just until moistened. Fold in chocolate chips. Fill greased or paper-lined muffin cups three-fourths full.

For topping, combine the flour, brown sugar and cinnamon in a small bowl. Cut in butter until mixture resembles coarse crumbs. Sprinkle over batter. Bake at 375° for 22-24 minutes or until a toothpick comes out clean. Cool for 5 minutes before removing from pans to wire racks. **Yield:** 15 muffins.

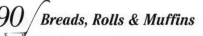

Bread Machine Rises To the Challenge

THE TEMPTING AROMA of bread baking is guaranteed to make mouths water! But these days, who has time? Not many of us, that's for sure!

With the convenience of a bread machine, you can treat your bunch to the delightful flavor of homemade yeast breads (and more) without all the fuss and bother of rolling out the dough and waiting patiently for it to rise. So stop loafing around and try one of these delicious recipes soon!

Calzone Rolls

(Pictured at far right)

Prep: 20 min. + rising   **Bake:** 20 min.

Big pizza flavor comes through in these rolls. This recipe makes two pans of rolls—you'll need 'em!
—Barb Downie, Peterborough, Ontario

    1-2/3 **cups water (70° to 80°)**
        2 **tablespoons nonfat dry milk powder**
        2 **tablespoons sugar**
        2 **tablespoons shortening**
    1-1/4 **teaspoons salt**
    4-1/2 **cups all-purpose flour**
    2-1/4 **teaspoons active dry yeast**
      1/2 **cup chopped onion**
      1/2 **cup sliced fresh mushrooms**
      1/2 **cup chopped green pepper**
      1/2 **cup chopped sweet red pepper**
        1 **tablespoon olive oil**
      1/3 **cup pizza sauce**
      1/2 **cup diced pepperoni**
        1 **cup (4 ounces) shredded pizza cheese blend**
      1/4 **cup chopped ripe olives**
        2 **tablespoons grated Parmesan cheese**

In bread machine pan, place the first seven ingredients in order suggested by manufacturer. Select dough setting (check dough after 5 minutes of mixing; add 1 to 2 tablespoons of water or flour if needed).

In a small skillet, saute the onion, mushrooms and peppers in oil until tender; cool. When bread machine cycle is completed, turn dough onto a lightly floured surface; divide in half. Let rest for 5 minutes.

Roll each portion into a 16-in. x 10-in. rectangle; spread with pizza sauce. Top with onion mixture, pepperoni, pizza cheese and olives. Roll up each rectangle jelly-roll style, starting with a long side; pinch seam to seal. Cut each into 12 slices (discard end pieces).

Place slices cut side down in two greased 9-in. round baking pans. Sprinkle with Parmesan. Cover and let rise until doubled, about 30 minutes. Bake at 375° for 18-22 minutes or until golden brown. Serve warm. **Yield:** 2 dozen.

Crescent Rolls

(Pictured at right)

Prep: 15 min. + rising   **Bake:** 20 min.

My mother-in-law bakes these buttery rolls for holiday meals. *—Joyce Guth, Mohnton, Pennsylvania*

      3/4 **cup plus 2 tablespoons warm milk (70° to 80°)**
      1/4 **cup water (70° to 80°)**
        1 **egg**
        6 **tablespoons butter, softened,** *divided*
        3 **cups bread flour**
        2 **tablespoons sugar**
        1 **teaspoon salt**
        2 **teaspoons active dry yeast**

In bread machine pan, place the milk, water, egg, 4 tablespoons butter, flour, sugar, salt and yeast in order suggested by manufacturer. Select dough setting (check dough after 5 minutes of mixing; add 1 to 2 tablespoons of water or flour if needed).

When cycle is completed, turn dough onto a lightly floured surface. Roll into a 12-in. circle. Melt remaining butter; brush over dough. Cut into 12 wedges. Roll up wedges from the wide end and place pointed side down 2 in. apart on greased baking sheets. Curve the ends to form crescents.

Cover and let rise in a warm place until doubled, about 20 minutes. Bake at 375° for 17-20 minutes. Remove to wire racks. **Yield:** 1 dozen.

Poppy Seed Onion Bread

(Pictured at right)

Prep: 10 min.   **Bake:** 3-4 hours + cooling

I rely on my bread machine to make this golden-crusted savory loaf. *—Sue Ashford, Bristol, Tennessee*

☑ Uses less fat, sugar or salt. Includes Nutritional Analysis and Diabetic Exchanges.

1-1/4 **cups water (70° to 80°)**
    2 **tablespoons butter, softened**
    2 **tablespoons brown sugar**
  1/4 **cup dried minced onion**
1-1/2 **teaspoons salt**
    1 **teaspoon poppy seeds**
  1/2 **teaspoon onion powder**
  1/2 **teaspoon pepper**
    3 **cups bread flour**
    2 **tablespoons nonfat dry milk powder**
    3 **teaspoons active dry yeast**

In bread machine pan, place all of the ingredients in order suggested by manufacturer. Select basic bread setting. Choose the crust color and loaf size if available.

Bake according to bread machine directions (check dough after 5 minutes of mixing; add 1 to 2 tablespoons of water or flour if needed). **Yield:** 1 loaf (1-1/2 pounds, 16 slices).

Nutritional Analysis: 1 slice equals 104 calories, 2 g fat (1 g saturated fat), 4 mg cholesterol, 242 mg sodium, 20 g carbohydrate, 1 g fiber, 4 g protein. **Diabetic Exchanges:** 1 starch, 1/2 fat.

WITH a bread machine, you don't "knead" hours to make Calzone Rolls, Crescent Rolls and Poppy Seed Onion Bread (shown above).

Cherry-Nut Tea Ring

(Pictured above)

Prep: 30 min. + rising   **Bake:** 30 min. + cooling

Let your bread machine prepare a lovely sweet dough, then roll it out and fill it for this pretty coffee cake.
—Claudeen Penry, Atkinson, Nebraska

> 3/4 cup warm milk (70° to 80°)
> 1/4 cup butter, melted
>   1 egg, beaten
>   3 tablespoons water (70° to 80°)
>   3 tablespoons sugar
> 3/4 teaspoon salt
> 3-1/3 cups bread flour
> 2-1/4 teaspoons active dry yeast
> **FILLING:**
> 1/4 cup sugar
> 1/4 cup packed brown sugar
>   3 tablespoons shortening
> 1/2 cup maraschino cherries, drained and
>   chopped
> 1/2 cup raisins
> 1/4 cup chopped walnuts
> **Confectioners' sugar**

In bread machine pan, place the first eight ingredients in order suggested by manufacturer. Select dough setting (check dough after 5 minutes of mixing; add 1 to 2 tablespoons of water or flour if needed).

For filling, combine the sugars in a small bowl; cut in shortening until crumbly. Stir in the cherries, raisins and walnuts; set aside. When cycle is completed, turn dough onto a lightly floured surface. Roll into a 20-in. x 10-in. rectangle; sprinkle with filling to within 1 in. of edges. Roll up tightly jelly-roll style, starting with a long side; seal ends.

Place in a greased 15-in. x 10-in. x 1-in. baking pan; pinch ends together to form a heart. With scissors, cut from outside edge two-thirds of the way toward center of ring at 1-in. intervals. Separate strips slightly; twist to allow filling to show. Cover and let rise until doubled, about 40 minutes.

Bake at 350° for 30-35 minutes or until golden brown, covering with foil to prevent overbrowning during the last 10 minutes. Remove to a wire rack to cool. Dust with confectioners' sugar. **Yield:** 1 loaf (2 pounds).

Editor's Note: If your bread machine has a time-delay feature, we recommend you do not use it for this recipe.

Honey Wheat Bread

Prep: 30 min. + rising   **Bake:** 25 min. + cooling

This bread is worth the effort. I usually send a loaf home with guests.   —Gayle Lewis, Yucaipa, California

> 1/3 cup vegetable oil
> 1/4 cup honey
> 1/4 cup raisins
> 1/4 cup plus 1 tablespoon brown sugar,
>   *divided*
> 1/2 cup boiling water
> 2-1/2 cups whole wheat flour
>   2 to 2-1/2 cups all-purpose flour
>   1 to 1-1/2 cups rye flour
> 1/2 cup nonfat dry milk powder
>   2 packages (1/4 ounce *each*) active dry
>   yeast
> 2-1/2 teaspoons salt
> 1-3/4 cups warm water (120° to 130°)
>   2 tablespoons cornmeal
>   1 tablespoon butter, melted

In a blender, combine oil, honey, raisins, 1/4 cup brown sugar and boiling water; cover and process until smooth. Cool to 120°-130°.

In a large mixing bowl, combine the whole wheat flour, 2 cups all-purpose flour, 1 cup rye flour, milk powder, yeast, salt and remaining brown sugar. Add raisin mixture and warm water; beat until smooth. Stir in enough remaining all-purpose and rye flour to form a soft dough.

Turn onto a surface floured with all-purpose flour; knead until smooth and elastic, 6-8 minutes. Place in a greased bowl, turning once to grease top. Cover and let rise in a warm place until doubled, about 1 hour.

Punch dough down. Turn onto a lightly floured surface; divide into fourths. Shape into four round loaves. Sprinkle greased baking sheets with cornmeal; place loaves on prepared pans. Let rise until doubled, about 30-45 minutes. Bake at 350° for 25-35 minutes or until dark brown. Remove from pans to wire racks. Brush with butter; cool. **Yield:** 4 loaves.

Cornmeal Pan Rolls

(Pictured on page 84)

Prep: 30 min. + rising   **Bake:** 15 min.

These delightful golden rolls are always requested at Thanksgiving and Christmas. The recipe is one we've enjoyed for years. —*Vivian Eccles, Gridley, Kansas*

✓ **Uses less fat, sugar or salt. Includes Nutritional Analysis and Diabetic Exchanges.**

    2-1/2 cups all-purpose flour
      1/2 cup cornmeal
        2 tablespoons sugar
        1 package (1/4 ounce) active dry yeast
        1 teaspoon salt
        1 cup water
        3 tablespoons butter, *divided*
        1 egg, beaten

In a large mixing bowl, combine the flour, cornmeal, sugar, yeast and salt. In a saucepan, heat water and 2 tablespoons butter to 120°-130°. Add to dry ingredients; beat until moistened. Add egg; beat on medium speed for 3 minutes.

Turn onto a floured surface; knead until smooth and elastic, about 6-8 minutes. Place in a greased bowl, turning once to grease top. Cover and let rise in a warm place until doubled, about 1 hour.

Punch dough down. Turn onto a lightly floured surface; divide into 18 pieces. Shape each piece into a ball. Place in a greased 13-in. x 9-in. x 2-in. baking pan or two 9-in. round baking pans. Cover and let rise in a warm place until doubled, about 30 minutes.

Bake at 400° for 15-20 minutes or until golden brown. Melt remaining butter; brush over rolls. Invert onto wire racks. **Yield:** 1-1/2 dozen.

Nutritional Analysis: 1 roll equals 105 calories, 2 g fat (1 g saturated fat), 17 mg cholesterol, 155 mg sodium, 18 g carbohydrate, 1 g fiber, 3 g protein. **Diabetic Exchanges:** 1 starch, 1/2 fat.

Herb-Cheese Yeast Bread

(Pictured at right)

Prep: 10 min.   **Bake:** 3-4 hours + cooling

For a variation, try other cheeses such as shredded cheddar or a blend of cheddar, Swiss and Co-Jack.
—*Linda Lundmark, Martinton, Illinois*

    1-1/3 cups water (70° to 80°)
        2 tablespoons butter, softened
      1/2 teaspoon salt
        3 teaspoons sugar
        1 teaspoon dried parsley flakes
      1/2 teaspoon dried basil
        3 cups bread flour
        1 cup whole wheat flour
        3 teaspoons active dry yeast
      2/3 cup shredded Swiss cheese
      1/4 cup grated Parmesan cheese

In bread machine pan, place the first nine ingredients in order suggested by manufacturer. Select basic bread setting. Choose crust color and loaf size if available.

Bake according to bread machine directions (check dough after 5 minutes of mixing; add 1 to 2 tablespoons of water or flour if needed).

Just before the final kneading (your bread machine may audibly signal this), add cheeses. **Yield:** 1 loaf (2 pounds).

Editor's Note: If your bread machine has a time-delay feature, we recommend you do not use it for this recipe.

Rhubarb Crumb Coffee Cake

(Pictured below)

Prep: 15 min.   **Bake:** 45 min. + cooling

Since rhubarb grows well in our frigid climate, I freeze a lot of it. I have plenty on hand to make this old-fashioned coffee cake and other rhubarb treats.   —Cindi Paulson
Anchorage, Alaska

  1/2 **cup butter, softened**
1-1/2 **cups sugar**
    2 **eggs**
    1 **teaspoon vanilla extract**
    2 **cups all-purpose flour**
    2 **teaspoons ground cinnamon**
    1 **teaspoon baking soda**
  1/4 **teaspoon ground nutmeg**
    1 **cup buttermilk**
    4 **cups chopped fresh *or* frozen rhubarb**
TOPPING:
    1 **cup all-purpose flour**
  1/2 **cup packed brown sugar**
    1 **teaspoon ground cinnamon**
  1/2 **cup cold butter**

In a large mixing bowl, cream butter and sugar. Add eggs, one at a time, beating well after each. Beat in vanilla. Combine dry ingredients; add to creamed mixture alternately with buttermilk. Stir in rhubarb. Pour into a greased 13-in. x 9-in. x 2-in. baking dish.

In a small bowl, combine the flour, brown sugar and cinnamon. Cut in butter until the mixture resembles coarse crumbs. Sprinkle over batter. Bake at 350° for 45-55 minutes or until a toothpick inserted near the center comes out clean. Cool on a wire rack. **Yield:** 16-20 servings.

Editor's Note: If using frozen rhubarb, measure rhubarb while still frozen, then thaw completely. Drain in a colander, but do not press liquid out.

Orange-Glazed Bunny Rolls

Prep: 45 min. + rising   **Bake:** 15 min. + cooling

I make these tender yeast rolls for special occasions. Orange marmalade gives the glaze a pleasant citrus flavor. Shape the rolls any way you like.   —Gerri Brown
Canfield, Ohio

    2 **packages (1/4 ounce *each*) active dry yeast**
  1/4 **cup warm water (110° to 115°)**
    1 **cup warm milk (110° to 115°)**
  1/2 **cup shortening**
    2 **eggs**
  1/3 **cup sugar**
  1/4 **cup orange juice**
    2 **tablespoons grated orange peel**
    1 **teaspoon salt**
    5 **to 5-1/2 cups all-purpose flour**
GLAZE:
    2 **cups confectioners' sugar**
  1/4 **cup water**
    1 **tablespoon orange marmalade**
  1/2 **teaspoon butter, softened**

In a large mixing bowl, dissolve yeast in warm water. Add the milk, shortening, eggs, sugar, orange juice, orange peel, salt and 3 cups flour; beat until smooth. Stir in enough remaining flour to form a soft dough.

Turn onto a floured surface; knead until smooth and elastic, about 6-8 minutes. Place in a greased bowl, turning once to grease top. Cover; let rise in a warm place until doubled, about 1 hour.

Punch dough down; turn onto a lightly floured surface. Divide into 13 pieces. Shape 12 pieces into 12-in. ropes. Fold each in half; twist top half of the open end twice to form ears. Place 2 in. apart on greased baking sheets. Shape remaining dough into 12 balls. Place one on the loop end of each roll to form a tail; press into dough. Cover and let rise until doubled, about 30 minutes.

Bake at 375° for 12-15 minutes or until golden brown. Cool on wire racks. In a small mixing bowl, combine the glaze ingredients; beat until blended. Spread over rolls. **Yield:** 1 dozen.

Giant Pretzels

(Pictured below)

Prep: 15 min. + rising **Bake:** 15 min.

When I make these pretzels, I never get any because my brother likes them so much he eats them all!
—Terra Wood, Lawrencetown, Nova Scotia

  1-1/2 **teaspoons active dry yeast**
   3/4 **cup warm water (110° to 115°)**
  1-1/2 **teaspoons sugar**
   3/4 **teaspoon salt**
  1-1/2 **cups all-purpose flour**
    2 **tablespoons butter, melted**
Coarse salt

In a large mixing bowl, dissolve yeast in warm water. Add sugar and salt. Stir in flour, 1/2 cup at a time, to form a soft dough. Turn onto a floured surface; knead until smooth and elastic, about 5 minutes (dough will be sticky). Place in a greased bowl, turning once to grease top. Cover and let rise in a warm place until doubled, about 1 hour.

Punch dough down and divide into six portions. On a lightly floured surface, roll each portion into a 14-in. rope; twist into a pretzel shape. Place on greased baking sheets. Brush with butter; sprinkle with coarse salt. Bake at 425° for 15-20 minutes or until golden brown. Remove to wire racks. Serve warm. **Yield:** 6 pretzels.

Sweet Potato Muffins

(Pictured above)

Prep: 15 min. **Bake:** 20 min.

Ground ginger and dried orange peel enhance the taste of these spiced muffins. I especially love the whipped ginger butter served alongside.   —Susan Bracken
State College, Pennsylvania

  1-1/2 **cups all-purpose flour**
    1 **cup plus 1 tablespoon sugar,** *divided*
    3 **teaspoons baking powder**
    3 **teaspoons grated orange peel**
  1-1/2 **teaspoons ground ginger**
    1 **teaspoon baking soda**
   1/4 **teaspoon salt**
    2 **eggs, lightly beaten**
    1 **cup cold mashed sweet potatoes**
      (prepared without milk *or* **butter)**
   1/4 **teaspoon ground cinnamon**
GINGER BUTTER:
   1/2 **cup butter, softened**
    2 **tablespoons finely chopped crystallized**
      ginger

In a large bowl, combine the flour, 1 cup sugar, baking powder, orange peel, ginger, baking soda and salt. Combine eggs and sweet potatoes; stir into dry ingredients just until moistened. Fill greased or paper-lined muffin cups two-thirds full. Combine cinnamon and remaining sugar; sprinkle over batter.

Bake at 400° for 18-22 minutes or until a toothpick comes out clean. Cool for 5 minutes before removing from pans to wire racks. In a small bowl, combine the ginger butter ingredients. Serve with warm muffins. **Yield:** 1 dozen.

In a large bowl, combine the flour, 3/4 cup brown sugar, baking powder, cinnamon, baking soda, pumpkin pie spice and salt. Whisk the eggs, pumpkin, milk, oil and 1 tablespoon syrup; stir into dry ingredients just until moistened. Fold in pecans.

In a small mixing bowl, beat cream cheese and remaining brown sugar and syrup until smooth. Gently stir into batter until mixture appears swirled.

Fill greased or paper-lined muffin cups about three-fourths full. Combine topping ingredients; sprinkle over batter. Bake at 400° for 20-25 minutes or until a toothpick comes out clean. Cool for 5 minutes before removing from pan to a wire rack. **Yield:** 1 dozen.

Garlic Cheese Breadsticks

Prep: 30 min. + rising   **Bake:** 15 min.

These slightly chewy breadsticks have plenty of garlic and cheese flavor. Whenever I make these breadsticks, my three daughters will eat every last one if I let them.
—Melinda Rhoads, Slippery Rock, Pennsylvania

☑ **Uses less fat, sugar or salt. Includes Nutritional Analysis and Diabetic Exchanges.**

 1-3/4 to 2-1/2 cups all-purpose flour
 1/4 cup toasted wheat germ
   1 package (1/4 ounce) active dry yeast
 1/2 teaspoon salt
   1 cup water
   1 tablespoon plus 2 teaspoons olive oil,
     divided
   1 tablespoon honey
   2 tablespoons minced fresh parsley *or* 2
     teaspoons dried parsley flakes
   1 tablespoon minced fresh basil *or* 1
     teaspoon dried basil
   2 to 4 garlic cloves, minced
 1/2 cup shredded part-skim mozzarella cheese
 1/2 cup shredded Parmesan cheese

In a large mixing bowl, combine 1-1/2 cups flour, wheat germ, yeast and salt. In a saucepan, heat the water, 1 tablespoon oil and honey to 120°-130°. Add to dry ingredients; beat just until moistened. Stir in enough remaining flour to form a soft dough.

Turn onto a lightly floured surface; knead until smooth and elastic, about 4-6 minutes. Cover and let rest for 10 minutes.

Roll into a 15-in. x 10-in. rectangle. Transfer to a greased 15-in. x 10-in. x 1-in. baking pan; press dough to edges of pan. Brush with remaining oil. Sprinkle with parsley, basil and garlic. Cover and let rise in a warm place until doubled, about 30 minutes.

Bake at 425° for 10 minutes. Sprinkle with cheeses. Bake 3-5 minutes longer or until cheese is melted

Maple Pumpkin Muffins

(Pictured above)

Prep: 20 min.   **Bake:** 20 min.

I love muffins, and these are among the most irresistible ones I have ever tasted. These go together in less than an hour. Best of all, the sweet aroma of pumpkin, brown sugar and maple syrup fills the house while they're baking.
—Stephanie Moon, Nampa, Idaho

   2 cups all-purpose flour
 3/4 cup plus 2 tablespoons packed brown
     sugar, *divided*
   2 teaspoons baking powder
   1 teaspoon ground cinnamon
 1/2 teaspoon baking soda
 1/2 teaspoon pumpkin pie spice
 1/4 teaspoon salt
   2 eggs
   1 cup canned pumpkin
 3/4 cup evaporated milk
 1/4 cup vegetable oil
   3 tablespoons maple syrup, *divided*
 1/2 cup chopped pecans *or* walnuts
   1 package (3 ounces) cream cheese,
     softened
TOPPING:
 1/4 cup chopped pecans *or* walnuts
   2 teaspoons brown sugar

and bread is golden brown. Cut into 20 strips. Serve warm. **Yield:** 20 breadsticks.

Nutritional Analysis: 2 breadsticks equals 163 calories, 5 g fat (2 g saturated fat), 6 mg cholesterol, 213 mg sodium, 23 g carbohydrate, 1 g fiber, 7 g protein. **Diabetic Exchange:** 1-1/2 starch.

Rhubarb Blueberry Muffins

Prep: 15 min.   **Bake:** 20 min.

We were camping, and I didn't have enough milk for my usual blueberry muffin recipe. I did have some sour cream and a bit of rhubarb, so I used those. The muffins were awesome, and now I make them often!   —Dorothy Ross
Ear Falls, Ontario

      1/4 **cup butter, softened**
      3/4 **cup sugar**
        1 **egg**
      1/4 **cup sour cream**
    1-1/2 **cups all-purpose flour**
        2 **teaspoons baking powder**
        1 **teaspoon salt**
      1/3 **cup milk**
        1 **cup fresh** *or* **frozen blueberries**
        1 **cup chopped fresh** *or* **frozen rhubarb**

In a small mixing bowl, cream butter and sugar. Add the egg and sour cream; mix well. Combine the flour, baking powder and salt; add to the creamed mixture alternately with milk. Fold in the blueberries and rhubarb.

Fill 12 greased or paper-lined muffin cups about two-thirds full. Bake at 400° for 20-25 minutes or until a toothpick comes out clean. Cool for 5 minutes before removing from pans to wire racks. **Yield:** 1 dozen.

Editor's Note: If using frozen blueberries, do not thaw before adding to batter. If using frozen rhubarb, measure rhubarb while still frozen, then thaw completely. Drain in a colander, but do not press liquid out.

Stollen Loaves

(Pictured at right)

Prep: 20 min. + rising   **Bake:** 35 min. + cooling

The recipe for these fresh-baked fruit-dotted loaves comes from my grandmother. They fill our house with a heavenly aroma that is such a part of the season.   —Tom Guenther
Oshkosh, Wisconsin

        3 **packages (1/4 ounce** *each***) active dry yeast**
      1/2 **cup warm water (110° to 115°)**
        1 **cup butter, softened**
        1 **cup sugar**
        2 **cups warm milk (110° to 115°)**
        2 **eggs**
   7 to 8 **cups all-purpose flour**
        1 **teaspoon salt**
        2 **cups mixed candied fruit**
        1 **cup raisins**
        1 **cup golden raisins**
      1/2 **cup sliced almonds**
Confectioners' sugar

In a small bowl, dissolve yeast in warm water. In a large mixing bowl, cream butter and sugar; gradually beat in milk. Stir in yeast mixture. Beat in eggs, 4 cups flour and salt until smooth. Add enough remaining flour to form a soft dough. Stir in candied fruit, raisins and almonds.

Turn onto a floured surface; knead until smooth and elastic, about 6-8 minutes (dough will be sticky). Place in a greased bowl, turning once to grease top. Cover and let rise in a warm place until nearly doubled, about 1 hour.

Punch dough down. Turn onto a lightly floured surface; divide into fourths. Shape each portion into a loaf. Place in four greased 8-in. x 4-in. x 2-in. loaf pans. Cover and let rise until doubled, about 1 hour.

Bake at 350° for 35-45 minutes or until golden brown. Remove from pans to wire racks to cool. Dust with confectioners' sugar. **Yield:** 4 loaves.

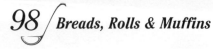

Blueberry Bonus!

WHEN the *Taste of Home* Test Kitchen staff tested blueberry recipes for a special feature in the August/September 2005 issue, they remembered some of the outstanding winners from our "Very Berry" recipe contest held in 1996. Here are three worth repeating!

Blueberry Streusel Coffee Cake

(Pictured below)

Prep: 20 min. **Bake:** 35 min. + cooling

This coffee cake smells wonderful as it bakes and tastes even better. —Lori Snedden, Sherman, Texas

>   2 cups all-purpose flour
>   3/4 cup sugar
>   2 teaspoons baking powder
>   1/4 teaspoon salt
>   1 egg
>   1/2 cup milk
>   1/2 cup butter, softened
>   1 cup fresh *or* frozen blueberries
>   1 cup chopped pecans
> STREUSEL TOPPING:
>   1/2 cup sugar
>   1/3 cup all-purpose flour
>   1/4 cup cold butter

In a large mixing bowl, combine the flour, sugar, baking powder and salt. Add egg, milk and butter; beat well. Fold in blueberries and pecans. Spread into a greased 9-in. square baking pan.

For topping, combine sugar and flour in a bowl; cut in butter until crumbly. Sprinkle over batter. Bake at 375° for 35-40 minutes or until a toothpick inserted near the center comes out clean. Cool on a wire rack. **Yield:** 9 servings.

Blueberry Basics

Here are some helpful tips for selecting and storing blueberries:

- Look for fresh berries that are firm, dry, plump and smooth-skinned and relatively free from leaves and stems. Berries should be deep purple-blue to blue-black; reddish berries aren't ripe, but may be used in cooking.

- Stay away from containers with juice stains, which may be a sign the berries are crushed and possibly moldy; soft watery fruit means the berries are overripe.

- Fresh berries should be stored covered in your refrigerator and washed just before using. Use them within 10 days of purchase.

Blueberry Sour Cream Pancakes

(Pictured below)

Prep: 20 min.   **Cook:** 30 min.

When our family of 10 goes blueberry picking, we have a bounty in no time. They taste great in these pancakes.
—*Paula Hadley, Forest Hill, Louisiana*

    1/2 cup sugar
      2 tablespoons cornstarch
      1 cup cold water
      4 cups fresh *or* frozen blueberries
PANCAKES:
      2 cups all-purpose flour
    1/4 cup sugar
      4 teaspoons baking powder
    1/2 teaspoon salt
      2 eggs
  1-1/2 cups milk
      1 cup (8 ounces) sour cream
    1/3 cup butter, melted
      1 cup fresh *or* frozen blueberries

For topping, in a large saucepan, combine sugar, cornstarch and water until smooth. Add blueberries. Bring to a boil over medium heat; cook and stir for 2 minutes or until thickened. Remove from the heat; cover and keep warm.

For pancakes, combine dry ingredients in a bowl. In another bowl, beat the eggs; stir in the milk, sour cream and butter. Stir into dry ingredients just until blended. Fold in blueberries.

Pour batter by 1/4 cupfuls onto a greased hot griddle; turn when bubbles form on top of pancakes. Cook until second side is golden brown. Serve with blueberry topping. **Yield:** about 20 pancakes (3-1/2 cups topping).

Blueberry French Toast

(Pictured above)

Prep: 30 min. + chilling   **Bake:** 55 min.

With luscious blueberries inside and in a sauce that drizzles over each slice, this French toast almost looks and tastes like a dessert! —*Patricia Walls, Aurora, Minnesota*

     12 slices day-old white bread, crusts removed
      2 packages (8 ounces *each*) cream cheese
      1 cup fresh *or* frozen blueberries
     12 eggs
      2 cups milk
    1/3 cup maple syrup *or* honey
SAUCE:
      1 cup sugar
      2 tablespoons cornstarch
      1 cup water
      1 cup fresh *or* frozen blueberries
      1 tablespoon butter

Cut bread into 1-in. cubes; place half in a greased 13-in. x 9-in. x 2-in. baking dish. Cut cream cheese into 1-in. cubes; place over bread. Top with blueberries and remaining bread cubes. In a large bowl, beat eggs. Add milk and syrup; mix well. Pour over bread mixture. Cover and chill for 8 hours or overnight.

Remove from refrigerator 30 minutes before baking. Cover; bake at 350° for 30 minutes. Uncover; bake 25-30 minutes longer or until center is set.

In a small saucepan, combine sugar, cornstarch and water until smooth. Bring to a boil over medium heat; cook and stir for 3 minutes. Stir in blueberries; reduce heat. Simmer for 8-10 minutes or until berries have burst. Stir in butter until melted. Serve with French toast. **Yield:** 6-8 servings (1-3/4 cups sauce).

Cookies, Bars & Candies

From traditional favorites to future stars of the cookie jar and candy tray, this pleasing selection provides something to satisfy every taste and occasion.

STOCK UP ON SWEETS. Clockwise from upper left: Blond Brownies a la Mode (p. 110), Delicate Mint Thins (p. 104), Nutty Chocolate Caramels (p. 102), Coffee 'n' Cream Brownies (p. 108) and Berry-Cream Cookie Snaps (p. 121).

Chocolate Heart Cookies

(Pictured above)

Prep: 30 min.   **Bake:** 10 min. + cooling

For a dramatic presentation, I dust dessert plates with cocoa powder and drizzle on a bit of melted raspberry fruit spread. I place a couple of these melt-in-your-mouth cookies in the center, along with some fresh raspberries, lemon zest and a sprig of mint. —*TerryAnn Moore Oaklyn, New Jersey*

    1 cup butter, softened
  1/2 cup sugar
    1 teaspoon vanilla extract
    2 cups all-purpose flour
  1/4 cup baking cocoa
    1 cup vanilla *or* white chips
    2 tablespoons shortening, *divided*
  1/2 cup semisweet chocolate chips

In a small mixing bowl, cream butter and sugar. Beat in vanilla. Combine the flour and cocoa; gradually add to creamed mixture. On a lightly floured surface, roll out dough to 1/4-in. thickness. Cut with a 3-in. heart-shaped cookie cutter. Place 2 in. apart on ungreased baking sheets. Bake at 375° for 8-10 minutes or until firm. Remove to wire racks to cool.

In a microwave-safe bowl, heat vanilla chips and 1 tablespoon shortening until melted, stirring frequently. Dip both sides of cookies into melted mixture. In another microwave-safe bowl, heat the chocolate chips and remaining shortening until melted, stirring frequently. Drizzle over the cookies. Place on wire racks to dry. **Yield:** about 2 dozen.

Nutty Chocolate Caramels

(Pictured on page 100)

Prep: 5 min.   **Cook:** 40 min. + cooling

My mother-in-law and her mother used this recipe and passed it on to me over 30 years ago. The caramels make a great gift during the holidays. —*Anita Gay Janesville, Wisconsin*

    2 teaspoons plus 1/4 cup butter, *divided*
  3/4 cup light corn syrup
  1/4 cup cold water
 1-1/2 cups sugar
    3 squares (1 ounce *each*) semisweet chocolate, chopped
  1/2 teaspoon salt
    1 cup half-and-half cream
    2 teaspoons vanilla extract
    1 cup chopped walnuts

Line an 8-in. square baking pan with foil. Grease with 1 teaspoon butter; set aside. Butter the sides of a heavy saucepan with 1 teaspoon butter; add the corn syrup, water, sugar, chocolate, salt and remaining butter. Cook and stir over medium heat until smooth and blended, about 6 minutes.

Gradually stir in cream. Cook and stir until mixture comes to a boil. Cook and stir until a candy thermometer reads 245° (firm-ball stage), about 25 minutes. Remove from the heat; stir in vanilla and walnuts. Pour into prepared pan. Cool; cut into squares.

Store in a covered container in the refrigerator. Remove from the refrigerator 1 hour before serving. **Yield:** 4 dozen (about 1-3/4 pounds).

Editor's Note: We recommend you test your candy thermometer before each use by bringing water to a boil; the thermometer should read 212°. Adjust recipe temperature up or down based on your test.

Lattice Blackberry Bars

(Pictured on back cover)

Prep: 45 min. + chilling   **Bake:** 40 min. + cooling

I pick blackberries—my son's favorite fruit—to make this dessert for family gatherings. Blueberries are a great substitute. —*Donna Miklavic, Butler, Pennsylvania*

    6 cups all-purpose flour
 1-1/4 cups sugar
 1-1/2 cups shortening
 1-1/4 cups sour cream
    1 egg
    1 egg yolk
    1 teaspoon vanilla extract
FILLING:
    2 cups plus 1 tablespoon sugar, *divided*

2/3 cup all-purpose flour
8 cups fresh *or* frozen unsweetened
   blackberries
1/4 cup butter, cubed
2 teaspoons ground cinnamon
1 egg, beaten

In a bowl, combine the flour and sugar. Cut in shortening until mixture resembles coarse crumbs. Combine sour cream, egg, egg yolk and vanilla until smooth; add to crumb mixture. Toss with a fork until dough forms a ball. Divide dough in half; cover with plastic wrap and refrigerate for 1 hour.

For filling, combine 2 cups sugar and flour in a large saucepan; add blackberries. Cook and stir over medium heat until mixture begins to boil; cook and stir 2 minutes longer. Remove from the heat; stir in butter and cinnamon. Cool slightly.

On a lightly floured surface, roll one portion of dough into a 17-in. x 12-in. rectangle; transfer to a greased 15-in. x 10-in. x 1-in. baking pan. Spread with filling. Roll remaining dough into a 15-in. x 10-in. rectangle; cut into 1/2-in. strips. Make a lattice crust over filling; seal and flute edges.

Brush egg over pastry. Sprinkle with remaining sugar. Bake at 350° for 40-45 minutes or until crust is golden and filling is bubbly. Cool on a wire rack. Slice into bars. **Yield:** 20 servings.

Butter Pecan Fudge

Prep: 20 min. + cooling

Toasted pecan halves add a nutty crunch to this creamy buttery fudge. I have given this candy, with its wonderful caramel flavor, as gifts at Christmastime for years and people always rave about it!
—Pam Smith
Alta Loma, California

1/2 cup butter
1/2 cup sugar
1/2 cup packed brown sugar
1/2 cup heavy whipping cream
1/8 teaspoon salt
1 teaspoon vanilla extract
2 cups confectioners' sugar
1 cup pecan halves, toasted and coarsely
   chopped

In a large heavy saucepan, combine the butter, sugars, cream and salt. Bring to a boil over medium heat, stirring occasionally. Boil for 5 minutes, stirring constantly. Remove from the heat; stir in vanilla. Stir in confectioners' sugar until smooth. Fold in pecans.

Spread into a buttered 8-in. square dish. Cool to room temperature. Cut into 1-in. squares. Store in an airtight container in the refrigerator. **Yield:** 1-1/4 pounds.

Hazelnut Brownies

(Pictured below)

Prep: 25 min.   **Bake:** 30 min. + chilling

I created these deep chocolate brownies by combining several recipes. After they cooled, I divided them up and put them in the freezer or we would have eaten the entire pan! They're now a family favorite.
—Becki Strader
Kennewick, Washington

1 cup butter, melted
2 cups sugar
2 teaspoons vanilla extract
4 eggs
1 cup all-purpose flour
3/4 cup baking cocoa
1/2 teaspoon baking powder
1/4 teaspoon salt
1/2 cup chopped hazelnuts
FROSTING:
2 cups (12 ounces) semisweet chocolate
   chips
1 cup heavy whipping cream *or* refrigerated
   hazelnut nondairy creamer
2 tablespoons butter
1/2 cup coarsely chopped hazelnuts

In a large mixing bowl, combine butter, sugar and vanilla. Add eggs, one at a time, beating well after each addition. Combine flour, cocoa, baking powder and salt; add to butter mixture and mix well. Fold in hazelnuts. Spread into a greased 13-in. x 9-in. x 2-in. baking pan. Bake at 350° for 30-35 minutes or until a toothpick inserted near the center comes out clean. Cool on a wire rack.

For frosting, in a microwave, heat chips and cream until chips are melted and mixture is smooth. Stir in butter until melted. Cover and refrigerate for 30 minutes or until the frosting achieves spreading consistency, stirring several times. Frost brownies. Sprinkle with hazelnuts. **Yield:** 2 dozen.

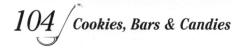

Chocolate Mallow Drops

(Pictured below)

Prep: 25 min.   **Bake:** 10 min. + cooling

I tell people these are so good and they are quick to agree after a taste.   —Marie Hattrup, The Dalles, Oregon

   1/2 **cup butter, softened**
     1 **cup sugar**
     1 **egg**
   1/2 **cup milk**
     1 **teaspoon vanilla extract**
1-3/4 **cups all-purpose flour**
   1/2 **cup baking cocoa**
   1/2 **teaspoon** *each* **baking soda and salt**
   1/2 **cup chopped pecans**
  18 **to 22 large marshmallows, halved**
FROSTING:
   1/4 **cup butter**
     2 **squares (1 ounce** *each***) unsweetened chocolate**
     1 **square (1 ounce) semisweet chocolate**
     2 **cups confectioners' sugar**
     3 **to 6 tablespoons brewed coffee**

In a large mixing bowl, cream butter and sugar. Beat in the egg, milk and vanilla until smooth. Combine the flour, cocoa, baking soda and salt; gradually add to creamed mixture. Stir in pecans.

   Drop by slightly rounded tablespoonfuls 2 in. apart onto ungreased baking sheets. Bake at 375° for 6 minutes. Press a marshmallow half, cut side down, onto each cookie. Bake 2 minutes longer or until marshmallows are softened. Remove to wire racks to cool.

   In a microwave-safe bowl, melt butter and chocolate squares; stir until smooth. Beat in the confectioners' sugar. Add enough coffee to achieve spreading consistency. Transfer frosting to a pastry or plastic bag; cut a small hole in one corner of bag. Pipe over cookies. **Yield:** about 3 dozen.

Peanut Butter Blondies

Prep: 30 min.   **Bake:** 35 min. + cooling

The kids I baby-sit for love these moist chewy bars. There's plenty of peanut butter flavor plus a yummy chocolate frosting.   —Karla Johnson, Tyler, Minnesota

   3/4 **cup creamy peanut butter**
   2/3 **cup butter, softened**
     1 **cup packed brown sugar**
   1/2 **cup sugar**
     2 **eggs**
     1 **teaspoon vanilla extract**
1-3/4 **cups all-purpose flour**
     1 **teaspoon baking powder**
   1/3 **cup milk**
     1 **cup peanut butter chips**
FROSTING:
   1/4 **cup butter, softened**
   1/4 **cup baking cocoa**
     2 **tablespoons milk**
     1 **tablespoon light corn syrup**
     1 **teaspoon vanilla extract**
1-1/2 **cups confectioners' sugar**
   1/3 **cup peanut butter chips**

In a large mixing bowl, cream the peanut butter, butter and sugars. Beat in eggs and vanilla. Combine the flour and baking powder; add to creamed mixture alternately with milk. Stir in chips.

   Spread into a greased 13-in. x 9-in. x 2-in. baking pan. Bake at 325° for 35-40 minutes or until a toothpick inserted near the center comes out clean (do not overbake). Cool on a wire rack.

   For frosting, in a small mixing bowl, combine the butter, cocoa, milk, corn syrup and vanilla. Gradually add confectioners' sugar; beat until smooth. Frost brownies. Sprinkle with chips. Cut into bars. **Yield:** 2 dozen.

Delicate Mint Thins

(Pictured on page 100)

Prep: 20 min. + chilling   **Bake:** 20 min. + cooling

Newly married, I needed something fancy to impress my relatives at a reunion and came up with these cookies. I got many compliments on their subtle flavor.
*   —Kristine McDaniel, Kettering, Ohio*

   1/2 **cup butter, softened**
   1/2 **cup sugar**
     1 **egg yolk**
   1/2 **teaspoon vanilla extract**
1-1/2 **cups all-purpose flour**
1-1/2 **teaspoons baking powder**
   1/8 **teaspoon salt**
     3 **tablespoons milk**

1 cup fresh mint, finely chopped
1-2/3 cups semisweet chocolate chips
1 tablespoon shortening

In a small mixing bowl, cream butter and sugar. Beat in egg yolk and vanilla. Combine the flour, baking powder and salt; add to creamed mixture alternately with milk. Stir in mint. Shape into two 8-in. rolls; wrap each in plastic wrap. Refrigerate for 2 hours or until firm.

Unwrap and cut into 1/4-in. slices. Place 1 in. apart on greased baking sheets. Bake at 350° for 8-12 minutes or until edges are golden. Remove to wire racks to cool.

In a microwave-safe bowl, melt the chocolate chips and shortening; stir until smooth. Dip each cookie halfway into chocolate; shake off excess. Place on waxed paper to harden. **Yield:** about 4-1/2 dozen.

Almond Truffle Brownies

Prep: 15 min.   **Bake:** 25 min. + chilling

This wonderful recipe is one my mom just had to share with me after she baked them. These fudgy almond delights are made in several steps, but the extra effort is well worth it!   —Lynn Snow, Taylors, South Carolina

1 package fudge brownie mix (13-inch
  x 9-Inch pan size)
1/2 cup water
1/2 cup vegetable oil
1 egg
3/4 cup chopped almonds
1 teaspoon almond extract
FILLING:
1 cup (6 ounces) semisweet chocolate chips
1 package (8 ounces) cream cheese, softened
1/4 cup confectioners' sugar
2 tablespoons milk
1/2 teaspoon almond extract
TOPPING:
1/2 cup semisweet chocolate chips
1/4 cup heavy whipping cream
1/2 cup sliced almonds, toasted

In a large bowl, combine the first six ingredients. Pour into a greased 13-in. x 9-in. x 2-in. baking pan. Bake at 350° for 23-25 minutes or until a toothpick inserted near the center comes out clean (do not overbake). Cool on a wire rack.

In a microwave, melt chocolate chips; stir until smooth. In a large mixing bowl, beat cream cheese and confectioners' sugar. Add milk, extract and melted chips; mix well. Spread over brownies. Refrigerate for 1 hour or until firm.

For topping, in a small saucepan, melt chips and cream over low heat, stirring occasionally. Spread over filling. Sprinkle with almonds. Refrigerate at least 1 hour longer before cutting. **Yield:** 1-1/2 dozen.

Peppermint Taffy

(Pictured above)

Prep: 1-3/4 hours + cooling

For a fun afternoon activity, get the kids or friends involved in an old-fashioned taffy pull. The soft chewy taffy has a mild minty flavor, and it won't stick to the wrapper.
—Elaine Chichura, Kingsley, Pennsylvania

2-1/2 cups sugar
1-1/2 cups light corn syrup
4 teaspoons white vinegar
1/4 teaspoon salt
1/2 cup evaporated milk
1/4 teaspoon peppermint oil
Red food coloring

Butter a 15-in. x 10-in. x 1-in. pan; set aside. In a heavy saucepan, combine the sugar, corn syrup, vinegar and salt. Cook and stir over low heat until sugar is dissolved. Bring to a boil over medium heat. Slowly add the milk; cook and stir until a candy thermometer reads 248° (firm-ball stage). Remove from the heat; stir in peppermint oil and food coloring, keeping face away from mixture, as odor is very strong.

Pour into prepared pan. Let stand for 8 minutes or until cool enough to handle. With well-buttered fingers, quickly pull candy until firm but pliable (color will become light pink). Pull into a 1/2-in. rope; cut into 1-in. pieces. Wrap each in waxed paper. **Yield:** 1-3/4 pounds.

Editor's Note: We recommend you test your candy thermometer before each use by bringing water to a boil; the thermometer should read 212°. Adjust recipe temperature up or down based on your test.

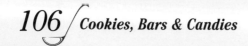

Anise Icebox Cookies

(Pictured above)

Prep: 25 min. + chilling   **Bake:** 10 min.

There's just the right accent of anise in these old-fashioned cookies.   —*Sharon Nichols, Brookings, South Dakota*

  1 cup butter, softened
  1 cup sugar
  1 cup packed brown sugar
  1 egg
2-1/2 cups all-purpose flour
  1 teaspoon baking soda
1/2 teaspoon salt
1/2 teaspoon ground cinnamon
1/2 teaspoon ground cloves
1/2 cup finely chopped pecans
  1 tablespoon aniseed

In a large mixing bowl, cream butter and sugars. Beat in egg. Combine the flour, baking soda, salt, cinnamon and cloves; gradually add to creamed mixture. Stir in pecans and aniseed. Shape into two 10-in. rolls; wrap each in plastic wrap. Refrigerate for 4 hours.

Unwrap; cut 1/4 in. off the ends of each roll. Cut dough into 1/4-in. slices. Place 2 in. apart on ungreased baking sheets. Bake at 375° for 8-10 minutes or until golden brown. Remove to wire racks to cool. **Yield:** about 5-1/2 dozen.

Gingerbread House Cookies

(Pictured at far right)

Prep: 40 min. + chilling   **Bake:** 10 min. + cooling

This is my favorite molasses cookie. I use the recipe at Christmas, Easter and Fourth of July, cutting shapes like houses, bunnies and stars.   —*Karen Haen*
Sturgeon Bay, Wisconsin

  1 cup shortening
1/2 cup sugar
1/2 cup packed brown sugar
  2 eggs
  1 cup molasses
  1 to 1-1/2 teaspoons grated orange peel
5-1/2 cups all-purpose flour
  3 teaspoons baking soda
3/4 teaspoon salt
3/4 teaspoon ground ginger
3/4 teaspoon ground cinnamon
1/2 teaspoon ground nutmeg
1/2 cup water
Frosting and food coloring of your choice

In a large mixing bowl, cream shortening and sugars. Add eggs, one at a time, beating well after each addition. Beat in molasses and orange peel. Combine flour, baking soda, salt and spices; add to creamed mixture alternately with water. Cover and refrigerate for 3 hours or until easy to handle.

On a lightly floured surface, roll out dough to 1/4-in. thickness. Cut with a 3-1/2-in. gingerbread house cookie cutter dipped in flour.

Place 1 in. apart on greased baking sheets. Bake at 350° for 8-10 minutes or until edges are firm. Cool for 2 minutes before removing to wire racks. Decorate cooled cookies as desired with tinted frosting. **Yield:** 4 dozen.

Lemon Angel Wings

(Pictured at right)

Prep: 20 min. + chilling   **Bake:** 20 min. + cooling

The light lemony flavor of these treats is wonderful and very impressive. They are quite showy on a cookie tray.
—*Charolette Westfall, Houston, Texas*

  1 cup cold butter
1-1/2 cups all-purpose flour
1/2 cup sour cream
  1 teaspoon grated lemon peel
 10 tablespoons sugar, *divided*

In a large bowl, cut butter into flour until crumbly. Stir in sour cream and lemon peel until well blended. Place on a piece of waxed paper; shape into a 4-1/2-in. square. Wrap in plastic wrap and refrigerate for at least 2 hours.

Cut dough into four 2-1/4-in. squares. Place one square on a piece of waxed paper sprinkled with 2 tablespoons sugar. Cover with another piece of waxed paper. Keep remaining squares refrigerated. Roll out dough into a 12-in. x 5-in. rectangle, turning often to coat with the sugar.

Lightly mark center of 12-in. side. Starting with a short side, roll up jelly-roll style to the center mark, peeling paper away while rolling. Repeat rolling from other short side, so the two rolls meet in the center and resemble a scroll.

Wrap well in plastic wrap and refrigerate. Repeat with remaining squares, using 2 tablespoons sugar for each. Chill for 1 hour.

Unwrap dough and cut into 1/2-in. slices; dip each side in remaining sugar. Place 2 in. apart on foil-lined baking sheets. Bake at 375° for 14 minutes or until golden brown. Turn cookies over; bake 5 minutes longer. Remove to wire racks to cool. **Yield:** 3 dozen.

Lime Meltaway Spritz

(Pictured below)

Prep: 20 min.   **Bake:** 10 min. + cooling

These sweet, tangy lime-flavored cookies really melt in your mouth. —*Beverly Coyde, Gusport, New York*

1 cup butter, softened
1/2 cup confectioners' sugar
1-3/4 cups all-purpose flour
1/4 cup cornstarch
1 tablespoon grated lime peel
1/2 teaspoon vanilla extract
Green food coloring, optional
LIME GLAZE:
1/2 cup confectioners' sugar
4 teaspoons lime juice
1/2 teaspoon grated lime peel, optional

In a mixing bowl, cream butter and confectioners' sugar until light and fluffy. Gradually beat in flour and cornstarch. Stir in lime peel and vanilla. Tint half of the dough green if desired.

Using a cookie press fitted with a ribbon disk, press dough into 12-in.-long strips 2 in. apart on un-greased baking sheets. Cut each strip into 3-in. pieces (do not separate pieces). Bake at 350° for 8-10 minutes or until edges are lightly browned. Cool for 2 minutes before removing to wire racks. Combine glaze ingredients; brush over cooled cookies. Let stand until set. **Yield:** about 3 dozen.

FUN SHAPES AND FLAVORS of Gingerbread House Cookies, Lemon Angel Wings and Lime Meltaway Spritz (shown above) add color and variety to holiday treats.

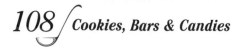

Hazelnut Toffee

(Pictured below)

Prep: 45 min. + cooling

This is one of my most-asked-for recipes. It's sweet and buttery with plenty of crunch. You could use dark, milk or even white chocolate. —Joanne Simpson, Portland, Oregon

  2 teaspoons plus 1 cup butter, *divided*
  1 cup sugar
  3 tablespoons water
  1 tablespoon light corn syrup
  1/3 cup chopped hazelnuts
TOPPING:
  2 cups (12 ounces) semisweet chocolate chips
  1/2 cup finely chopped hazelnuts

Line a 13-in. x 9-in. x 2-in. pan with foil; coat the foil with nonstick cooking spray and set aside. Butter the sides of a large heavy saucepan with 2 teaspoons butter. Cube remaining butter; place in pan. Add the sugar, water and corn syrup. Cook and stir until mixture turns golden brown and a candy thermometer reads 300° (hard-crack stage).

Remove from the heat; stir in hazelnuts. Pour into prepared pan without scraping; spread evenly. Let stand at room temperature until cool, about 1 hour.

In a microwave-safe bowl, melt chocolate chips. Spread evenly over toffee. Sprinkle with hazelnuts, pressing down gently. Let stand for 1 hour. Break into bite-size pieces. Store in the refrigerator. **Yield:** 1-3/4 pounds.

Editor's Note: We recommend you test your candy thermometer before each use by bringing water to a boil; the thermometer should read 212°. Adjust recipe temperature up or down based on your test.

Chocolate Peanut Squares

Prep: 20 min. + cooling

If you're a fan of peanut butter cups, you'll enjoy these two-layer treats. A slightly crunchy graham cracker and peanut butter layer is topped with a smooth coating of melted chocolate chips and peanut butter. —Nicole Trudell
Fort Langley, British Columbia

  2 cups confectioners' sugar
  3/4 cup creamy peanut butter
  2/3 cup graham cracker crumbs
  1/2 cup butter, melted
TOPPING:
  2/3 cup semisweet chocolate chips
  4-1/2 teaspoons creamy peanut butter
  1/2 teaspoon butter

Line a 9-in. square pan with foil and butter the foil; set aside. In a large bowl, combine confectioners' sugar, peanut butter, graham cracker crumbs and butter. Spread into prepared pan.

Combine topping ingredients in a microwave-safe bowl; heat until melted. Spread over peanut butter layer. Refrigerate until cool. Using foil, lift out of pan. Cut into 1-in. squares. Store in an airtight container in the refrigerator. **Yield:** about 1-1/2 pounds.

Coffee 'n' Cream Brownies

(Pictured on page 100)

Prep: 25 min.   **Bake:** 25 min. + cooling

A friend gave me the recipe for these rich cake-like brownies topped with a coffee-enhanced filling and a chocolate glaze. —Michelle Tiemstra, Lacombe, Alberta

  1/2 cup butter, cubed
  3 squares (1 ounce *each*) unsweetened chocolate, chopped
  2 eggs
  1 cup sugar
  1 teaspoon vanilla extract
  2/3 cup all-purpose flour
  1/4 teaspoon baking soda
FILLING:
  1 tablespoon heavy whipping cream
  1 teaspoon instant coffee granules
  2 tablespoons butter, softened
  1 cup confectioners' sugar
GLAZE:
  1 cup (6 ounces) semisweet chocolate chips
  1/3 cup heavy whipping cream

In a saucepan over low heat, melt butter and chocolate; cool slightly. In a small mixing bowl, beat eggs, sugar and vanilla; stir in the chocolate mixture. Combine

rosette with fork and remove iron. Fry for 1-2 minutes on each side or until golden brown. Remove to a wire rack covered with paper towels. Repeat with remaining batter. Sprinkle with confectioners' sugar before serving. **Yield:** about 2-1/2 dozen.

Creamy Cashew Brownies

(Pictured below)

Prep: 15 min. **Bake:** 25 min. + chilling

These brownies have a fudge-like texture and a rich cream cheese topping. Cashews and a hot fudge swirl make the pretty bars special. —*Karen Wagner, Danville, Illinois*

 1 **package fudge brownie mix (13-inch x 9-inch pan size)**
 1/3 **cup water**
 1/4 **cup vegetable oil**
 1 **egg**
 1 **cup (6 ounces) semisweet chocolate chips**
TOPPING:
 2 **packages (8 ounces *each*) cream cheese, softened**
 1-1/2 **cups confectioners' sugar**
 1 **teaspoon vanilla extract**
 1 **cup salted cashews, coarsely chopped**
 1/2 **cup hot fudge ice cream topping, warmed**

In a large bowl, combine the brownie mix, water, oil and egg. Stir in chips. Spread into a greased 13-in. x 9-in. x 2-in. baking pan. Bake at 350° for 25-27 minutes or until a toothpick inserted near the center comes out clean (do not overbake). Cool on a wire rack.

For topping, in a large mixing bowl, beat the cream cheese, confectioners' sugar and vanilla until smooth. Spread over brownies. Sprinkle with cashews; drizzle with hot fudge topping. Refrigerate before cutting. Store in the refrigerator. **Yield:** 2 dozen.

flour and baking soda; add to the chocolate mixture. Spread into a greased 8-in. square baking pan. Bake at 350° for 25-30 minutes or until a toothpick inserted near the center comes out clean (do not overbake). Cool on a wire rack.

For filling, combine cream and coffee granules in a small bowl; stir until coffee is dissolved. In a small mixing bowl, beat butter and confectioners' sugar. Add coffee mixture; beat until creamy. Spread over brownies.

In a small saucepan, combine the chips and cream. Cook and stir over low heat until the chocolate is melted and mixture is thickened. Cool slightly. Carefully spread over filling. Let stand for 30 minutes or until glaze is set. Cut into squares. Store in refrigerator. **Yield:** 16 servings.

Rosettes

(Pictured above)

Prep: 5 min. **Cook:** 1 hour + cooling

Shaped like delicate snowflakes, these crisp rosettes make a lovely winter dessert. —*Rita Christianson Glenburn, North Dakota*

 2 **eggs**
 1 **cup milk**
 1 **teaspoon sugar**
 1/4 **teaspoon salt**
 1 **cup all-purpose flour**
Oil for deep-fat frying
Confectioners' sugar

In a small mixing bowl, beat the eggs, milk, sugar and salt. Add flour; beat until smooth. In a deep-fat fryer or electric skillet, heat 2-1/2 in. of oil to 375°. Place rosette iron in hot oil for 30 seconds.

Blot iron on paper towels, then dip iron in batter to three-fourths the way up the sides (do not let batter run over top of iron). Immediately place in hot oil; loosen

Rosebud Butter Cookies

(Pictured above)

Prep: 30 min. + chilling   **Bake:** 20 min. + cooling

When an occasion calls for flowers, why not make them edible? These unique cookies make lovely gifts. They're pretty in yellow, too—just change the food coloring.
—Cheryl Phelps, Greenfield, Indiana

   1/3 **cup butter, softened**
     1 **cup sugar**
     2 **eggs**
     2 **teaspoons vanilla extract**
2-1/4 **cups all-purpose flour**
   1/2 **teaspoon salt**
   1/2 **teaspoon baking powder**
Red paste food coloring
     1 **cup vanilla frosting**
Green paste food coloring

In a small mixing bowl, cream butter and sugar. Beat in eggs and vanilla. Combine the flour, salt and baking powder; gradually add to creamed mixture. Tint dough red. Shape into a ball. Wrap in plastic wrap; refrigerate overnight.

Shape dough into 3/4-in. balls. Place 2 in. apart on greased baking sheets; flatten to 1/4-in. thickness. With a sharp knife, cut two slits at the top of each circle, forming a flower bud. Pinch the bottom of each bud, forming the stem end.

Bake at 350° for 8-10 minutes or until set. Remove to wire racks to cool completely. Tint frosting green. Using a small leaf tip, pipe leaves onto the stem end of each flower. **Yield:** about 6-1/2 dozen.

Blond Brownies a la Mode

(Pictured on page 100)

Prep: 25 min.   **Bake:** 25 min. + cooling

We have a lot of church socials and I'm always looking for something new and different to prepare. These brownies, drizzled with a sweet maple sauce, are a sure hit…with or without the ice cream.
—Pat Parker
Chester, South Carolina

   3/4 **cup butter, softened**
     2 **cups packed brown sugar**
     4 **eggs**
     2 **teaspoons vanilla extract**
     2 **cups all-purpose flour**
     2 **teaspoons baking powder**
     1 **teaspoon salt**
1-1/2 **cups chopped pecans**
MAPLE CREAM SAUCE:
     1 **cup maple syrup**
     2 **tablespoons butter**
   1/4 **cup evaporated milk**
Vanilla ice cream and chopped pecans

In a mixing bowl, cream butter and brown sugar. Add eggs, one at a time, beating well after each addition. Beat in vanilla. Combine the flour, baking powder and salt; gradually add to creamed mixture. Stir in pecans. Spread into a greased 13-in. x 9-in. x 2-in. baking pan.

Bake at 350° for 25-30 minutes or until a toothpick inserted near the center comes out clean. Cool on a wire rack.

For sauce, combine syrup and butter in a saucepan. Bring to a boil; cook and stir for 3 minutes. Remove from the heat; stir in milk. Cut brownies into squares; cut in half if desired. Place on dessert plates with a scoop of ice cream. Top with sauce; sprinkle with pecans. **Yield:** 20 servings.

Caramel Truffles

Prep: 1 hour + chilling

These candies disappear as fast as I can make them. The five-ingredient microwave recipe is easy and fun to make. Packaged with ribbon, they make a pretty gift.
—Charlotte Midthun, Granite Falls, Minnesota

  26 **caramels**
    1 **cup milk chocolate chips**
 1/4 **cup heavy whipping cream**
1-1/3 **cups semisweet chocolate chips**
    1 **tablespoon shortening**

Line an 8-in. square dish with plastic wrap and set aside. In a microwave-safe bowl, combine the caramels, milk chocolate chips and cream. Microwave, uncovered, on high for 1 minute; stir. Microwave 1 minute longer, stirring every 15 seconds or until caramels are melted and mixture is smooth. Spread into prepared dish; refrigerate for 1 hour or until firm.

Using plastic wrap, lift candy out of pan. Cut into 30 pieces; roll each piece into a 1-in. ball. Cover and refrigerate for 1 hour or until firm.

In a microwave-safe bowl, melt semisweet chips and shortening; stir until smooth. Dip caramels in chocolate and place on waxed paper-lined baking sheets. Refrigerate until firm. **Yield:** 2-1/2 dozen.

Editor's Note: This recipe was tested with Hershey caramels in a 1,100-watt microwave.

Fudgy Oat Brownies

Prep: 30 min. **Bake:** 35 min. + cooling

These cake-like brownies have a rich crunchy oat crust and a smooth homemade chocolate frosting. A packaged brownie mix makes the recipe easy to prepare. You can make it even easier by using canned frosting.
—*Diana Otterson, Canandaigua, New York*

```
1-1/2  cups quick-cooking oats
  3/4  cup all-purpose flour
  3/4  cup packed brown sugar
  1/4  teaspoon baking soda
  1/4  teaspoon salt
  3/4  cup butter, melted
    1  package fudge brownie mix (13-inch
         x 9-inch pan size)
FROSTING:
    3  tablespoons butter
1-1/2  squares (1-1/2 ounces) unsweetened
         chocolate, chopped
2-1/4  cups confectioners' sugar
    3 to 4 tablespoons hot water
1-1/2  teaspoons vanilla extract
```

In a bowl, combine the oats, flour, brown sugar, baking soda and salt. Stir in butter until combined. Press into an ungreased 13-in. x 9-in. x 2-in. baking pan. Bake at 350° for 10-11 minutes or until puffed and edges are lightly browned.

Meanwhile, prepare the brownie mix according to package directions for cake-like brownies. Spread the batter over crust. Bake 25-30 minutes longer or until a toothpick inserted near the center comes out clean.

For frosting, in a small saucepan, melt butter and chocolate over low heat; stir until smooth. Remove from the heat; immediately stir in confectioners' sugar, 2 tablespoons water and vanilla until smooth. Add the remaining water; stir until smooth. Immediately spread over brownies. Cool on a wire rack until firm. Cut into bars. **Yield:** 3 dozen.

Elegant Dipped Cherries

(Pictured below)

Prep: 1-1/4 hours + freezing

Here's a sure way to impress holiday guests. These sweet maraschino cherries are wrapped in unsweetened chocolate, then dipped in melted vanilla chips. A chocolate drizzle dresses them up for serving on a festive plate of sweets.
—*Sedora Brown, Waynesboro, Virginia*

```
    1  jar (10 ounces) maraschino cherries with
         stems, well drained
    3  tablespoons butter, melted
    2  tablespoons light corn syrup
    1  square (1 ounce) unsweetened chocolate,
         melted
    2  teaspoons half-and-half cream
    2  cups confectioners' sugar
    1  cup vanilla or white chips
2-1/2  teaspoons shortening, divided
  1/2  cup semisweet chocolate chips
```

Pat cherries dry with paper towels and set aside. In a bowl, combine the butter, corn syrup, unsweetened chocolate and cream. Stir in the confectioners' sugar.

Knead until smooth. Roll into 18 balls; flatten each into a 2-in. circle. Wrap each circle around a cherry and lightly roll in hands. Place cherries, stem side up, in a shallow paper-lined container. Cover and freeze for at least 2 hours.

The day before serving, remove the cherries from freezer. In a microwave-safe bowl, melt vanilla chips and 1-1/2 teaspoons shortening; stir until smooth.

Holding onto the stem, dip each cherry into vanilla mixture; set on waxed paper to dry. Melt chocolate chips and remaining shortening; stir until smooth. Drizzle over the candies. Refrigerate until firm. Store candies in an airtight container. **Yield:** 1-1/2 dozen.

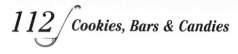

Peanut Lover's Brownies

(Pictured below)

Prep: 30 min.   **Bake:** 30 min. + chilling

Peanut butter lovers won't be able to eat just one of these delectable dessert squares. These chocolaty brownies are sandwiched between a graham cracker crust and peanut butter mousse. They're irresistible!
—April Phillips
Lafayette, Indiana

- 1/2 cup butter, softened
- 3/4 cup all-purpose flour
- 1/2 cup graham cracker crumbs
- 1/4 cup sugar
- 1/2 cup salted peanuts, chopped

BROWNIE LAYER:
- 3/4 cup butter, cubed
- 4 squares (1 ounce *each*) unsweetened chocolate, chopped
- 4 eggs
- 2 cups sugar
- 2 teaspoons vanilla extract
- 1 cup all-purpose flour

PEANUT CREAM TOPPING:
- 1 cup creamy peanut butter
- 1 carton (12 ounces) frozen whipped topping, thawed
- 12 miniature peanut butter cups, coarsely chopped

Line a 13-in. x 9-in. x 2-in. baking pan with foil; grease the foil. In a small mixing bowl, combine the butter, flour, cracker crumbs and sugar; press into prepared pan. Bake at 350° for 10-12 minutes or until set. Cool on a wire rack. Sprinkle peanuts over crust.

In a microwave, melt the butter and chocolate; stir until smooth. In a mixing bowl, combine the eggs, sugar, vanilla and chocolate mixture. Add flour; mix well. Spread over crust. Bake for 30-40 minutes or until a toothpick inserted near the center comes out clean. Cool on a wire rack.

For topping, warm peanut butter for 30 seconds in a microwave. Gradually fold in whipped topping; spread over brownies. Refrigerate for 1 hour. Sprinkle with chopped peanut butter cups. Using foil, lift brownies out of pan; remove foil. Cut into squares. Store in the refrigerator. **Yield:** 2 dozen.

Butter Mints

Prep: 30 min. + cooling   **Cook:** 25 min.

These heavenly nuggets are out of this world! My mom has made the melt-in-your-mouth mints for as long as I can remember, usually for holidays and special occasions. She made them for my wedding, and people were still talking about them a year later.
—Mindee Williams
Spanish Fork, Utah

- 3 cups sugar
- 1 cup water
- 1 cup butter, softened
- 1/4 teaspoon peppermint oil
- 3 to 5 drops green food coloring

Butter a 15-in. x 10-in. x 1-in. pan; refrigerate. In a large heavy saucepan with a lid, combine the sugar, water and butter with a wooden spoon. Cook and stir over high heat until sugar is dissolved.

Bring to a boil; cover and cook over medium heat for 3 minutes to allow steam to wash sugar crystals down. Uncover; cook over medium heat, without stirring, until a candy thermometer reads 260° (hard-ball stage).

Remove from the heat; stir in peppermint oil and food coloring, keeping face away from mixture, as odor is very strong. Pour into chilled pan without scraping. Let stand undisturbed for several minutes.

With a rubber spatula, gently fold the edges of hot candy into the center to soften. Continue folding edges into the center until candy is cool enough to handle.

With well-buttered fingers, form candy into a ball, then begin stretching and pulling. Continue pulling and stretching until candy becomes porous and satiny, about 5 minutes. Pull out into a 1/2-in. rope. Using buttered scissors, cut candy into 1/2-in. pieces. For best results, place candy in airtight containers for at least 24 hours before serving. **Yield:** about 1-1/2 pounds.

Editor's Note: We recommend that you test your candy thermometer before each use by bringing water to a boil; the thermometer should read 212°. Adjust recipe temperature up or down based on your test.

ing to be boxed up and couldn't believe I made them. He said they looked like they came from a candy shop. That's the best compliment I've ever received.
—*Carrie Burke, Conway, Massachusetts*

   1 teaspoon plus 1 cup butter, *divided*
   1 cup light corn syrup
2-1/4 cups packed brown sugar
   1/8 teaspoon salt
   1 can (14 ounces) sweetened condensed
     milk
   1 teaspoon vanilla extract
1-1/2 pounds pecan halves, toasted
   3/4 cup milk chocolate chips
   3/4 cup semisweet chocolate chips
   4 teaspoons shortening

Line baking sheets with waxed paper; lightly coat with nonstick cooking spray and set aside. Butter the sides of a heavy saucepan with 1 teaspoon butter. Cube remaining butter; place in pan. Add corn syrup, brown sugar and salt. Cook and stir until sugar is melted.

Gradually stir in milk. Cook and stir over medium heat until mixture comes to a boil. Cook and stir until a candy thermometer reads 248° (firm-ball stage), about 16 minutes. Remove from the heat; stir in vanilla. Gently stir in pecans. Drop by rounded teaspoonfuls onto prepared baking sheets. Refrigerate until firm, about 12 minutes.

In a microwave-safe bowl, melt the chips and shortening; stir until smooth. Drizzle over clusters. Chill until firm. Store in the refrigerator. **Yield:** about 6 dozen.

Editor's Note: We recommend you test your candy thermometer before each use by bringing water to a boil; the thermometer should read 212°. Adjust recipe temperature up or down based on your test.

Rosemary Raisin Cookies

(Pictured above)

Prep: 15 min. **Bake:** 10 min.

These buttery cookies are one of my favorites. I added the rosemary and substituted golden raisins for the regular raisins in the original recipe. —*Sue Gronholz Beaver Dam, Wisconsin*

   1/2 cup butter, softened
   1/2 cup shortening
 1-1/2 cups sugar
     2 eggs
     1 tablespoon minced fresh rosemary
     1 tablespoon grated lemon peel
   1/2 teaspoon lemon extract
 3-1/2 cups all-purpose flour
 1-1/2 teaspoons cream of tartar
 1-1/2 teaspoons baking soda
   1/2 teaspoon salt
     1 cup golden raisins

In a large mixing bowl, cream butter, shortening and sugar. Add eggs, one at a time, beating well after each addition. Stir in the rosemary, lemon peel and extract. Combine the flour, cream of tartar, baking soda and salt; gradually add to creamed mixture. Stir in raisins.

Roll into 1-in. balls. Place on ungreased baking sheets. Flatten with a fork. Bake at 400° for 8-10 minutes or until golden brown. Remove to wire racks to cool. **Yield:** about 8 dozen.

Pecan Clusters

(Pictured at right)

Prep: 1-1/4 hours + chilling

I made these "turtle-like" concoctions one Christmas for a sweets exchange. My dad saw them on the counter wait-

Simply Scrumptious From-Scratch Brownies

MOIST and chewy, fudgy or fluffy, those sensational squares we simply call "brownies" accomplish a not-so-simple feat: They tickle just about everyone's fancy.

Whether you enjoy the dense texture of a basic fudgy brownie or the ooey-gooeyness of cake-like versions frosted to creamy perfection, brownies do the trick when you want a fast-to-fix snack or dessert that's oh, so delicious.

You can mix and bake a batch of delectable chocolaty bars in minutes. Or you can take the time to assemble luscious layered brownies or bolster the batter with an assortment of ingredients—from nuts and chips to caramel and peanut butter.

With so many choices, your family will never tire of these sweet squares. Even guests will say "Yum" when you set a dressed-up brownie in front of them. Drizzled with a rich sauce, sprinkled with berries or topped with homemade whipped cream, this all-time favorite will delight as much as any elaborate dessert.

Just try the Decadent Brownie Pie on the opposite page or one of our contest-winning recipes in this chapter, and you'll know what we mean!

Tips from Our Kitchen

Follow these baking tips from our Test Kitchen home economists and make your brownies the perfect treat! But be prepared to make more because they'll be gone before you know it.

- Measure ingredients accurately.
- Avoid overmixing the batter.
- Dark-colored pans can cause overbrowning, so stick with dull aluminum baking pans or glass baking dishes.
- Coat the pan with nonstick cooking spray or grease the pan.
- Preheat your oven 10-15 minutes before baking the brownies and center the pan in the middle of the oven. Check your brownies when the minimum baking time has been reached.

More Tips

Seasoned brownie-baking *Taste of Home* readers offer these sweet suggestions:

To give boxed brownie mix extra flavor, I add a tablespoon of instant coffee granules to the batter. —Tracy Knight
Knoxville, Tennessee

I wrap brownies individually in plastic wrap and place them in a basket on the counter. This keeps them fresh longer...and they're ready to be packed into lunch boxes the next day. —Caroline Engelbert
Ann Arbor, Michigan

Out of unsweetened baking chocolate? You can substitute 3 tablespoons cocoa plus 1 tablespoon vegetable oil or shortening for each 1-ounce square of unsweetened chocolate. —Diane Moss, Ottawa, Illinois

Brush Up on Brownie Baking

If your brownies don't bake up to your expectations, one of these could be the reason why...

Uneven
- Batter wasn't spread evenly in the pan.
- The oven rack wasn't level.

Overbaked
- If you use a pan larger than the one called for in the recipe, brownies will be thin and dry.
- Oven temperature was too high.
- Next time, check brownies sooner than the baking time called for in the recipe.

Too Gummy
- You used a pan that was smaller than called for.

Too Tough
- Dry ingredients were overmixed. Stir them in with a wooden spoon until moistened.

Crumbles When Cut
- Make sure that the brownies are completely cooled before cutting them.
- Do not use a sawing motion when cutting.
- Warm the knife blade in hot water, dry and cut. Clean and rewarm the knife after each cut.

Decadent Brownie Pie

I have no doubt you'll love this favorite of mine. This is the richest brownie you'll ever taste. You can dress it up with different toppings.
—Stephanie Vozzo
Belvidere, New Jersey

    2/3 **cup butter, softened**
1-1/4 **cups sugar**
    1/2 **cup light corn syrup**
     2 **eggs**
1-1/4 **cups all-purpose flour**
    1/2 **cup baking cocoa**
    1/2 **teaspoon salt**
     3 **tablespoons milk**
     2 **cups chopped walnuts**
GANACHE:
     1 **cup heavy whipping cream**
     8 **squares (1 ounce** *each***) semisweet chocolate, chopped**
Optional toppings—mint Andes candies, raspberries and fresh mint, caramel ice cream topping and whipped cream

In a mixing bowl, cream butter and sugar. Add corn syrup; mix well. Add eggs, one at a time, beating well after each addition. Combine the flour, cocoa and salt; add to creamed mixture alternately with milk. Fold in walnuts. Spread into a greased 10-in. springform pan. Bake at 325° for 55-60 minutes or until a toothpick inserted 1 in. from the side of pan comes out clean. Cool on a wire rack.

For ganache, in a saucepan, bring cream to a boil. Remove from heat; stir in chocolate until melted. Cool completely.

Remove sides of springform pan. Place a wire rack over waxed paper; set brownie on rack. Pour ganache over brownie; spread over top and let drip down sides. Let stand until set. Cut into wedges; garnish with desired toppings. Store in refrigerator. **Yield:** 10-12 servings.

Brownie Biography

The name "brownie" comes from the traditional brown color of the bars.

Linda Stradley, co-author of *What's Cooking America*, notes that the first batch of brownies might have been created accidentally when a cook omitted the baking powder from a chocolate cake recipe.

The first very known published recipe for "brownies" appeared in the 1897 Sears, Roebuck catalog.

Brownies are classified as a bar cookie that tastes like a rich chocolate cake but is cut into squares.

center of each square. Cut through dough from each corner of square to within 1/2 in. of center. Fold alternating points to each center to form a pinwheel; pinch gently at center to seal. Gently press a whole cranberry in center of each one.

Bake at 350° for 12-15 minutes or until lightly browned around edges. Remove to wire racks to cool. Dust with confectioners' sugar. **Yield:** 2 dozen.

Ginger Cranberry Pinwheels

(Pictured above)

Prep: 20 min. + chilling   **Bake:** 15 min. + cooling

Here's a nice Christmas cookie with a different shape. They are fun to make and very delicious. —Laurel Doughty
Fryeburg, Maine

    1 cup butter, softened
    1 package (8 ounces) cream cheese, softened
  1/4 cup sugar
2-1/2 cups all-purpose flour
FILLING:
  1/2 cup fresh *or* frozen cranberries
  1/4 cup sugar
    1 tablespoon water
  1/4 cup orange marmalade
  1/4 teaspoon ground ginger
   24 whole fresh cranberries
Confectioners' sugar

In a mixing bowl, cream the butter, cream cheese and sugar. Gradually beat in flour. Cover and refrigerate for 1 hour. In a saucepan, bring 1/2 cup cranberries, sugar and water to a boil over medium heat. Reduce heat; simmer, uncovered, for 5-6 minutes or until berries pop. Remove from the heat; stir in marmalade and ginger. Set aside.

Divide dough in half. On a floured surface, roll each portion into a 16-in. x 12-in. rectangle. Let stand for 20 minutes. With a sharp knife or pastry wheel, cut dough into 4-in. squares. Place 3 in. apart on lightly greased baking sheets. Spoon 1 teaspoon of filling into the

Rich Chocolate Cake Bars

Prep: 15 min.   **Bake:** 20 min. + cooling

These cake-like brownies work well for large gatherings and are quick to make. —Kathy Kittell, Lenexa, Kansas

  1/2 cup butter, softened
    1 cup sugar
    4 eggs
    1 teaspoon vanilla extract
    1 can (16 ounces) chocolate syrup
    1 cup all-purpose flour
  1/2 teaspoon baking powder
  1/4 teaspoon salt
  1/2 cup chopped nuts
GLAZE:
    1 cup sugar
  1/3 cup milk
  1/3 cup butter, cubed
  1/2 cup semisweet chocolate chips
    1 teaspoon vanilla extract

In a large mixing bowl, cream the butter and sugar. Add eggs and vanilla; mix well. Stir in syrup. Combine the flour, baking powder and salt; add to creamed mixture and mix well. Stir in nuts. Pour into a greased 15-in. x 10-in. x 1-in. baking pan.

Bake at 350° for 20-22 minutes or until a toothpick inserted near the center comes out clean. For glaze, combine the sugar, milk and butter in a heavy saucepan. Bring to a boil over medium heat; boil for 1 minute.

Remove from the heat. Add chips and vanilla; beat with a wooden spoon until smooth. Spread over warm bars. Cool on a wire rack before cutting. **Yield:** about 3 dozen.

Mocha Mousse Brownies

Prep: 40 min.   **Bake:** 15 min. + chilling

Chocolate is one of my favorite foods, and these goodies are the perfect pairing of coffee-flavored mousse and fudge brownies. —Stacy Waller, Eagan, Minnesota

  2/3 cup semisweet chocolate chips
  1/2 cup butter
    1 cup plus 2 tablespoons sugar

2 eggs
1/4 cup hot water
2 tablespoons instant coffee granules
1/2 cup all-purpose flour
1/2 cup baking cocoa
1 teaspoon baking powder

MOCHA MOUSSE:
1 envelope unflavored gelatin
1/4 cup cold water
2 tablespoons instant coffee granules
1 package (3 ounces) cream cheese, softened
1/4 cup sweetened condensed milk
1/2 cup semisweet chocolate chips, melted
1 cup heavy whipping cream

In a saucepan over low heat, melt the chips and butter; pour into a mixing bowl. Beat in sugar until smooth. Add eggs, one at a time, beating well after each addition. Combine hot water and coffee granules; add to chocolate mixture. Combine the flour, cocoa and baking powder; beat into chocolate mixture.

Spread into a greased 13-in. x 9-in. x 2-in. baking pan. Bake at 350° for 15-20 minutes or until a toothpick inserted near the center comes out clean (brownies will be thin). Cool on a wire rack.

For mousse, in a saucepan, sprinkle gelatin over cold water; let stand for 1 minute. Cook and stir over low heat until gelatin is dissolved. Remove from the heat; stir in coffee granules until dissolved.

In a small mixing bowl, beat cream cheese until smooth; beat in milk and melted chips. In a chilled mixing bowl, beat whipping cream and gelatin mixture until soft peaks form. Fold into cream cheese mixture. Spread over brownies. Cover and refrigerate for 3 hours or until firm. Cut into squares. **Yield:** 2 dozen.

Irish Mint Brownies

(Pictured at right)

Prep: 45 min.   **Bake:** 30 min. + chilling

These layered treats are great for St. Patrick's Day. The brownies are topped with a mint flavored mousse and bittersweet chocolate icing.
—Lori Risdal
Sioux City, Iowa

1 cup butter, cubed
4 squares (1 ounce *each*) bittersweet chocolate, chopped
4 eggs
2 cups sugar
2 teaspoons vanilla extract
1-1/2 cups all-purpose flour
1 cup (6 ounces) double dark chocolate chips *or* semisweet chocolate chips
1/2 cup chopped walnuts

FILLING:
4 squares (1 ounce *each*) white baking chocolate, chopped
1/4 cup refrigerated Irish creme nondairy creamer
1 cup heavy whipping cream
15 mint Andes candies, chopped

ICING:
12 squares (1 ounce *each*) bittersweet chocolate, chopped
1 cup heavy whipping cream
2 tablespoons butter

In a saucepan over low heat, melt butter and bittersweet chocolate; cool slightly. In a bowl, beat eggs, sugar and vanilla. Stir in chocolate mixture. Gradually add flour until blended. Stir in chips and walnuts. Spread into a greased 13-in. x 9-in. x 2-in. baking pan. Bake at 350° for 30-35 minutes or until a toothpick inserted near the center comes out clean (do not overbake). Cool on a wire rack.

In a saucepan, combine white chocolate and creamer. Cook and stir over low heat until smooth; remove from heat. Refrigerate 30-40 minutes or until chilled. In a mixing bowl, beat cream until soft peaks form; fold into chocolate mixture. Beat on medium until stiff peaks form, about 4 minutes. Fold in candies. Spread over brownies. Cover; refrigerate.

In a small saucepan, combine bittersweet chocolate and cream. Cook and stir over low heat until chocolate is melted and smooth; remove from heat. Stir in butter until melted. Cool to room temperature. Carefully spread over filling. Cover and refrigerate for 1 hour or until icing is set. Cut into bars. Store in refrigerator. **Yield:** 2-1/2 dozen.

Lemon Curd Cookies

(Pictured below)

Prep: 30 min. + chilling   **Bake:** 10 min. + cooling

I've made these cookies for years…and like to give them out to family and friends.   —Carole Vogel
Allison Park, Pennsylvania

      1 cup butter, softened
   3/4 cup sugar
      1 egg
      1 teaspoon lemon extract
      1 teaspoon vanilla extract
2-1/2 cups all-purpose flour
   1/2 teaspoon baking soda
   1/2 teaspoon salt
      1 cup ground pecans, toasted
FILLING:
1-1/2 cups sugar
      2 tablespoons cornstarch
   1/8 teaspoon salt
   1/2 cup lemon juice
      4 egg yolks, beaten
      6 tablespoons butter, cubed
      2 teaspoons grated lemon peel
Confectioners' sugar

In a large mixing bowl, cream butter and sugar. Beat in egg and extracts. Combine the flour, baking soda and salt; gradually add to creamed mixture. Stir in pecans. Divide dough in half; shape into logs. Wrap each in plastic wrap. Refrigerate for 1-2 hours or until firm.

On a floured surface, roll each portion to 1/8-in. thickness. Cut with a 3-in. fluted round cookie cutter dipped in flour. With a floured 1/2-in. round cookie cutter, cut out the centers of half of the cookies. (Reroll small cutouts if desired.) Place solid and cutout cookies 1 in. apart on ungreased baking sheets. Bake at 350° for 10-12 minutes or until lightly browned. Remove to wire racks to cool.

In a saucepan, combine the sugar, cornstarch and salt. Stir in lemon juice until smooth. Cook and stir until slightly thickened and bubbly, about 2 minutes. Stir a small amount into egg yolks. Return all to the pan; bring to a gentle boil, stirring constantly. Cook and stir 2 minutes longer or until mixture reaches 160° and coats the back of a metal spoon.

Remove from the heat; stir in butter and lemon peel. Pour into a bowl; cover surface with plastic wrap. Chill for 2-3 hours (mixture will be thick).

Spread 1 tablespoon filling over solid cookies; top with cutout cookies, pressing down lightly. Sprinkle with confectioners' sugar. Store in the refrigerator. **Yield:** 1-1/2 dozen.

Frosted Cookie Brownies

Prep: 30 min.   **Bake:** 40 min. + cooling

With a crisp cookie crust and fluffy frosting, these brownies are the most requested treats at our house.
—Alicia French, Crestline, California

      1 tube (18 ounces) refrigerated chocolate chip cookie dough
      3 cups miniature marshmallows
      2 cups (12 ounces) semisweet chocolate chips
      1 cup butter, cubed
      4 eggs
      2 teaspoons vanilla extract
      1 cup all-purpose flour
   1/2 teaspoon baking powder
   1/4 teaspoon salt
      1 cup chopped walnuts
FROSTING:
      2 cups miniature marshmallows
      6 tablespoons milk
   1/4 cup butter
      2 squares (1 ounce *each*) unsweetened chocolate, chopped
      3 cups confectioners' sugar

Press cookie dough into a greased 13-in. x 9-in. x 2-in. baking pan. Bake at 350° for 10 minutes.

In a large saucepan, combine the marshmallows, chips and butter; cook and stir over low heat until melted and smooth. Transfer to a bowl; cool. Beat in eggs and vanilla. Combine the flour, baking powder and salt; stir into marshmallow mixture. Stir in nuts; spread over cookie crust. Bake for 30-35 minutes or until a toothpick inserted near the center comes out clean. Cool on a wire rack.

Combine marshmallows, milk, butter and chocolate in a saucepan. Cook and stir over low heat until smooth. Remove from heat; beat in confectioners' sugar. Frost brownies. Cut into bars. **Yield:** 15 servings.

Hint-of-Berry Bonbons

(Pictured above)

Prep: 1-1/2 hours + chilling

You'll have a hard time eating just one of these heavenly sweets. Inside the rich milk chocolate coating is a fudgy center with a hint of strawberry. —*Brenda Hoffman Stanton, Michigan*

  1 **package (8 ounces) cream cheese, softened**
  1 **cup milk chocolate chips, melted and cooled**
3/4 **cup crushed vanilla wafers (about 40 wafers)**
1/4 **cup strawberry preserves**
 15 **ounces milk chocolate candy coating, chopped**
  2 **squares (1 ounce *each*) white baking chocolate**

In a large mixing bowl, beat the cream cheese until fluffy. Beat in melted chocolate chips. Stir in wafer crumbs and preserves. Cover and refrigerate for 2 hours or until easy to handle.

Divide mixture in half. Return one portion to refrigerator. Shape the remaining mixture into 1-in. balls. Refrigerate. Repeat with remaining mixture. In a microwave-safe bowl, melt candy coating. Dip balls in coating; place on waxed paper-lined baking sheets. Refrigerate until set.

In a microwave-safe bowl, melt white chocolate; stir until smooth. Transfer to a heavy-duty resealable plastic bag; cut a small hole in a corner of bag. Driz-zle white chocolate over candies. Store in the refrigerator. **Yield:** about 4-1/2 dozen.

Pecan Swirls

(Pictured below)

Prep: 25 min. + chilling **Bake:** 10 min. + cooling

Cream cheese makes these cookies rich and tender and the sweet filling showcases pecans. —*Wanda Rascoe Shreveport, Louisiana*

   2 **cups butter, softened**
   2 **packages (8 ounces *each*) cream cheese, softened**
   2 **teaspoons vanilla extract**
   4 **cups all-purpose flour**
 1/2 **teaspoon salt**
2-1/4 **cups finely chopped pecans**
1-1/3 **cups sugar**

In a large mixing bowl, cream butter and cream cheese until smooth. Beat in vanilla. Combine flour and salt; gradually add to creamed mixture. Divide into three portions. Wrap each in plastic wrap; refrigerate for 2 hours or until easy to handle.

On a lightly floured surface, roll each portion into a 16-in. x 9-in. rectangle. Combine pecans and sugar; sprinkle over dough to within 1/2 in. of edges. Roll up each rectangle tightly jelly-roll style, starting with a long side. Wrap in plastic wrap; refrigerate for 2 hours.

Unwrap and cut into 3/8-in. slices. Place 2 in. apart on lightly greased baking sheets. Bake at 400° for 12-14 minutes or until lightly browned. Remove to wire racks to cool. **Yield:** 7 dozen.

Cookie Dough Truffles

(Pictured below)

Prep: 1 hour + chilling

The flavorful filling at the center of these yummy candies tastes like genuine chocolate chip cookie dough…without the worry of raw eggs. That's what makes them so appealing. Plus, they're easy to make.
—Lanita Dedon
Slaughter, Louisiana

- 1/2 cup butter, softened
- 3/4 cup packed brown sugar
- 2 cups all-purpose flour
- 1 can (14 ounces) sweetened condensed milk
- 1 teaspoon vanilla extract
- 1/2 cup miniature semisweet chocolate chips
- 1/2 cup chopped walnuts
- 1-1/2 pounds semisweet chocolate candy coating, chopped

In a mixing bowl, cream the butter and brown sugar until light and fluffy. Add the flour, milk and vanilla; mix well. Stir in the chocolate chips and walnuts. Shape into 1-in. balls; place on waxed paper-lined baking sheets. Loosely cover and refrigerate for 1-2 hours or until firm.

In a microwave-safe bowl, melt candy coating, stirring often until smooth. Dip balls in coating; place on waxed paper-lined baking sheets. Refrigerate until firm, about 15 minutes. If desired, remelt remaining candy coating and drizzle over candies. Store in the refrigerator. **Yield:** 5-1/2 dozen.

Butterscotch Hard Candy

Prep: 10 min.　**Cook:** 30 min. + cooling

We think these irresistible bites are better than the store-bought variety…and they sure don't last long!
—Darlene Smithers, Elkhart, Indiana

- 2-1/2 cups sugar
- 3/4 cup water
- 1/2 cup light corn syrup
- 1 cup butter, cubed
- 1/4 cup honey
- 1/2 teaspoon salt
- 1/2 teaspoon rum extract

Butter a 15-in. x 10-in. x 1-in. baking pan; set aside. In a heavy saucepan, combine the sugar, water and corn syrup. Cover and bring to a boil over medium heat without stirring. Cook, uncovered, until a candy thermometer reads 270° (soft-crack stage). Add the butter, honey, salt and extract; stir constantly until the mixture reaches 300° (hard-crack stage).

Remove from the heat. Pour into prepared pan without scraping; do not spread. Cool for 1-2 minutes or until the candy is almost set. Score into 1-in. squares; cool completely. Break squares apart. Store in an airtight container. **Yield:** 1-1/2 pounds.

Editor's Note: We recommend you test your candy thermometer before each use by bringing water to a boil; the thermometer should read 212°. Adjust recipe temperature up or down based on your test.

Meringue Coconut Brownies

Prep: 30 min.　**Bake:** 30 min. + cooling

Looking for an ooey-gooey brownie that's delicious and different? This sweet recipe features a shortbread-like crust and a brown sugar meringue with chocolate, coconut and nuts.
—Diane Bridge, Clymer, Pennsylvania

- 3/4 cup butter, softened
- 1-1/2 cups packed brown sugar, *divided*
- 1/2 cup sugar
- 3 eggs, *separated*
- 1 teaspoon vanilla extract
- 2 cups all-purpose flour
- 1 teaspoon baking powder
- 1/4 teaspoon baking soda
- 1/4 teaspoon salt
- 2 cups (12 ounces) semisweet chocolate chips
- 1 cup flaked coconut
- 3/4 cup chopped walnuts

In a large mixing bowl, cream the butter, 1/2 cup brown sugar and sugar. Add egg yolks and vanilla. Beat on medium speed for 2 minutes.

Combine flour, baking powder, baking soda and salt; add to creamed mixture and mix well (the batter will be thick). Spread into a greased 13-in. x 9-in. x 2-in. baking pan. Sprinkle with chocolate chips, coconut and walnuts.

In a small mixing bowl, beat egg whites until soft peaks form. Gradually beat in remaining brown sugar, 1 tablespoon at a time. Beat until stiff peaks form. Spread over the top.

Bake at 350° for 30-35 minutes or until a toothpick inserted near the center comes out clean. Cool on a wire rack. Cut into bars. Store in refrigerator. **Yield:** 3 to 3-1/2 dozen.

Berry-Cream Cookie Snaps

(Pictured on page 100)

Prep: 40 min. + chilling **Bake:** 30 min. + cooling

My mom and I made up this tasty recipe by combining two others. These cute cookies are crispy on the outside and light and fluffy inside. —Crystal Briddick
Colfax, Illinois

    4 **ounces cream cheese, softened**
  1/4 **cup sugar**
    2 **tablespoons seedless strawberry jam**
  1/4 **cup heavy whipping cream, whipped**
    1 **to 3 drops red food coloring, optional**
BATTER:
  1/2 **cup sugar**
  1/3 **cup all-purpose flour**
    2 **egg whites**
  1/4 **teaspoon vanilla extract**
  1/8 **teaspoon salt**
  1/4 **cup butter, melted and cooled**
  1/2 **cup chopped fresh strawberries**
Additional sugar

For filling, in a small mixing bowl, combine cream cheese, sugar and jam until blended. Fold in whipped cream and food coloring if desired. Chill.

In a bowl, whisk the sugar, flour, egg whites, vanilla and salt until smooth. Whisk in butter until blended. Line baking sheets with parchment paper. Preparing four cookies at a time, drop batter by 1-1/2 teaspoonfuls 4 in. apart onto prepared pan. Bake at 400° for 5-8 minutes or until edges are lightly browned.

Immediately remove one cookie at a time from parchment and form into a tube around a greased clean round wooden clothespin. Press lightly to seal; hold until set, about 20 seconds. Remove cookie from clothespin; place on waxed paper to cool. Continue with remaining cookies. If cookies become too cool to shape, return to oven for 1 minute to soften. Repeat with remaining batter.

Just before serving, pipe or spoon filling into cookie shells. Dip end of each into strawberries and additional sugar. Refrigerate leftovers. **Yield:** about 2 dozen.

Zebra Butter Cookies

(Pictured above)

Prep: 20 min. + chilling **Bake:** 10 min.

For a jungle or animal theme party, these striped cookies are a lot of fun. They are real eye-catchers. I started with a horse cookie cutter...and got exotic! —Shannon Wade
Kansas City, Kansas

  1-1/4 **cups butter, softened**
      1 **cup sugar**
    2/3 **cup confectioners' sugar**
      1 **egg**
      1 **teaspoon vanilla extract**
      3 **cups all-purpose flour**
    1/4 **teaspoon salt**
    1/4 **cup baking cocoa**

In a large mixing bowl, cream butter and sugars. Beat in egg and vanilla. Combine flour and salt; gradually add to the creamed mixture. Divide dough in half. Add cocoa to one half; mix well. Roll each half between waxed paper into a 9-in. square. Cut both squares into three 3-in. strips. Cut the strips in half lengthwise to make six 4-1/2-in. x 3-in. rectangles.

Place one cream-colored rectangle on a large piece of plastic wrap; top with a chocolate rectangle. Repeat layers five times. Wrap in plastic wrap and refrigerate for 2 hours. Unwrap and cut stack widthwise into eighteen 1/4-in. slices.

Cut each slice with a horse-shaped cookie cutter dipped in flour. Place 1 in. apart on ungreased baking sheets. Bake at 375° for 8-10 minutes or until edges are lightly golden. Let stand for 2 minutes before removing to wire racks to cool. **Yield:** 1-1/2 dozen.

BAKE delicious Caramel Chocolate Cookies and Chocolate-Mint Creme Cookies (shown above) for your bunch this holiday season.

Chocolate-Mint Creme Cookies

(Pictured above)

Prep: 20 min.   **Bake:** 10 min. + cooling

I recommend this recipe with an enthusiastic "Delicious!" Your cookie munchers are sure to agree.
—*Gaylene Anderson, Sandy, Utah*

```
1-1/2  cups packed brown sugar
  3/4  cup butter, cubed
    2  tablespoons water
    2  cups (12 ounces) semisweet chocolate
       chips
    2  eggs
    3  cups all-purpose flour
1-1/4  teaspoons baking soda
    1  teaspoon salt
```
FILLING:
```
  1/3  cup butter, softened
    3  cups confectioners' sugar
    3 to 4 tablespoons milk
  1/8  teaspoon peppermint extract
```
Dash salt

In a small saucepan, combine the brown sugar, butter and water. Cook and stir over medium heat until sugar is dissolved. Remove from the heat; stir in the chocolate chips until melted and smooth. Transfer to a large mixing bowl; cool slightly.

Add eggs, one at a time, beating well after each addition. Combine the flour, baking soda and salt; gradually add to chocolate mixture. Drop by rounded teaspoonfuls onto greased baking sheets. Bake at 350° for 8-10 minutes or until set. Remove to wire racks; flatten slightly. Cool completely.

Combine filling ingredients; spread on the bottom of half of the cookies. Top with remaining cookies. Store in the refrigerator. **Yield:** 4 dozen.

Caramel Chocolate Cookies

(Pictured above)

Prep: 25 min. + chilling   **Bake:** 10 min. + cooling

I'm noted for my Christmas cookies, and this recipe is my absolute all-time favorite.
—*Joan Williams*
Eatontown, New Jersey

```
  1/2  cup butter, softened
    1  cup sugar
    1  egg
  1/3  cup milk
    2  squares (1 ounce each) unsweetened
       chocolate, melted and cooled
    1  teaspoon vanilla extract
```

2 cups all-purpose flour
1/2 teaspoon baking powder
1/2 teaspoon salt
12 caramels, quartered
FROSTING:
1-1/2 cups confectioners' sugar
1 square (1 ounce) unsweetened chocolate, melted and cooled
2 tablespoons light corn syrup
2 to 3 tablespoons hot water
Chopped pecans, optional

In a large mixing bowl, cream the butter and sugar. Beat in the egg, milk, chocolate and vanilla. Combine the flour, baking powder and salt; gradually add to the creamed mixture. Cover and refrigerate overnight or until easy to handle.

Shape rounded tablespoonfuls of dough around caramel pieces. Place 2 in. apart on ungreased baking sheets. Bake at 400° for 6-8 minutes or until set. Remove to wire racks to cool.

In a mixing bowl, combine the confectioners' sugar, chocolate, corn syrup and enough water to achieve desired spreading consistency. Frost cookies. Sprinkle with pecans if desired. **Yield:** 4 dozen.

Cherry Snowballs

Prep: 15 min. **Bake:** 20 min. + cooling

These simple cookies have a delicate buttery flavor complemented by the cherry surprise in the center. They've become a holiday favorite for my family. —Joy Schuster
Glentana, Montana

1 cup butter, softened
1/2 cup confectioners' sugar
2 cups all-purpose flour
1 jar (6 ounces) maraschino cherries without stems, drained and halved
Additional confectioners' sugar

In a mixing bowl, cream butter and confectioners' sugar; gradually add flour. Shape a tablespoonful of dough around each cherry, forming a ball. Place 1 in. apart on ungreased baking sheets.

Bake at 325° for 18-20 minutes or until the bottoms are browned. Roll warm cookies in confectioners' sugar. Cool on wire racks. **Yield:** about 2-1/2 dozen.

Coconut Snowmen

(Pictured at right)

Prep: 4 hours + chilling

My mom made her basic coconut candy recipe for years, but I took it a step further and created jolly snowman

heads. These cute little characters are worth the extra effort because they're always a big hit!* —Donell Mayfield
Rio Rancho, Minnesota

4 cups flaked coconut, coarsely chopped
3-3/4 cups confectioners' sugar
2/3 cup sweetened condensed milk
1/4 cup butter, softened
1-1/2 cups vanilla *or* white chips
2 packages (11-1/2 ounces *each*) milk chocolate chips
1 package (10-1/2 ounces) large marshmallows
Black, orange and red decorator icing
Green leaf-shaped decorator candies

In a large mixing bowl, combine coconut, confectioners' sugar, milk and butter. Shape into 1-1/4-in. balls; place on waxed paper-lined baking sheets. Loosely cover and chill for 1-1/4 hours or until firm.

In a microwave-safe bowl, melt vanilla chips; stir until smooth. Dip balls in melted chips; place on waxed paper-lined baking sheets. Chill until firm, about 15 minutes. Set aside remaining melted vanilla chips.

Melt the chocolate chips; stir until smooth. For hats, dip each marshmallow in chocolate; place on a waxed paper-lined baking sheet, allowing excess to drip down. Swirl the marshmallows in chocolate on waxed paper to create hat brims. Chill until firm, about 15 minutes.

Level the top of coated coconut balls. Attach marshmallow hats, using reserved melted vanilla chips. With black icing, add eyes and a mouth to each face; with orange icing, add a nose. Use red icing and leaf candies for holly on hats. Store in an airtight container. **Yield:** 4 dozen.

Cakes & Pies

The hardest task in
making any of these
decadent cakes and pies is
waiting to indulge in a piece!

HARD TO RESIST. Clockwise from upper left: Banana Split Brownie Pie (p. 128), Berry Pinwheel Cake (p. 126), Black Pepper Pound Cake (p. 134), Cherry-Cream Crumble Pie (p. 128) and Berry-Glazed Chocolate Cake (p. 132).

Bavarian Strawberry Pie

(Pictured above)

Prep: 15 min. **Bake:** 30 min. + chilling

A coconut crust and pretty fluffy filling make this dessert special. When the strawberries ripen here in the Hudson Valley, many churches feature them at festivals.
—Kathryn Anderson, Wallkill, New York

2-1/2 cups flaked coconut
1/3 cup butter, melted
1 quart fresh strawberries, sliced
3/4 cup sugar
1 envelope unflavored gelatin
1/2 cup cold water
2 teaspoons lemon juice
1 cup heavy whipping cream, whipped

In a small bowl, combine coconut and butter. Press onto the bottom and up the sides of a greased 9-in. pie plate. Bake at 300° for 30-35 minutes or until lightly browned (cover edges loosely with foil to prevent overbrowning if necessary). Cool on a wire rack.

In a large bowl, combine strawberries and sugar; let stand for 15 minutes. In a small saucepan, sprinkle gelatin over cold water; let stand for 1 minute. Cook and stir over medium heat until gelatin is dissolved; stir in lemon juice. Stir into strawberry mixture. Cool to room temperature. Fold in whipped cream. Pour into crust. Refrigerate for at least 4 hours before slicing. **Yield:** 6-8 servings.

Berry Pinwheel Cake

(Pictured on page 125)

Prep: 30 min. **Bake:** 10 min. + chilling

Perfect for special meals, this lovely chiffon cake is a nice change from strawberry shortcake. Don't be afraid to try this jelly-roll-style dessert...it's easy to make. Plus, the waxed paper-lined pan helps make cleanup a breeze!
—Becky Ruff, Monona, Iowa

4 egg yolks
2 eggs
1/2 cup sugar
4-1/2 teaspoons water
2 teaspoons vegetable oil
1 teaspoon vanilla extract
1 cup cake flour
1 teaspoon baking powder
1/2 teaspoon salt
Confectioners' sugar
FILLING:
1 cup heavy whipping cream
1 tablespoon sugar
3 tablespoons lemon curd
2 cups chopped fresh strawberries

In a large mixing bowl, beat the egg yolks, eggs and sugar until thick and lemon-colored. Beat in the water, oil and vanilla. Combine flour, baking powder and salt; gradually add to egg mixture. Grease a 15-in. x 10-in. x 1-in. baking pan and line with waxed paper; grease and flour the paper. Spread batter into pan.

Bake at 375° for 10-12 minutes or until the cake springs back when lightly touched. Cool for 5 minutes. Turn cake onto a kitchen towel dusted with confectioners' sugar. Peel off waxed paper. Roll up cake in towel jelly-roll style, starting with a short side. Cool on a wire rack.

In a mixing bowl, beat cream until soft peaks form; add sugar, beating until stiff. Fold in lemon curd; gradually fold in strawberries. Unroll cake; spread filling evenly to within 1/2 in. of edges. Roll up again; dust with confectioners' sugar. Cover and chill for 1 hour before serving. Refrigerate leftovers. **Yield:** 8 servings.

Texas Pecan Pie

Prep: 25 min. **Bake:** 45 min. + cooling

I won a blue ribbon for this pie at the Texas State Fair. In the military for over 20 years, I didn't really start cooking until after I retired. Now I enjoy spending my time in the kitchen. —Pat King, Brownwood, Texas

1 cup all-purpose flour
1/4 teaspoon salt
1/3 cup shortening
3 tablespoons cold water
FILLING:
1-1/4 cups chopped pecans
1 cup plus 1 tablespoon light corn syrup

3 eggs
1/2 cup plus 1 tablespoon sugar
1-1/2 teaspoons vanilla extract
Pinch salt

In a bowl, combine the flour and salt; cut in shortening until crumbly. Gradually add cold water, tossing with a fork until a ball forms. Roll out pastry to fit a 9-in. pie plate. Transfer pastry to pie plate. Trim pastry to 1/2 in. beyond edge of plate; flute edges. Sprinkle with pecans; set aside.

In a small mixing bowl, beat the corn syrup, eggs, sugar, vanilla and salt until well blended. Pour over pecans. Bake at 350° for 45-50 minutes or until a knife inserted near the center comes out clean. Cool on a wire rack. **Yield:** 6-8 servings.

Almond Pear Tart

Prep: 15 min. **Bake:** 20 min. + cooling

I had never seen a "pie without a pan" until my daughter brought back this wonderful recipe from a Rotary Club exchange program in Belgium. —C.B. LaMay
Capitan, New Mexico

Pastry for single-crust pie (9 inches)
3/4 cup plus 2 teaspoons sugar, *divided*
3 tablespoons all-purpose flour
4 cups sliced peeled fresh pears (about 4 medium)
3 tablespoons sliced almonds

Roll out pastry into a 10-in. circle. Place on an ungreased baking sheet. In a bowl, combine 3/4 cup sugar and flour; add pears and toss to coat. Place in center of pastry; spread to within 2 in. of edges. Fold edges up and slightly crimp.

Sprinkle with remaining sugar. Bake at 450° for 15 minutes or until pears are tender. Sprinkle with almonds; bake 5 minutes longer. Cool slightly before cutting into wedges. **Yield:** 8 servings.

Chocolate Lover's Cake

(Pictured at right)

Prep: 30 min. **Bake:** 1-1/4 hours

My aunt often made a sour cream pound cake. I've added chips and the glaze. —Nancy Zimmerman
Cape May Court House, New Jersey

1 cup butter, softened
3 cups sugar
6 eggs
1-1/2 teaspoons vanilla extract
1/2 teaspoon almond extract

2-1/2 cups all-purpose flour
1/2 cup baking cocoa
1/4 teaspoon baking soda
1 cup (8 ounces) sour cream
2 cups (12 ounces) semisweet chocolate chips
GLAZE:
2/3 cup semisweet chocolate chips
1/3 cup heavy whipping cream
1/4 cup butter, cubed
1 cup confectioners' sugar
1/8 to 1/4 teaspoon almond extract
1/4 cup chopped almonds

In a large mixing bowl, cream butter and sugar until light and fluffy, about 5 minutes. Add eggs, one at a time, beating well after each addition. Stir in extracts. Combine the flour, cocoa and baking soda; add to creamed mixture alternately with sour cream. Beat just until combined. Stir in chocolate chips.

Pour into a greased and floured 10-in. fluted tube pan. Bake at 325° for 75-90 minutes or until a toothpick inserted near the center comes out clean. Cool for 10 minutes before removing from pan to a wire rack to cool completely.

Combine the chocolate chips, cream and butter in a saucepan. Cook; stir over low heat until smooth. Cool slightly. Gradually whisk in confectioners' sugar. Stir in extract. Drizzle over cake. Sprinkle with almonds. **Yield:** 12 servings.

Raspberry Cream Torte

(Pictured below)

Prep: 25 min.   **Bake:** 35 min. + cooling

I've always tried to eat low-fat foods, including desserts like this one. It's truly delicious—but there's not too much guilt with the indulgence!—Amy Freitag, Stanford, Illinois

☑ **Uses less fat, sugar or salt. Includes Nutritional Analysis and Diabetic Exchanges.**

- 1 package (16 ounces) angel food cake mix
- 1 carton (12 ounces) frozen whipped topping, thawed
- 1 carton (6 ounces) raspberry yogurt
- 1/3 cup confectioners' sugar
- 1 pint fresh raspberries

Prepare and bake cake according to package directions, using an ungreased 10-in. tube pan. Immediately invert pan onto a wire rack; cool completely, about 1 hour.

In a large bowl, gently combine the whipped topping, yogurt and confectioners' sugar until blended. Run a knife around side of cake and remove from pan. Split cake into thirds horizontally. Place bottom layer on a serving plate; spread with 1 cup topping mixture. Top with second cake layer; spread with 1 cup topping mixture.

Top with remaining cake layer. Frost top and sides of cake with remaining topping mixture. Garnish with raspberries. Refrigerate leftovers. **Yield:** 14 servings.

Nutritional Analysis: 1 slice (prepared with reduced-fat whipped topping and fat-free raspberry yogurt) equals 206 calories, 3 g fat (3 g saturated fat), 1 mg cholesterol, 246 mg sodium, 40 g carbohydrate, 1 g fiber, 4 g protein. **Diabetic Exchanges:** 2 starch, 1/2 fruit.

Cherry-Cream Crumble Pie

(Pictured on page 124)

Prep: 20 min.   **Bake:** 45 min. + cooling

I created this yummy recipe for a cherry pie contest at the San Diego County Fair when I was first married in 1984. It won the blue ribbon.   —Marian Hollingsworth
La Mesa, California

- 1/2 cup sugar
- 3 tablespoons all-purpose flour
- 2 cans (15 ounces *each*) pitted tart cherries, drained
- 1 cup (8 ounces) sour cream
- 1 egg, beaten
- 1/4 teaspoon almond extract
- 1 unbaked pastry shell (9 inches)

TOPPING:
- 1/2 cup quick-cooking oats
- 1/3 cup all-purpose flour
- 1/3 cup packed brown sugar
- 1/4 teaspoon ground cinnamon
- 1/4 cup cold butter
- 1/2 cup chopped pecans

In a large bowl, combine the sugar, flour, cherries, sour cream, egg and extract; stir well. Spoon into the pastry shell. Bake at 400° for 20 minutes.

For topping, combine the oats, flour, brown sugar and cinnamon in a bowl; cut in butter until mixture resembles coarse crumbs. Stir in pecans. Sprinkle over filling. Cover edges of crust to prevent overbrowning. Bake for 25-30 minutes or until topping is lightly browned. Cool on a wire rack for 1 hour. Store in the refrigerator. **Yield:** 8 servings.

Banana Split Brownie Pie

(Pictured on page 124)

Prep: 30 min. + freezing   **Bake:** 30 min. + freezing

I often use Neapolitan in place of three different ice cream flavors to make this luscious dessert.
—Tanna Walker, Salina, Kansas

- 4 ounces German sweet chocolate, chopped
- 1/2 cup butter, cubed
- 3 eggs

1 cup sugar
1/2 teaspoon vanilla extract
1/2 cup all-purpose flour
1-1/3 cups vanilla ice cream
1-2/3 cups chocolate ice cream
1-2/3 cups strawberry ice cream
2 medium firm bananas, sliced
1 cup fresh strawberries, sliced
1/2 to 3/4 cup hot fudge ice cream topping, warmed
1/2 to 3/4 cup strawberry ice cream topping
1/4 to 1/2 cup toffee bits *or* almond brickle chips
Whipping cream and sliced almonds

In a microwave, melt chocolate and butter; stir until smooth. Cool. In a small mixing bowl, beat the eggs, sugar, vanilla and cooled chocolate mixture. Add flour; mix well. Spread into a greased 9-in. springform pan. Bake at 350° for 30-35 minutes or until a toothpick inserted near the center comes out clean. Cool on a wire rack. Cover and freeze until firm.

Using 1/3 cup for each scoop, place four scoops of vanilla ice cream, five scoops of chocolate ice cream and five scoops of strawberry ice cream on a waxed paper-lined baking sheet. Freeze until firm. Place vanilla scoops in center of brownie crust; alternate scoops of chocolate and strawberry around edge. Cover and freeze until firm.

Just before serving, remove sides of pan. Arrange bananas and strawberries over ice cream. Drizzle with hot fudge and strawberry toppings. Sprinkle with toffee bits. Garnish with whipped cream and almonds. **Yield:** 10 servings.

Chocolate Carrot Cake

(Pictured above right)

Prep: 35 min. **Bake:** 25 min. + cooling

Finely shredding the carrots gives this cake an extra-nice texture. The walnuts sprinkled on top add crunch.
—Pamela Brown, Williamsburg, Michigan

2 cups all-purpose flour
2 cups sugar
1/2 cup baking cocoa
1 teaspoon baking soda
1/2 teaspoon salt
4 eggs
1-1/4 cups vegetable oil
3 cups finely shredded carrots
FROSTING:
1 package (8 ounces) cream cheese, softened
1/2 cup butter, softened

3-3/4 cups confectioners' sugar
1/4 cup baking cocoa
3 teaspoons vanilla extract
1/4 cup chopped walnuts
1/4 cup semisweet chocolate chips

Line two 9-in. round baking pans with waxed paper; grease the paper and set aside. In a large mixing bowl, combine the flour, sugar, cocoa, baking soda and salt. Add the eggs, oil and carrots; beat until combined. Pour into prepared pans.

Bake at 350° for 25-30 minutes or until a toothpick inserted near the center comes out clean. Cool for 10 minutes before removing from pans to wire racks to cool completely.

For frosting, in a large mixing bowl, beat cream cheese and butter until fluffy. Beat in the confectioners' sugar, cocoa and vanilla until smooth. Place one cake layer on a serving plate; spread with half of the frosting. Repeat layers. Sprinkle with nuts and chocolate chips. **Yield:** 12-16 servings.

Choosing Carrots

Select smooth, firm and well-shaped carrots that are bright orange to orange-red. Green shoots on trimmed carrots or yellow tips may be signs of age and poor flavor.

Carrots can be kept in the refrigerator 3 weeks or more. Carrots that are limp have lost their moisture.

Frozen Strawberry Pie

(Pictured below)

Prep: 25 min. + freezing

This recipe makes two attractive pies using store-bought chocolate crumb crusts. I work full-time, so I like the fact that this yummy pie can be made ahead. I serve each slice with a dollop of whipped cream, a strawberry and chocolate curls.
— *Awynne Thurstenson*
Siloam Springs, Arkansas

> 1 package (8 ounces) cream cheese, softened
> 1 cup sugar
> 1 teaspoon vanilla extract
> 4 cups chopped fresh strawberries
> 1 carton (12 ounces) frozen whipped topping, thawed
> 1/2 cup chopped pecans, toasted
> 2 chocolate crumb crusts (9 inches)

In a large mixing bowl, beat the cream cheese, sugar and vanilla until smooth. Beat in the strawberries. Fold in the whipped topping and pecans. Pour into crusts. Cover and freeze for 3-4 hours or until firm. Remove from the freezer 15-20 minutes before serving. **Yield:** 2 pies (6 servings each).

Layered Carrot Cake

Prep: 50 min.   **Bake:** 30 min. + cooling

I never liked carrot cake until I tried this one. The rich, moist cake with orange-flavored frosting is now a family tradition for special occasions. Sometimes I add cranberries with the raisins. —*Anna Morgan, Eatonville, Washington*

> 1 package (18-1/4 ounces) yellow cake mix
> 1 package (3.4 ounces) instant vanilla pudding mix
> 2 teaspoons ground cinnamon
> 4 eggs
> 2/3 cup orange juice
> 1/2 cup vegetable oil
> 3 cups grated carrots
> 1/2 cup raisins
> 1/2 cup chopped walnuts

ORANGE CREAM CHEESE FROSTING:
> 1 package (8 ounces) cream cheese, softened
> 1/2 cup butter, softened
> 3 cups confectioners' sugar
> 1 to 2 tablespoons orange juice
> 1 tablespoon grated orange peel

In a large mixing bowl, combine cake mix, pudding mix and cinnamon. Whisk the eggs, orange juice and oil; add to dry ingredients. Beat until well blended. Stir in the carrots, raisins and nuts (batter will be thick).

Pour batter into two greased and floured 9-in. round baking pans. Bake at 350° for 30-35 minutes or until a toothpick inserted near the center comes out clean. Cool for 10 minutes before removing from pans to wire racks to cool completely.

For frosting, in a small mixing bowl, beat the cream cheese and butter until fluffy. Add the confectioners' sugar, orange juice and orange peel; beat until well blended. Spread frosting between layers and over top and sides of cake. Store in the refrigerator. **Yield:** 12-14 servings.

Blueberry Angel Cupcakes

(Pictured above right)

Prep: 15 min. + standing   **Bake:** 15 min. + cooling

Like angel food cake, these yummy cupcakes don't last long at my house. They're so light and airy that they melt in your mouth. —*Kathy Kittell, Lenexa, Kansas*

✓ **Uses less fat, sugar or salt. Includes Nutritional Analysis and Diabetic Exchanges.**

> 11 egg whites
> 1 cup plus 2 tablespoons cake flour
> 1-1/2 cups sugar, *divided*
> 1-1/4 teaspoons cream of tartar
> 1/2 teaspoon salt
> 1 teaspoon vanilla extract
> 1 teaspoon grated lemon peel
> 1-1/2 cups fresh *or* frozen blueberries

GLAZE:
> 1 cup confectioners' sugar
> 3 tablespoons lemon juice

2 eggs
1 teaspoon vanilla extract
2 cups all-purpose flour
3 tablespoons plus 1-1/2 teaspoons baking cocoa
1 teaspoon baking soda
1/2 cup buttermilk
1 cup water
1/2 cup vegetable oil

FILLING:
2 packages (8 ounces *each*) cream cheese, softened
2/3 cup sugar
1/4 cup heavy whipping cream
1/4 teaspoon almond extract
1 can (21 ounces) cherry pie filling, *divided*

In a large mixing bowl, cream butter and sugar. Add eggs, one at a time, beating well after each addition. Beat in vanilla. Combine the flour, cocoa and baking soda; add to creamed mixture alternately with buttermilk. Beat in water and oil until smooth.

Pour into two greased and floured 9-in. heart-shaped baking pans. Bake at 350° for 20-25 minutes or until a toothpick inserted near the center comes out clean. Cool for 10 minutes before removing from pans to wire racks to cool completely.

In a mixing bowl, beat cream cheese and sugar until fluffy. Beat in cream and extract. Place one cake on a serving plate; spread with half of cream cheese mixture. Refrigerate for 10 minutes. Top with 1 cup pie filling and second cake; spread with remaining cream cheese mixture. Make a heart-shaped indentation in center of cake; fill with remaining pie filling. Refrigerate until serving. **Yield:** 12 servings.

Place egg whites in a large mixing bowl; let stand at room temperature for 30 minutes. Sift together flour and 1/2 cup sugar three times; set aside.

Beat egg whites until foamy. Add cream of tartar and salt; beat until soft peaks form. Add vanilla and lemon peel. Gradually beat in the remaining sugar, about 2 tablespoons at a time, beating well after each addition; beat until stiff glossy peaks form. Gradually fold in flour mixture, about 1/2 cup at a time. Fold in blueberries.

Fill paper-lined muffin cups three-fourths full. Bake at 375° for 14-17 minutes or until cupcakes spring back when lightly touched. Immediately remove from pans to wire racks to cool completely.

In a small bowl, whisk confectioners' sugar and lemon juice until smooth. Brush over cupcakes. Let stand until set. **Yield:** 2-1/2 dozen.

Nutritional Analysis: 1 cupcake equals 76 calories, trace fat (trace saturated fat), 0 cholesterol, 60 mg sodium, 18 g carbohydrate, trace fiber, 2 g protein. **Diabetic Exchange:** 1 starch.

Editor's Note: If using frozen blueberries, do not thaw before adding to the batter.

My Truelove Cake

(Pictured at right)

Prep: 30 min.   **Bake:** 20 min. + cooling

Like my mother and my grandmother, I have special recipes for every occasion. For Valentine's Day—one of my favorite holidays—this beautiful cake is an outstanding treat. —Beverly Coyde, Gasport, New York

1/2 cup butter, softened
2 cups sugar

Maple Pumpkin Torte

(Pictured below)

Prep: 20 min. **Bake:** 20 min. + cooling

This dessert always gets rave reviews. When people ask where I bought the cake, I smile and say that it was made with love in my own kitchen. —Dianna Wara
Washington, Illinois

- 1 package (18-1/2 ounces) white cake mix
- 3/4 cup all-purpose flour, *divided*
- 1 teaspoon ground cinnamon
- 1 cup water
- 3/4 cup canned pumpkin
- 1/3 cup vegetable oil
- 2 eggs
- 2 tablespoons brown sugar
- 1-1/3 cups vanilla *or* white chips
- 1/4 cup chopped pecans

FROSTING:
- 1 cup butter-flavored shortening
- 1 package (2 pounds) confectioners' sugar
- 3/4 cup milk
- 2 teaspoons vanilla extract
- 1 to 1-1/2 teaspoons maple flavoring

Grease three 9-in. round baking pans; line with waxed paper. Grease the paper and set aside. In a large mixing bowl, combine the cake mix, 1/2 cup flour and cinnamon. Add the water, pumpkin, oil and eggs; beat well.

Transfer a third of the batter to a small mixing bowl; beat in brown sugar and remaining flour. Stir in chips and pecans. Pour into one prepared pan. Divide the plain batter between the two remaining pans.

Bake at 350° for 20-30 minutes or until a toothpick inserted near the center comes out clean. Cool for 10 minutes before removing from pans to wire racks to cool completely.

For frosting, in a large mixing bowl, cream shortening and confectioners' sugar. Beat in the milk, vanilla and maple flavoring. Place one plain cake on a serving platter; spread with frosting. Top with the pumpkin-nut cake; frost. Top with remaining cake; spread remaining frosting over top and sides of cake. **Yield:** 12-14 servings.

No-Bake Cheesecake Pie

Prep: 20 min. + chilling

You won't miss the traditional graham cracker crust with this fluffy lemon dessert. The texture is wonderful and the citrus taste is great...plus it's easy as pie to prepare. —Normajo Reynolds, Goldthwaite, Texas

✓ **Uses less fat, sugar or salt. Includes Nutritional Analysis and Diabetic Exchanges.**

- 2 tablespoons graham cracker crumbs, *divided*
- 1 package (.3 ounce) sugar-free lemon gelatin
- 2/3 cup boiling water
- 1 package (8 ounces) reduced-fat cream cheese, cubed
- 1 cup 1% cottage cheese
- 2 cups reduced-fat whipped topping

Coat the bottom and sides of a 9-in. pie plate with nonstick cooking spray. Sprinkle with 1 tablespoon cracker crumbs; set aside.

In a small bowl, dissolve gelatin in boiling water; cool slightly. Pour into a blender; add cream cheese and cottage cheese. Cover and process until smooth. Transfer to a large bowl. Fold in whipped topping. Pour into prepared pie plate. Sprinkle with remaining cracker crumbs. Cover and refrigerate until set. **Yield:** 8 servings.

Nutritional Analysis: 1 piece equals 131 calories, 7 g fat (5 g saturated fat), 17 mg cholesterol, 207 mg sodium, 8 g carbohydrate, trace fiber, 7 g protein. **Diabetic Exchanges:** 1-1/2 fat, 1/2 fat-free milk.

Berry-Glazed Chocolate Cake

(Pictured on page 124)

Prep: 15 min. **Bake:** 45 min. + cooling

This recipe was given to me by my niece and is wickedly delicious! It is really quite easy to prepare. —Betty Checkett, St. Louis, Missouri

- 1 package (18-1/4 ounces) devil's food cake mix
- 1 package (3.9 ounces) instant chocolate pudding mix

4 eggs
3/4 cup water
1/2 cup apple juice
1/2 cup vegetable oil
1 teaspoon rum extract
1 cup (6 ounces) semisweet chocolate chips
RASPBERRY GLAZE:
1/4 cup seedless raspberry jam
2 tablespoons apple juice
1/2 teaspoon rum extract
CHOCOLATE ICING:
2 tablespoons baking cocoa
1/4 cup heavy whipping cream
2 tablespoons butter, melted
1 cup confectioners' sugar
1 teaspoon vanilla extract

In a large mixing bowl, combine the first seven ingredients; beat on low speed for 30 seconds. Beat on medium for 2 minutes. Stir in chocolate chips. Pour into a greased and floured 10-in. fluted tube pan. Bake at 350° for 45-50 minutes or until a toothpick comes out clean. Cool for 10 minutes before removing from pan to a wire rack to cool completely.

In a small saucepan, combine the glaze ingredients. Cook and stir over low heat until smooth. Brush over cake. Let stand for 10 minutes or until set.

Place cocoa in a small saucepan. Stir in cream and butter until smooth. Cook and stir over low heat for 2 minutes or until thickened. Remove from heat; stir in confectioners' sugar and vanilla until smooth. Cool slightly; drizzle over cake. Let stand until set. **Yield:** 12 servings.

for 2 minutes or until thickened. Cool. Spread over cream cheese layer. Refrigerate until serving. **Yield:** 6-8 servings.

Saucy Cranberry Cake

(Pictured above)

Prep: 15 min. **Bake:** 55 min.

The fresh cranberries in this dessert add a little zing! I ask my mom to bake this cake for me every year on my birthday. I also love to make it at Christmastime.
—Lisa Seehafer, Appleton, Wisconsin

3 tablespoons butter, softened
1 cup sugar
1 egg
2 cups all-purpose flour
1 teaspoon salt
1 teaspoon baking powder
1 cup milk
2 cups fresh *or* frozen cranberries, thawed
CARAMEL BUTTER SAUCE:
1/2 cup butter
1 cup packed brown sugar
1 cup heavy whipping cream

In a small mixing bowl, beat butter and sugar until crumbly, about 2 minutes. Beat in egg. Combine the flour, salt and baking powder; add to butter mixture alternately with milk. Fold in cranberries. Pour into a greased 9-in. square baking dish. Bake at 350° for 55-60 minutes or until a toothpick inserted near the center comes out clean.

In a small saucepan, melt butter; stir in brown sugar and cream. Bring to a boil, stirring constantly. Serve over warm cake. **Yield:** 12 servings.

Cream Cheese Blueberry Pie

Prep: 20 min. + cooling

"Yum!" is what I always hear when people bite into this luscious blueberry pie. —*Lisieux Bauman*
Cheektowaga, New York

4 ounces cream cheese, softened
1/2 cup confectioners' sugar
1/2 cup heavy whipping cream, whipped
1 pastry shell (9 inches), baked
2/3 cup sugar
1/4 cup cornstarch
1/2 cup water
1/4 cup lemon juice
3 cups fresh *or* frozen blueberries

In a small mixing bowl, beat cream cheese and confectioners' sugar until smooth. Fold in whipped cream. Spread into pastry shell.

In a large saucepan, combine the sugar, cornstarch, water and lemon juice until smooth; stir in blueberries. Bring to a boil over medium heat; cook and stir

Butterfly Cupcakes

(Pictured below)

Prep: 30 min.   **Bake:** 20 min. + cooling

Dessert takes wing with this fun recipe. I simply cut the cupcake tops to resemble butterflies and decorate.
—*Joyce Turley, Slaughters, Kentucky*

1 package (18-1/4 ounces) chocolate cake mix
1 cup cold milk
1 package (3.9 ounces) instant chocolate pudding mix
1 carton (8 ounces) frozen whipped topping, thawed
Pastel sprinkles
Black shoestring licorice, cut into 2-inch pieces

Prepare and bake cake mix according to package directions for cupcakes; cool completely. Slice off the top fourth of each cupcake; cut slices in half. Set aside.

In a bowl, whisk the milk and pudding mix for 2 minutes; let stand for 2 minutes or until soft-set. Fold in whipped topping. Spoon 2 tablespoons pudding mixture onto each cupcake.

For wings, place two reserved cupcake halves, rounded edges together, in pudding mixture. Gently press sprinkles into wings (cupcakes should be moist enough for candy to stick). For antennae, insert two licorice pieces into each cupcake. **Yield:** 2 dozen.

Black Pepper Pound Cake

(Pictured on page 125)

Prep: 20 min.   **Bake:** 70 min. + cooling

I once had a recipe for this cake from the early 1900s but lost it, so I adapted my grandma's pound cake recipe.
—*Sue Gronholz, Beaver Dam, Wisconsin*

1 cup butter, softened
3 cups sugar
3 teaspoons coarsely ground pepper
2 teaspoons lemon extract
6 eggs
3 cups all-purpose flour
1 cup heavy whipping cream
Confectioners' sugar, optional

In a large mixing bowl, cream the butter and sugar. Beat in pepper and extract. Add eggs, one at a time, beating very well after each addition. Add flour alternately with cream; mix well.

Pour into a greased and floured 10-in. fluted tube pan. Bake at 325° for 70-75 minutes or until a toothpick inserted near the center comes out clean. Cool for 10 minutes before removing from pan to a wire rack to cool completely. Dust with the confectioners' sugar if desired. **Yield:** 16 servings.

Peach-Topped Cake

Prep: 20 min. + chilling   **Bake:** 10 min. + chilling

This bright-orange dessert is perfect for summer menus or anytime. —*Chris Lafser, Richmond, Virginia*

✓ **Uses less fat, sugar or salt. Includes Nutritional Analysis and Diabetic Exchanges.**

2 tablespoons butter, softened
1/2 cup sugar
1 egg
1/2 teaspoon vanilla extract
3/4 cup cake flour
3/4 teaspoon baking powder
1/4 teaspoon salt
1/4 cup fat-free milk
TOPPING:
1 envelope unflavored gelatin
1-3/4 cups cold water, *divided*
1/4 cup sugar
1 envelope sugar-free orange soft drink mix
2 medium ripe peaches, thinly sliced *or* 1 can (15 ounces) sliced peaches
1/2 cup reduced-fat whipped topping

In a small mixing bowl, beat butter and sugar until crumbly. Beat in egg and vanilla. Combine flour, baking powder and salt; add to sugar mixture alternately with milk. Spread into a 9-in. springform pan coated with nonstick cooking spray. Bake at 350° for 10-15 minutes or until a toothpick inserted near center comes out clean. Cool on a wire rack.

Austrian Hazelnut Torte

(Pictured below)

Prep: 20 min. **Bake:** 25 min. + cooling

This unusual but delicious flourless torte has a distinctive nutty flavor with a hint of orange. Its luscious cream filling and topping is accented with citrus.
—Isobel Hudson, Pembroke, Ontario

   6 **eggs,** *separated*
   1 **cup sugar**
   1 **cup finely chopped hazelnuts, toasted**
3/4 **cup dry bread crumbs**
   2 **tablespoons orange juice**
1/8 **teaspoon salt**
   2 **cups heavy whipping cream, whipped**
Additional hazelnuts, halved, optional

In a large mixing bowl, beat egg yolks and sugar until light lemon-colored. Stir in the chopped hazelnuts, bread crumbs and orange juice. In another mixing bowl, beat egg whites and salt until stiff peaks form; fold into hazelnut mixture.

Spoon into a greased 9-in. springform pan. Bake at 350° for 25-30 minutes or until a toothpick inserted near the center comes out clean. Cool for 10 minutes before removing from the pan to a wire rack to cool completely.

Split the cake into two layers. Spread half of the whipped cream over one layer; top with the remaining layer and whipped cream. Garnish with halved hazelnuts if desired. **Yield:** 10-12 servings.

   Editor's Note: This recipe does not use flour.

In a small saucepan, sprinkle gelatin over 1/2 cup cold water. Let stand for 1 minute. Stir in sugar and soft drink mix; cook and stir over low heat until gelatin is dissolved. Transfer to a large bowl; stir in remaining cold water. Refrigerate until partially set, about 1-1/2 hours.

Line outside of springform pan with foil. Arrange peaches over top of cake. Pour gelatin over the peaches. Chill overnight. Just before serving, remove the foil and sides of pan. Garnish with whipped topping. Refrigerate leftovers. **Yield:** 12 servings.

   Nutritional Analysis: 1 piece equals 121 calories, 3 g fat (2 g saturated fat), 23 mg cholesterol, 103 mg sodium, 22 g carbohydrate, trace fiber, 2 g protein. **Diabetic Exchanges:** 1 fruit, 1/2 starch, 1/2 fat.

Almond-Fudge Custard Pie

(Pictured above)

Prep: 15 min. **Bake:** 30 min. + cooling

Rich chocolate and a hint of almond team up in this creamy pie. —Marie Hattrup, The Dalles, Oregon

3/4 **cup sugar**
1/3 **cup baking cocoa**
1/8 **teaspoon salt**
   3 **eggs**
1-1/2 **cups half-and-half cream**
3/4 **teaspoon almond extract**
   1 **pastry shell (9 inches), baked**
Whipped cream
Toasted sliced almonds

In a bowl, combine the sugar, cocoa and salt. In another bowl, beat eggs, cream and extract just until combined. Stir into dry ingredients until blended. Carefully pour into pastry shell.

Bake at 350° for 30-35 minutes or until a knife inserted near the center comes out clean. Cool on a wire rack. Garnish with whipped cream and almonds. Store in the refrigerator. **Yield:** 6-8 servings.

Just Desserts

You might want to eat dessert first after seeing these scrumptious crisps and cobblers, layered trifles, luscious cheesecakes and much more!

SAVE ROOM FOR THEM. Clockwise from upper left: Cinnamon Roll Cherry Cobbler (p. 138), Pumpkin Freeze with Mincemeat (p. 148), Caramel Apple Crunch (p. 140), Banana Cream Eclairs (p. 142) and Two-Tone Cheesecake (p. 144).

Ladyfinger Cheesecake

(Pictured below)

Prep: 25 min. + chilling

My mom got this recipe from a friend, and after we tried it, we promised we'd never make cheesecake any other way. —Marcia Savery, New Bedford, Massachusetts

- 4-1/2 **cups sliced fresh strawberries (about 2 pounds)**
- 2 **tablespoons plus 2 cups sugar, *divided***
- 3 **packages (3 ounces *each*) ladyfingers, split**
- 4 **packages (8 ounces *each*) cream cheese, softened**
- 2 **cups heavy whipping cream**

In a bowl, combine strawberries and 2 tablespoons sugar. Cover; refrigerate for at least 1 hour. Meanwhile, arrange 25 split ladyfingers around the edges of a lightly greased 10-in. springform pan. Place 25 more on the bottom; set aside.

In a large mixing bowl, beat cream cheese until smooth. Gradually beat in the remaining sugar. In a large bowl, beat cream until stiff peaks form. Gradually fold into cream cheese mixture.

Spoon half of the cream cheese mixture into prepared pan. Spread with half of strawberry mixture to within 1 in. of edges. Cover; refrigerate remaining strawberry mixture. Arrange remaining ladyfingers over top. Spoon remaining cream cheese mixture over ladyfingers. Cover; refrigerate overnight. Remove sides of pan. Serve with reserved strawberry mixture. **Yield:** 14 servings.

Cinnamon Roll Cherry Cobbler

(Pictured on page 136)

Prep: 30 min. **Bake:** 25 min. + cooling

I hadn't had this dessert in years, so when I found my mother's recipe, I had to make it to see if it was as good as I remembered…and it was! —Betty Zorn, Eagle, Idaho

- 1 **can (14-1/2 ounces) pitted tart cherries**
- 1/2 **cup sugar**
- 2 **tablespoons cornstarch**
- 1/2 **cup water**
- 3 **tablespoons red-hot candies**

CINNAMON ROLL TOPPING:
- 1-1/2 **cups all-purpose flour**
- 6 **tablespoons brown sugar, *divided***
- 2 **teaspoons baking powder**
- 1/2 **teaspoon salt**
- 1/4 **cup shortening**
- 1 **egg, lightly beaten**
- 1/4 **cup milk**
- 1 **tablespoon butter, softened**
- 1/3 **cup finely chopped pecans**
- 1/2 **teaspoon ground cinnamon**

LEMON GLAZE:
- 1/2 **cup confectioners' sugar**
- 1 **tablespoon lemon juice**

Drain cherries, reserving juice; set cherries aside. In a small saucepan, combine sugar, cornstarch, water and reserved juice until smooth. Stir in red-hot candies. Bring to a boil, stirring constantly; cook 1-2 minutes longer or until thick and bubbly and red-hot candies are melted. Stir in cherries; heat through. Transfer to a greased 8-in. square baking dish.

In a bowl, combine flour, 3 tablespoons brown sugar, baking powder and salt. Cut in shortening until crumbly. Combine egg and milk; stir into crumb mixture until blended. Turn onto a lightly floured surface; knead 3-4 times. Roll into a 14-in. x 10-in. rectangle. Spread with butter; sprinkle with pecans. Combine cinnamon and remaining brown sugar; sprinkle over top.

Roll up jelly-roll style, starting with a short side. Cut into eight slices; place cut side down over cherry filling. Bake at 400° for 25-30 minutes or until golden brown. Cool for 10 minutes. Combine glaze ingredients; drizzle over cobbler. **Yield:** 8 servings.

Cran-Apple Crisp

(Pictured above right)

Prep: 30 min. **Bake:** 35 min. + cooling

An easy-to-make eggnog sauce gives this crunchy oat-topped fruit crisp a distinctive flavor. The apples and cranberries make it a natural for autumn celebrations and hol-

iday meals. We like it so much though that I serve it year-round. —Mary Lou Timpson, Centennial Park, Arizona

- **2 snack-size cups (4 ounces *each*) vanilla pudding**
- **1 cup eggnog**
- **3/4 cup sugar**
- **2 tablespoons all-purpose flour**
- **5 cups thinly sliced peeled tart apples**
- **2 cups fresh *or* frozen cranberries, thawed**

TOPPING:
- **1 cup quick-cooking oats**
- **3/4 cup packed brown sugar**
- **2/3 cup all-purpose flour**
- **1/2 teaspoon ground cinnamon**
- **1/2 cup cold butter**

In a small bowl, combine the pudding and eggnog until blended; cover and refrigerate until serving. In a large bowl, combine the sugar and flour. Add apples and cranberries; toss to coat. Transfer to an ungreased 13-in. x 9-in. x 2-in. baking dish.

In a large bowl, combine oats, brown sugar, flour and cinnamon; cut in butter until crumbly. Sprinkle over fruit mixture. Bake at 375° for 35-40 minutes or until filling is bubbly and topping is golden brown. Cool for 10 minutes. Serve with eggnog sauce. **Yield:** 12-14 servings.

Editor's Note: This recipe was tested with commercially prepared eggnog.

Cherry Chocolate Cups

(Pictured at right)

Prep: 30 min. + chilling

These outstanding treats taste like you spent hours working on them. —Michelle Smith, Sykesville, Maryland

- **2-1/2 squares (2-1/2 ounces) semisweet chocolate**
- **2 teaspoons shortening, *divided***
- **2-1/2 squares (2-1/2 ounces) white baking chocolate**
- **1/2 cup dried cherries, chopped**
- **1/2 cup boiling water**
- **1/4 teaspoon almond extract**
- **1 package (8 ounces) cream cheese, softened**
- **3 tablespoons confectioners' sugar**
- **1 drop red food coloring**
- **1/4 teaspoon grated lemon peel**

In a microwave, melt semisweet chocolate and 1 teaspoon shortening. Brush evenly on the inside of 12 paper or foil miniature muffin cup liners. Repeat with white baking chocolate and remaining shortening. Chill until firm, about 25 minutes. Meanwhile, in a bowl, combine cherries, water and extract; let stand for 5 minutes. Drain, reserving liquid.

In a small mixing bowl, combine cream cheese, confectioners' sugar, food coloring, lemon peel and 2 tablespoons reserved cherry liquid; beat on medium-low speed for 2 minutes or until smooth. Fold in cherries.

Cut a small hole in the corner of a pastry or plastic bag; insert a tip. Fill with cherry mixture. Pipe into chocolate cups. Refrigerate for 1 hour or until firm. Carefully remove from liners. **Yield:** 2 dozen.

greased 13-in. x 9-in. x 2-in. dish with bottom pastry halves, cut side up; spread with 3-1/2 cups strawberry cream. Top with 1 cup of sliced berries. Cover with pastry tops, cut side down.

Spread with remaining strawberry cream. Sprinkle with remaining berries. Drizzle with strawberry syrup if desired. Refrigerate leftovers. **Yield:** 9 servings.

Caramel Apple Crunch

(Pictured on page 136)

Prep: 25 min.   **Bake:** 45 min. + cooling

I combined ingredients from various apple crisp recipes to create this one. I like to use tart apples because they provide a balance to the sweetness of the caramels.
—*Melissa Williams, Peoria, Illinois*

> 8 **cups sliced peeled tart apples**
> 33 **caramels,** *divided*
> 2 **tablespoons plus 2 teaspoons milk,** *divided*
> 3/4 **cup all-purpose flour**
> 3/4 **cup quick-cooking oats**
> 3/4 **cup packed brown sugar**
> 1/2 **cup chopped walnuts**
> 1/8 **teaspoon salt**
>
> **Dash ground cinnamon**
> 1/2 **cup cold butter**
>
> **Vanilla ice cream, optional**

Place apples in a greased 13-in. x 9-in. x 2-in. baking dish. In a heavy saucepan or microwave, melt 25 caramels with 2 tablespoons milk, stirring often; drizzle over apples. In a bowl, combine flour, oats, brown sugar, walnuts, salt and cinnamon; cut in butter until mixture resembles coarse crumbs. Sprinkle over apples.

Bake at 375° for 45-50 minutes or until golden brown. Cool for 10 minutes. Meanwhile, in a heavy saucepan or microwave, melt remaining caramels with remaining milk, stirring often until smooth. Drizzle over dessert and ice cream if desired. **Yield:** 12-16 servings.

Carrot Cheesecake

(Pictured at right)

Prep: 25 min.   **Bake:** 65 min. + chilling

My family loves this creamy make-ahead dessert. Unlike traditional cheesecake, I sprinkle a streusel topping over the filling. It needs to be refrigerated overnight but is well worth the wait. —*Misty Wellman, Scottsdale, Arizona*

> 2 **cups graham cracker crumbs**
> 1/4 **cup sugar**
> 1/3 **cup butter, melted**

Strawberry Puff Pastry Dessert

(Pictured above)

Prep: 30 min.   **Bake:** 15 min. + cooling

My failed attempt to make a triple-layer strawberry malt mousse resulted in this scrumptious dessert. I don't use puff pastry often, but it was simple to work with. My husband declared it one of the best desserts ever.
—*Anna Ginsberg, Austin, Texas*

> 1 **package (17.3 ounces) frozen puff pastry**
> 5 **cups sliced fresh strawberries,** *divided*
> 6 **squares (1 ounce** *each***) white baking chocolate**
> 1 **package (8 ounces) cream cheese, softened**
> 1 **teaspoon vanilla extract**
> 1 **cup confectioners' sugar**
> 1/3 **cup malted milk powder**
> 2 **cups heavy whipping cream, whipped**
>
> **Strawberry syrup, optional**

Thaw one puff pastry sheet (save remaining sheet for another use). Unfold pastry; cut lengthwise into three 3-in.-wide strips. Cut each strip into thirds, making nine squares. Place 1 in. apart on ungreased baking sheets. Bake at 400° for 11-13 minutes or until golden brown. Remove to wire racks to cool.

Place 2-1/2 cups strawberries in a blender; cover and puree. Set aside. In a large microwave-safe mixing bowl, melt the white chocolate; cool slightly. Add cream cheese and vanilla; beat until smooth. Beat in the confectioners' sugar and malted milk powder until smooth. Stir in the puree. Fold in whipped cream.

Split pastry squares in half horizontally. Line an un-

FILLING:
- 3 packages (8 ounces *each*) cream cheese, softened
- 1-1/4 cups sugar
- 2 tablespoons brown sugar
- 3 eggs, lightly beaten
- 1/4 cup heavy whipping cream
- 2 tablespoons cornstarch
- 1 tablespoon sour cream
- 1-1/2 teaspoons vanilla extract
- 1 teaspoon lemon juice
- 1/2 teaspoon ground cinnamon
- 1-1/3 cups chopped carrots, cooked and pureed

TOPPING:
- 1 cup graham cracker crumbs
- 2 tablespoons brown sugar
- 1-1/2 teaspoons ground cinnamon
- 1/4 cup butter, melted

In a small bowl, combine crumbs and sugar; stir in butter. Press onto the bottom and 2 in. up the sides of a greased 9-in. springform pan. Place on a baking sheet. Bake at 350° for 6-8 minutes. Cool on a wire rack.

In a large mixing bowl, beat cream cheese and sugars until smooth. Add eggs; beat on low speed just until combined. Stir in cream, cornstarch, sour cream, vanilla, lemon juice and cinnamon. Fold in carrots.

Pour into crust. Place pan on a double thickness of heavy-duty foil (about 16 in. square). Securely wrap foil around pan. Place in a larger baking pan. Add 1 in. of hot water to larger pan. Bake at 350° for 55-60 minutes until center is just set.

Combine topping ingredients; sprinkle over filling. Bake 7-10 minutes longer. Remove pan from water bath. Cool on a wire rack for 10 minutes. Carefully run a knife around edge of pan to loosen; cool 1 hour longer. Refrigerate overnight. Remove sides of pan. **Yield:** 10-12 servings.

Frozen Orange Delight

(Pictured above)

Prep: 15 min. + freezing

Knowing that a diabetic friend would be attending our cookout, I concocted this sorbet-like dessert. I've also made it with sugar-free cherry and raspberry gelatin.
—Diane Daniel, Birmingham, Alabama

✓ **Uses less fat, sugar or salt. Includes Nutritional Analysis and Diabetic Exchanges.**

- 1 package (.3 ounce) sugar-free orange gelatin
- 1/2 cup boiling water
- 1-1/2 cups unsweetened pineapple juice, chilled
- 2 cups reduced-fat whipped topping

In a bowl, dissolve gelatin in boiling water. Stir in pineapple juice. Refrigerate for 20-30 minutes or until slightly thickened.

Fold in whipped topping. Fill cylinder of ice cream freezer two-thirds full; freeze according to manufacturer's directions. Allow to ripen in ice cream freezer or firm up in the refrigerator freezer for 2-4 hours before serving. **Yield:** 4 servings (1 quart).

Nutritional Analysis: 1 cup equals 140 calories, 4 g fat (4 g saturated fat), 0 cholesterol, 6 mg sodium, 23 g carbohydrate, trace fiber, trace protein. **Diabetic Exchanges:** 1-1/2 fruit, 1 fat.

Banana Cream Eclairs

(Pictured on page 136)

Prep: 40 min.   **Bake:** 25 min. + cooling

To surprise my banana-loving family, I made this dessert for a reunion, where it stood out among the usual fare. These special treats are both something to look at and mouth-watering delicious. —Ruby Williams, Bogalusa, Louisiana

    1 cup water
  1/2 cup butter, cubed
  1/4 cup sugar
  1/2 teaspoon salt
    1 cup all-purpose flour
    4 eggs
FILLING:
2-1/2 cups heavy whipping cream
    3 tablespoons sugar
    1 teaspoon vanilla extract
    3 to 4 medium firm bananas
GLAZE:
  1/2 cup confectioners' sugar
    2 tablespoons baking cocoa
    2 tablespoons butter, melted
    1 teaspoon vanilla extract
    1 to 2 tablespoons boiling water
  1/2 cup finely chopped pecans

In a large saucepan, bring the water, butter, sugar and salt to a boil. Add flour all at once and stir until a smooth ball forms. Remove from the heat; let stand for 5 minutes. Add eggs, one at a time, beating well after each addition. Continue beating until dough is smooth and shiny.

Insert a 3/4-in. round tip into a pastry bag; add dough. Pipe 3-in. strips about 3 in. apart on a greased baking sheet. Bake at 400° for 25-30 minutes or until golden brown. Remove to wire racks. Immediately split puffs open; remove tops and set aside. Discard soft dough from inside. Cool puffs.

In a large mixing bowl, beat cream until it begins to thicken. Add sugar and vanilla; beat until stiff peaks form. In another bowl, mash bananas; gently fold in whipped cream. Pipe or spoon into eclairs.

In a small bowl, combine the confectioners' sugar, cocoa, butter and vanilla. Add enough water to make a thin glaze. Spread over eclairs. Sprinkle with pecans. Serve immediately. Refrigerate leftovers. **Yield:** 16 servings.

Rosemary Citrus Sorbet

(Pictured below left)

Prep: 10 min.   **Freeze:** 1-3/4 hours

*This pretty pink dessert bursts with the fresh flavors of grapefruit, lime and rosemary.   —Becky Baird
Salt Lake City, Utah*

  1/2 cup sugar
  1/2 cup water
1-1/2 teaspoons packed fresh rosemary leaves
  1/2 cup pink grapefruit juice
    1 teaspoon lime juice

In a small saucepan, bring the sugar, water and rosemary to a boil. Remove from the heat; let stand for 2 minutes. Strain and discard rosemary. Stir in the grapefruit juice and lime juice.

Pour into a shallow 1-qt. dish; cover and freeze for 45 minutes or until edges begin to firm. Stir and return to freezer. Repeat every 30 minutes or until slushy, about 1 hour. **Yield:** 2 servings.

Double-Berry Crisp

(Pictured above right)

Prep: 20 min.   **Bake:** 25 min. + cooling

*This sweet-tart treat has an extra-crispy topping, thanks to the addition of cornflakes. Orange juice and orange peel accent the blueberry-raspberry flavor. —Bernadette Beaton
Goose River, Prince Edward Island*

    1 cup sugar
  1/4 cup cornstarch
    2 tablespoons orange juice
    1 teaspoon grated orange peel

2 cups fresh *or* frozen raspberries
2 cups fresh *or* frozen blueberries
1 cup old-fashioned oats
1/2 cup cornflakes
1/2 cup packed brown sugar
1/2 teaspoon ground cinnamon
1/4 teaspoon salt
1/4 cup butter, melted

In a saucepan, combine sugar, cornstarch, orange juice, orange peel and berries until blended. Bring to a boil; cook and stir for 2 minutes or until thickened and bubbly. Pour into a greased 8-in. square baking dish.

In a bowl, combine the oats, cornflakes, brown sugar, cinnamon and salt; stir in butter. Sprinkle over berry mixture. Bake at 350° for 25-30 minutes or until filling is bubbly. Cool for 10 minutes before serving. **Yield:** 6 servings.

Editor's Note: If using frozen raspberries, do not thaw before adding to the blueberry mixture.

Strawberry Swirl Cheesecake

(Pictured at right)

Prep: 1 hour **Bake:** 1-1/4 hours + chilling

This melt-in-your-mouth delight is doubly delicious, with two creamy layers...one strawberry, one vanilla. To avoid cracking, run the knife just through the very top when swirling the strawberry puree. —Mary Ellen Friend
Ravenswood, West Virginia

1-1/4 cups all-purpose flour
1 tablespoon sugar
1 teaspoon grated lemon peel
1/2 cup cold butter

FILLING:
4 packages (8 ounces *each*) cream cheese, softened
1-1/3 cups sugar
2 tablespoons all-purpose flour
2 tablespoons heavy whipping cream
4 eggs, lightly beaten
1 tablespoon lemon juice
2 teaspoons vanilla extract
1 cup pureed fresh strawberries, *divided*
8 to 10 drops red food coloring, optional

In a bowl, combine flour, sugar and lemon peel; cut in butter until crumbly. Pat dough onto the bottom and 1 in. up the sides of a greased 9-in. springform pan. Place on a baking sheet. Bake at 325° for 15-20 minutes or until lightly browned. Cool on a wire rack.

In a large mixing bowl, beat the cream cheese, sugar, flour and cream until smooth. Add eggs; beat on low speed just until combined. Beat in lemon juice and vanilla just until blended. Pour 2-1/2 cups batter into a bowl; set aside.

Stir 3/4 cup pureed strawberries and food coloring if desired into remaining batter. Pour into crust. Place pan on a double thickness of heavy-duty foil (about 16 in. square). Securely wrap foil around pan. Place in a large baking pan. Add 1 in. of hot water to larger pan. Bake for 35 minutes.

Carefully pour reserved batter over bottom layer. Spoon remaining pureed berries over batter. Carefully cut through top layer only with a knife to swirl. Bake 40-50 minutes longer or until center is almost set. Remove pan from water bath. Cool on a wire rack for 10 minutes. Carefully run a knife around edge of pan to loosen; cool 1 hour longer. Refrigerate overnight. **Yield:** 12 servings.

Almond Fruit Crisp

(Pictured above)

Prep: 35 min. + standing **Bake:** 20 min. + cooling

Sliced almonds give extra crunch to these yummy individual crisps made with plums and nectarines or peaches. We love desserts, but this one has to be our very favorite. I usually serve it with ice cream. —Elizabeth Sicard Summerfield, Florida

   1-1/2 pounds nectarines *or* peaches, cubed
   1-1/2 pounds red plums, cubed
      1/4 cup lemon juice
        1 cup sugar
        2 tablespoons quick-cooking tapioca
Dash salt
ALMOND TOPPING:
        1 cup all-purpose flour
      1/2 cup sugar
      1/2 teaspoon baking powder
Dash salt
      1/4 cup cold butter
        3 tablespoons almond paste
        1 egg, lightly beaten
      1/4 teaspoon almond extract
      1/3 cup sliced almonds

In a large bowl, combine the nectarines and plums. Drizzle with lemon juice; toss to coat. Combine the sugar, tapioca and salt; sprinkle over fruit and toss to coat evenly. Let stand for 15 minutes. Spoon into 10 greased 6-oz. custard cups.

In a bowl, combine the flour, sugar, baking powder and salt. Cut in butter and almond paste until crumbly. Combine egg and extract; stir into crumb mixture just until blended. Sprinkle over fruit. Top with almonds.

Place cups on a baking sheet coated with nonstick cooking spray. Bake, uncovered, at 400° for 20-25 minutes or until fruit is bubbly and topping is golden brown. Cool for 15-20 minutes before serving. **Yield:** 10 servings.

Two-Tone Cheesecake

(Pictured on page 136)

Prep: 25 min. **Bake:** 1-1/4 hours + cooling

Looking to create an original for the 2002 Alaska State Fair contest, I came up with this creamy cheesecake. It won Grand Champion! —Cindi Paulson, Anchorage, Alaska

   1-1/2 cups chocolate graham cracker crumbs
        6 tablespoons sugar
        6 tablespoons butter, melted
FILLING:
        4 packages (8 ounces *each*) cream cheese, softened
   1-3/4 cups sugar
      3/4 cup heavy whipping cream
        4 eggs, lightly beaten
        6 squares (1 ounce *each*) semisweet chocolate, melted and cooled
TOPPING:
        4 squares (1 ounce *each*) semisweet chocolate, finely chopped
      1/2 cup heavy whipping cream

In a bowl, combine cracker crumbs, sugar and butter. Press onto the bottom of a greased 10-in. springform pan. Place on a baking sheet. Bake at 325° for 10 minutes. Cool on a wire rack.

In a large mixing bowl, beat cream cheese and sugar until smooth. Gradually beat in cream. Add eggs; beat on low speed just until combined.

Remove 3-1/2 cups to a small bowl; gently stir in melted chocolate. Pour over crust. Carefully pour remaining filling over chocolate layer. Return to baking sheet. Bake at 325° for 65-75 minutes or until center is almost set.

Cool on a wire rack for 10 minutes. Carefully run a knife around edge of pan to loosen; cool 1 hour longer. Meanwhile, place chopped chocolate in a small bowl.

In a small saucepan, bring cream to a boil. Pour over chocolate; whisk until smooth. Cool slightly; pour over cheesecake. Cover and chill overnight. Remove sides of pan. Refrigerate leftovers. **Yield:** 12 servings.

Strawberry Rhubarb Cobbler

(Pictured at right)

Prep: 25 min. **Bake:** 20 min. + cooling

This ruby red cobbler has an old-fashioned look and flavor that can't be beat. Tender golden-brown biscuits top the thick filling that's loaded with fruit.
—Sabrina Musk
Caledonia, Michigan

> 3/4 cup sugar
> 2 tablespoons cornstarch
> 1/8 teaspoon salt
> 3 cups chopped fresh *or* frozen rhubarb
> 1-1/2 cups sliced fresh strawberries
> TOPPING:
> 1 cup all-purpose flour
> 1 tablespoon sugar
> 1-1/2 teaspoons baking powder
> 1/4 teaspoon salt
> 1/4 cup cold butter
> 1 egg, lightly beaten
> 1/4 cup milk
> Additional sugar

In a large saucepan, combine the sugar, cornstarch and salt. Add rhubarb and strawberries; toss to coat. Let stand for 5 minutes. Bring to a boil; cook and stir for 1 minute. Pour into a greased 8-in. square baking dish.

In a bowl, combine the flour, sugar, baking powder and salt; cut in butter until mixture resembles coarse crumbs. Combine egg and milk; stir into dry ingredients just until moistened. Drop by tablespoonfuls onto fruit. Sprinkle with additional sugar.

Bake at 400° for 20-25 minutes or until filling is bubbly and topping is golden brown. Cool for 10 minutes before serving. **Yield:** 6-8 servings.

Editor's Note: If using frozen rhubarb, measure rhubarb while still frozen, then thaw completely. Drain in a colander, but do not press liquid out.

Fruit Pizza Supreme

(Pictured above)

Prep: 30 min.   **Bake:** 10 min. + chilling

I like to prepare this easy, colorful treat first thing in the morning when we're expecting guests that evening.
—Nina Vilhauer, Mina, South Dakota

> 1 tube (18 ounces) refrigerated sugar cookie dough
> 2 packages (8 ounces *each*) cream cheese, softened
> 1 cup confectioners' sugar
> 1 teaspoon vanilla extract
> 1 carton (8 ounces) frozen whipped topping, thawed
> 1 cup fresh strawberries, halved
> 1 cup seedless red grapes
> 1 cup fresh blueberries
> 2 kiwifruit, peeled and sliced
> 1 can (11 ounces) mandarin oranges, drained
> 1 cup sugar
> 3 tablespoons cornstarch
> 1 cup orange juice
> 1/4 cup unsweetened pineapple juice

Pat cookie dough onto bottom of an ungreased 15-in. x 10-in. x 1-in. baking pan. Bake at 350° for 10-12 minutes or until golden. Cool completely on wire rack.

In a large mixing bowl, beat cream cheese, confectioners' sugar and vanilla until smooth. Fold in whipped topping. Spread over the crust. Arrange fruit on top.

In a saucepan, combine the sugar, cornstarch, orange juice and pineapple juice until smooth. Bring to a boil; cook and stir for 2 minutes or until thickened. Cool; drizzle over fruit. Refrigerate until chilled. **Yield:** 20 servings.

Trifles Steal Center Stage

SERVED in a pretty glass bowl or footed trifle dish, cubed cake, creamy filling and pretty fruit layers make a sweet centerpiece.

Cappuccino Cherry Trifle

(Pictured below)

Prep: 20 min.   **Cook:** 15 min. + chilling

This is a rich dessert that's as pretty to look at as it is good to eat. It's the perfect complement to any meal.
—*Katie Sloan, Charlotte, North Carolina*

    3/4 **cup sugar**
    1/4 **cup cornstarch**
      2 **tablespoons instant coffee granules**
      1 **tablespoon baking cocoa**
1-1/2 **cups milk**
      2 **tablespoons water**
      4 **egg yolks, beaten**
      2 **teaspoons vanilla extract**
2-3/4 **cups heavy whipping cream**
      2 **loaves (10-3/4 ounces *each*) frozen pound cake, thawed and cut into 1-inch cubes**

      1 **can (15 ounces) pitted dark sweet cherries**
      1 **cup (6 ounces) semisweet chocolate chips**

For custard, combine the sugar, cornstarch, coffee granules and cocoa in a large saucepan. Stir in milk and water until smooth. Bring to a boil over medium heat; cook and stir for 1-2 minutes or until thick and bubbly.

Remove from the heat. Stir a small amount of hot mixture into yolks; return all to the pan, stirring constantly. Bring to a gentle boil; cook and stir 2 minutes longer. Remove from the heat; gently stir in vanilla. Refrigerate until cool.

In a large mixing bowl, beat the cream until stiff peaks form. Fold 2-1/2 cups whipped cream into cooled custard. Set aside the remaining whipped cream for garnish.

Place half of the cake cubes in a 3-qt. trifle bowl. Drain the cherries, reserving juice; sprinkle cake with 3-4 tablespoons cherry juice. Top with half of the cherries, 1/3 cup chocolate chips and half of the custard mixture. Repeat layers. Garnish with reserved whipped cream and remaining chocolate chips. **Yield:** 12-14 servings.

Six-Fruit Trifle

(Pictured above right)

Prep: 20 min.   **Bake:** 20 min. + chilling

For a large group, try doubling this recipe and layering it in a punch bowl. Let guests serve themselves. Don't be surprised if the bowl gets licked clean! —*Verna Peterson Omaha, Nebraska*

      1 **package (9 ounces) yellow cake mix**
      1 **can (20 ounces) pineapple tidbits, drained**
      2 **medium firm bananas, sliced**
      2 **medium peaches *or* nectarines, peeled and sliced**
      2 **cups sliced fresh strawberries, *divided***
      2 **cups cold milk**
      1 **package (3.4 ounces) instant vanilla pudding mix**
      1 **cup heavy whipping cream**
      1 **tablespoon sugar**
    1/2 **cup fresh blueberries**
      2 **kiwifruit, peeled and sliced**

Prepare and bake cake mix according to package directions, using a 9-in. round baking pan. Cool; cut into 1-in. cubes. In a bowl, combine the pineapple, ba-

In a large mixing bowl, beat the milk, water and extract until blended. Add pudding mix; whisk for 2 minutes. Let stand for 2 minutes or until soft-set. Cover and chill until mixture is partially set. Fold in the whipped cream.

Place half of the cake cubes in a 2-qt. glass serving bowl. Top with half of the cream mixture. Carefully spread with jam. Sprinkle with 1 cup raspberries. Layer with remaining cake cubes, cream mixture and raspberries. Garnish with chocolate curls and mint. **Yield:** 14-16 servings.

✓ *Trifle Trivia*

We have the British to thank for the trifle, a luscious layered treat steeped in tradition.

"Trifle" is from the Middle English word "trufle"...which means something of little importance. That definition hardly fits this stunning dessert!

In the 18th century, when preparing this dessert, English cooks started with dry cake, soaking it in sherry or brandy to add moisture. (Even today, many trifle recipes call for dousing cake or ladyfingers—even if they aren't dry—with spirits.) The cake was then surrounded with a vanilla-flavored custard sauce (creme anglaise). Over time, fruit was added.

nanas, peaches and 1/2 cup strawberries. In another bowl, whisk milk and pudding mix for 2 minutes; let stand for 2 minutes or until soft-set. In a mixing bowl, beat cream until soft peaks form. Add sugar; beat until stiff peaks form.

In a 3-qt. trifle bowl, layer half of the cake cubes, fruit mixture, pudding and whipped cream. Repeat layers. Top with blueberries, kiwi and remaining strawberries. Cover and refrigerate for 4 hours or overnight. **Yield:** 12-14 servings.

Raspberry Cream Trifle

(Pictured at right)

Prep/Total Time: 30 min.

Here's a dessert that's delicious, simple and inviting. You can vary the flavor by substituting strawberries or peaches (with preserves to match) for the raspberries.
—*Donna Huitema, Whitby, Ontario*

1 can (14 ounces) sweetened condensed milk, chilled
1 cup cold water
1 teaspoon almond extract
1 package (3.4 ounces) instant vanilla pudding mix
2 cups heavy whipping cream, whipped
1 angel food cake (7 inches), cut into 1-inch cubes
2 tablespoons seedless raspberry jam
2 cups fresh raspberries
Chocolate curls and fresh mint

Apple Crumble

(Pictured above)

Prep: 30 min.   **Bake:** 40 min. + cooling

While visiting friends in New Zealand, I watched this dessert being made. Back at home, I came up with my own version. —Carol Simpkins, Santa Cruz, California

  8 sheets phyllo dough (14 inches x 9 inches)
Butter-flavored nonstick cooking spray
  1/2 cup packed brown sugar
  2 tablespoons all-purpose flour
  1/2 teaspoon ground ginger
  1/2 teaspoon ground cinnamon
  4 medium tart apples, peeled and sliced
TOPPING:
  1/2 cup all-purpose flour
  1/2 cup packed brown sugar
  1/2 cup soft whole wheat bread crumbs
  1/4 teaspoon ground ginger
  1/4 teaspoon ground cinnamon
  1/2 cup cold butter
  1/4 cup slivered almonds

Cut phyllo sheets in half; spritz with butter-flavored spray. Layer phyllo, sprayed side up, in a greased 8-in. square baking dish. In a large bowl, combine the brown sugar, flour, ginger and cinnamon; add apples and toss to coat. Spoon over phyllo dough.

In a bowl, combine the flour, brown sugar, bread crumbs, ginger and cinnamon; cut in butter until mixture resembles coarse crumbs. Add almonds; sprinkle over apple mixture. Bake at 350° for 40-45 minutes or until filling is bubbly and topping is golden. Cool for 10 minutes before serving. **Yield:** 9 servings.

Frozen Strawberry Yogurt

Prep: 15 min. + freezing

After losing 60 pounds, I wanted a lower-fat version of the ice cream I make in my ice cream freezer. Even my co-workers enjoyed this recipe. —Teri Van Wey
Salina, Kansas

☑ **Uses less fat, sugar or salt. Includes Nutritional Analysis and Diabetic Exchanges.**

  2 cups (16 ounces) fat-free plain yogurt
  2 cups pureed fresh strawberries
  1 can (14 ounces) fat-free sweetened condensed milk
  1 cup fat-free milk
  3 teaspoons vanilla extract

In a large bowl, combine all ingredients. Fill cylinder of ice cream freezer two-thirds full; freeze according to manufacturer's directions. Refrigerate remaining mixture until ready to freeze.

Allow to ripen in ice cream freezer or firm up in refrigerator freezer 2-4 hours before serving. Remove from the freezer 30-45 minutes before serving. **Yield:** 1-1/2 quarts.

Nutritional Analysis: 1/2 cup equals 130 calories, trace fat (trace saturated fat), 3 mg cholesterol, 68 mg sodium, 27 g carbohydrate, 1 g fiber, 6 g protein. **Diabetic Exchanges:** 1 fruit, 1 fat-free milk.

Pumpkin Freeze with Mincemeat

(Pictured on page 136)

Prep: 24 min. + freezing

I love serving this dessert at fall gatherings, especially Thanksgiving. After a bountiful meal, a refreshing treat like this is always appreciated. —Donna Gonda
North Canton, Ohio

  1 cup canned pumpkin
  1/2 cup packed brown sugar
  1/4 teaspoon salt
  1/4 teaspoon ground cinnamon
  1/8 teaspoon ground cloves
  1 quart vanilla ice cream, softened
MINCEMEAT SAUCE:
  1 package (9 ounces) condensed mincemeat
1-1/2 cups water
  1/2 cup apricot nectar
  1 tablespoon grated orange peel

In a large bowl, combine pumpkin, brown sugar, salt, cinnamon and cloves. Fold in ice cream. Fill individual molds or foil-lined muffin cups. Cover and freeze for 24 hours.

For sauce, crumble mincemeat into a saucepan; add water. Cook and stir until mixture comes to a rolling boil; boil for 1 minute. Cool to room temperature. Stir in apricot nectar and orange peel. Unmold pumpkin mixture or remove foil from cups. Serve over mincemeat sauce. **Yield:** 8 servings.

Blueberry Cornmeal Cobbler

(Pictured below)

Prep: 20 min. + standing   **Bake:** 35 min.

Corn bread, blueberries and maple syrup butter give this special dessert a taste that's different from any cobbler you've had before. I came across the recipe years ago.
—Judy Watson, Tipton, Indiana

- 4 **cups fresh blueberries**
- 1 **cup plus 2 tablespoons sugar**
- 1 **tablespoon quick-cooking tapioca**
- 2 **teaspoons grated lemon peel**
- 1 **teaspoon ground cinnamon**
- 1/4 **to 1/2 teaspoon ground nutmeg**
TOPPING:
- 1/2 **cup butter, softened,** *divided*
- 1 **cup confectioners' sugar**
- 1 **egg**
- 1 **cup all-purpose flour**
- 1/2 **cup cornmeal**
- 2 **teaspoons baking powder**
- 1/2 **teaspoon baking soda**
- 1/2 **teaspoon salt**
- 3/4 **cup buttermilk**
- 2 **tablespoons maple syrup**

In a large bowl, combine blueberries, sugar, tapioca, lemon peel, cinnamon and nutmeg. Let stand for 15 minutes. Pour into a greased 11-in. x 7-in. x 2-in. baking dish.

In a small mixing bowl, beat 1/4 cup butter and confectioners' sugar. Add egg; beat well. Combine the flour, cornmeal, baking powder, baking soda and salt; add to creamed mixture alternately with buttermilk, beating just until combined. Pour over berry mixture. Bake at 375° for 35-40 minutes or until a toothpick inserted near the center comes out clean.

In a small saucepan, melt remaining butter over low heat. Remove from the heat; stir in the syrup. Brush over corn bread. Broil 4-6 in. from the heat for 1-2 minutes or until bubbly. Serve warm. **Yield:** 12 servings.

Cranberry Ice Cream

(Pictured above)

Prep: 20 min. + freezing

A traditional treat for Christmas, this recipe was my great-grandmother's. She liked to serve it in pretty parfait glasses along with the meal.   —Nona Dumas, Wilmar, Arkansas

- 2 **cups fresh** *or* **frozen cranberries**
- 1/2 **cup water**
- 4 **cups milk**
- 4 **cups sugar**
- 2 **cups heavy whipping cream**
- 1 **cup orange juice**
- 1/2 **cup lemon juice**

In a large saucepan, cook cranberries and water over medium heat until the berries pop, about 15 minutes. Strain; discard seeds and skins. Cool completely. Meanwhile, in a large saucepan, heat milk to 175°; stir in sugar until dissolved. Cool. Stir in the cream, juices and cranberry mixture.

Fill cylinder of ice cream freezer; freeze according to manufacturer's directions. Refrigerate remaining mixture until ready to freeze. Allow to ripen in ice cream freezer or firm up in the refrigerator freezer for 2-4 hours before serving. **Yield:** 3 quarts.

Fruit Salad Cheesecake

(Pictured below)

Prep: 30 min. + chilling

I have enjoyed this recipe since the 1960s, when my in-laws' dear neighbor shared it. Similar to a fruit fluff, this yummy dessert has a macaroon crust and plenty of fruit and nuts in the filling. —Pamela O'Brien
Greenville, Michigan

      1 can (20 ounces) crushed pineapple,
          drained
      1 cup sugar
  1/2 cup cold water
      2 envelopes unflavored gelatin
      1 package (8 ounces) cream cheese, cubed
1-1/2 cups crushed crisp macaroons
      2 tablespoons butter, melted
      2 cups halved seedless grapes
      1 can (11 ounces) mandarin oranges,
          drained
      1 jar (10 ounces) maraschino cherries,
          drained and chopped
  1/2 cup finely chopped pecans *or* walnuts
      2 cups whipped topping

In a small saucepan, cook pineapple and sugar over medium heat for 5 minutes or until heated through. Place cold water in a bowl; sprinkle with gelatin. Let stand for 1 minute. Stir into the warm pineapple mixture. Reduce heat to low; add cream cheese. Cook and stir until cream cheese is melted and mixture is blended. Remove from the heat; cool completely.

In a small bowl, combine macaroon crumbs and butter. Press onto the bottom of a greased 9-in. springform pan; set aside. Stir the grapes, oranges, cherries and nuts into cream cheese mixture. Fold in the whipped topping. Pour into prepared pan. Cover and refrigerate overnight. Remove sides of pan before serving. **Yield:** 12 servings.

Ginger-Lime Pear Cobbler

Prep: 25 min.   **Bake:** 50 min. + cooling

We have a huge pear tree in our yard, which is why I came up with this recipe. The tart lime, sweet pears and tangy ginger are a winning combination. —Heather Naas
Lompoc, California

  3/4 cup sugar
  1/8 teaspoon ground ginger
      5 cups sliced peeled fresh pears
      2 tablespoons finely chopped crystallized
          ginger
      2 tablespoons lime juice
  1/2 cup butter, melted
BATTER:
  3/4 cup all-purpose flour
  1/2 cup sugar
      2 teaspoons baking powder
      1 teaspoon grated lime peel
  1/8 teaspoon salt
Pinch ground ginger
  3/4 cup milk

In a large bowl, combine sugar and ground ginger. Stir in the pears, crystallized ginger and lime juice; set aside.

Pour the butter into an ungreased 11-in. x 7-in. x 2-in. baking dish. In a small bowl, combine the flour, sugar, baking powder, lime peel, salt and ginger. Stir in milk. Pour over butter (do not stir). Spoon pear mixture over the top.

Bake at 350° for 50-55 minutes or until bubbly and golden brown. Cool for 10 minutes before serving. **Yield:** 8-10 servings.

Fluffy Raspberry Torte

(Pictured on back cover)

Prep: 25 min. + chilling

Relatives at our reunion were quick to request the recipe when I brought this torte that's chock-full of fresh berries. —Dorothy Meyer, Markesan, Wisconsin

      2 cups graham cracker crumbs
  1/2 cup butter, melted

batches, process the sugar syrup and watermelon in a food processor. Transfer to a large bowl; stir in lemonade concentrate. Cover and refrigerate until chilled.

Fill cylinder of ice cream freezer two-thirds full; freeze according to manufacturer's directions. Refrigerate remaining mixture until ready to freeze. Allow to ripen in ice cream freezer or firm up in the refrigerator freezer for 2-4 hours before serving. **Yield:** about 2-1/2 quarts.

Ice Cream Sandwich Dessert

(Pictured below)

Prep: 10 min. + freezing

It takes 10 minutes tops to prepare this cool treat, but it tastes like you spent a lot of time creating it.
—Cathie Valentine, Graniteville, South Carolina

17 miniature ice cream sandwiches, *divided*
1 jar (12 ounces) caramel ice cream topping
1 carton (12 ounces) frozen whipped topping, thawed
1/4 cup chocolate syrup
1 Symphony candy bar (7 ounces), chopped

Arrange 14 ice cream sandwiches in an ungreased 13-in. x 9-in. x 2-in. dish. Cut remaining sandwiches in half lengthwise, and fill in the spaces in the dish.

Spread with caramel and whipped toppings. Drizzle with chocolate syrup. Sprinkle with chopped candy bar. Cover and freeze for at least 45 minutes. Cut into squares. **Yield:** 15-18 servings.

1/4 cup sugar
1 package (16 ounces) miniature marshmallows
1 cup milk
2 cups heavy whipping cream, whipped
4 cups fresh raspberries
1/2 cup chopped pecans

In a small bowl, combine the cracker crumbs, butter and sugar. Set aside 1/4 cup for topping. Press remaining crumb mixture onto the bottom and 1-1/2 in. up the sides of a 9-in. springform pan; set aside.

In a large saucepan, combine marshmallows and milk. Cook and whisk over medium-low heat until marshmallows are melted and mixture is smooth. Cool. Fold in whipped cream, raspberries and pecans.

Pour into prepared crust. Top with remaining crumb mixture. Cover and refrigerate overnight. Remove sides of pan. **Yield:** 12 servings.

Watermelon Sorbet

(Pictured above)

Prep: 25 min. + freezing

After scooping out the watermelon for this pretty pink sorbet, I freeze the rind shell to use as a serving bowl for the scoops. We also put out bowls of chocolate chips and jimmies so our guests can sprinkle on their own "seeds."
—Heidi Grable, Raleigh, North Carolina

4 cups water
2 cups sugar
8 cups cubed seedless watermelon
1 can (12 ounces) frozen pink lemonade concentrate, thawed

In a large saucepan, bring water and sugar to a boil. Cook and stir until sugar is dissolved. Cool slightly. In

Blueberry Sauce for Sorbet

Prep: 15 min. + chilling

We enjoy this refreshing and lovely dessert on warm days at our summer home. —Kay Tanberg
Two Harbors, Minnesota

✓ **Uses less fat, sugar or salt. Includes Nutritional Analysis and Diabetic Exchanges.**

- 2 tablespoons cornstarch
- 1 cup water
- 4 cups fresh blueberries
- 3 tablespoons sugar
- 3 tablespoons lemon juice
Lemon sorbet
Additional blueberries, optional

In a large saucepan, combine the cornstarch and water until smooth. Stir in blueberries, sugar and lemon juice. Bring to a boil; cook and stir for 1 minute or until thickened. Cool slightly. Transfer mixture to a blender; cover and process until smooth. Strain and discard seeds. Pour sauce into a bowl; cover and chill.

To serve, spoon sauce over scoops of sorbet. Garnish with additional blueberries if desired. Refrigerate leftover sauce. **Yield:** about 3 cups.

Nutritional Analysis: 2 tablespoons sauce (calculated without sorbet) equals 23 calories, trace fat (trace saturated fat), 0 cholesterol, 2 mg sodium, 6 g carbohydrate, 1 g fiber, trace protein. **Diabetic Exchange:** 1/2 fruit.

Strawberry Popovers

(Pictured above)
Prep: 20 min.   **Bake:** 30 min.

These tender popovers "pop up" nicely in the oven and hold a delicate cream filling dotted with fresh chopped strawberries. If you don't have a popover pan on hand, you might try muffin cups. —Sandra Vanthoff
San Diego, California

- 1 cup heavy whipping cream
- 1/3 cup sugar
- 1 teaspoon vanilla extract
- 2 cups chopped fresh strawberries
POPOVERS:
- 4-1/2 teaspoons shortening
- 4 eggs
- 2 cups milk
- 2 cups all-purpose flour
- 1 tablespoon sugar
- 1 teaspoon salt

In a mixing bowl, beat cream until it begins to thicken. Add sugar and vanilla; beat until stiff peaks form. Fold in the strawberries. Cover and refrigerate until serving.

Using 1/2 teaspoon shortening for each cup, grease the bottoms and sides of nine popover cups. In a small mixing bowl, beat eggs; beat in milk. Add the flour, sugar and salt; beat until smooth (do not overbeat). Fill prepared cups half full.

Bake at 450° for 15 minutes. Reduce heat to 350°; bake 15 minutes longer or until very firm. Immediately cut a slit in the top of each popover to allow steam to escape. Spoon strawberry filling into popovers. Serve immediately. **Yield:** 9 servings.

Peach Cobbler

(Pictured below right)
Prep: 20 min. + standing   **Bake:** 50 min. + cooling

Convenient canned peaches make this cobbler quick to assemble. The tender cake-like topping pairs nicely with the sweet fruit filling and butterscotch sauce. The sauce should always be served warm. —Ellen Merick
North Pole, Alaska

- 2 cans (29 ounces *each*) sliced peaches
- 1/2 cup packed brown sugar
- 6 tablespoons quick-cooking tapioca
- 1 teaspoon ground cinnamon, optional
- 1 teaspoon lemon juice
- 1 teaspoon vanilla extract
TOPPING:
- 1 cup all-purpose flour
- 1 cup sugar
- 1 teaspoon baking powder
- 1/2 teaspoon salt
- 1/4 cup cold butter
- 2 eggs, beaten

BUTTERSCOTCH SAUCE:
  1/2 **cup packed brown sugar**
    2 **tablespoons all-purpose flour**
  1/8 **teaspoon salt**
  1/4 **cup butter, melted**
    2 **tablespoons lemon juice**
Vanilla ice cream, optional

Drain peaches, reserving 1/2 cup syrup for the sauce. In a large bowl, combine peaches, brown sugar, tapioca, cinnamon if desired, lemon juice and vanilla. Transfer to an ungreased 11-in. x 7-in. x 2-in. baking dish. Let stand for 15 minutes.

In a large bowl, combine the flour, sugar, baking powder and salt; cut in butter until mixture resembles coarse crumbs. Stir in eggs. Drop by spoonfuls onto peach mixture; spread evenly. Bake at 350° for 50-55 minutes or until filling is bubbly and a toothpick inserted in topping comes out clean. Cool for 10 minutes.

In a small saucepan, combine the brown sugar, flour, salt, butter and reserved peach syrup. Bring to a boil over medium heat; cook and stir for 1 minute or until thickened. Remove from the heat; add lemon juice. Serve with cobbler and ice cream if desired. **Yield:** 10-12 servings.

Chocolate Berry Cheesecake

(Pictured above right and on back cover)

Prep: 20 min. **Bake:** 55 min. + chilling

A fruity sauce accents this fudgy cheesecake, making it perfect for holidays and celebrations. —Lisa Varner
Greenville, South Carolina

  1 **cup crushed chocolate wafers (about 20 wafers)**
  2 **tablespoons butter, melted**

  3 **packages (8 ounces *each*) cream cheese, softened**
1/2 **cup sugar**
  1 **tablespoon cornstarch**
  2 **cups (12 ounces) semisweet chocolate chips, melted and cooled**
1/2 **cup heavy whipping cream**
  1 **teaspoon vanilla extract**
  4 **eggs, lightly beaten**
RASPBERRY SAUCE:
  2 **tablespoons sugar**
  2 **teaspoons cornstarch**
1/2 **cup cranberry juice**
  1 **package (12 ounces) frozen unsweetened raspberries, thawed**

Combine wafer crumbs and butter. Press onto the bottom of a greased 9-in. springform pan; set aside. In a mixing bowl, beat cream cheese on low speed until smooth. Combine sugar and cornstarch; beat into cream cheese. Stir in the chocolate, cream and vanilla. Add eggs; beat on low just until combined.

Pour into prepared pan. Place on a double thickness of heavy-duty foil (about 16 in. square). Securely wrap foil around pan. Place in a large baking pan. Add 1 in. of hot water to larger pan.

Bake at 325° for 55-60 minutes or until center is just set. Cool on a wire rack for 10 minutes. Carefully run a knife around edge of pan to loosen; cool 1 hour longer. Refrigerate for 4 hours or overnight.

In a saucepan, combine sugar, cornstarch and cranberry juice until smooth. Bring to a boil over medium heat; cook and stir for 1 minute. Remove from heat; stir in raspberries. Cool completely. Remove sides of pan. Serve cheesecake with raspberry sauce. Refrigerate leftovers. **Yield:** 12-14 servings.

Walnut Baklava

(Pictured below)

Prep: 1-1/4 hours   **Bake:** 45 min. + cooling

My family can't get enough of this traditional sweet and nutty Greek pastry.
—*Josie Bochek*
Sturgeon Bay, Wisconsin

    4 cups finely chopped walnuts
1/4 cup sugar
    1 tablespoon ground cinnamon
    1 cup butter, melted
    1 package (16 ounces) frozen phyllo dough, thawed
SYRUP:
    1 cup sugar
1/2 cup water
1/4 cup honey
    1 teaspoon lemon juice
    1 teaspoon vanilla extract

In a bowl, combine the walnuts, sugar and cinnamon; set aside. Grease a 13-in. x 9-in. x 2-in. baking dish with some of the melted butter. Unroll phyllo dough sheets (keep dough covered with plastic wrap while assembling).

Place one sheet of phyllo in baking dish; brush with butter. Top with a second sheet; brush with butter. Fold short ends under to fit the dish. Sprinkle with about 1/4 cup nut mixture. Repeat 18 times, layering two sheets, brushing with butter and sprinkling with nut

mixture. Top with remaining dough; brush with butter. Cut into 2-in. diamonds with a sharp knife.

Bake at 350° for 45-55 minutes or until golden brown. Meanwhile, in a saucepan, combine the syrup ingredients; bring to a boil. Reduce heat; simmer, uncovered, for 10 minutes. Pour over warm baklava. Cool on a wire rack. **Yield:** about 3 dozen.

Editor's Note: This recipe was tested with Athenos phyllo dough. The phyllo sheets measure 14 in. x 9 in.

Homemade Sugar Cones

Prep: 15 min.   **Bake:** 20 min. + cooling

I often sprinkle sliced almonds on the circles of batter before baking these crunchy cones.   —*Ellen Osborne*
Clarksville, Tennessee

    2 egg whites
1/2 cup sugar
3/4 cup all-purpose flour
1/4 cup butter, melted

In a mixing bowl, beat egg whites on medium speed until soft peaks form. Gradually beat in sugar. Beat in flour and butter just until blended.

Line a baking sheet with parchment paper. Draw two 7-in. circles on paper. Drop 3 tablespoons of batter in the center of each circle; spread batter to edges. Bake at 400° for 6-8 minutes or until edges are golden brown.

Place the cookies, bottom side up, on a paper towel-lined work surface. To shape cone, begin with one edge and roll cookie a third of the way toward the center; roll a third of the opposite side over the rolled portion. Shape top of cone. Place seam side down on a wire rack to cool completely.

Return second cookie to oven for 1-2 minutes if necessary before rolling. Repeat with remaining batter to make four more cones. **Yield:** 6 cones.

Strawberry Cream Crepes

(Pictured above far right)

Prep: 25 min. + chilling   **Cook:** 1 hour

I always feel like a French chef when I serve these pretty crepes. Although they take a little time to prepare, they're well worth the effort. My guests are always impressed.
—*Debra Latta, Port Matilda, Pennsylvania*

1-1/2 cups milk
    3 eggs
    2 tablespoons butter, melted
1/2 teaspoon lemon extract
1-1/4 cups all-purpose flour
    2 tablespoons sugar

Dash salt
TOPPING:
    1/2 cup sugar
    2 tablespoons cornstarch
    3/4 cup water
    1 tablespoon lemon juice
    1 teaspoon strawberry extract
    1/4 teaspoon red food coloring, optional
    4 cups sliced fresh strawberries
FILLING:
    1 cup heavy whipping cream
    1 package (8 ounces) cream
      cheese, softened
    2 cups confectioners' sugar
    1 teaspoon vanilla extract

In a large mixing bowl, combine milk, eggs, butter and extract. Combine flour, sugar and salt; add to milk mixture and beat until smooth. Cover and refrigerate for 1 hour.

Heat a lightly greased 8-in. nonstick skillet. Stir batter; pour 2 tablespoons into center of skillet. Lift and tilt pan to coat bottom evenly. Cook until top appears dry; turn and cook 15-20 seconds longer. Remove to a wire rack. Repeat with remaining batter, greasing skillet as needed. When cool, stack crepes with waxed paper or paper towels in between.

In a small saucepan, combine the sugar and cornstarch; stir in water and lemon juice until smooth. Bring to a boil over medium heat; cook and stir for 1 minute or until thickened. Stir in extract and food coloring if desired. Cool. Add strawberries.

In a small mixing bowl, beat the cream until stiff peaks form; set aside. In a large mixing bowl, beat the cream cheese, confectioners' sugar and vanilla until smooth; fold in the whipped cream. Spoon 2 rounded tablespoons of the filling down the center of each crepe; roll up. Top with strawberry topping. **Yield:** 22 crepes.

YOUR FAMILY will agree, Strawberry Tartlets and Strawberry Cream Crepes (shown above) are the pick of the crop.

Strawberry Tartlets

(Pictured above right)

Prep: 25 min.   **Bake:** 10 min. + cooling

This elegant-looking dessert is easy to make, and the cute wonton "cups" can be made in advance. They're a different way to present fresh strawberries when entertaining. The recipe is easy to double, too. —Joy Van Meter
Thornton, Colorado

  12 wonton wrappers
   3 tablespoons butter, melted
  1/3 cup packed brown sugar
  3/4 cup Mascarpone cheese
   2 tablespoons honey
   2 teaspoons orange juice
   3 cups fresh strawberries, sliced
Whipped cream and fresh mint, optional

Brush one side of each wonton wrapper with butter. Place brown sugar in a shallow bowl; press buttered side of wontons into sugar to coat. Press wontons sugared side up into greased muffin cups. Bake at 325° for 7-9 minutes or until edges are lightly browned. Remove to a wire rack to cool.

In a bowl, combine the cheese, honey and orange juice. Spoon about 1 tablespoon of mixture into each wonton cup. Top with strawberries. Garnish with whipped cream and mint if desired. **Yield:** 1 dozen.

Apple Blueberry Cobbler

(Pictured above)

Prep: 20 min. + cooling   **Bake:** 35 min.

Serve this old-fashioned dessert warm or cold with whipped topping or ice cream.
                              —Clara Dumke
                              Plant City, Florida

    1 tablespoon butter, melted
    9 gingersnap cookies, crushed
FILLING:
    4 large tart apples, peeled
    1 tablespoon butter
3/4 cup sugar
3/4 teaspoon ground cinnamon
1/8 teaspoon ground ginger
    3 cups fresh blueberries
    2 tablespoons lemon juice
    1 tablespoon grated orange peel
TOPPING:
    1 cup all-purpose flour
    3 tablespoons brown sugar
    6 tablespoons cold butter

Spread butter on bottom of an 8-in. square baking dish. Sprinkle with gingersnap crumbs; press gently. Set aside.

    Cut each apple into 16 wedges. In a large skillet, saute apples in butter until crisp-tender, about 10 minutes. Remove from the heat; cool for 10 minutes. Combine the sugar, cinnamon and ginger; sprinkle

over apples and mix well. Place blueberries in a bowl. Sprinkle with lemon juice and orange peel; toss gently to mix well.

    For topping, combine flour and brown sugar in a bowl; cut in butter until crumbly. Spoon apple mixture into baking dish. Top with blueberries and topping (dish will be full). Bake at 350° for 35-40 minutes or until bubbly. **Yield:** 6-8 servings.

Pineapple Doughnut Dessert

Prep/Total Time: 15 min.

End your day around the fire with this dessert. When we can't go camping, we sometimes pitch a tent in the yard for the kids and grill this treat.
                              —Christy Hinrichs
                              Parkville, Missouri

    5 cake doughnuts
    3 tablespoons butter, softened
2/3 cup packed brown sugar
    1 can (20 ounces) sliced pineapple, drained
10 maraschino cherries

Cut doughnuts in half horizontally; spread with butter. For each packet, place two doughnut halves cut side up on a 12-in. square of heavy-duty foil.

    Sprinkle each with about 1 tablespoon of brown sugar. Top each with a pineapple slice; place a cherry in the center. Seal foil tightly. Grill over indirect medium heat for 2-4 minutes or until heated through. **Yield:** 10 servings.

Cherry Cheesecake Ice Cream

Prep: 25 min. + freezing

You don't need an ice cream maker for this pretty home-made treat.
                              —Lisa Allen, Joppa, Alabama

    2 packages (8 ounces *each*) cream cheese, softened
1/3 cup lemon juice
    1 teaspoon vanilla extract
    2 cans (14 ounces *each*) sweetened condensed milk
    4 cups half-and-half cream
    6 eggs, beaten
    2 cups heavy whipping cream
    3 cups granola
    2 cans (21 ounces *each*) cherry pie filling

In a large mixing bowl, beat the cream cheese, lemon juice and vanilla. Add milk and mix well; set aside.

    In a large saucepan, heat the half-and-half to 175°; whisk a small amount into eggs. Return all to the pan, whisking constantly. Cook and stir over low heat until mixture reaches 160° and coats the back of a metal spoon. Remove from the heat; cool slightly. Stir in the whipping cream; beat into cream cheese mixture (mixture will be thin).

Divide granola between two greased 13-in. x 9-in. x 2-in. dishes. Top with cream mixture and pie filling. Cover and freeze overnight. **Yield:** 3-1/2 quarts.

Raspberry Pear Crisp

(Pictured below)

Prep: 15 min.   **Bake:** 25 min. + cooling

We grow our own luscious red raspberries and feast on them fresh and freeze them for winter. This recipe combines the berries with fresh pears and a crunchy cereal topping.   —Fancheon Resler, Bluffton, Indiana

```
2  cups sliced peeled fresh pears
2  cups fresh or frozen raspberries
3/4  cup packed brown sugar, divided
1  teaspoon ground cinnamon, divided
1/2  cup all-purpose flour
3  tablespoons cold butter
1  cup cranberry almond whole grain cereal,
   lightly crushed
```
Vanilla ice cream, optional

In a large bowl, combine the pears, raspberries, 1/4 cup brown sugar and 1/2 teaspoon cinnamon. Spoon into a greased 9-in. pie plate.

In a small bowl, combine flour and remaining brown sugar and cinnamon; cut in butter until mixture resembles coarse crumbs. Stir in cereal. Sprinkle over fruit. Bake at 375° for 25-30 minutes or until filling is bubbly and topping is golden brown. Cool for 10 minutes. Serve with ice cream if desired. **Yield:** 6 servings.

Editor's Note: If using frozen raspberries, do not thaw before adding to the fruit mixture.

Pavlova

(Pictured above)

Prep: 45 min.   **Bake:** 1 hour + standing

This is a sweet showstopper that originates in Australia. Make a meringue nest, fill it with luscious almond cream and top it with fresh fruit.   —Jane Shapton, Tustin, California

```
3  egg whites
1/4  teaspoon cream of tartar
1/4  teaspoon salt
3/4  cup sugar
2  cups heavy whipping cream
1  teaspoon almond extract
```
Assorted fresh fruit

Place egg whites in a small mixing bowl; let stand at room temperature for 30 minutes. Line a baking sheet with parchment paper; set aside.

Add cream of tartar and salt to egg whites; beat on medium speed until soft peaks form. Gradually beat in sugar, 1 tablespoon at a time, on high until stiff peaks form.

Spread into a 9-in. circle on prepared pan, forming a shallow well in the center. Bake at 225° for 1 to 1-1/4 hours or until meringue is dry and firm to the touch and lightly browned. Turn oven off; leave meringue in oven for 1 to 1-1/2 hours.

Just before serving, beat cream and almond extract in a small mixing bowl until stiff peaks form. Spoon into the meringue shell. Top with fresh fruit. **Yield:** 8-10 servings.

Rhubarb Crunch

(Pictured below)

Prep: 20 min.   **Bake:** 1 hour

This treat features my perennial spring favorite, rhubarb. I can't wait each year to make it!
—Charlene Griffin
Minocqua, Wisconsin

     1 cup all-purpose flour
     1 cup old-fashioned oats
     1 cup packed brown sugar
     1 teaspoon ground cinnamon
   1/2 cup cold butter
     4 cups diced fresh rhubarb
 1-1/3 cups sugar
     2 teaspoons cornstarch
     1 cup cold water
     1 teaspoon vanilla extract
Vanilla ice cream, optional

In a large bowl, combine the first four ingredients. Cut in butter until mixture resembles coarse crumbs. Press half of the mixture into a greased 8-in. square baking dish. Set remaining crumb mixture aside for topping. Sprinkle rhubarb over crust; set aside.

In a small saucepan, combine the sugar and cornstarch; gradually whisk in water until smooth. Bring to a boil; cook and stir for 2 minutes or until thickened.

Remove from the heat; whisk in vanilla. Pour over rhubarb. Sprinkle with reserved crumb mixture. Bake, uncovered, at 350° for 1 hour or until bubbly and lightly browned. Serve warm with ice cream if desired.
Yield: 6-8 servings.

Streusel Squash Dessert

Prep: 1 hour   **Bake:** 55 min. + chilling

I call this my "I Won't Tell Them It's Squash if You Don't" dessert. The holiday treat features a praline-like topping.
—Teri Rasey-Bolf, Cadillac, Michigan

 1-1/2 cups all-purpose flour
   1/4 cup sugar
   1/4 cup confectioners' sugar
   1/2 cup cold butter
STREUSEL TOPPING:
   1/4 cup packed brown sugar
     2 tablespoons all-purpose flour
     1 teaspoon ground cinnamon
     2 tablespoons cold butter
     1 cup chopped pecans
FILLING:
     1 medium butternut squash (4 pounds), peeled, seeded and cubed
     1 cup sugar
   1/3 cup packed brown sugar
   1/4 cup cornstarch
     3 teaspoons ground cinnamon
     1 teaspoon salt
     1 teaspoon ground ginger
   1/2 teaspoon ground nutmeg
   1/2 teaspoon ground cloves
     2 cans (12 ounces *each*) evaporated milk
     4 eggs
Whipped cream and additional cinnamon, optional

In a bowl, combine flour and sugars; cut in butter until crumbly. Press into an ungreased 13-in. x 9-in. x 2-in. baking dish. Bake at 350° for 15-20 minutes or until edges begin to brown. In a small bowl, combine brown sugar, flour and cinnamon; cut in butter until crumbly. Stir in pecans; set aside.

Place squash in a large saucepan and cover with water; bring to a boil. Reduce heat; cover and simmer for 15-20 minutes or until tender. Drain. Transfer to a blender or food processor; cover. Process until smooth.

In a large mixing bowl, combine the sugars, cornstarch and seasonings. Gradually beat in 4 cups squash, milk and eggs until smooth (save any remaining squash for another use). Pour over crust. Sprinkle with topping.

Bake at 350° for 55-65 minutes or until a knife inserted near the center comes out clean. Cool on a wire rack. Cover and refrigerate overnight. Garnish with whipped cream and additional cinnamon if desired.
Yield: 15-18 servings.

Coconut Cream Dessert

(Pictured above)

Prep: 20 min.   **Bake:** 20 min. + chilling

This refreshing dessert satisfies the sweet tooth. My sister gave me the recipe years ago. —Deanna Richter Elmore, Minnesota

  1 **cup all-purpose flour**
  2 **tablespoons sugar**
1/2 **cup cold butter**
1/2 **cup chopped pecans**
FILLING:
  1 **package (8 ounces) cream cheese, softened**
  1 **cup confectioners' sugar**
  1 **carton (12 ounces) frozen whipped topping, thawed,** *divided*
  4 **cups cold milk**
  3 **packages (3.4 ounces** *each***) instant coconut cream pudding mix**
1/2 **cup flaked coconut, toasted**

In a bowl, combine the flour and sugar; cut in butter until crumbly. Stir in the pecans. Press into a greased 13-in. x 9-in. x 2-in. baking dish. Bake at 325° for 20-25 minutes or until edges are lightly browned. Cool on a wire rack.

In a small mixing bowl, beat the cream cheese and confectioners' sugar until smooth; fold in 1 cup whipped topping. Spread over the crust. In a bowl, whisk milk and pudding mixes for 2 minutes; let stand for 2 minutes or until soft-set. Spread over cream cheese mixture. Top with remaining whipped topping. Sprinkle with coconut. Refrigerate overnight. **Yield:** 15 servings.

Blackberry Cobbler

(Pictured at right)

Prep: 15 min.   **Bake:** 45 min. + cooling

I've tweaked this recipe a few times, and everyone enjoys it. You can use frozen blackberries, but fresh are best. The lime zest really complements the sweet fruit, and the sour cream pastry is delightful. —Kimberly Reisinger, Spring, Texas

  6 **cups fresh** *or* **frozen blackberries**
1/2 **cup sugar**
  3 **tablespoons cornstarch**
  1 **teaspoon grated lime peel**
SOUR CREAM PASTRY:
1-1/3 **cups all-purpose flour**
  3 **tablespoons sugar,** *divided*
3/4 **teaspoon baking powder**
1/2 **teaspoon salt**
1/4 **teaspoon baking soda**
  7 **tablespoons cold butter,** *divided*
1/2 **cup sour cream**
1/4 **cup heavy whipping cream**

Place the blackberries in a large bowl. Combine the sugar, cornstarch and lime peel; sprinkle over berries and gently toss to coat. Pour into a greased 9-in. square baking dish.

In a large bowl, combine the flour, 2 tablespoons sugar, baking powder, salt and baking soda; cut in 5 tablespoons butter until crumbly. Combine sour cream and heavy cream; gradually add to crumb mixture, tossing with a fork until mixture forms a ball. Roll out to fit top of baking dish; place pastry over filling. Trim and seal edges; cut slits in top. Melt remaining butter; brush over pastry. Sprinkle with remaining sugar.

Bake, uncovered, at 375° for 30 minutes. Cover and bake 15-20 minutes longer or until filling is bubbly and crust is golden brown. Cool for 15 minutes before serving. **Yield:** 6-8 servings.

Editor's Note: If using frozen blackberries, do not thaw before assembling cobbler.

Potluck Pleasers

The line at the buffet table is sure to form fast when you contribute any of the large-quantity dishes served up here. Cooking for a crowd has never been easier!

FABULOUS CONTRIBUTIONS. Clockwise from upper left: Grape Turkey Salad, Raspberry Vinaigrette, Cottage Potatoes and Chunky Pecan Bars (pp. 168-169); Frosted Pumpkin Gems (p. 170); Giant Green Salad (p. 170); Cranberry Bog Bars (p. 162) and Brunch Strata, Sausage Bacon Bites, Glazed Fruit Bowl and Walnut Pear Coffee Cake (pp. 164-165).

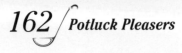

Cranberry Bog Bars

(Pictured on page 160)

Prep: 25 min.   **Bake:** 25 min. + cooling

Sweet and chewy, these fun bars combine the flavors of oats, cranberries, brown sugar and pecans. I like to sprinkle the squares with confectioners' sugar before serving.
—Sally Wakefield, Bruceton Mills, West Virginia

1-1/4   cups butter, softened, *divided*
1-1/2   cups packed brown sugar, *divided*
3-1/2   cups old-fashioned oats, *divided*
  1   cup all-purpose flour
  1   can (16 ounces) whole-berry cranberry
       sauce
1/2   cup finely chopped pecans

In a large mixing bowl, cream 1 cup butter and 1 cup brown sugar; stir in 2-1/2 cups oats and flour. Press into a greased 13-in. x 9-in. x 2-in. baking pan. Spread with cranberry sauce.

In a microwave-safe bowl, melt remaining butter; stir in the pecans and remaining brown sugar and oats. Sprinkle over cranberry sauce. Bake at 375° for 25-30 minutes or until lightly browned. Cool on a wire rack. Cut into bars. **Yield:** 3 dozen.

Spicy Pork Chili

(Pictured at far right)

Prep: 10 min.   **Cook:** 2 hours

Loaded with white beans and cubes of pork, this chili has plenty of bite. But if it's not spicy enough for you, top servings with shredded jalapeno Jack cheese and finely diced onions.   —Larry Laatsch, Saginaw, Michigan

☑ **Uses less fat, sugar or salt. Includes Nutritional Analysis and Diabetic Exchanges.**

1-1/2   pounds pork tenderloin, cubed
  2   large onions, diced
  4   celery ribs, diced
  2   tablespoons butter
  6   cans (15-1/2 ounces *each*) great northern
       beans, rinsed and drained
  4   cans (14-1/2 ounces *each*) chicken
       broth
  2   cups water
  2   jalapeno peppers, seeded and chopped
  2   teaspoons chili powder
1/2   teaspoon *each* white pepper, cayenne
       pepper, ground cumin and pepper
  2   garlic cloves, minced
1/2   teaspoon salt
1/4   teaspoon dried parsley flakes
1/4   teaspoon hot pepper sauce, optional

  1   cup (4 ounces) shredded Monterey Jack
       cheese

In a Dutch oven, cook the pork, onions and celery in butter until meat is browned. Stir in the beans, broth, water, jalapenos, spices, garlic, salt, parsley and hot pepper sauce if desired. Bring to a boil. Reduce heat; cover and simmer for 1-1/2 hours.

Uncover; simmer 30-40 minutes longer or until chili reaches desired consistency. Sprinkle with cheese. **Yield:** 15 servings.

Nutritional Analysis: 1-1/2 cups (prepared with reduced-sodium chicken broth and reduced-fat cheddar cheese) equals 247 calories, 6 g fat (3 g saturated fat), 35 mg cholesterol, 871 mg sodium, 29 g carbohydrate, 9 g fiber, 21 g protein. **Diabetic Exchanges:** 2 starch, 2 lean meat.

Editor's Note: When cutting or seeding hot peppers, use rubber or plastic gloves to protect your hands. Avoid touching your face.

Carrot Cabbage Slaw

(Pictured at right)

Prep/Total Time: 20 min.

This crunchy salad with a homemade honey mayonnaise dressing is light and complements almost any main dish.   —Geordyth Sullivan, Miami, Florida

  4   cups shredded cabbage
  2   cups shredded carrots
  2   medium Golden Delicious apples, diced
  1   cup raisins
1/2   cup chopped walnuts
1/2   cup honey
  1   tablespoon lemon juice
  1   cup (8 ounces) sour cream
1/4   teaspoon salt
1/8   teaspoon pepper
1/8 to 1/4 teaspoon ground nutmeg, optional

In a large serving bowl, combine the cabbage, carrots, apples, raisins and walnuts. In a small bowl, combine the honey and lemon juice until smooth. Stir in the sour cream, salt, pepper and nutmeg if desired. Stir into cabbage mixture. Serve or chill. **Yield:** 12 servings.

Pecan Corn Muffins

(Pictured at right)

Prep: 20 min.   **Bake:** 15 min.

These dressed-up cornmeal muffins are chock-full of chopped pecans. Served warm with jalapeno pepper

jelly, they make a zippy accompaniment to a bowl of chili or a brunch buffet. —*Shirley Glaab*
Hattiesburg, Mississippi

1-1/4 cups yellow cornmeal
1 cup sugar
3/4 cup all-purpose flour
2 teaspoons baking powder
1/4 teaspoon salt
2 eggs, beaten
1 cup milk
1/2 cup butter, melted
1 cup chopped pecans
Jalapeno pepper jelly

In a large bowl, combine the cornmeal, sugar, flour, baking powder and salt. Combine the eggs, milk and butter; stir into dry ingredients just until moistened. Fold in pecans.

Fill greased or paper-lined muffin cups two-thirds full. Bake at 400° for 15-18 minutes or until a toothpick comes out clean. Cool for 5 minutes before removing from pans to wire racks. Serve warm with pepper jelly. **Yield:** 16 muffins.

WHEN COOL WINDS start to blow, head to the kitchen and whip up Spicy Pork Chili, Carrot Cabbage Slaw and Pecan Corn Muffins (shown above) for your clan.

MUNCH a taste-tempting brunch menu at your next potluck with Brunch Strata, Sausage Bacon Bites, Glazed Fruit Bowl and Walnut Pear Coffee Cake (shown above).

Brunch Strata

(Pictured above and on page 160)

Prep: 45 min. **Bake:** 35 min. + standing

Ham, zucchini, mushrooms and cheese flavor this rich, hearty egg dish. It adds appeal to a breakfast or lunch buffet and cuts easily, too. —Arlene Butler, Ogden, Utah

   3 cups sliced fresh mushrooms
   3 cups chopped zucchini
   2 cups cubed fully cooked ham
1-1/2 cups chopped onions
1-1/2 cups chopped green peppers
   2 garlic cloves, minced
 1/3 cup vegetable oil
   2 packages (8 ounces *each*) cream cheese, softened
 1/2 cup half-and-half cream
 12 eggs
   4 cups cubed day-old bread
   3 cups (12 ounces) shredded cheddar cheese
   1 teaspoon salt
 1/2 teaspoon pepper

In a large skillet, saute the mushrooms, zucchini, ham, onions, green peppers and garlic in oil until vegetables are tender. Drain and pat dry; set aside.

In a large mixing bowl, beat the cream cheese and cream until smooth. Beat in the eggs. Stir in the bread, cheese, salt, pepper and vegetable mixture.

Pour into two greased 11-in. x 7-in. x 2-in. baking dishes. Bake, uncovered, at 350° for 35-40 minutes or until a knife inserted near the center comes out clean. Let stand for 10 minutes before serving. **Yield:** 2 casseroles (8 servings each).

Sausage Bacon Bites

(Pictured at left and on page 160)

Prep: 20 min. + chilling   **Bake:** 35 min.

These tasty morsels are perfect with almost any egg dish or as finger food that party guests can just pop into their mouths.   —*Pat Waymire, Yellow Springs, Ohio*

3/4 pound sliced bacon
2 packages (8 ounces *each*) brown-and-serve sausage links
1/2 cup plus 2 tablespoons packed brown sugar, *divided*

Cut bacon strips widthwise in half; cut sausage links in half. Wrap a piece of bacon around each piece of sausage. Place 1/2 cup brown sugar in a shallow bowl; roll sausages in sugar. Secure each with a toothpick. Place in a foil-lined 15-in. x 10-in. x 1-in. baking pan. Cover and refrigerate for 4 hours or overnight.

Sprinkle with 1 tablespoon of brown sugar. Bake at 350° for 35-40 minutes or until the bacon is crisp, turning once. Sprinkle with the remaining brown sugar. **Yield:** about 3-1/2 dozen.

Glazed Fruit Bowl

(Pictured at left and on page 160)

Prep/Total Time: 30 min.

This fruit salad combines summer favorites such as cantaloupe, honeydew and strawberries into a refreshing side dish.   —*Christine Wilson, Sellersville, Pennsylvania*

✓ Uses less fat, sugar or salt. Includes Nutritional Analysis and Diabetic Exchanges.

2 cans (20 ounces *each*) unsweetened pineapple chunks
2 packages (3 ounces *each*) cook-and-serve vanilla pudding mix
2-1/2 cups orange juice
1 small cantaloupe, cubed
3-1/2 cups cubed honeydew
2 cups fresh strawberries, halved
2 cups fresh blueberries
2 cups seedless grapes
2 medium firm bananas, sliced

Drain pineapple, reserving 1 cup juice; set pineapple aside. (Discard remaining juice or save for another use.) In a large saucepan, combine the pudding mix, pineapple juice and orange juice. Cook and stir over medium heat until mixture boils and thickens. Remove from the heat; cool.

In a large bowl, combine the pineapple, melon, berries, grapes and bananas. Drizzle with the pudding mixture. Refrigerate until serving. **Yield:** 25 servings.

Nutritional Analysis: 3/4 cup (prepared with sugar-free pudding mix) equals 82 calories, trace fat (trace saturated fat), 0 cholesterol, 43 mg sodium, 20 g carbohydrate, 2 g fiber, 1 g protein. **Diabetic Exchange:** 1-1/2 fruit.

Walnut Pear Coffee Cake

(Pictured at far left and on page 160)

Prep: 30 min.   **Bake:** 50 min. + cooling

This moist coffee cake goes great with a cup of coffee at breakfast but also makes a delicious snack or dessert. When I bring it to work, it disappears in minutes.   —*Darlene Spalding, Lynden, Washington*

1 cup chopped walnuts
1/3 cup packed brown sugar
1 teaspoon ground cinnamon
1/3 cup all-purpose flour
1/4 cup cold butter
FILLING:
2 medium ripe pears, peeled and sliced (about 2 cups)
2 teaspoons lemon juice
1/2 cup butter, softened
1 cup sugar
2 eggs
1 teaspoon vanilla extract
1-3/4 cups all-purpose flour
3/4 teaspoon baking powder
1/2 teaspoon baking soda
1/4 teaspoon salt
1 cup (8 ounces) sour cream
1/2 cup chopped walnuts

In a bowl, combine walnuts, brown sugar and cinnamon; set aside. Place flour in a small bowl; cut in butter until mixture resembles coarse crumbs. Stir in 3/4 cup of nut mixture; set aside for topping. Set aside remaining nut mixture for filling.

Toss pears with the lemon juice; set aside. In a small mixing bowl, cream the butter and sugar. Add eggs, one at a time, beating well after each addition. Beat in vanilla. Combine the flour, baking powder, baking soda and salt; add to creamed mixture alternately with sour cream.

Spread two-thirds of batter into a greased 9-in. springform pan. Top with reserved nut mixture, pears and remaining batter. Sprinkle with walnuts and reserved topping mixture.

Bake at 350° for 50-55 minutes or until a toothpick inserted near the center comes out clean. Cool on a wire rack for 10 minutes. Carefully run a knife around edge of pan to loosen; remove sides of pan. Cool for 1 hour before cutting. **Yield:** 12 servings.

Cinnamon Roll Coffee Cakes

(Pictured below)

Prep: 40 min. + rising **Bake:** 20 min. + cooling

The whole house smelled wonderful whenever my mom made these mouth-watering coffee cakes. Now, I bake them for holidays and special gatherings. They also make great gifts. —Tracy Sorrentino, Commerce, Michigan

> 2 packages (1/4 ounce *each*) active dry yeast
> 1/3 cup warm water (110° to 115°)
> 1 cup warm milk (110° to 115°)
> 1 cup butter, melted
> 2 eggs, beaten
> 1/2 cup sugar
> 1 teaspoon salt
> 5-1/2 to 6-1/4 cups all-purpose flour
> FILLING:
> 1 cup butter, softened
> 1/2 cup packed brown sugar
> 1 tablespoon ground cinnamon
> 1-1/2 cups chopped pecans
> ICING:
> 1-1/2 cups confectioners' sugar
> 1/2 teaspoon vanilla extract
> 2 to 3 tablespoons milk

In a large mixing bowl, dissolve yeast in warm water. Add the milk, butter, eggs, sugar, salt and 3 cups flour; beat until smooth. Stir in enough remaining flour to form a soft dough. Turn onto a lightly floured surface; knead until smooth and elastic, about 6-8 minutes. Place in a greased bowl, turning once to grease top. Cover and let rise in a warm place until doubled, about 1 hour.

Punch dough down; turn onto a floured surface. Divide into four portions. Roll each portion into a 12-in. x 8-in. rectangle. In a mixing bowl, cream the butter, brown sugar and cinnamon. Spread over each rectangle to within 1/2 in. of edges. Sprinkle with pecans. Roll up each jelly-roll style, starting with a long side; pinch seam to seal.

Place each roll seam side down in a greased 15-in. x 10-in. x 1-in. baking pan; pinch ends together to form a ring. With scissors, cut from an outside edge two-thirds of the way toward center of ring at 1-in. intervals. Separate strips slightly; twist to allow filling to show, slightly overlapping previous strip.

Cover and let rise in a warm place until doubled, about 30 minutes. Bake at 350° for 20-25 minutes or until golden brown. Remove from pans to wire racks to cool. Combine icing ingredients; drizzle over coffee cakes. May be frozen for up to 2 months. **Yield:** 4 coffee cakes.

Chunky Blue Cheese Dressing

Prep/Total Time: 10 min.

This flavorful full-bodied dressing is better than any bottled dressing I've ever tasted...and it's easy to prepare, too. I found the recipe in a church cookbook.
—Leona Luecking, West Burlington, Iowa

> 1/4 cup milk
> 3 cups mayonnaise
> 1 cup (8 ounces) sour cream
> 4 ounces crumbled blue cheese
> 2 teaspoons garlic salt

Place the milk, mayonnaise, sour cream, blue cheese and garlic salt in a blender. Cover and process until smooth. Refrigerate until serving. **Yield:** about 4 cups.

Cucumber Potato Salad

(Pictured above right)

Prep: 30 min. + chilling

Because it seems to appeal to so many, this creamy salad is one of my favorite crowd-size recipes. I've taken it to potlucks and picnics...and it's always a hit.
—Marlene Muckenhirn, Delano, Minnesota

5 pounds red potatoes
4 celery ribs, sliced
1 bunch green onions, sliced
2 tablespoons dill weed
2 teaspoons salt
2 cups mayonnaise
1 bottle (16 ounces) cucumber ranch salad dressing

Place potatoes in a large kettle; cover with water. Bring to a boil. Reduce heat; cover and simmer for 20-25 minutes or until tender. Drain and cool. Cut potatoes into small cubes.

In a large serving bowl, combine the potatoes, celery, onions, dill and salt. In a small bowl, whisk mayonnaise and salad dressing until blended. Pour over potato mixture and stir gently to coat. Cover; refrigerate for at least 6 hours before serving. **Yield:** 36 servings (about 3/4 cup each).

Mint Chip Freeze

(Pictured at right)

Prep: 30 min. + chilling

I'm a retired home economics teacher and have quite a collection of recipes from my classes. My students really liked this refreshing frozen dessert made with ice cream and sandwich cookies.
—Mrs. Robert Lamb
Daleville, Indiana

2 packages (14 ounces *each*) cream-filled chocolate sandwich cookies, crushed
1/2 cup butter, melted
1 can (12 ounces) evaporated milk
1 cup sugar
1/2 cup butter, cubed
2 squares (1 ounce *each*) unsweetened baking chocolate
1 gallon mint chocolate chip ice cream, softened
1 carton (16 ounces) frozen whipped topping, thawed
Shaved chocolate

In a large bowl, combine the cookie crumbs and butter. Press into two 13-in. x 9-in. x 2-in. dishes. Refrigerate for 30 minutes.

In a small saucepan, combine the milk, sugar, butter and chocolate. Cook and stir over medium heat until thickened and bubbly, about 12 minutes. Remove from the heat; cool completely.

Spread ice cream over each crust. Spoon cooled chocolate sauce over top; evenly spread to cover. Freeze until firm. Spread with whipped topping. Desserts may be frozen for up to 2 months. Remove from the freezer 10 minutes before cutting. Garnish with shaved chocolate. **Yield:** 2 desserts (15-18 servings each).

Grape Turkey Salad

(Pictured at far right and on page 160)

Prep: 20 min. + chilling

To maintain freshness, serve this make-ahead salad on a chilled platter. —*Sue Ross, Casa Grande, Arizona*

☑ **Uses less fat, sugar or salt. Includes Nutritional Analysis and Diabetic Exchanges.**

- 12 cups cubed cooked turkey breast
- 2 pounds green grapes, halved
- 5-1/4 cups diced celery
- 1 to 1-1/2 cups chopped pecans, toasted
- 3 green onions, sliced
- 2 cups mayonnaise
- 1-1/2 cups chicken broth
- 3/4 cup vinaigrette
- 1 tablespoon prepared mustard

In a very large bowl, combine the turkey, grapes, celery, pecans and onions. In a small bowl, whisk mayonnaise, broth, vinaigrette and mustard until smooth. Pour over turkey mixture and mix well. Cover and chill for at least 4 hours before serving. Refrigerate leftovers. **Yield:** 20 servings (about 1 cup each).
Nutritional Analysis: 1 cup (prepared with fat-free mayonnaise and 1 cup pecans) equals 232 calories, 8 g fat (1 g saturated fat), 75 mg cholesterol, 391 mg sodium, 14 g carbohydrate, 2 g fiber, 27 g protein. **Diabetic Exchanges:** 3 lean meat, 1 fruit.

Raspberry Vinaigrette

(Pictured at far right and on page 160)

Prep/Total Time: 20 min.

When making this sweet dressing, figure on 2 tablespoons of dressing for each 1-cup serving of salad greens.
—*Betty Miller, Angola, Indiana*

- 2 jars (12 ounces *each*) seedless raspberry preserves
- 1-1/4 cups sugar, *divided*
- 1/2 cup water
- 1/3 cup chopped sweet onion
- 1/4 cup balsamic vinegar
- 1 tablespoon dried tarragon
- 1 tablespoon curry powder
- 1 teaspoon white pepper
- 1 teaspoon pepper
- 1 cup olive oil
- Torn mixed salad greens

In a large saucepan, bring preserves and 3/4 cup sugar to a boil. Remove from heat; cool slightly. Transfer to a blender. Add the water, onion, vinegar, tarragon, curry powder, white pepper, pepper and remaining sugar; cover and process until smooth. While processing, gradually add oil in a steady stream. Serve with salad greens. **Yield:** about 4 cups.

Cottage Potatoes

(Pictured at right and on page 160)

Prep: 20 min.   **Bake:** 55 min.

I often make this for our family reunions…and there's never any left. —*Mary Sholtis, Ashtabula, Ohio*

- 12 large potatoes, peeled and diced
- 8 ounces process cheese (Velveeta), cubed
- 1 large onion, finely chopped
- 1 large green pepper, diced
- 1 jar (2 ounces) diced pimientos, drained
- 1 slice bread, torn
- 3 tablespoons minced fresh parsley, *divided*
- 1/2 teaspoon salt
- 1/2 cup milk
- 1/2 cup butter, melted
- 1-1/2 cups cornflakes, crushed

Place potatoes in a large saucepan or Dutch oven; cover with water. Bring to a boil; reduce heat to medium. Cover and cook for 5-7 minutes or until tender; drain. In a bowl, combine cheese, onion, green pepper, pimientos, bread, 2 tablespoons parsley and salt.

In a greased shallow 4-qt. baking dish, layer a third of the potatoes and a third of cheese mixture. Repeat layers twice. Pour milk and butter over all; sprinkle with cornflake crumbs. Cover and bake at 350° for 45 minutes. Uncover; bake 10-15 minutes longer or until bubbly and top is golden. Sprinkle with remaining parsley. **Yield:** 12-14 servings.

Chunky Pecan Bars

(Pictured at right and on page 160)

Prep: 15 min.   **Bake:** 20 min. + cooling

Most folks can't eat just one of these rich gooey bars that taste like chocolate pecan pie. —*Hazel Baldner, Austin, Minnesota*

- 1-1/2 cups all-purpose flour
- 1/2 cup packed brown sugar
- 1/2 cup cold butter
- FILLING:
- 3 eggs
- 3/4 cup sugar
- 3/4 cup dark corn syrup
- 2 tablespoons butter, melted

1 teaspoon vanilla extract
1-3/4 cups semisweet chocolate chunks
1-1/2 cups coarsely chopped pecans

In a small bowl, combine the flour and brown sugar; cut in butter until crumbly. Press into a greased 13-in. x 9-in. x 2-in. baking pan. Bake at 350° for 10-15 minutes or until golden brown.

Meanwhile, in a large bowl, whisk the eggs, sugar, corn syrup, butter and vanilla until blended. Stir in chocolate chunks and pecans. Pour over crust. Bake for 20-25 minutes or until set. Cool completely on a wire rack. Cut into bars. Store in an airtight container in the refrigerator. **Yield**: about 6 dozen.

CELEBRATE warm weather with picnic-pleasing dishes such as Grape Turkey Salad, Raspberry Vinaigrette, Cottage Potatoes and Chunky Pecan Bars (shown above).

Chunky Chicken Veggie Soup

(Pictured below)

Prep: 25 min.   **Cook:** 25 min.

Catering to a Christmas crowd or a huddle of hungry Super Bowl fans? Try this hot savory soup loaded with veggies, chicken and seasonings. Ladle it up with warm bread for a hearty stick-to-your-ribs meal in a bowl.
— *Sundra Hauc, Bogalusa, Louisiana*

 8 **cups chicken broth**
 6 **medium carrots, sliced**
 2 **medium onions, chopped**
 2 **small zucchini, chopped**
 4 **garlic cloves, minced**
 6 **cups cubed cooked chicken**
 2 **cans (28 ounces *each*) crushed tomatoes**
 1 **can (14-1/2 ounces) diced tomatoes, undrained**
 1 **can (10 ounces) diced tomatoes with green chilies, undrained**
 1 **can (8 ounces) tomato sauce**
 4 **teaspoons sugar**
 1 **teaspoon salt**
 1 **teaspoon celery salt**
 1 **teaspoon Creole seasoning**
1/2 **teaspoon pepper**

In a large soup kettle, bring the broth, carrots and onions to a boil. Reduce heat; simmer, uncovered, for 5 minutes. Add the zucchini and garlic; simmer 5 minutes longer or until vegetables are crisp-tender. Stir in all of the remaining ingredients and heat through. **Yield:** 20 servings.

Frosted Pumpkin Gems

(Pictured on page 160)

Prep: 20 min.   **Bake:** 30 min. + cooling

If I don't hold back my four hungry sons, they'll eat a third of the batch of these moist and tender mini muffins before I get them frosted!
— *Becky Carnahan
Mauldin, South Carolina*

 1 **can (15 ounces) solid-pack pumpkin**
 3 **eggs**
1/2 **cup vegetable oil**
 2 **teaspoons ground cinnamon**
 1 **teaspoon baking soda**
 1 **package (18-1/4 ounces) yellow cake mix**
 1 **to 2 cans (12 ounces *each*) whipped cream cheese frosting**

In a mixing bowl, combine the pumpkin, eggs, oil, cinnamon and baking soda. Add cake mix; beat on low speed for 1 minute or until combined. Beat on high for 2 minutes.

Fill paper-lined miniature muffin cups two-thirds full. Bake at 350° for 12-16 minutes or until a toothpick comes out clean. Cool for 5 minutes before removing from pans to wire racks to cool completely. Spread with frosting. **Yield:** 7 dozen.

Giant Green Salad

(Pictured on page 160)

Prep/Total Time: 30 min.

I tried this refreshing salad at a friend's house and just couldn't wait to have the recipe. It makes a beautiful presentation for holidays.
— *Rebecca Cook Jones
Henderson, Nevada*

 3 **tablespoons butter**
 4 **cups walnut halves**
1/4 **cup sugar**
 4 **bunches romaine, torn**
16 **cups torn leaf lettuce**
 6 **cups dried cranberries**
 4 **medium sweet yellow peppers, diced**
 4 **cups (16 ounces) crumbled feta cheese**
Coarsely ground pepper, optional
DRESSING:
 4 **envelopes Italian salad dressing mix**
 2 **cups vegetable oil**
 1 **cup balsamic vinegar**
3/4 **cup water**

In a large heavy skillet, melt the butter. Add walnuts; cook over medium heat until toasted, about 4 minutes. Sprinkle with sugar; cook and stir for 2-4 minutes or until sugar is melted. Spread on foil to cool.

Nutritional Analysis: 1/4 cup equals 22 calories, 1 g fat (trace saturated fat), 0 cholesterol, 2 mg sodium, 3 g carbohydrate, 1 g fiber, 1 g protein. **Diabetic Exchange:** Free food.

Editor's Note: When cutting or seeding hot peppers, use rubber or plastic gloves to protect your hands. Avoid touching your face.

Red Cream Soda Punch

(Pictured below)

Prep: 5 min. + chilling

The bright coral color and sweet citrusy flavor make this fizzy punch a hit…and there's plenty to go around!
—Naomi Cross, Millwood, Kentucky

    4 quarts cold water
    2 cans (12 ounces *each*) frozen orange juice
      concentrate, thawed
    1 can (12 ounces) frozen lemonade
      concentrate, thawed
  1/2 cup sugar
    1 bottle (2 liters) red cream soda, chilled

In a large punch bowl or several pitchers, combine the water, concentrates and sugar; stir until sugar is dissolved. Refrigerate for 2 hours or until chilled. Just before serving, stir in the cream soda. **Yield:** about 7 quarts.

Editor's Note: This recipe was tested with Barq's Red Cream Soda.

Meanwhile, in several large salad bowls, combine the romaine, lettuce, cranberries, yellow peppers, cheese and pepper if desired. In a jar with a tight-fitting lid, combine the dressing ingredients; shake well. Drizzle over salad and toss to coat. Sprinkle with sugared walnuts. **Yield:** 85 servings.

Watermelon Salsa

(Pictured above)

Prep/Total Time: 25 min.

A burst of fresh flavor is yours in this unique summer salsa sparked with cilantro, basil and mint. —Ann Chan
Augusta, Georgia

✓ Uses less fat, sugar or salt. Includes Nutritional Analysis and Diabetic Exchanges.

    4 cups diced seedless watermelon
    1 cup diced green pepper
    1 cup diced sweet red pepper
    1 cup diced red onion
    1 cup sliced fresh carrots
    2 jalapeno peppers, seeded and cut into
      rings
    2 tablespoons rice wine vinegar
    1 tablespoon canola oil
    1 cup chopped fresh cilantro
    2 tablespoons chopped fresh mint
    2 tablespoons chopped fresh basil
  1/4 cup unsalted chopped peanuts

In a large bowl, combine the first 11 ingredients. Cover and refrigerate until serving. Just before serving, sprinkle with peanuts. **Yield:** about 8-1/2 cups.

FOLKS will quickly fall in line when the potluck menu features savory Barbecued Brisket, tender Marinated Vegetables, Oat Pan Rolls and Paradise Pineapple Pie (shown above).

Barbecued Brisket

(Pictured above)

Prep: 10 min. + marinating
Cook: 5 hours + standing

These tender slices of beef can be served as a main dish for Sunday dinner or as barbecued beef sandwiches for a potluck. —Mildred Burk, Parker, Kansas

  1 bottle (10 ounces) soy sauce
  1 tablespoon Liquid Smoke, optional
  2 teaspoons pepper
  2 teaspoons Worcestershire sauce
  1 teaspoon garlic salt
  1 teaspoon onion salt
  1 teaspoon celery salt
  1 fresh beef brisket (about 5 pounds)
BARBECUE SAUCE:
  1 bottle (14 ounces) ketchup
  1 to 2 tablespoons sugar
  1 tablespoon cider vinegar
1-1/2 teaspoons prepared mustard
  1 teaspoon Worcestershire sauce
  1 teaspoon soy sauce

In a large resealable plastic bag, combine the first seven ingredients. Add the brisket. Seal bag and turn to coat; refrigerate for 8 hours or overnight.

Drain and discard marinade. Place brisket on a large sheet of heavy-duty foil; seal tightly. Place in a 15-in. x 10-in. x 1-in. baking pan coated with nonstick cooking spray. Bake at 325° for 4 hours or until meat is tender.

Remove brisket; let stand for 20 minutes. Thinly slice meat across the grain. Place in an ungreased 13-in. x 9-in. x 2-in. baking dish. Combine sauce ingredients; pour over meat. Cover and bake for 1 hour or until heated through. Brisket may be frozen for up to 3 months. **Yield:** 12 servings.

Editor's Note: This is a fresh beef brisket, not corned beef.

Marinated Vegetables

(Pictured at left)

Prep: 25 min. + chilling

A tangy dressing makes this refreshing vegetable blend especially pleasing. Sometimes I add thinly sliced carrots, zucchini or pearl onions. —Priscilla Weaver
Hagerstown, Maryland

    3/4 cup lemon juice
    3/4 cup vegetable oil
      3 tablespoons sugar
      1 tablespoon salt
  1-1/2 teaspoons dried oregano
    1/2 teaspoon pepper
      1 can (15 ounces) whole baby corn, rinsed
        and drained
      1 cup halved brussels sprouts, cooked
      1 cup halved fresh mushrooms
      1 cup fresh cauliflowerets
      1 cup fresh snow peas, halved
      1 cup cherry tomatoes
      1 cup sliced sweet yellow pepper
      1 cup sliced sweet red pepper

In a bowl, whisk the lemon juice, oil, sugar, salt, oregano and pepper. Pour into a large resealable plastic bag; add the vegetables. Seal bag and turn to coat; refrigerate for 6 hours or overnight. **Yield:** 12 servings.

Oat Pan Rolls

(Pictured at left)

Prep: 30 min. + rising   **Bake:** 30 min.

I've made so many of these delicious rolls that I think I could make them blindfolded! I always take about 200
of them to the senior citizens' dinner at our church. After shaping the rolls, you can freeze them…then just thaw and bake when you need them. —Debbie Johnson
Centertown, Missouri

      2 cups quick-cooking oats
    2/3 cup packed brown sugar
    1/4 cup butter, cubed
      1 tablespoon salt
  2-1/2 cups boiling water
      2 packages (1/4 ounce *each*) active
        dry yeast
    1/2 cup warm water (110° to 115°)
  5-1/2 to 6 cups all-purpose flour
Additional butter, melted

In a bowl, combine oats, brown sugar, butter and salt; stir in boiling water. Cool to 110°-115°. In a large mixing bowl, dissolve yeast in warm water; let stand for 5 minutes. Add oat mixture and 2 cups flour; beat until smooth. Stir in enough remaining flour to form a soft dough.

Turn onto a floured surface; knead until smooth and elastic, about 6-8 minutes. Place in a greased bowl, turning once to grease top. Cover and let rise in a warm place until doubled, about 1 hour.

Punch dough down. Turn onto a lightly floured surface; divide into 20 pieces. Place in a greased 13-in. x 9-in. x 2-in. baking pan. Cover and let rise until doubled, about 45 minutes. Bake at 350° for 30-35 minutes or until golden brown. Remove from pan to a wire rack; brush with melted butter. **Yield:** 20 rolls.

Paradise Pineapple Pie

(Pictured at far left)

Prep: 20 min. + chilling

This quick-to-fix recipe makes two yummy pies that will be a hit at any carry-in dinner. Lemon juice and pineapple flavor the fluffy filling that's topped with a sprinkling of coconut. I like to garnish with a sprig of fresh mint.
—Bonnie Baumgardner, Sylva, North Carolina

      1 can (14 ounces) sweetened condensed milk
      1 carton (12 ounces) frozen whipped
        topping, thawed
      1 can (20 ounces) crushed pineapple,
        drained
    1/3 cup lemon juice
      2 graham cracker crusts (8 inches)
      1 cup flaked coconut, toasted

Place the milk in a bowl; fold in whipped topping. Add pineapple and lemon juice; stir for 2 minutes or until slightly thickened. Pour into crusts. Sprinkle with coconut. Cover and refrigerate for at least 2 hours. **Yield:** 2 pies (6 servings each).

Pumpkin Pies for a Gang

(Pictured below)

Prep: 50 min. **Bake:** 1 hour + cooling

Come fall, pumpkin pie always comes to mind. Guests love this traditional treat, and the recipe is perfect for a large gathering—it fills eight pie shells! —Edna Hoffman Hebron, Indiana

    4 packages (15 ounces *each*) refrigerated
      pie pastry
   16 eggs, beaten
    4 cans (29 ounces *each*) solid-pack pumpkin
  1/2 cup dark corn syrup
    9 cups sugar
1-1/4 cups all-purpose flour
    1 cup nonfat dry milk powder
    4 teaspoons salt
    4 teaspoons *each* ground ginger, cinnamon
      and nutmeg
    1 teaspoon ground cloves
    2 quarts milk

Unroll pastry; line eight 9-in. pie plates with one sheet of pastry. Flute edges; set aside. In a large bowl, combine the eggs, pumpkin and corn syrup. In two large bowls, combine the sugar, flour, milk powder, salt, ginger, cinnamon, nutmeg and cloves; stir half of the pumpkin mixture into each bowl. Gradually stir in milk until smooth.

Pour into pie shells. Bake at 350° for 60-70 minutes or until a knife inserted near the center comes out clean. Cool on wire racks. Store in the refrigerator. **Yield:** 8 pies (6-8 servings each).

Gingerbread with Raisin Sauce

Prep: 30 min. **Bake:** 30 min. + cooling

What's nicer on a cold winter day than the spicy aroma of warm gingerbread filling the house? Drizzled with a rich raisin sauce, the wonderfully moist texture of this old-time favorite is good any time of year. Folks can't get enough! —Julia Livingston, Frostproof, Florida

2-1/2 cups shortening
2-1/2 cups sugar
    8 eggs
    5 cups molasses
   10 cups all-purpose flour
    3 tablespoons ground cinnamon
    2 tablespoons baking powder
    2 tablespoons ground ginger
2-1/2 teaspoons baking soda
    1 teaspoon salt
    3 cups water
RAISIN SAUCE:
2-1/2 cups packed brown sugar
  1/2 cup plus 2 tablespoons sugar
  1/2 cup plus 2 tablespoons all-purpose flour
    1 teaspoon salt
    8 cups water
    3 cups golden raisins
  1/2 cup plus 2 tablespoons butter

In a very large mixing bowl, cream the shortening and sugar. Add eggs, one at a time, beating well after each addition. Beat in molasses. Combine flour, cinnamon, baking powder, ginger, baking soda and salt; add to creamed mixture alternately with water. Mix well.

Transfer to four greased 13-in. x 9-in. x 2-in. baking pans. Bake at 350° for 30-40 minutes or until a toothpick comes out clean. Cool on wire racks.

For sauce, in a Dutch oven, combine the sugars, flour and salt. Gradually stir in water. Bring to a boil, stirring constantly. Reduce heat; add raisins. Simmer for 10 minutes or until raisins are plump, stirring occasionally.

Remove from the heat. Stir in butter until melted. Serve warm with gingerbread. **Yield:** 4 cakes (20 servings each) and about 10 cups sauce.

Cheesy Spaghetti Bake

(Pictured above right)

Prep: 45 min. **Bake:** 40 min.

With all the favorite ingredients of spaghetti and meat sauce, this recipe makes two hearty family-style casseroles. It's great for casual entertaining or a potluck. —Sue Braunschweig, Delafield, Wisconsin

    1 pound uncooked spaghetti, broken
      into 3-inch pieces

4 pounds ground beef
2 large onions, chopped
1 large green pepper, chopped
4 cups milk
4 cans (10-3/4 ounces *each*) condensed tomato soup, undiluted
2 cans (10-3/4 ounces *each*) condensed cream of mushroom soup, undiluted
4 cups (16 ounces) shredded sharp cheddar cheese, *divided*

Cook spaghetti according to package directions. Drain and place in two greased 13-in. x 9-in. x 2-in. baking dishes; set aside.

In two Dutch ovens or stockpots, cook the beef, onions and green pepper over medium heat until meat is no longer pink; drain. To each pot, add 2 cups of milk, two cans of tomato soup, one can of mushroom soup and 1 cup of cheese. Bring to a boil.

Spoon over spaghetti (spaghetti will absorb liquid during baking). Sprinkle with remaining cheese. Bake, uncovered, at 350° for 40-45 minutes or until bubbly and the tops are lightly browned. **Yield:** 2 casseroles (12 servings each).

Sweet-Sour Vegetable Salad

(Pictured at right)

Prep: 25 min. + chilling

I quickly assemble this marinated medley using canned veggies. It's excellent for potlucks, accompanied by yeast rolls, corn bread muffins or Parmesan cheese squares.
—Lucille Terry, Frankfort, Kentucky

2 cups sugar
1-1/2 cups cider vinegar
1 cup vegetable oil
2 teaspoons salt
2 teaspoons white pepper
2 cans (15-1/4 ounces *each*) small peas, drained
2 cans (11 ounces *each*) shoepeg corn, drained
1 can (16 ounces) kidney beans, rinsed and drained
1 can (15-1/4 ounces) lima beans, drained
1 can (14-1/2 ounces) cut green beans, drained
1 can (14 ounces) water-packed artichoke hearts, rinsed, drained and halved
2 jars (4-1/2 ounces *each*) sliced mushrooms, drained
1 can (8 ounces) sliced water chestnuts, drained
2 cups thinly sliced celery
1 cup chopped onion
1 cup chopped sweet red pepper
1 cup chopped green pepper
1 jar (7 ounces) diced pimientos, drained

For the dressing, combine the sugar, vinegar, oil, salt and pepper in a large saucepan. Bring to a boil. Remove from the heat; cool. In a large bowl, combine the remaining ingredients. Drizzle with dressing and toss to coat. Cover and chill for 8 hours. Serve with a slotted spoon. **Yield:** 24 servings.

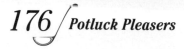
Baked Taco Chicken

(Pictured at far right)

Prep: 10 min. **Bake:** 55 min.

The mildly seasoned chicken pieces could be pan-fried or deep-fried, but we like oven baking the best.
—*Helen Grimli, Browns Valley, Minnesota*

    1 cup all-purpose flour
    2 envelopes taco seasoning
  1/2 teaspoon salt
    2 eggs
    2 tablespoons milk
    2 broiler/fryer chickens (3 to 4 pounds *each*),
      cut up

In a large resealable plastic bag, combine the flour, taco seasoning and salt. In a shallow bowl, beat eggs and milk. Dip chicken pieces in egg mixture, then place in bag and shake to coat.

Place bone side down in a greased 15-in. x 10-in. x 1-in. baking pan. Bake, uncovered, at 350° for 55-60 minutes or until juices run clear. **Yield:** 12 servings.

Cheesy Onion Focaccia

(Pictured at far right)

Prep: 1 hour + rising **Bake:** 15 min.

With melted cheddar and Parmesan cheese on top, this bread tastes best when served warm.
—*Christina Romanyshyn, Granbury, Texas*

  3/4 cup water (70° to 80°)
    2 tablespoons olive oil
    1 teaspoon salt
    2 cups bread flour
    1 tablespoon sugar
1-1/2 teaspoons active dry yeast
    2 medium onions, sliced and quartered
    3 garlic cloves, minced
  1/4 cup butter
    2 teaspoons Italian seasoning
    1 cup (4 ounces) shredded cheddar cheese
    2 tablespoons grated Parmesan cheese

In bread machine pan, place the first six ingredients in order suggested by manufacturer. Select dough setting (check dough after 5 minutes of mixing; add 1 to 2 tablespoons of water or flour if needed).

When the cycle is completed, turn dough onto a lightly greased 12-in. pizza pan; pat into a 10-in. circle. Cover and let rise in a warm place until doubled, about 30 minutes. Meanwhile, in a large skillet, saute onions and garlic in butter for 18-20 minutes or until golden brown. Stir in the Italian seasoning; cook 1 minute longer.

Using the end of a wooden spoon handle, make deep indentations 1 in. apart in dough. Top with onion mixture and cheeses. Bake at 400° for 15-18 minutes or until golden brown. Serve warm. **Yield:** 12 servings.

Pretty Picnic Salad

(Pictured at right)

Prep/Total Time: 30 min.

A homemade vinaigrette seasoned with thyme and garlic coats this colorful salad that you'll make again and again. —*Paula Marchesi, Lenhartsville, Pennsylvania*

    5 medium red potatoes (about 1-3/4 pounds)
  1/2 pound fresh green beans, cut into 2-inch
      pieces
    1 medium sweet red pepper, cut into strips
    1 cup frozen corn, thawed
    1 celery rib, thinly sliced
    1 medium carrot, shredded
    3 green onions, thinly sliced
1-1/2 cups cubed mozzarella cheese
VINAIGRETTE:
  2/3 cup olive oil
    2 garlic cloves, minced
  1/4 cup white wine vinegar
    2 tablespoons minced fresh thyme
    1 to 1-1/2 teaspoons salt
  1/2 teaspoon sugar
  1/2 teaspoon garlic powder
  1/2 teaspoon pepper

Cut potatoes into 1/2-in. slices; cut each slice into four pieces. Place in a large saucepan and cover with water. Bring to a boil. Reduce heat; cover and cook for 15-20 minutes or until tender.

Meanwhile, place beans in a small saucepan and cover with water. Bring to a boil. Reduce heat; cover and cook for 8-10 minutes or until crisp-tender. Drain potatoes and beans.

In a large bowl, combine red pepper, corn, celery, carrot, onions and cheese. Add potatoes and beans. In a small bowl, whisk vinaigrette ingredients. Pour over vegetable mixture; toss to coat. Serve at room temperature or chilled. **Yield:** 12 servings.

Creamy Fruit Delight

(Pictured above right)

Prep: 25 min. + chilling

Everyone will want to save room for this fun make-ahead dessert that uses convenient canned fruit and pie filling. —*Leota Recknor, Ash Grove, Missouri*

PICNICS, parties and other fun-filled occasions make the perfect settings for serving this lip-smacking menu of Baked Taco Chicken, Cheesy Onion Focaccia, Pretty Picnic Salad and Creamy Fruit Delight (shown above).

1 package (8 ounces) cream cheese, softened
1 jar (6 ounces) peach baby food
1/2 teaspoon ground ginger
1/4 to 1/2 teaspoon ground nutmeg
1 can (21 ounces) peach pie filling
1 can (15 ounces) fruit cocktail, drained
1 can (11 ounces) mandarin oranges, drained
1/4 cup crushed pineapple

1 carton (8 ounces) frozen whipped topping, thawed
1 cup miniature marshmallows
1/2 cup chopped walnuts

In a large mixing bowl, beat cream cheese until smooth. Add the baby food, ginger and nutmeg; mix well. Stir in the pie filling, fruit cocktail, oranges and pineapple. Fold in whipped topping, marshmallows and nuts. Cover and refrigerate overnight. **Yield:** 12 servings.

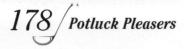

Hearty Spaghetti

(Pictured below)

Prep: 20 min.   **Cook:** 1 hour

This spaghetti will feed a crowd. For easy transport, assemble pasta and sauce in an insulated carrier.
—Julia Livingston, Frostproof, Florida

- 5 pounds ground beef
- 5 medium onions, chopped
- 1 bunch celery, chopped
- 8 cans (14-1/2 ounces *each*) diced tomatoes, drained
- 2 cans (6 ounces *each*) tomato paste
- 1 cup Worcestershire sauce
- 1/2 cup sugar
- 4 tablespoons salt
- 4 pounds uncooked spaghetti

In two large Dutch ovens or soup kettles, cook the beef, onions and celery over medium heat until meat is no longer pink; drain.

Stir in the tomatoes, tomato paste, Worcestershire sauce, sugar and salt. Bring to a boil. Reduce heat; cover and simmer for 1 hour, stirring occasionally.

Cook spaghetti according to package directions; drain. Serve with meat sauce. **Yield:** 25 servings (about 3/4 cup meat sauce with 3/4 cup spaghetti).

Whole Wheat Braids

Prep: 20 min. + rising   **Bake:** 45 min. + cooling

There's nothing like fresh bread to complete a meal. I've had very good results with this recipe. Braiding the dough makes a pretty presentation.
—Suella Miller
LaGrange, Indiana

- 3 packages (1/4 ounce *each*) active dry yeast
- 3 cups warm water (110° to 115°)
- 1/2 cup sugar
- 3 eggs
- 1/3 cup vegetable oil
- 1 tablespoon salt
- 5 cups whole wheat flour
- 4 to 4-1/2 cups all-purpose flour

In a mixing bowl, dissolve yeast in warm water. Add the sugar, eggs, oil, salt and whole wheat flour; beat until smooth. Add enough all-purpose flour to form a soft dough. Turn onto a floured surface; knead until smooth and elastic, about 6-8 minutes. Place in a greased bowl, turning once to grease top. Cover and let rise in a warm place until doubled, about 1 hour.

Punch dough down. Divide into nine pieces; shape each piece into a 14-in. rope and braid three ropes together. Place in three greased 8-in. x 4-in. x 2-in. loaf pans. Cover and let rise until doubled, about 30 minutes. Bake at 350° for 40-45 minutes. Remove from pans to cool on wire racks. **Yield:** 3 loaves (16 slices each).

Creamy Italian Spiral Salad

(Pictured above right)

Prep: 30 min. + chilling

I have accumulated some delicious recipes that serve large numbers, like this colorful and delicious pasta salad. The flavors blend so well, and there's plenty of creamy dressing. *—Marlene Muckenhirn, Delano, Minnesota*

- 2 packages (16 ounces *each*) multicolored spiral pasta
- 1 medium bunch broccoli, cut into florets
- 1 medium head cauliflower, cut into florets
- 1 package (10 ounces) frozen peas and carrots, thawed
- 2 cups cherry tomatoes, quartered
- 1 cup shredded Parmesan cheese

2 cups (8 ounces) shredded Swiss cheese
1 cup small-curd cottage cheese
1/3 cup grated Parmesan cheese
Paprika

In a large skillet, cook sausage and onion over medium heat for 4-5 minutes or until meat is no longer pink; drain. Stir in chives.

On a lightly floured surface, unroll crescent dough into one long rectangle; seal seams and perforations. Cut into 48 pieces. Press onto the bottom and up the sides of greased miniature muffin cups. Fill each with about 2 teaspoons of sausage mixture. In a large bowl, combine the eggs and cheeses. Spoon 2 teaspoonfuls over sausage mixture. Sprinkle with paprika.

Bake at 375° for 20-25 minutes or until a knife inserted in the center comes out clean. Cool for 5 minutes before removing from pans to wire racks. Serve warm. Refrigerate leftovers. **Yield:** 4 dozen.

Potluck Pointers

When going to a potluck, take your food in a disposable container so you don't have to worry about leaving the dish behind. If you're the host, supply disposable containers for guests to take leftovers home.

At large gatherings, display a list of ingredients with each dish to clue in any guests who have food allergies.

6 green onions, chopped
1/2 cup chopped green pepper
1 can (2-1/4 ounces) sliced ripe olives, drained
2 bottles (16 ounces *each*) creamy Italian salad dressing

Cook pasta according to package directions; drain and rinse in cold water. In a large bowl, combine the pasta, broccoli, cauliflower, peas and carrots, tomatoes, Parmesan cheese, onions, green pepper and olives. Add the dressing; mix well. Cover and refrigerate for 2-3 hours or until chilled. **Yield:** 30 (3/4-cup) servings.

Mini Sausage Quiches

(Pictured at right)

Prep: 25 min. **Bake:** 20 min.

These bite-size quiches are loaded with sausage and cheese, and their crescent roll crusts make preparation a snap. Serve these bite-sized treats at any brunch or potluck gathering. —Jan Mead, Milford, Connecticut

1/2 pound bulk hot Italian sausage
2 tablespoons dried minced onion
2 tablespoons minced chives
1 tube (8 ounces) refrigerated crescent rolls
4 eggs, lightly beaten

POTLUCK PLEASERS like Angel Hair Shrimp Bake, Overnight Floret Salad, yummy Apricot Empanadas and bright Red 'n' Green Gelatin (shown above) add sparkle to celebrations.

Angel Hair Shrimp Bake

(Pictured above)

Prep: 25 min. **Bake:** 25 min. + standing

Shrimp and pasta blend beautifully with the herbs, salsa and three kinds of cheese in this hearty layered casserole. The shrimp make this dish special enough for guests, but your family is sure to enjoy it, too. —Susan Davidson
Elm Grove, Wisconsin

 Uses less fat, sugar or salt. Includes Nutritional Analysis and Diabetic Exchanges.

    1 package (9 ounces) refrigerated angel hair
      pasta
1-1/2 pounds uncooked medium shrimp, peeled
      and deveined
  3/4 cup crumbled feta cheese
  1/2 cup shredded Swiss cheese
    1 jar (16 ounces) chunky salsa

1/2 **cup shredded Monterey Jack cheese**
3/4 **cup minced fresh parsley**
1 **teaspoon dried basil**
1 **teaspoon dried oregano**
2 **eggs**
1 **cup half-and-half cream**
1 **cup (8 ounces) plain yogurt**

In a greased 13-in. x 9-in. x 2-in. baking dish, layer half of the pasta, shrimp, feta cheese, Swiss cheese and salsa. Repeat layers. Sprinkle with Monterey Jack cheese, parsley, basil and oregano.

In a small bowl, whisk the eggs, half-and-half cream and yogurt; pour over the casserole. Bake, uncovered, at 350° for 25-30 minutes or until shrimp turn pink and pasta is tender. Let stand for 5 minutes before serving. **Yield:** 12 servings.

Nutritional Analysis: 1 serving (prepared with reduced-fat Swiss and Monterey Jack cheeses and fat-free half-and-half) equals 230 calories, 6 g fat (3 g saturated fat), 135 mg cholesterol, 556 mg sodium, 23 g carbohydrate, 1 g fiber, 22 g protein. **Diabetic Exchanges:** 2-1/2 lean meat, 1-1/2 starch.

Overnight Floret Salad

(Pictured at left)

Prep: 25 min. + chilling

Bacon and sunflower kernels lend extra crunch to this colorful combination of onions, cauliflower and broccoli. With its slightly sweet dressing, this salad's a great way to get kids to eat their veggies.
—*Elizabeth Wenzl*
Eugene, Oregon

1 **small head cauliflower, broken into small florets (6 cups)**
1 **bunch broccoli, broken into small florets (4 cups)**
1 **bunch green onions, thinly sliced**
1/2 **cup sugar**
1/2 **cup mayonnaise**
1/3 **cup cider vinegar**
1/2 **cup sunflower kernels**
6 **bacon strips, cooked and crumbled**

In a bowl, combine the cauliflower, broccoli, onions, sugar, mayonnaise and vinegar. Cover and refrigerate overnight. Just before serving, stir in the sunflower kernels and bacon. **Yield:** 10 servings.

Apricot Empanadas

(Pictured above left)

Prep: 30 min. + chilling **Bake:** 15 min.

These cute handheld desserts are flaky and tender outside with a flavorful fruit filling inside. They take a little time to make, but you'll know they're worth it when the compliments start flowing.
—*Jeaune Hadl*
Lexington, Kentucky

1 **cup butter, softened**
2 **packages (3 ounces** *each*) **cream cheese, softened**
2 **cups all-purpose flour**
2 **teaspoons grated lemon peel**
6 **tablespoons apricot jam**
Cinnamon-sugar

In a small mixing bowl, cream butter and cream cheese until light and fluffy. Gradually beat in the flour and lemon peel. Shape dough into a ball. Cover and refrigerate overnight.

Remove dough from the refrigerator 1 hour before rolling. On a lightly floured surface, roll the dough into a 17-1/2-in. x 12-1/2-in. rectangle; cut into 2-1/2-in. squares.

Spoon 1/2 teaspoon jam onto each square. Brush edges with water; fold pastry over filling, forming a triangle. Seal edges well with a fork.

Place on greased baking sheets. Sprinkle with cinnamon-sugar. Bake at 375° for 15-18 minutes or until golden brown. Remove to wire racks. Refrigerate leftovers. **Yield:** 35 empanadas.

Red 'n' Green Gelatin

(Pictured at far left)

Prep: 20 min. + chilling

Brighten up your Christmas buffet table with this cheery salad. You can change the colors of the gelatin to fit other holidays, too. For the Fourth of July, I use red and blue gelatin with blueberry pie filling.
—*Ruth Yaple McKee*
Orlando, Florida

1 **package (3 ounces) lime gelatin**
2 **cups boiling water,** *divided*
1 **can (8 ounces) crushed pineapple, undrained**
2 **cups large marshmallows**
1 **package (3 ounces) cherry gelatin**
1 **cup cherry pie filling**

In a small bowl, dissolve lime gelatin in 1 cup boiling water. Let stand for 2 minutes. Stir in pineapple. Pour into an 11-in. x 7-in. x 2-in. dish. Top with marshmallows. Cover and refrigerate until set.

In a small bowl, dissolve cherry gelatin in remaining boiling water. Let stand for 2 minutes. Stir in pie filling; pour over marshmallows. Cover and refrigerate until set. **Yield:** 12 servings.

Cooking for One or Two

The deliciously downsized recipes—main dishes, sides, breads, desserts and more—featured in this convenient chapter won't leave you with a fridge full of leftovers!

THE PERFECT SIZE. Clockwise from upper left: Tuscan Salmon Pasta (p. 196); Chicken on Rainbow Rice (p. 190); Lemon-Studded Artichokes (p. 185); Stuffed Pork Tenderloin, Baked Garlic Green Beans and Mixed Fruit Shortcakes (pp. 188-189) and Petite Lasagna, Apple Spinach Salad and Blueberry Cornmeal Pudding (pp. 194-195).

Holiday Game Hens

(Pictured below)

Prep: 40 min.　**Bake:** 40 min.

These golden-brown birds are tender and juicy, and stuffed with a savory mixture of pork, apple and raisins. I've had this recipe for some time, and it always makes a great meal. ——*Delia Kennedy, Deer Park, Washington*

>　2　**Cornish game hens (20 ounces** *each***)**
>　1　**medium lemon, cut in half**
> 1/2　**teaspoon salt**
> 1/4　**teaspoon pepper**
>　1　**bacon strip, diced**
> 1/4　**pound ground pork**
> 1/2　**cup diced apple**
>　1　**tablespoon raisins**
>　1　**tablespoon chicken broth**

Rub each Cornish hen inside and out with cut lemon. Sprinkle each cavity with salt and pepper; set aside. In a small skillet, cook the bacon over medium heat until crisp. Remove to paper towels; drain, reserving drippings.

In a saucepan, cook the pork over medium heat until no longer pink; drain. Stir in the apple, raisins, broth and bacon. Loosely stuff into hens; skewer openings and tie drumsticks together.

In the reserved drippings, brown hens on all sides. Place on a rack in a shallow roasting pan. Tuck wings under hens. Bake, uncovered, at 425° for 40-45 minutes or until juices run clear and a meat thermometer reads 180°. **Yield:** 2 servings.

Grapefruit Lettuce Salad

(Pictured below)

Prep/Total Time: 15 min.

A light vinaigrette flavored with cilantro and grapefruit juice drapes this tangy salad. You can make the vinaigrette ahead because it keeps well in the refrigerator. ——*Vivian Haen, Menomonee Falls, Wisconsin*

✓ **Uses less fat, sugar or salt. Includes Nutritional Analysis and Diabetic Exchanges.**

>　2　**tablespoons pink grapefruit juice**
>　1　**tablespoon olive oil**
> 1-1/2　**teaspoons red wine vinegar**
> 1/2　**teaspoon honey**
> 1-1/2　**teaspoons minced fresh cilantro**
>　2　**cups torn Bibb** *or* **Boston lettuce**
>　1　**medium pink grapefruit, peeled and sectioned**

In a small bowl, whisk the grapefruit juice, oil, vinegar and honey; stir in cilantro. In a salad bowl, toss lettuce and grapefruit. Drizzle with dressing; gently toss to coat. **Yield:** 2 servings.

Nutritional Analysis: 1 serving equals 120 calo-

TWO is the perfect number when you're dishing up this special menu featuring Holiday Game Hens, Grapefruit Lettuce Salad and Toffee Apple Crunch (shown below).

ries, 7 g fat (1 g saturated fat), 0 cholesterol, 5 mg sodium, 14 g carbohydrate, 2 g fiber, 1 g protein. **Diabetic Exchanges:** 2 vegetable, 1-1/2 fat.

Toffee Apple Crunch

(Pictured below left)

Prep/Total Time: 15 min.

You'll be licking your lips after one bite of this crunchy combination of apple, toffee bits and pecans over a cool scoop of ice cream. —Ray Eutler, Greenville, Texas

 1 medium tart apple, peeled and cubed
 1 tablespoon butter
 1/8 teaspoon ground cinnamon
TOPPING:
 2 tablespoons all-purpose flour
 1 tablespoon brown sugar
 1 tablespoon butter, softened
 2 tablespoons finely chopped pecans
 1 tablespoon English toffee bits *or* almond brickle chips
Dash ground cinnamon
Vanilla ice cream

In a microwave-safe bowl, combine apple, butter and cinnamon; cover and microwave on high for 2 minutes. Stir; cover and let stand while preparing topping.

 In another microwave-safe bowl, combine flour and brown sugar. Stir in butter. Add the pecans, toffee bits and cinnamon. Microwave, uncovered, on high for 1-1/2 to 2 minutes, stirring twice. Spoon apple mixture over ice cream; sprinkle with topping. **Yield:** 1 serving.

 Editor's Note: This recipe was tested in a 1,100-watt microwave.

Lemon-Studded Artichokes

(Pictured on page 182)

Prep/Total Time: 30 min.

For a change-of-pace side dish or appetizer, microwave some artichokes. I flavor them with lemon slices and garlic butter, which is great for dipping. —Lorraine Galazyk
South Surrey, British Columbia

 2 medium artichokes
 1 tablespoon lemon juice
 1 medium lemon, sliced
 1/2 cup plus 2 tablespoons butter, melted
 2 to 4 garlic cloves, minced

Rinse artichokes well; trim stems. With scissors, snip 1 in. off the tops. Snip the tip end from each leaf. Brush cut edges with the lemon juice. Spread artichoke leaves

open. Using a small knife, carefully cut around each center choke. Scoop out and discard the fuzzy centers.

 Cut each of the lemon slices into six wedges; place between artichoke leaves. Place artichokes in an 8-in. microwave-safe dish. Combine butter and garlic; pour over artichokes. Cover and microwave on high for 10-12 minutes or until artichokes are tender. Let stand for 5 minutes. Serve with garlic butter from the dish. **Yield:** 2 servings.

 Editor's Note: This recipe was tested in a 1,100-watt microwave.

Banana Oat Pancakes

(Pictured above)

Prep/Total Time: 20 min.

I concocted these pancakes using a muffin recipe. We love them topped with strawberry jam or maple syrup for breakfast. —Janie Obermier, St. Joseph, Missouri

 1-1/3 cups all-purpose flour
 3/4 cup old-fashioned oats
 1 tablespoon sugar
 2 teaspoons baking powder
 1/2 teaspoon ground cinnamon
 1 egg
 1-1/3 cups milk
 1 cup mashed ripe banana
 2 tablespoons vegetable oil
Maple syrup

In a large bowl, combine the flour, oats, sugar, baking powder and cinnamon. Combine the egg, milk, banana and oil; stir into dry ingredients just until moistened.

 Pour batter by 1/4 cupfuls onto a greased hot griddle. Turn when bubbles form on top; cook until second side is golden brown. Serve with syrup. **Yield:** 6 pancakes.

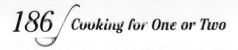

Jam 'n' Cream French Toast

(Pictured below)

Prep/Total Time: 10 min.

My grandmother used to make this for me when I was a child. You can use other flavors of jam, too.
— B. MacKinnon, Kodak, Tennessee

    2 tablespoons cream cheese, softened
    2 thick slices cinnamon-raisin bread
    2 tablespoons strawberry jam
    1 egg
    1 tablespoon butter
Maple syrup, optional

Spread cream cheese on one slice of bread. Spread jam on the other slice; place jam side down over the cream cheese. In a shallow bowl, beat egg. Dip both sides of bread into egg.

In a skillet, melt butter; cook bread for 3-4 minutes on each side or until golden brown. Serve with syrup if desired. **Yield:** 1 serving.

Sweetheart Steaks

(Pictured at far right)

Prep: 10 min.   **Cook:** 50 min.

I created this recipe when I was planning a steak dinner and wanted a barbecue sauce to go with it. Try the sauce on pork and chicken. —Dolores Jensen, Arnold, Missouri

    3 tablespoons Catalina salad dressing
    3 tablespoons honey
    3 tablespoons apricot preserves
    3 tablespoons grape jelly
    2 tablespoons minced chives
    2 tablespoons balsamic vinegar
    2 tablespoons olive oil
    2 tablespoons ketchup
    1 tablespoon soy sauce
    3 garlic cloves, minced
    1 teaspoon ground mustard
    1 teaspoon Worcestershire sauce
  1/2 teaspoon salt
  1/2 teaspoon crushed red pepper flakes
  1/4 teaspoon pepper
    2 beef tenderloin steaks (1-1/2 to 2 inches thick)

In a small saucepan, combine the first 15 ingredients. Bring to a boil. Reduce heat; simmer, uncovered, for 30 minutes, stirring occasionally. Set aside 1/4 cup sauce for serving and keep warm.

Place steaks on a broiler pan; top with some of the remaining sauce. Broil 4-6 in. from the heat for 10-16 minutes on each side or until meat reaches desired doneness (for medium-rare, a meat thermometer should read 145°; medium, 160°; well-done, 170°), basting occasionally with remaining sauce. Serve with reserved sauce. **Yield:** 2 servings.

Cheese-Stuffed Potatoes

(Pictured at right)

Prep: 15 min.   **Bake:** 1 hour

Cottage cheese is the "secret" ingredient in this creamy side dish. I make two potatoes, one for dinner and one for lunch the next day. —Janet English, Pittsburgh, Pennsylvania

    2 medium baking potatoes
    1 small onion, finely chopped
    2 tablespoons water
  1/2 cup cottage cheese
  1/4 cup buttermilk
    3 tablespoons grated Parmesan cheese
Salt and pepper to taste
    2 tablespoons thinly sliced green onion

Bake potatoes at 400° for 1 hour or until tender. Cut a thin slice off the top of each potato and discard. Scoop out pulp, leaving a thin shell. In a small mixing bowl, mash pulp; set aside.

In a small skillet, cook and stir onion in water for 2-3 minutes or until tender. Add mashed potatoes, cottage cheese, buttermilk, Parmesan cheese, salt and pepper. Stir until blended and heated through. Spoon into potato shells. Sprinkle with green onion. **Yield:** 2 servings.

CELEBRATE Valentine's Day with a special dinner for two that features Sweetheart Steaks, Cheese-Stuffed Potatoes and Valentine Cakes (shown above).

Valentine Cakes

(Pictured above)

Prep: 30 min.   **Bake:** 15 min. + cooling

These individual chocolate layer cakes are a sweet way to say "I love you" even when it's not Valentine's Day.
—Dixie Terry, Goreville, Illinois

3/4 cup all-purpose flour
1/4 cup sugar
1/4 cup packed brown sugar
 3 tablespoons baking cocoa
1/2 teaspoon baking soda
1/8 teaspoon salt
1/2 cup water
 3 tablespoons vegetable oil
1/2 teaspoon white vinegar
1/2 teaspoon vanilla extract
FROSTING:
1-1/3 cups confectioners' sugar
 2 tablespoons baking cocoa
2 to 3 tablespoons milk
2 tablespoons butter, melted
1/4 teaspoon vanilla extract
Decorator icing and confetti candies

In a mixing bowl, combine the first six ingredients. Add water, oil, vinegar and vanilla. Pour into a greased and floured 8-in. square baking dish. Bake at 350° for 15-20 minutes or until a toothpick inserted near center comes out clean. Cool for 10 minutes before removing from pan to a wire rack to cool completely.

In a mixing bowl, beat confectioners' sugar, cocoa, milk, butter and vanilla until smooth; set aside. Transfer cake to a work surface. Using a 3- to 3-1/2-in. heart-shaped cookie cutter, gently cut out four heart-shaped cakes (set cake trimmings aside for another use).

Place one heart on a serving plate; spread with some frosting. Top with a second cake; frost top and sides. Repeat with remaining cakes and frosting. Decorate with icing and candies. **Yield:** 2 servings.

Stuffed Pork Tenderloin

(Pictured below and on page 182)

Prep: 20 min. **Bake:** 50 min.

My grandmother often prepared this dish for Sunday dinner. She loved to cook and eat, especially when she had someone to share her food with. —Mary Ann Marino
West Pittsburg, Pennsylvania

- 1 pork tenderloin (3/4 to 1 pound)
- 1/2 cup chopped onion
- 2 tablespoons butter
- 1 cup soft bread crumbs
- 1/4 cup minced fresh parsley
- 1/4 teaspoon rubbed sage
- 1/4 teaspoon dried rosemary, crushed
- 1/4 teaspoon salt
- 1/8 teaspoon pepper
- 1 egg, lightly beaten
- 1 bacon strip

Make a lengthwise slit about three-fourths of the way through tenderloin; open tenderloin so it lies flat. Flatten to 1/4-in. thickness; set aside.

In a small skillet, saute onion in butter until tender. Add bread crumbs; saute until crumbs are golden brown. Remove from heat. Stir in parsley, sage, rosemary, salt, pepper and enough egg to moisten the ingredients.

Spread stuffing on one long side of tenderloin to within 1/4 in. of edges. Close meat and place bacon on top; tie with kitchen string. Place on a rack in a shallow roasting pan. Bake, uncovered, at 350° for 50-60 minutes or until a meat thermometer reads 160°. Let stand 5 minutes before slicing. **Yield:** 2 servings.

Baked Garlic Green Beans

(Pictured below and on page 182)

Prep/Total Time: 20 min.

DOUBLY DELICIOUS meal of Stuffed Pork Tenderloin, Baked Garlic Green Beans and Mixed Fruit Shortcakes (shown below) is a treat for two.

This flavorful dish dresses up frozen green beans with onion, cheese, bread crumbs and garlic. It's easy enough to serve any day of the week.
—Marilyn Farmer
Centerville, Utah

☑ **Uses less fat, sugar or salt. Includes Nutritional Analysis and Diabetic Exchanges.**

    1 tablespoon olive oil
1-1/2 teaspoons cider vinegar
    1 teaspoon dried minced onion
    1 garlic clove, minced
  1/4 teaspoon salt
Dash pepper
1-1/2 cups frozen cut green beans, thawed
    1 tablespoon dry bread crumbs
    1 tablespoon grated Parmesan cheese
    1 teaspoon butter, melted

In a small bowl, combine the oil, vinegar, onion, garlic, salt and pepper. Add the beans; toss to coat. Transfer to a greased 3-cup baking dish. Combine the bread crumbs, Parmesan cheese and butter; sprinkle over beans. Bake, uncovered, at 350° for 10-15 minutes or until heated through. **Yield:** 2 servings.

Nutritional Analysis: 3/4 cup (prepared with reduced-fat butter) equals 126 calories, 9 g fat (2 g saturated fat), 5 mg cholesterol, 491 mg sodium, 9 g carbohydrate, 2 g fiber, 3 g protein. **Diabetic Exchanges:** 2 vegetable, 1-1/2 fat.

Mixed Fruit Shortcakes

(Pictured at left and on page 182)
Prep/Total Time: 30 min.

This delightful downsized recipe makes just two biscuit-like shortcakes. Fill them with fresh fruit of your choice and top with whipped cream for an impressive dinner finale.
—Sue Ross, Casa Grande, Arizona

    1 cup mixed fresh berries
  1/2 cup sliced fresh peaches *or* nectarines
    4 teaspoons sugar, *divided*
  1/2 cup all-purpose flour
  3/4 teaspoon baking powder
  1/8 teaspoon salt
    2 tablespoons shortening
    3 tablespoons milk
Whipped cream

In a bowl, combine berries, peaches and 2 teaspoons sugar; set aside. In another bowl, combine the flour, baking powder and salt; cut in shortening until mixture is crumbly. Stir in milk just until moistened. Drop by 1/3 cupfuls 2 in. apart onto an ungreased baking sheet. Flatten into 2-1/2-in. circles. Sprinkle with remaining sugar.

Bake at 425° for 10-12 minutes or until golden

brown. Remove to a wire rack to cool. Split shortcakes in half horizontally. Spoon fruit onto bottoms; replace tops. Garnish with whipped cream. **Yield:** 2 servings.

Thai Shrimp and Cabbage

(Pictured above)
Prep/Total Time: 15 min.

This spicy shrimp is absolutely wonderful served over shredded cabbage. When I'm in a hurry, I use packaged coleslaw mix instead. It's a welcome change from rice.
—Beth Malchiodi, Brooklyn, New York

    1 cup shredded cabbage
    3 teaspoons vegetable oil, *divided*
    1 slice onion, halved
    1 garlic clove, minced
    8 uncooked large shrimp, peeled and deveined
    2 tablespoons water
    1 tablespoon soy sauce
    1 tablespoon minced fresh cilantro
  1/8 teaspoon crushed red pepper flakes

In a small skillet, stir-fry cabbage in 1 teaspoon oil for 2 minutes or until tender. Remove and keep warm. In the same skillet, stir-fry onion and garlic in the remaining oil until tender. Add the shrimp, water and soy sauce; stir-fry for 2-3 minutes or until shrimp turn pink. Stir in cilantro and pepper flakes. Serve over cabbage. **Yield:** 1 serving.

Crab-Stuffed Sole

(Pictured below)

Prep/Total Time: 20 min.

There's a pleasant lemony tang to this seafood entree. For side dishes, try broccoli or asparagus.
—*Judie Anglen, Riverton, Wyoming*

      1/4 **cup butter**
 4-1/2 **teaspoons all-purpose flour**
      1/2 **cup chicken broth**
      1/4 **teaspoon dill weed**
        1 **to 3 teaspoons lemon juice**
FILLETS:
        1 **egg, lightly beaten**
        1 **package (8 ounces) imitation crabmeat, flaked**
      1/4 **cup finely chopped celery**
        3 **tablespoons dry bread crumbs**
        1 **tablespoon grated Parmesan cheese**
        1 **teaspoon butter, melted**
        2 **sole *or* orange roughy fillets (6 ounces *each*)**

For dill sauce, melt the butter in a microwave-safe bowl; stir in flour until smooth. Stir in the broth and dill until blended. Microwave, uncovered, on high for 2-3 minutes, stirring after each minute, until sauce comes to a boil and is thickened. Stir in the lemon juice; keep warm.

In a bowl, combine egg, crab, celery, bread crumbs, Parmesan cheese and butter. Spoon onto the center of each fillet; roll up fish around filling. Place in a 9-in. round microwave-safe dish. Cover with waxed paper. Microwave on high for 5-6 minutes or until fish flakes easily with a fork and a thermometer inserted into stuffing reads 160°. Serve with the dill sauce. **Yield:** 2 servings.

Editor's Note: This recipe was tested in a 1,100-watt microwave.

Chicken on Rainbow Rice

(Pictured on page 182)

Prep: 20 min. + marinating   **Grill:** 10 min.

Chicken breasts can make a variety of interesting dishes. Here, I enhance the meat with a lightly seasoned marinade and rice pilaf.   —*Bill Hilbrich, St. Cloud, Minnesota*

 1/4 **cup olive oil**
    2 **tablespoons lime *or* lemon juice**
    1 **boneless skinless chicken breast half**
 1/4 **cup *each* chopped onion, sweet red pepper and green pepper**
    1 **tablespoon butter**
    1 **cup cooked long grain rice**
 1/4 **teaspoon salt**
Dash pepper

In a small resealable plastic bag, combine the oil and lime juice; add chicken. Seal bag and turn to coat; refrigerate for at least 1 hour.

Drain and discard marinade. Grill chicken, uncovered, over medium heat for 5-7 minutes on each side or until juices run clear.

Meanwhile, in a skillet, saute onion and peppers in butter until tender. Stir in rice, salt and pepper; heat through. Serve with chicken. **Yield:** 1 serving.

Smoked Turkey Pizza

(Pictured above right)

Prep/Total Time: 20 min.

A chewy prebaked crust makes quick work of this tasty one-serving pizza. I use out-of-the-ordinary toppings including cranberry sauce and turkey. It's a great way to use up holiday leftovers.   —*Lisa Varner, Greenville, South Carolina*

1/8 teaspoon ground allspice
1 can (8 ounces) tomato sauce
1/4 cup chicken broth
2 teaspoons balsamic vinegar
1-1/2 teaspoons dried basil
4 tablespoons grated Parmesan *or* Romano cheese, *divided*

Cut tops off peppers; remove seeds. Place peppers cut side down on a microwave-safe plate; cover with plastic wrap. Microwave on high for 2-3 minutes or until crisp-tender; set aside.

In a small skillet, cook beef and onion over medium heat until meat is no longer pink; drain. Remove from heat; stir in rice, parsley, salt, cayenne and allspice.

In a small saucepan, bring tomato sauce and broth to a boil. Stir in vinegar, basil and 3 tablespoons Parmesan cheese; stir about 1/2 cup sauce into rice mixture. Spoon into peppers. Place in a greased shallow 1-qt. baking dish.

Cover and bake at 350° for 30 minutes. Sprinkle with remaining Parmesan cheese. Bake, uncovered, for 5-10 minutes or until peppers are tender. Serve with remaining sauce. **Yield:** 2 servings.

Editor's Note: This recipe was tested in a 1,100-watt microwave.

1 prebaked mini Italian bread shell crust
1/4 cup whole-berry cranberry sauce
1 tablespoon chopped onion
1/3 cup shredded Monterey Jack cheese
2 ounces thinly sliced deli smoked turkey, cut into strips
1 teaspoon chopped walnuts

Place the crust on a baking sheet or pizza pan. Spread with cranberry sauce; sprinkle with onion and cheese. Arrange turkey over cheese; sprinkle with walnuts. Bake at 375° for 10-15 minutes or until cheese is melted. **Yield:** 1 serving.

Herb-Stuffed Red Peppers

(Pictured at right)

Prep: 25 min. **Bake:** 35 min.

We love to experiment with new dishes. We found this recipe on-line but we didn't have some of the ingredients. So we improvised! —Luke and Brenda Joyner
Pateros, Washington

2 large sweet red peppers
1/2 pound ground beef
1/2 cup chopped onion
1-1/2 cups cooked brown rice
1 tablespoon dried parsley flakes
3/4 teaspoon salt
1/8 to 1/4 teaspoon cayenne pepper

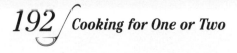

Asparagus Ham Fettuccine

(Pictured below)

Prep/Total Time: 20 min.

This entree is quick to fix for every day but is also perfect as a special meal to share with another person.
—*Rebecca Baird, Salt Lake City, Utah*

    4 ounces uncooked fettuccine
1/2 pound fresh asparagus, trimmed and cut into 1/2-inch pieces
1/2 pound fully cooked ham, julienned
1/4 cup chopped walnuts
    1 green onion, chopped
    2 tablespoons minced fresh sage *or* 2 teaspoons rubbed sage
1/4 teaspoon pepper
    2 tablespoons olive oil
    1 cup (4 ounces) shredded cheddar cheese

Cook fettuccine according to package directions. Meanwhile, in a large saucepan, bring 4 cups water to a boil; add asparagus. Cover and cook for 3 minutes. Drain and immediately place in ice water; drain and set aside.

In a skillet, saute the ham, walnuts, onion, sage and pepper in oil until onion is tender. Add asparagus; cook and stir for 1 minute. Drain fettuccine; toss with ham mixture. Sprinkle with cheese. **Yield:** 2 servings.

Chicken Biscuit Bake

(Pictured at far right)

Prep: 20 min.   **Bake:** 30 min.

This recipe looks fussy but doesn't take long to assemble...plus it gives me time to put my feet up and read the paper while it bakes. It's nice served with just a salad and some fruit. —*Gail Cory-Betz, Newport, Washington*

1/2 cup plus 1 tablespoon all-purpose flour
1/2 teaspoon baking powder
Dash salt
    3 tablespoons cold butter
    2 tablespoons beaten egg
1/4 cup buttermilk
FILLING:
    2 tablespoons butter
    2 tablespoons all-purpose flour
    1 cup milk
    1 tablespoon chicken bouillon granules
Dash poultry seasoning
Dash onion powder
1/2 cup cubed cooked chicken
1/2 cup frozen mixed vegetables
1/2 cup small-curd cottage cheese

In a bowl, combine flour, baking powder and salt; cut in butter until mixture resembles coarse crumbs. Set aside 1 teaspoon beaten egg; stir remaining egg into buttermilk. Add to crumb mixture; stir until dough forms a ball.

Turn onto a floured surface; knead 10 times or until smooth. Divide dough in half. On a lightly floured surface, roll out one portion to fit the bottom of a greased 1-qt. baking dish. Place in dish.

In a small saucepan, melt butter over medium heat. Stir in flour until smooth. Gradually add the milk, bouillon, poultry seasoning and onion powder. Bring to a boil; cook and stir for 1-2 minutes or until thickened. Remove from the heat. Stir in the chicken, vegetables and cottage cheese. Pour into baking dish.

Roll out the remaining dough to fit the top of the dish; place over the filling. Brush with reserved egg. Bake at 350° for 30-35 minutes or until crust is golden brown. **Yield:** 2 servings.

Creamy Banana Lettuce Salad

(Pictured above right)

Prep/Total Time: 10 min.

I dress up salad greens with fruit, nuts and a yummy banana dressing. —*Nancye Thompson, Paducah, Kentucky*

✓ **Uses less fat, sugar or salt. Includes Nutritional Analysis and Diabetic Exchanges.**

    1 large firm banana, sliced
1/2 teaspoon lemon juice
    3 tablespoons mayonnaise
1/2 teaspoon sugar
    2 cups torn mixed salad greens
    5 fresh strawberries, sliced
    1 tablespoon salted peanuts, chopped

SET A TABLE for two with delicious Chicken Biscuit Bake, Creamy Banana Lettuce Salad and Sand Dollar Cookies (shown above).

Lightly toss banana slices with the lemon juice. Place 1/4 cup in a small bowl; mash. Stir in the mayonnaise and sugar.

In a salad bowl, combine the salad greens, strawberries and remaining banana slices; toss. Top with dressing; sprinkle with peanuts. **Yield:** 2 servings.

Nutritional Analysis: 1-1/2 cups (prepared with fat-free mayonnaise and sugar substitute) equals 124 calories, 3 g fat (1 g saturated fat), 2 mg cholesterol, 214 mg sodium, 24 g carbohydrate, 4 g fiber, 3 g protein. **Diabetic Exchanges:** 1-1/2 fruit, 1 fat.

Sand Dollar Cookies

(Pictured above)

Prep: 15 min. + chilling   **Bake:** 15 min.

When the military relocated our family, my children had never lived near the beach before. I came up with this special treat with a beach theme—it made our move a lot more fun.   —Michelle Duncan, Callaway, Florida

3/4 cup butter, softened
1/3 cup confectioners' sugar
4-1/2 teaspoons sugar
2 teaspoons almond extract
1-1/3 cups all-purpose flour
1/4 teaspoon salt
1 egg, beaten
Slivered almonds
Cinnamon-sugar

In a mixing bowl, cream butter and sugars. Beat in extract. Combine the flour and salt; gradually add to creamed mixture. Cover and refrigerate for 1 hour or until easy to handle.

Roll dough between waxed paper to 1/8-in. thickness. Cut with a 3-1/2-in. round cookie cutter dipped in flour. Using a floured spatula, place 1 in. apart on ungreased baking sheets. Brush with egg. Decorate with almonds and sprinkle with cinnamon-sugar.

Bake at 325° for 12-16 minutes or until edges begin to brown. Cool for 2 minutes before removing to wire racks. **Yield:** 9 cookies.

Petite Lasagna

(Pictured below and on page 182)

Prep: 30 min.   **Bake:** 30 min. + standing

Store-bought spaghetti sauce simplifies preparation of this loaf-size lasagna. With a salad on the side, a serving of this Italian-style casserole makes a hearty meal.
—*Kathy Coble, Missouri City, Texas*

   5 **lasagna noodles**
1/2 **pound ground beef**
1/4 **cup** *each* **chopped onion, green pepper and fresh mushrooms**
   1 **jar (14 ounces) meatless spaghetti sauce**
   1 **egg, beaten**
3/4 **cup ricotta cheese**
   2 **tablespoons grated Parmesan cheese**
   2 **tablespoons minced fresh parsley**
1-1/2 **teaspoons Italian seasoning**
   1 **cup (4 ounces) shredded mozzarella cheese**

Cook noodles according to package directions. Meanwhile, in a large skillet, cook the beef, onion, green pepper and mushrooms over medium heat until meat is no longer pink; drain. Stir in the spaghetti sauce. Cook over low heat for 5 minutes, stirring occasionally. In a small bowl, combine the egg, ricotta cheese, Parmesan cheese, parsley and Italian seasoning. Drain noodles.

Spread 1/4 cup meat sauce in a greased 8-in. x 4-in. x 2-in. loaf pan. Trim noodles to fit pan. Place two noodles over meat sauce; layer with a third of the cheese mixture, a third of the remaining meat sauce and 1/3 cup mozzarella cheese. Repeat layers twice, using noodle trimmings in top layer.

Bake, uncovered, at 350° for 30-35 minutes or until heated through and cheese is melted. Let stand for 5 minutes before cutting. **Yield:** 2 servings.

Apple Spinach Salad

(Pictured below and on page 182)

Prep/Total Time: 15 min.

Apple, onion and bacon flavor this crunchy salad. After eating a similar salad at a restaurant, I concocted my own.
—*Roberta Ashcraft, Twin Falls, Idaho*

DUOS will delight in Petite Lasagna, Apple Spinach Salad and Blueberry Cornmeal Pudding (shown below).

✓ Uses less fat, sugar or salt. Includes Nutritional Analysis and Diabetic Exchanges.

    2 cups fresh spinach, torn
    1 medium apple, chopped
    2 bacon strips, cooked and crumbled
    2 red onion slices, separated into rings
    2 tablespoons chopped nuts
DRESSING:
    2 tablespoons lime juice
    2 tablespoons honey
    1 tablespoon vegetable oil
    1/2 teaspoon Worcestershire sauce
    1/4 teaspoon celery seed
    1/4 teaspoon chili powder
    1/4 teaspoon pepper
Dash hot pepper sauce

In a salad bowl, toss spinach, apple, bacon, onion and nuts. In a jar with a tight-fitting lid, combine dressing ingredients; shake well. Drizzle over salad; toss to coat. Refrigerate any remaining dressing. **Yield:** 2 servings.

Nutritional Analysis: 1-1/2 cups of dressed salad equals 268 calories, 15 g fat (2 g saturated fat), 5 mg cholesterol, 144 mg sodium, 33 g carbohydrate, 4 g fiber, 5 g protein. **Diabetic Exchanges:** 2-1/2 fat, 2 vegetable, 1-1/2 fruit.

Blueberry Cornmeal Pudding

(Pictured at left and on page 182)

Prep/Total Time: 20 min.

When I want something that will satisfy my sweet tooth, I make this pleasing pudding topped with blueberry sauce.
        —Lillian Julow, Gainesville, Florida

    1 cup fresh *or* frozen unsweetened
        blueberries, thawed
    1/2 cup sugar, *divided*
    2 cups milk
    6 tablespoons yellow cornmeal
    3/4 teaspoon grated lemon peel
    1/2 teaspoon vanilla extract
    1/4 teaspoon salt

In a small microwave-safe bowl, combine blueberries and 1/4 cup sugar. Microwave, uncovered, on high for 3 minutes or until sugar is dissolved, stirring once.

In a 3-qt. microwave-safe bowl, combine the milk, cornmeal, lemon peel and remaining sugar. Cover and microwave on high for 7 minutes or until thickened, stirring every 2 minutes. Stir in the vanilla and salt. Pour into dessert dishes; cool slightly. Top with blueberry sauce. **Yield:** 2 servings.

Editor's Note: This recipe was tested in a 1,100-watt microwave.

Mini Salmon Loaf

(Pictured above)

Prep: 15 min. **Bake:** 40 min.

This nicely textured salmon loaf accompanied by a pleasing dill sauce is perfect for two. I've made it many, many times.   —Patricia Gould, Canaan, New Hampshire

    3/4 cup chopped celery
    1/2 cup chopped onion
    2 tablespoons vegetable oil
    1 can (7-1/2 ounces) salmon, drained, bones
        and skin removed
    1 egg, lightly beaten
    2 tablespoons milk
    1 cup soft bread crumbs
    1/4 teaspoon salt
    1/4 teaspoon pepper
DILL SAUCE:
    1/2 cup mayonnaise
    1/4 cup sour cream
    1 tablespoon lemon juice
    1 tablespoon milk
    2 teaspoons snipped fresh dill
    1/2 teaspoon sugar
    1/8 teaspoon pepper

In a skillet, saute celery and onion in oil until tender. In a bowl, combine the salmon, egg, milk, bread crumbs, salt, pepper and celery mixture. Transfer to a greased 5-3/4-in. x 3-in. x 2-in. loaf pan.

Bake at 350° for 40-45 minutes or until a knife inserted near the center comes out clean. In a small bowl, combine the sauce ingredients. Serve with salmon loaf. **Yield:** 2 servings.

Tuscan Salmon Pasta

(Pictured below and on page 182)

Prep/Total Time: 20 min.

White kidney beans and plum tomatoes are tossed with salmon and linguine in this fast-to-fix entree that works for special dinners or every day. —*Dianne Alvine Toms River, New Jersey*

    4 ounces uncooked linguine
    1 salmon fillet (10 ounces), cut into 1-inch cubes
    1 teaspoon minced fresh rosemary
    5 tablespoons olive oil, *divided*
  3/4 cup white kidney *or* cannellini beans, rinsed and drained
    2 small plum tomatoes, chopped
    6 garlic cloves, minced
Salt and pepper to taste

Cook linguine according to package directions. Meanwhile, in a small skillet, saute the salmon and rosemary in 2 tablespoons oil for 5 minutes or until salmon flakes easily with a fork.

Add the beans, tomatoes, garlic, salt and pepper; heat through. Drain linguine and place in a bowl. Add salmon mixture; toss gently. Drizzle with remaining oil. **Yield:** 2 servings.

Miniature Ham Loaf

(Pictured at right)

Prep: 15 min. **Bake:** 30 min.

Shredded carrots add color and flavor to this downsized ham loaf. A buttery glaze and slices of pineapple put the finishing touches on this satisfying entree.
  —*Carol Dunne, Middle Village, New York*

    1 egg
    1 small carrot, shredded
  1/4 cup chopped onion
  1/3 cup seasoned bread crumbs
    1 tablespoon dried parsley flakes
    1 teaspoon prepared mustard
  1/2 pound ground fully cooked ham
    1 can (8 ounces) unsweetened sliced pineapple
    1 tablespoon brown sugar
    1 teaspoon cornstarch
    1 tablespoon butter
    1 tablespoon lemon juice

In a bowl, combine first six ingredients. Crumble ham over mixture and mix well. Shape into a loaf and place in a greased baking dish. Bake at 350° for 20 minutes.

Meanwhile, drain pineapple, reserving juice; set pineapple aside. In a small saucepan, combine the brown sugar, cornstarch and reserved juice until smooth. Bring to a boil; cook and stir for 1 minute or until thickened. Stir in butter and lemon juice.

Brush over ham loaf; top with three pineapple slices. (Save remaining pineapple for another use.) Bake 10-15 minutes longer or until a meat thermometer reads 160°. Let stand for 5 minutes before slicing. **Yield:** 2 servings.

Goldenrod Broccoli

(Pictured above right)

Prep/Total Time: 20 min.

This broccoli tastes delicious and looks so pretty when served. The sauce is light and mellow. —*Glynis Belec Drayton, Ontario*

    2 cups fresh broccoli spears
    1 hard-cooked egg
  1-1/2 teaspoons butter
    2 teaspoons all-purpose flour
  1/4 teaspoon salt
Dash pepper
  1/4 cup evaporated milk
    3 tablespoons water
  1/4 cup mayonnaise
    2 tablespoons shredded cheddar cheese
Dash Worcestershire sauce

DOWNSIZED comfort food like Miniature Ham Loaf, Goldenrod Broccoli and Praline Sweet Potatoes (shown above) is a real treat!

Place broccoli in a steamer basket; place in a small saucepan over 1 in. of water. Bring to a boil; cover and steam for 5-8 minutes or until crisp-tender. Meanwhile, cut egg in half; remove yolk and finely crumble. Chop egg white; set aside.

In a saucepan, melt butter. Stir in flour, salt and pepper until smooth; gradually add milk and water. Bring to a boil; cook and stir 1-2 minutes or until thickened. Reduce heat to low; add mayonnaise, cheese and Worcestershire. Cook and stir until smooth. Remove from the heat; stir in reserved egg white. Spoon over broccoli; sprinkle with crumbled egg yolk. **Yield:** 2 servings.

Praline Sweet Potatoes

(Pictured above)

Prep/Total Time: 30 min.

I like to serve these creamy potatoes alongside ham. Chopped pecans add crunch to the sweet brown sugar topping. —Ruth Peterson, Jenison, Michigan

    1 cup mashed sweet potatoes
    2 tablespoons milk
    1 egg yolk
1/4 teaspoon salt
Dash pepper
    1/4 cup packed brown sugar
    2 tablespoons butter, melted
    2 tablespoons corn syrup
    2 tablespoons chopped pecans

In a small mixing bowl, combine the sweet potatoes, milk, egg yolk, salt and pepper. Transfer to a greased shallow 2-cup baking dish.

In a small microwave-safe bowl, combine the brown sugar, butter and corn syrup until blended; cover and microwave on high for 1 minute or until the sugar is dissolved. Spoon over the sweet potatoes. Sprinkle with the pecans. Bake, uncovered, at 350° for 20-22 minutes or until a knife comes out clean. **Yield:** 2 servings.

    Editor's Note: This recipe was tested in a 1,100-watt microwave.

'My Mom's Best Meal'

Six daughters fondly recall—and share the recipes for—the meals made by their moms that they treasure the most.

TOP PICKS. Clockwise from upper left: International Cuisine (p. 216), From-Scratch Favorites (p. 204), Memorable Sunday Supper (p. 220) and Friday Fish Fry (p. 212).

Her mother's home-cooked meals fostered full stomachs, fond memories and enduring family ties.

By Denise Bitner, Reedsville, Pennsylvania

WHETHER cooking for a family of four or a large group, my mother, Lynn Dippery (above), has always been able to make a simple meal taste like it's fit for a king.

When my sister, Dana, and I were growing up, Mom made dinnertime special. Her wonderful evening meals resulted not only in full stomachs but in countless hours of relaxation and conversation—shared times that encouraged a family closeness we maintain today.

One of my favorite menus features Peppered Beef Tenderloin, Fruit 'n' Nut Tossed Salad, Creamed Onions, Crisp Sweet Pickles and Peanut Butter Pie.

Peppered Beef Tenderloin, perfect for a holiday meal, is moist and delicious with a crispy coating. The pepper rub gives this tender beef a bit of a zippy taste.

Fruit 'n' Nut Tossed Salad is a delightful combination of sweet and salty flavors. It's Dana's favorite dish. The oil-and-vinegar dressing lends a lovely sheen to the tossed ingredients, making the salad an attractive addition to a festive menu.

With its sweet taste, Creamed Onions is the one recipe I request for my birthdays and holidays. The onions have a mild flavor, and there's plenty of the rich creamy sauce.

My mom's delicious Crisp Sweet Pickles, a Christmas tradition, are quick and easy to make since they start with a jar of purchased dill pickles and then are just "dressed up." They would make a nice gift from the kitchen in a pretty glass jar.

Everyone loves Mom's yummy Peanut Butter Pie—it's the perfect ending to a meal. It's sure to satisfy your sweet tooth!

Whenever I smell or taste these delicious dishes, I think of home and all of the wonderful memories of growing up. I hope you enjoy this memorable family meal.

PICTURED AT LEFT: Peppered Beef Tenderloin, Fruit 'n' Nut Tossed Salad, Creamed Onions, Crisp Sweet Pickles and Peanut Butter Pie (recipes are on the next page).

Fruit 'n' Nut Tossed Salad

Prep: 20 min.   **Cook:** 30 min. + cooling

- 1/4 **cup olive oil**
- 2 **tablespoons plus 2 teaspoons sugar**
- 2 **tablespoons white vinegar**
- 1 **tablespoon minced fresh parsley**
- 1/4 **teaspoon salt**
- **Dash hot pepper sauce**
- **SALAD:**
- 1/3 **cup sugar**
- 1 **cup pecan halves**
- 2 **tablespoons butter**
- 4 **cups torn fresh spinach**
- 4 **cups torn romaine**
- 1 **can (15 ounces) mandarin oranges, drained**
- 2 **celery ribs, chopped**
- 1 **cup sliced fresh strawberries**
- 4 **green onions, chopped**

For dressing, in a small bowl, whisk the oil, sugar, vinegar, parsley, salt and hot pepper sauce until blended. Cover and refrigerate.

In a heavy skillet, melt sugar over medium-low heat without stirring until golden brown, about 30 minutes. Add pecans and butter; stir constantly until butter is melted and pecans are coated. Remove from the heat. Pour onto a foil-lined baking sheet; cool completely. Break pecans apart if necessary.

In a salad bowl, combine spinach, romaine, oranges, celery, strawberries and onions. Just before serving, drizzle with dressing; toss to coat. Top with sugared pecans. **Yield:** 8-10 servings.

Peppered Beef Tenderloin

Prep: 10 min.   **Bake:** 45 min. + standing

- 3 **tablespoons coarsely ground pepper**
- 2 **tablespoons olive oil**
- 1 **tablespoon grated lemon peel**
- 1 **teaspoon salt**
- 2 **garlic cloves, minced**
- 1 **whole beef tenderloin (3 to 4 pounds)**

Combine the pepper, oil, lemon peel, salt and garlic; rub over tenderloin. Place on a greased rack in a foil-lined roasting pan.

Bake, uncovered, at 400° for 45-65 minutes or until beef reaches desired doneness (for medium-rare, a meat thermometer should read 145°; medium, 160°; well-done, 170°). Cover and let stand for 10 minutes before slicing. **Yield:** 10-12 servings.

1 tablespoon dried minced onion
1 tablespoon celery seed

Cut pickles into 1/2-in. slices; return to the jar. Add the remaining ingredients. Cover and shake until coated. Refrigerate for at least 1 week, shaking occasionally. Serve with a slotted spoon. **Yield:** 1 quart.

Peanut Butter Pie

Prep: 10 min. + chilling

1 package (8 ounces) cream cheese, softened
2/3 cup peanut butter
1 tablespoon milk
2 cups confectioners' sugar
1 carton (12 ounces) frozen whipped topping, thawed
2 graham cracker crusts (9 inches *each*)
Dry roasted peanuts

In a large mixing bowl, beat the cream cheese, peanut butter and milk until smooth. Gradually beat in confectioners' sugar. Fold in whipped topping. Spoon into crusts. Cover and refrigerate for at least 4 hours before serving. Sprinkle with peanuts. **Yield:** 2 pies (6-8 servings each).

Creamed Onions

Prep: 10 min.   **Cook:** 30 min.

6 large onions, sliced
1 cup butter
2 tablespoons all-purpose flour
2 teaspoons salt
1/2 teaspoon white pepper
2 cups milk

In a large skillet or Dutch oven, saute onions in butter until tender and golden brown, about 25 minutes. Remove with a slotted spoon. Add flour, salt and pepper to skillet; stir until smooth. Gradually stir in milk until blended.

Bring to a boil; cook and stir for 2 minutes or until thickened. Reduce heat to medium. Return onions to the pan; heat through. **Yield:** 8-10 servings.

Crisp Sweet Pickles

(Pictured on page 201)

Prep: 10 min. + chilling

1 jar (32 ounces) whole kosher dill pickles, drained
1-1/4 cups sugar
3 tablespoons cider vinegar

Her mom's natural knack for cooking has served up superb meals and fond memories.

By Daria Burcar, Rochester, Michigan

WHEN I'm asked to describe my mother, Blanche Herbster (above), the words friendly, nurturing and deeply religious come to mind. But she's also funny, vivacious and a wonderful cook.

My mom has always cooked from scratch, and every night she would serve our family a complete meal—meat, potatoes, salad, two vegetables and a delectable dessert. My brother, Ric, sisters, Dina and Joline, and I have warm recollections of those evening meals, but we each have our own favorites.

My favorite menu has to be Mom's Down-Home Meat Loaf, Greens and Sprouts Salad, Red Potatoes with Beans and Fresh Strawberry Pie. Whenever I smell the appealing aroma of this meal, it transports me back to when I was 12.

Down-Home Meat Loaf is the perfect comfort food, and it's just as good the next day in a sandwich. The Greens and Sprouts Salad, with its sweet-tangy dressing, complements the meat loaf so well. Mom loves vegetables, so we were exposed to everything from asparagus to zucchini when we were growing up. In fact, my two sisters are now vegetarians.

The microwave makes Red Potatoes with Beans a quick and easy dish to prepare. Tossed with onion and Italian dressing, it tastes great cold or warm.

Nothing compares to Mom's pretty Fresh Strawberry Pie. My mother is a registered nurse and worked for a wealthy family as a private duty nurse in the 1950s. The family's cook would not share her recipes, including the one for this pie. So, when Mom knew it was on the menu, she took her coffee break in the kitchen and memorized the recipe while the cook prepared it. She has tweaked it over the years and sometimes substitutes raspberries.

Mom has a natural ability to add a pinch of this and a dash of that and make a superb meal every time. I hope you'll find this meal of hers just as delicious as I do!

PICTURED AT LEFT: Down-Home Meat Loaf, Greens and Sprouts Salad, Red Potatoes with Beans and Fresh Strawberry Pie (recipes are on the next page).

Greens and Sprouts Salad

Prep/Total Time: 20 min.

- 1 package (10 ounces) fresh baby spinach
- 3 cups torn leaf lettuce
- 2 hard-cooked eggs, chopped
- 5 bacon strips, cooked and crumbled
- 1 can (28 ounces) bean sprouts, drained
- 1 can (8 ounces) sliced water chestnuts, drained
- 1/2 cup chow mein noodles

FRENCH DRESSING:
- 1/2 cup vegetable oil
- 1/2 cup sugar
- 1/3 cup ketchup
- 2 tablespoons cider vinegar
- 1-1/2 teaspoons Worcestershire sauce
- 1/8 teaspoon salt
- 1 small onion, cut into wedges

In a large salad bowl, toss the spinach, lettuce, eggs, bacon, bean sprouts and water chestnuts. Sprinkle with chow mein noodles. In a blender, combine the dressing ingredients; cover and process until blended. Serve with salad. **Yield:** 8 servings.

Down-Home Meat Loaf

Prep: 15 min.   **Bake:** 1-1/4 hours + standing

- 2 eggs, beaten
- 1/4 cup milk
- 2 cups soft bread crumbs
- 3/4 cup finely chopped onion
- 1/3 cup finely chopped green pepper
- 2 tablespoons prepared horseradish
- 1-1/2 teaspoons salt
- 1 teaspoon ground mustard
- 2 pounds ground beef
- 1/4 cup ketchup

In a bowl, combine the first eight ingredients. Crumble beef over mixture and mix well. Press into a greased 9-in. x 5-in. x 3-in. loaf pan.

Bake at 350° for 1 hour. Spread with ketchup; bake 15-20 minutes longer or until a meat thermometer reads 160° and meat is no longer pink. Let stand for 10 minutes before slicing. Meat loaf may be frozen for up to 3 months. **Yield:** 8 servings.

Red Potatoes with Beans

Prep/Total Time: 20 min.

✓ Uses less fat, sugar or salt. Includes Nutritional Analysis and Diabetic Exchanges.

1-1/3 pounds fresh green beans, trimmed
1/3 cup water
6 small red potatoes, cut into wedges
1/2 cup chopped red onion
1/2 cup Italian salad dressing

Place the beans and water in a 2-qt. microwave-safe dish. Cover and microwave on high for 6-8 minutes or until tender.

Meanwhile, place the potatoes in a large saucepan and cover with water. Bring to a boil. Reduce heat; cover and cook for 5-7 minutes or until tender. Drain beans and potatoes; place in a bowl. Add onion and dressing; toss to coat. Yield: 8 servings.

Nutritional Analysis: 3/4 cup (prepared with fat-free Italian dressing) equals 49 calories, trace fat (trace saturated fat), 1 mg cholesterol, 220 mg sodium, 11 g carbohydrate, 1 g fiber, 2 g protein. **Diabetic Exchange:** 2 vegetable.

Editor's Note: This recipe was tested in a 1,100-watt microwave.

Fresh Strawberry Pie

Prep: 30 min. + chilling   **Bake:** 15 min. + chilling

1-1/3 cups all-purpose flour
1/4 teaspoon salt
1/2 cup shortening
4 teaspoons plus 1 tablespoon milk, *divided*
4 teaspoons water
1 package (8 ounces) cream cheese, softened
2 tablespoons sugar
1 to 1-1/2 quarts fresh strawberries, sliced
GLAZE:
1/2 cup sugar
1 tablespoon cornstarch
Dash salt
1-3/4 cups water
1 package (3 ounces) strawberry gelatin

In a bowl, combine the flour and salt; cut in shortening until mixture resembles coarse crumbs. Combine 4 teaspoons milk and water; gradually add to crumb mixture, tossing with a fork until dough forms a ball. Refrigerate for 30 minutes.

Roll out pastry to fit a 9-in. pie plate. Transfer pastry to pie plate. Trim pastry to 1/2 in. beyond edge of plate; flute edge of pastry. Line unpricked pastry shell with a double thickness of heavy-duty foil. Bake at 450° for 8 minutes. Remove foil; bake 7 minutes longer. Cool completely on a wire rack.

In a small mixing bowl, beat the cream cheese, sugar and remaining milk until smooth. Spread over the bottom of crust; arrange strawberries over the top.

In a saucepan, combine the sugar, cornstarch, salt and water until smooth. Bring to a boil; cook and stir for 2 minutes or until thickened. Remove from the heat; stir in gelatin until dissolved. Chill until partially set. Pour over berries. Refrigerate until set. **Yield:** 8 servings.

Her mom's best meal, an annual birthday dinner, was a long-lasting gift for this daughter.

By Genny Monchamp, Redding, California

SOME of my favorite memories as a child revolve around the kitchen table of my mother, Margaret Sherer (above). I grew up on a remote Indian reservation in northwest California (my brother, Riley, and stepfather are Native American). With the closest restaurant an hour away, Mom's kitchen was the choice for most of our meals.

She made home-cooked meals for breakfast, lunch and dinner almost every day of the week. Since the supermarket was also an hour away, Mom became a master of improvisation. Some of our favorite recipes evolved because she had to adjust recipes to accommodate the ingredients she had on hand.

Birthdays were the highlight of the year because Riley and I could choose anything we wanted for dinner. My choice was Mom's savory Fried Chicken Strips, cooked to golden perfection in a crunchy cracker coating. Waiting for the strips to cool was almost more than I could bear.

There were no better accompaniments than her Poppy Seed Pasta Salad and Round Whole Wheat Loaves followed by Chocolate Torte.

Mom found ways to incorporate fresh fruits and vegetables from her garden into almost every meal. That's how she created Poppy Seed Pasta Salad. Wherever she takes this salad, she's asked for the recipe.

The smell of fresh baked bread often greeted people as they entered our house. Mom's buttery Round Whole Wheat Loaves are hands down the best whole wheat bread I've ever tasted.

Her triple-layered Chocolate Torte was the crown jewel of my birthday celebration. Because Mom baked from scratch, I didn't know there was such a thing as boxed cake mix until I was 10 years old.

Even though I live in a city with fast-food restaurants on every corner, I share home-cooked meals with my own family almost every night. One thing Mom taught me is that a real "taste of home" can't be bought at a drive-thru window.

PICTURED AT LEFT: Fried Chicken Strips, Poppy Seed Pasta Salad, Round Whole Wheat Loaves and Chocolate Torte (recipes are on the next page).

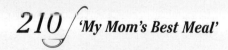

1 can (3.8 ounces) sliced ripe olives, drained
1/2 cup fresh broccoli florets
1/2 cup fresh cauliflowerets
1/4 cup julienned yellow summer squash
1 bottle (12 ounces) poppy seed salad dressing
1/4 cup sunflower kernels

Cook pasta according to package directions; drain and rinse in cold water. Place in a large serving bowl; add the tomatoes, olives, broccoli, cauliflower and squash. Drizzle with dressing and toss to coat.

Cover and refrigerate for 2 hours or overnight. Just before serving, sprinkle with sunflower kernels. **Yield:** 6 servings.

Round Whole Wheat Loaves

Prep: 30 min. + rising   **Bake:** 30 min. + cooling

1 cup milk
3/4 cup shortening
1/2 cup honey
2 teaspoons salt
4-1/2 cups all-purpose flour
1-1/2 cups whole wheat flour
2 packages (1/4 ounce *each*) active dry yeast
3/4 cup warm water (110° to 115°)
3 eggs
1 teaspoon butter, melted

Fried Chicken Strips

Prep/Total Time: 20 min.

2-2/3 cups crushed saltines (about 80 crackers)
1 teaspoon garlic salt
1/2 teaspoon dried basil
1/2 teaspoon paprika
1/8 teaspoon pepper
1 egg
1 cup milk
1-1/2 pounds boneless skinless chicken breasts, cut into 1/2-inch strips
Oil for deep-fat frying

In a shallow bowl, combine the first five ingredients. In another shallow bowl, beat egg and milk. Dip chicken into egg mixture, then cracker mixture.

In an electric skillet or deep-fat fryer, heat oil to 375°. Fry chicken, a few strips at a time, for 2-3 minutes on each side or until golden brown. Drain on paper towels. **Yield:** 6 servings.

Poppy Seed Pasta Salad

Prep: 30 min. + chilling

1 package (12 ounces) tricolor spiral pasta
1 cup halved cherry tomatoes

1/2 teaspoon baking powder
1/2 teaspoon salt
FILLING:
   1 cup heavy whipping cream
1/4 cup confectioners' sugar
   1 teaspoon vanilla extract
FROSTING:
   1 cup (6 ounces) semisweet chocolate chips
   1 cup butter, cubed
1/2 cup heavy whipping cream
2-1/2 cups confectioners' sugar

In a large mixing bowl, cream butter and sugar. Add eggs, one at a time, beating well after each addition. Beat in vanilla. Whisk cocoa and water until smooth. Combine flour, baking soda, baking powder and salt; add to creamed mixture alternately with cocoa mixture. Beat until smooth.

Pour into three greased and floured 9-in. round baking pans. Bake at 350° for 25-30 minutes or until a toothpick comes out clean. Cool for 10 minutes; remove from pans to wire racks.

In a mixing bowl, beat cream, confectioners' sugar and vanilla on high speed until soft peaks form. Chill until firm.

In a saucepan, melt chips and butter over medium heat; stir in cream. Remove from the heat; stir in confectioners' sugar. Chill for at least 1 hour or until completely cooled. Beat with electric mixer to achieve spreading consistency.

Spread half of the filling over one cake layer; top with second layer and remaining filling. Top with third layer; frost top and sides of cake. Chill for 2 hours before cutting. **Yield:** 10-12 servings.

In a large saucepan, bring milk to a boil over medium heat, stirring constantly. Remove from the heat. Stir in the shortening, honey and salt until shortening is melted. Cool to 110° to 115°. Combine the flours; set aside.

In a large mixing bowl, dissolve yeast in warm water. Add milk mixture and eggs. Beat in half of the flour mixture until smooth. Stir in enough remaining flour mixture to form a soft dough.

Turn onto a floured surface; knead until smooth and elastic, about 6-8 minutes. Place in a greased bowl, turning once to grease top. Cover and let rise in a warm place until doubled, about 1 hour.

Punch dough down. Turn onto a lightly floured surface; divide in half. Shape into round loaves. Place each loaf on a greased baking sheet. Cover and let rise until doubled, about 35 minutes. With a sharp knife, make a deep X in top of each piece of dough.

Bake at 375° for 30-35 minutes or until golden brown. Remove from pans to wire racks; brush with butter. Cool completely. **Yield:** 2 loaves.

Chocolate Torte

(Also pictured on front cover)

Prep: 30 min. **Bake:** 25 min. + cooling

   1 cup butter, softened
2-1/2 cups sugar
   4 eggs
1-1/2 teaspoons vanilla extract
   1 cup baking cocoa
   2 cups boiling water
2-3/4 cups all-purpose flour
   2 teaspoons baking soda

She's hooked on her mom's delicious family fish-fry menu served on Friday evenings at the lake.

By Julie Jahnke, Green Lake, Wisconsin

MY MOM, Margaret Peterson (above) from Bloomington, Minnesota, never has to fish for compliments when she cooks a meal...especially when we are on vacation.

Every year, our family spends a week at a lake in northern Minnesota. We've been doing this for 16 years. With my brother and four sisters as well as all our spouses and children, there are now 14 of us.

We all enjoy fishing because my dad taught us when we were young. So the finale of the week is, appropriately, a fish fry. Dad used to say Mom's Fried Fish was the finest he'd ever tried. Sadly, he is no longer with us, but we share fond memories of Dad all during our stay at the lake.

Once the fresh fish is cleaned, Mom dips it in an egg wash and rolls it in crushed crackers. My brother, Jim, cooks it outdoors in a deep fryer to a delicious golden brown.

Mom also prepares her tarter sauce and Parsley Red Potatoes. I help her by peeling and slicing the potatoes. The easy-to-prepare spuds cook up tender and buttery on the stove.

She makes Crunchy Floret Salad the night before so the creamy dressing marinates the vegetables. The pretty combination always gets raves.

Mom's Apple Crisp rounds out this satisfying meal. The aroma of baking apples and cinnamon always brings everyone to her cabin. We like this dessert served warm, topped with mounded clouds of whipped cream.

Family is so important to my mom. She did her best to have all eight of us at the dinner table every evening when we were growing up.

I'm in awe of how much my mom has done for us over the years. I've told her many times that if I can be half the mother she has been, I'll consider myself a success. I hope you'll enjoy her fish-fry menu as much as we do!

PICTURED AT LEFT: Mom's Fried Fish, Parsley Red Potatoes, Crunchy Floret Salad and Mom's Apple Crisp (recipes are on the next page).

Parsley Red Potatoes

Prep/Total Time: 25 min.

2 **pounds red potatoes**
1-1/2 **teaspoons salt**
1/3 **cup butter, cubed**
2 **tablespoons minced fresh parsley**

Peel off a strip around each potato if desired. Place in a large saucepan; cover with water. Add salt. Bring to a boil; reduce heat. Cover and cook for 15 minutes or until tender; drain. Add butter and parsley; toss until butter is melted. **Yield:** 6 servings.

Crunchy Floret Salad

Prep/Total Time: 20 min.

3 **cups fresh broccoli florets**
1-1/2 **cups fresh cauliflowerets**
1/2 **pound sliced bacon, cooked and crumbled**
1 **cup mayonnaise**
2 to 3 **tablespoons sugar**
2 **tablespoons cider vinegar**
1/4 **teaspoon salt**
1-1/2 **cups (6 ounces) shredded cheddar cheese**

Mom's Fried Fish

Prep/Total Time: 30 min.

2 **eggs, beaten**
1-1/2 **cups crushed saltines (about 45 crackers)**
2 **pounds whitefish fillets, cut in half lengthwise**
Oil for deep-fat frying
TARTAR SAUCE:
1 **cup mayonnaise**
2 **tablespoons sweet pickle relish**
1 **tablespoon finely chopped onion**

Place eggs and cracker crumbs in separate shallow bowls. Dip fillets into eggs, then coat with crumbs. Let stand for 5 minutes.

In an electric skillet or deep-fat fryer, heat oil to 375°. Fry fillets, a few at a time, for 2 minutes on each side or until fish is golden brown and flakes easily with a fork. Drain on paper towels. In a small bowl, combine the tartar sauce ingredients. Serve with fish. **Yield:** 6 servings.

until crumbly. Sprinkle over apples, pressing down to smooth top.

Slowly pour water over the top; sprinkle with remaining cinnamon. Bake, uncovered, at 400° for 40-45 minutes or until apples are tender. Serve warm. **Yield:** 8 servings.

Deep Frying

To allow for bubbling up and splattering, the pot in which you deep fry should be filled no more than halfway with oil.

The temperature of the oil is important and can mean the difference between success and disaster. If the oil isn't hot enough, food will absorb it and become greasy; if it's too hot, the food will burn. The most accurate method of testing the temperature is with a deep-frying thermometer.

It's best to fry food in small batches. Large amounts of food will lower the oil temperature, which means it's more likely to soak into the food.

In a large bowl, combine the broccoli, cauliflower and bacon. In a small bowl, whisk the mayonnaise, sugar, vinegar and salt. Pour over salad and mix well. Cover and refrigerate until serving. Stir in the cheese. **Yield:** 6-8 servings.

Mom's Apple Crisp

Prep: 25 min.   **Bake:** 40 min.

    5 medium tart apples, peeled and sliced
1-1/4 cups sugar, *divided*
1-3/4 teaspoons ground cinnamon, *divided*
    1 cup all-purpose flour
    1 teaspoon baking powder
  1/2 teaspoon salt
  1/2 cup cold butter
    1 cup water

In a bowl, combine the apples, 1/4 cup sugar and 1 teaspoon cinnamon. Transfer to a greased 8-in. square baking dish. In a small bowl, combine the flour, baking powder, salt and remaining sugar; cut in butter

Her mother's from-scratch cooking deliciously combines Syrian and Italian cultures.

By Weda Mosellie, Phillipsburg, New Jersey

SOMETIMES cultures clash, but in my family, they blended beautifully when my mom was in the kitchen. My mother, Mamie Pullo Mosellie (above), has always loved the foods of her Italian heritage …just as much as my Syrian dad, Anthony, enjoyed his culture's foods.

When my sister, Christine, and I were growing up, Mom often combined the two cuisines with delicious results. And definitely, everything was made from scratch, including what I think is her best meal: Lamb and Beef Kabobs, Cilantro Potatoes, Syrian Salad and Pistachio Apricot Bars.

Grilled Lamb and Beef Kabobs, seasoned with a lemon juice and olive oil marinade, can be served on or off the skewers. In bad weather, we cook them in a 400° oven for 25-40 minutes. Mom's tender, well-seasoned Cilantro Potatoes make the perfect side dish. Fresh cilantro gives great flavor to these easy-to-prepare skillet potatoes.

Syrian Salad marries Italian and Syrian ingredients such as Greek olives, prosciutto, and feta and mozzarella cheeses with traditional salad fixings. We enjoy making "salad sandwiches" by spooning the mixture into pita bread pockets.

The yummy Pistachio Apricot Bars provide a sweet end to this colorful meal. Mom tops a pistachio crust with apricot preserves and more chopped nuts to make these moist, buttery, shortbread-like bars.

Some of my earliest memories are of Mom cooking. Like her mother before her, she'd tell me to watch what she was doing so I'd "learn to cook."

Mom and I still live in the family home. My sister is just a few miles away. My mother mostly cooks for holidays and when we yearn for a Syrian meal. Otherwise, I do the cooking.

I love to cook and have even won some cooking contests, but I owe my success to Mom. Although I have learned a lot from her, no one can touch her cooking. I hope you'll give her recipes a try!

PICTURED AT LEFT: Lamb and Beef Kabobs, Cilantro Potatoes, Syrian Salad and Pistachio Apricot Bars (recipes are on the next page).

On eight metal or soaked wooden skewers, alternately thread the lamb, beef, onions, red peppers and mushrooms. Grill, covered, over medium-hot heat for 5-6 minutes on each side or until meat reaches desired doneness and vegetables are tender. Serve with pita bread. **Yield:** 8 servings.

Cilantro Potatoes

Prep: 25 min.   **Cook:** 20 min.

- 1 **bunch fresh cilantro, chopped**
- 1 **garlic clove, minced**
- 1/4 **cup olive oil**
- 3 **pounds potatoes, peeled and cubed**
- 1/2 **teaspoon salt**

In a large skillet, cook the cilantro and garlic in oil over medium heat for 1 minute. Add the potatoes; cook and stir for 20-25 minutes or until tender and lightly browned. Drain. Sprinkle with salt. **Yield:** 8 servings.

Syrian Salad

Prep/Total Time: 50 min.

- 4 **cups torn iceberg lettuce**
- 2 **cups torn romaine**

Lamb and Beef Kabobs

Prep: 25 min. + marinating   **Grill:** 10 min.

- 1/4 **cup minced fresh parsley**
- 2 **tablespoons olive oil**
- 4 **teaspoons salt**
- 2 **teaspoons pepper**
- 2 **teaspoons lemon juice**
- 2 **pounds boneless lamb, cut into 1-1/2-inch cubes**
- 1 **pound boneless beef sirloin steak, cut into 1-1/2-inch cubes**
- 6 **small onions, cut into wedges**
- 2 **medium sweet red peppers, cut into 1-inch pieces**
- 16 **large fresh mushrooms**
- 6 **pita breads (6 inches), cut into wedges**

In a small bowl, combine the first five ingredients. Place the lamb and beef in a large resealable plastic bag; add half of the marinade. Place the vegetables in another large resealable plastic bag; add the remaining marinade. Seal bags and turn to coat; refrigerate for 1 hour.

In a jar with a tight-fitting lid, combine dressing ingredients; shake well. Drizzle over salad and toss to coat. **Yield:** 8 servings.

Pistachio Apricot Bars

Prep: 15 min.   **Bake:** 25 min. + cooling

- 1 cup butter, softened
- 1 cup sugar
- 1 egg
- 1 teaspoon vanilla extract
- 2-1/2 cups all-purpose flour
- 1/2 cup chopped pistachios
- 1 jar (18 ounces) apricot preserves

Additional chopped pistachios, optional

In a small mixing bowl, cream butter and sugar. Beat in the egg and vanilla. Gradually add flour. Stir in pistachios. Press into a greased 13-in. x 9-in. x 2-in. baking dish. Spread with preserves.

Bake at 350° for 25-30 minutes or until edges begin to brown. Cool on a wire rack. Cut into bars. Garnish with additional pistachios if desired. **Yield:** 2-1/2 dozen.

- 1-1/2 cups chopped seeded cucumbers
- 3 plum tomatoes, seeded and chopped
- 1/2 pound fresh mozzarella, cubed
- 2/3 cup chopped red onion
- 1 jar (4-1/2 ounces) marinated artichoke hearts, drained and quartered
- 1/2 cup canned garbanzo beans *or* chickpeas, rinsed and drained
- 1 can (2-1/4 ounces) sliced ripe olives, drained
- 1/3 cup Greek olives, drained
- 1/3 cup sliced stuffed olives, drained
- 4 thin slices hard salami, julienned
- 4 thin slices prosciutto, julienned
- 1/2 cup crumbled feta cheese
- 1/3 cup grated Parmesan cheese

DRESSING:

- 1/2 cup olive oil
- 1/4 cup lemon juice
- 1 anchovy fillet, finely chopped
- 1 tablespoon garlic powder
- 1 tablespoon dried oregano
- 1 tablespoon minced fresh cilantro

Pepper to taste

In a large salad bowl, combine the first 13 ingredients. Sprinkle salad with both the feta and Parmesan cheeses.

Stuffed pork roasts were the centerpiece of her mom's special Sunday noontime meals.

By Lois Frazee, Gardnerville, Nevada

I'VE SPENT part of my life teaching college-level nutrition classes and taste-testing for a federal research lab. But my fondest food-related memories center on my mother's kitchen.

My mom, Sarah Catterson (above), taught school for a short time before I was born. From then on, she was devoted full-time to taking care of her family—me, brother Donald and our dad, Frehn, who was a chemical engineer.

There weren't a lot of convenience foods back then, so Mom made everything from scratch. I liked to help her, and I learned to cook in the process.

On Sundays, our big meal was served at noon, and Mom often served a roast. Her best was Pork Tenderloin with Stuffing, served with Apple Zucchini Salad, Parsnip Pancakes and Gelatin Dessert Squares.

Pork Tenderloin with Stuffing was so special-looking that Mom served it for company, too. If you like, prepare it with her stuffing recipe or use one of your own.

I think she came up with her refreshing Apple Zucchini Salad because the colors looked so pretty in a glass bowl.

Mom liked parsnips, so she sometimes substituted them in her potato pancake recipe to make Parsnip Pancakes. Parsnips, rutabaga and other root vegetables were plentiful in Winnipeg, Manitoba, where we lived at the time.

A friend gave Mom the recipe for Gelatin Dessert Squares. She'd make them when neighbors came to play bridge.

It was the Depression era, so Mom made the most of the food we had. She'd grind up leftover roast from Sunday dinner with gravy for sandwiches.

I inherited Mom's love of cooking and still enjoy preparing meals when my own children visit. I have two daughters, a son and five grandchildren.

I hope you'll share Mom's menu with your family and enjoy it as much as we have.

PICTURED AT LEFT: Pork Tenderloin with Stuffing, Apple Zucchini Salad, Parsnip Pancakes and Gelatin Dessert Squares (recipes are on the next page).

Spoon stuffing onto one tenderloin. Top with the second tenderloin; tie with kitchen string. Place on a rack in a shallow roasting pan. Bake, uncovered, at 350° for 50-60 minutes or until a meat thermometer inserted into meat reads 160°. Let stand for 5 minutes before slicing. **Yield:** 6 servings.

Apple Zucchini Salad

Prep/Total Time: 10 min.

✓ Uses less fat, sugar or salt. Includes Nutritional Analysis and Diabetic Exchanges.

- 2 medium red apples, chopped
- 2 small zucchini, chopped
- 1/2 cup coarsely chopped walnuts
- 2/3 cup Italian salad dressing

In a serving bowl, combine the apples, zucchini and walnuts; add salad dressing and toss to coat. Serve immediately. **Yield:** 6 servings.

Nutritional Analysis: 2/3 cup (prepared with fat-free salad dressing) equals 114 calories, 6 g fat (1 g saturated fat), 1 mg cholesterol, 383 mg sodium, 13 g carbohydrate, 2 g fiber, 3 g protein. **Diabetic Exchanges:** 1 vegetable, 1 fat, 1/2 fruit.

Pork Tenderloin with Stuffing

Prep: 20 min.   **Bake:** 50 min.

- 4 celery ribs, chopped
- 1 small onion, chopped
- 2 tablespoons butter
- 6 cups cubed day-old bread (1/2-inch cubes)
- 1/2 teaspoon salt
- 1/4 teaspoon pepper
- 2 pork tenderloins (1 pound *each*)
- 2 tablespoons vegetable oil

In a small skillet, saute celery and onion in butter until tender. In a bowl, combine the bread cubes, celery mixture, salt and pepper; set aside.

Cut a lengthwise slit down the center of each tenderloin to within 1/2 in. of bottom. Open tenderloins so they lie flat; cover with plastic wrap. Flatten to 1/2-in. thickness. In a large skillet, brown pork in oil on both sides over medium-high heat.

In a jar with a tight-fitting lid, combine dressing ingredients; shake well. Drizzle over salad and toss to coat. **Yield:** 8 servings.

Pistachio Apricot Bars

Prep: 15 min.   **Bake:** 25 min. + cooling

  1 cup butter, softened
  1 cup sugar
  1 egg
  1 teaspoon vanilla extract
2-1/2 cups all-purpose flour
  1/2 cup chopped pistachios
  1 jar (18 ounces) apricot preserves
Additional chopped pistachios, optional

In a small mixing bowl, cream butter and sugar. Beat in the egg and vanilla. Gradually add flour. Stir in pistachios. Press into a greased 13-in. x 9-in. x 2-in. baking dish. Spread with preserves.

Bake at 350° for 25-30 minutes or until edges begin to brown. Cool on a wire rack. Cut into bars. Garnish with additional pistachios if desired. **Yield:** 2-1/2 dozen.

1-1/2 cups chopped seeded cucumbers
  3 plum tomatoes, seeded and chopped
1/2 pound fresh mozzarella, cubed
2/3 cup chopped red onion
  1 jar (4-1/2 ounces) marinated artichoke hearts, drained and quartered
1/2 cup canned garbanzo beans *or* chickpeas, rinsed and drained
  1 can (2-1/4 ounces) sliced ripe olives, drained
1/3 cup Greek olives, drained
1/3 cup sliced stuffed olives, drained
  4 thin slices hard salami, julienned
  4 thin slices prosciutto, julienned
1/2 cup crumbled feta cheese
1/3 cup grated Parmesan cheese
DRESSING:
1/2 cup olive oil
1/4 cup lemon juice
  1 anchovy fillet, finely chopped
  1 tablespoon garlic powder
  1 tablespoon dried oregano
  1 tablespoon minced fresh cilantro
Pepper to taste

In a large salad bowl, combine the first 13 ingredients. Sprinkle salad with both the feta and Parmesan cheeses.

Stuffed pork roasts were the centerpiece of her mom's special Sunday noontime meals.

By Lois Frazee, Gardnerville, Nevada

I'VE SPENT part of my life teaching college-level nutrition classes and taste-testing for a federal research lab. But my fondest food-related memories center on my mother's kitchen.

My mom, Sarah Catterson (above), taught school for a short time before I was born. From then on, she was devoted full-time to taking care of her family—me, brother Donald and our dad, Frehn, who was a chemical engineer.

There weren't a lot of convenience foods back then, so Mom made everything from scratch. I liked to help her, and I learned to cook in the process.

On Sundays, our big meal was served at noon, and Mom often served a roast. Her best was Pork Tenderloin with Stuffing, served with Apple Zucchini Salad, Parsnip Pancakes and Gelatin Dessert Squares.

Pork Tenderloin with Stuffing was so special-looking that Mom served it for company, too. If you like, prepare it with her stuffing recipe or use one of your own.

I think she came up with her refreshing Apple Zucchini Salad because the colors looked so pretty in a glass bowl.

Mom liked parsnips, so she sometimes substituted them in her potato pancake recipe to make Parsnip Pancakes. Parsnips, rutabaga and other root vegetables were plentiful in Winnipeg, Manitoba, where we lived at the time.

A friend gave Mom the recipe for Gelatin Dessert Squares. She'd make them when neighbors came to play bridge.

It was the Depression era, so Mom made the most of the food we had. She'd grind up leftover roast from Sunday dinner with gravy for sandwiches.

I inherited Mom's love of cooking and still enjoy preparing meals when my own children visit. I have two daughters, a son and five grandchildren.

I hope you'll share Mom's menu with your family and enjoy it as much as we have.

PICTURED AT LEFT: Pork Tenderloin with Stuffing, Apple Zucchini Salad, Parsnip Pancakes and Gelatin Dessert Squares (recipes are on the next page).

Spoon stuffing onto one tenderloin. Top with the second tenderloin; tie with kitchen string. Place on a rack in a shallow roasting pan. Bake, uncovered, at 350° for 50-60 minutes or until a meat thermometer inserted into meat reads 160°. Let stand for 5 minutes before slicing. **Yield:** 6 servings.

Apple Zucchini Salad

Prep/Total Time: 10 min.

✓ Uses less fat, sugar or salt. Includes Nutritional Analysis and Diabetic Exchanges.

- 2 medium red apples, chopped
- 2 small zucchini, chopped
- 1/2 cup coarsely chopped walnuts
- 2/3 cup Italian salad dressing

In a serving bowl, combine the apples, zucchini and walnuts; add salad dressing and toss to coat. Serve immediately. **Yield:** 6 servings.

Nutritional Analysis: 2/3 cup (prepared with fat-free salad dressing) equals 114 calories, 6 g fat (1 g saturated fat), 1 mg cholesterol, 383 mg sodium, 13 g carbohydrate, 2 g fiber, 3 g protein. **Diabetic Exchanges:** 1 vegetable, 1 fat, 1/2 fruit.

Pork Tenderloin with Stuffing

Prep: 20 min. **Bake:** 50 min.

- 4 celery ribs, chopped
- 1 small onion, chopped
- 2 tablespoons butter
- 6 cups cubed day-old bread (1/2-inch cubes)
- 1/2 teaspoon salt
- 1/4 teaspoon pepper
- 2 pork tenderloins (1 pound *each*)
- 2 tablespoons vegetable oil

In a small skillet, saute celery and onion in butter until tender. In a bowl, combine the bread cubes, celery mixture, salt and pepper; set aside.

Cut a lengthwise slit down the center of each tenderloin to within 1/2 in. of bottom. Open tenderloins so they lie flat; cover with plastic wrap. Flatten to 1/2-in. thickness. In a large skillet, brown pork in oil on both sides over medium-high heat.

Parsnip Pancakes

Prep/Total Time: 30 min.

- 2 pounds parsnips, peeled
- 1 teaspoon salt
- 1/2 cup chopped onion
- 1/4 cup all-purpose flour
- 1 egg, lightly beaten
- 1 tablespoon minced chives

Place parsnips in a large saucepan and cover with water; add salt. Bring to a boil over medium-high heat. Reduce heat; cover and cook for 15-20 minutes or until tender. Drain and place parsnips in a large bowl; mash. Stir in the onion, flour, egg and chives.

Drop batter by 1/4 cupfuls onto a well-greased hot griddle. Flatten with a spatula. Fry until golden brown; turn and cook until second side is lightly browned. Drain on paper towels. **Yield:** 6 servings.

Gelatin Dessert Squares

Prep: 20 min. + chilling   **Bake:** 10 min. + cooling

- 1 cup all-purpose flour
- 1/2 cup finely chopped pecans
- 1/4 cup packed brown sugar
- 1/2 cup butter, melted
- 2 packages (8 ounces *each*) cream cheese, softened
- 3/4 cup sugar
- 1 carton (8 ounces) frozen whipped topping, thawed
- 2 packages (3 ounces *each*) raspberry gelatin
- 2 cups boiling water
- 2 cups cold water

In a bowl, combine the flour, pecans and brown sugar; stir in butter. Press into an ungreased 13-in. x 9-in. x 2-in. baking dish. Bake at 350° for 10-13 minutes or until lightly browned. Cool on a wire rack.

In a large mixing bowl, beat cream cheese and sugar until smooth; fold in whipped topping. Spread over crust. Cover and refrigerate for 1 hour.

In a bowl, dissolve gelatin in boiling water; stir in cold water. Spoon over cream cheese layer. Refrigerate until firm. Cut into squares. **Yield:** 12-16 servings.

Editors' Meals

Taste of Home is edited by 1,000 cooks across North America. Here, you'll "meet" some of those cooks who share a family-favorite meal.

HOME COOKING. Clockwise from upper left: Fun Pizza Party! (p. 238), Lip-Smacking Chicken Menu (p. 242), Favorite Easter Foods (p. 230) and Savory Steak Dinner (p. 246).

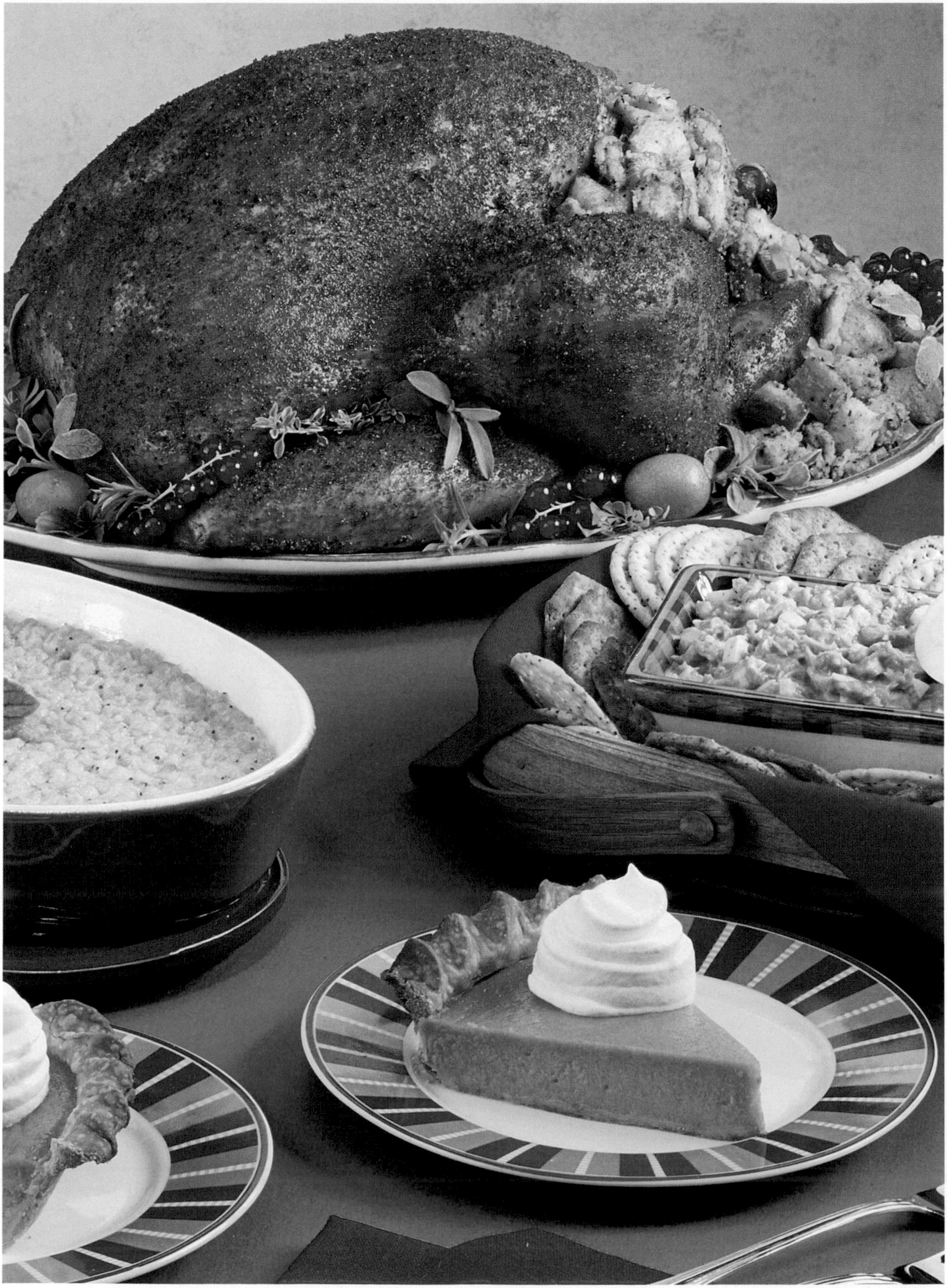

Merry Christmas Meal

One of our 1,000 field editors shares her best-loved
holiday menu along with helpful tips.

By Peggy West, Georgetown, Delaware

I LOVE to have family and friends over, especially at holiday time. Most of our relatives tend to gather at our home for special occasions since cooking and decorating for the different seasons are my passions.

Our Christmas dinner may vary some from year to year as I try out a new dish or two on my husband, Eugene, and the crowd. But Crab-Egg Cracker Spread, Sage-Rubbed Roast Turkey, Baked Corn Pudding and Lemony Sweet Potato Pie are traditional favorites they've come to expect.

I grew up on the Eastern shore, where crabmeat was plentiful. Mom always made the Crab-Egg Cracker Spread at the holidays. Since it's such a hit, I serve this appetizer often. It's delicious on small bread slices and toasted bread chips as well as crackers...and makes a great chunky dip for vegetables.

I love bringing my best roast turkey and dressing to the holiday table. Golden brown and seasoned with sage and paprika, the turkey meat is moist, tender and delicious. The herb rub I use on the turkey forms a thin crust as it bakes. To keep it from breaking apart, use a tube baster instead of a brush. I always get compliments on the flavorful seasoning.

Baked Corn Pudding is a recipe from a church cookbook. I love the sweet corn flavor in this delicious side dish. To give it extra-fresh flavor, I use frozen corn from our garden instead of canned kernel corn. It has a pleasant custard-like consistency.

The recipe for Lemony Sweet Potato Pie came from a wonderful old-fashioned cook, my sister's mother-in-law. I recall going to her home on Christmas a few times when she cooked on a woodstove (she preferred it to her gas stove). The aromas and tastes of those delicious foods are a mouth-watering memory.

I asked her for the pie recipe, then added a little lemon flavoring since lemon is Eugene's favorite—it's what makes this pie unique.

My mother and grandmother were both very good cooks and have influenced my cooking style. Mom was a great baker and taught me from-scratch methods for cakes and pies.

During the summer months of my childhood, I stayed with my father's parents during the day. I stood on a chair in the kitchen to "help" as Grandma canned and froze garden produce and made jams and preserves.

Now that Eugene and I are both retired, we spend lots of time in our own garden in spring and summer. We like to freeze vegetables we've raised and can relishes—especially pepper relish.

I'm enjoying being home full-time and having more time to spend with my two grown stepchildren and other family members. Eugene and I also go antiquing and shop at flea markets for treasures to sell in a couple of booths that we rent in a local antiques mall.

When the weather turns colder, I turn my attention inside, decorating our home and planning hearty menus. I hope you'll enjoy the one I'm sharing here as much as we do. Happy holidays!

Holiday Dinner Countdown

PLANNING AHEAD for a holiday gathering reduces stress and lets the hostess enjoy herself, too. Here's a checklist that Peggy suggests:

- At least 3 weeks before the party, plan the menu and start a running list of groceries and other necessities.
- Purchase all nonperishable items well in advance—often you can catch a sale on seasonal ingredients such as frozen turkeys, cranberries, sweet potatoes and such.
- A few days in advance, polish silver, locate special serving pieces and press the tablecloth.
- The day before, make sure the house is clean and in good order.
- Set the table the night before or get up early the day of the party and do it first thing.
- Enjoy celebrating with your guests!

PICTURED AT LEFT: Crab-Egg Cracker Spread, Sage-Rubbed Roast Turkey, Baked Corn Pudding and Lemony Sweet Potato Pie (recipes are on the next page).

Sage-Rubbed Roast Turkey

Prep: 30 min.   **Bake:** 3-1/2 hours + standing

    1 turkey (13 to 15 pounds)
    3 tablespoons butter, softened
    4 teaspoons salt
    2 teaspoons pepper
    1 teaspoon rubbed sage
    1 teaspoon paprika
STUFFING:
    2 celery ribs, chopped
    1 large onion, chopped
  1/2 cup butter
    1 loaf (1 pound) day-old bread, cubed
      (about 11 cups)
    3 teaspoons rubbed sage
    1 teaspoon salt
    1 teaspoon pepper
 1-1/4 to 1-3/4 cups chicken broth

Pat turkey dry. Combine the butter, salt, pepper, sage and paprika; rub over the outside and inside of turkey. In a skillet, saute celery and onion in butter until tender. In a large bowl, combine the bread cubes, celery mix-

Crab-Egg Cracker Spread

Prep: 15 min. + chilling

  1/3 cup mayonnaise
  1/3 cup chili sauce
    1 tablespoon prepared horseradish
    1 garlic clove, minced
  1/2 teaspoon prepared mustard
  1/4 to 1/2 teaspoon hot pepper sauce
  1/2 teaspoon salt
    2 cans (6 ounces *each*) crabmeat, drained,
      flaked and cartilage removed *or* 1-1/2 cups
      flaked fresh *or* frozen crabmeat
    2 hard-cooked eggs, finely chopped
Assorted crackers

In a bowl, combine the mayonnaise, chili sauce, horseradish, garlic, mustard, hot pepper sauce and salt. Stir in the crab and eggs. Cover and refrigerate for at least 2 hours before serving. Serve with crackers.
Yield: 2-1/2 cups.

Lemony Sweet Potato Pie

Prep: 20 min.   **Bake:** 50 min.

2 cups mashed cooked sweet potatoes
3 eggs
1 can (5 ounces) evaporated milk
1/4 cup water
1/4 cup butter, melted
1-1/2 teaspoons vanilla extract
1/2 teaspoon lemon extract
1 cup sugar
1 unbaked pastry shell (9 inches)
Whipped cream

Press mashed sweet potatoes through a sieve or food mill. In a bowl, whisk the eggs, milk, water, butter and extracts. Stir in the sugar and sweet potatoes. Pour into crust.

Bake at 375° for 30 minutes. Cover edges loosely with foil. Bake 20-30 minutes longer or until a knife inserted near the center comes out clean. Cool on a wire rack. Serve pie with whipped cream. Refrigerate leftovers. **Yield:** 6-8 servings.

ture, sage, salt and pepper. Add enough broth to moisten; toss gently. Just before baking, loosely stuff turkey. Skewer turkey openings; tie drumsticks together. Place breast side up on a rack in a roasting pan.

Bake at 350° for 3-1/2 to 4 hours or until a meat thermometer reads 180° for the turkey and 165° for the stuffing, basting occasionally with pan drippings. Cover loosely with foil if turkey browns too quickly. Cover and let stand for 20 minutes before removing stuffing and carving turkey. **Yield:** 10-12 servings (8 cups stuffing).

Baked Corn Pudding

Prep: 10 min.   **Bake:** 45 min.

1/2 cup sugar
3 tablespoons all-purpose flour
3 eggs
1 cup milk
1/4 cup butter, melted
1/2 teaspoon salt
1/2 teaspoon pepper
1 can (15-1/4 ounces) whole kernel corn, drained
1 can (14-3/4 ounces) cream-style corn

In a bowl, combine the sugar and flour. Whisk in the eggs, milk, butter, salt and pepper. Stir in the corn and cream-style corn. Pour into a greased 1-1/2-qt. baking dish. Bake, uncovered, at 350° for 45-50 minutes or until a knife inserted near the center comes out clean. **Yield:** 10 servings.

Favorite Easter Foods

This field editor celebrates Easter and the arrival of spring with a home-style ham dinner.

By Lavonn Bormuth, Westerville, Ohio

EASTER has always been a special time for my husband, Jeff, and me to gather with our relatives for a very wonderful meal. As the family sits around the dinner table, we thank God for His many blessings and enjoy each other and good food. Usually we linger for hours, talking and—more importantly—laughing together.

Ham with Cherry Sauce, Golden Scalloped Potatoes, Almond-Orange Tossed Salad and Double-Crust Rhubarb Pie are my all-time favorite Easter foods.

My mother-in-law taught me how to make the delightful cherry sauce for my baked ham. Different from the standard brown sugar glaze, it is fruity tasting and its bright ruby color stands out. Brown sugar still plays an important role, however. I combine it with maple syrup and ground mustard, then rub the mixture over the scored ham before baking it.

Golden Scalloped Potatoes are a must with ham. We all love the great taste of the rich cream sauce in this dish. I like this casserole best when it bakes to a golden brown. The recipe is also from my mother-in-law.

My mother introduced me to Almond-Orange Tossed Salad. Mandarin oranges are a refreshing addition to the greens and sugared almonds in this pretty salad. And I love the pleasant sweet dressing!

I started cooking in junior high home economics classes, and my mother taught my two sisters and me how to bake. When we were in high school, Mom went to work full-time, and getting dinner started was up to us. We'd get the meat roasting…pull together a few side dishes…and when Mom and Dad arrived, dinner was ready.

The recipe for Double-Crust Rhubarb Pie—an old-fashioned spring comfort food—came from a church cookbook. What makes this pie different from the traditional rhubarb pie is the custard filling.

I never really appreciated spring until I moved from southern California, where the seasons never change drastically, to Ohio in 1983. Now I can better understand the connection between Easter and spring—they both celebrate a new beginning and new life.

I was born and raised in Chula Vista, a San Diego suburb, and met Jeff when he was stationed in the Navy and came to the church I attended. Jeff is a meat-and-potatoes kind of guy, and I like to cook for him. However, the daring part of my personality comes out when I try new recipes. I love to experiment!

When we go to a potluck, friends tell me they look for the most unusual dish on the buffet and say that it must be mine. For some of our family gatherings, all the cooks agree to bring only new items. That's when I turn to *Taste of Home*, because I know the recipes are tried and true—and they always turn out!

Besides cooking, I enjoy scrapbooking. I make custom photo albums for gifts and also sell some by special order.

I do hope you'll enjoy the cherished recipes I'm sharing here as much as we do. Happy Easter!

Lavonn's Hints for a Carefree Dinner

LAVONNE usually makes the cherry sauce for the ham the night before and reheats it on the stove or in the microwave. This saves time in the kitchen after you arrive home for dinner from church.

For the scalloped potatoes, she peels the whole potatoes the night before and seals them in a resealable bag with the air removed so they don't turn brown. In the morning, she slices them and assembles the casserole. You can also add diced onions and/or cheese to the dish for variety.

To get a head start on the salad, Lavonn mixes the lettuce, celery and green onions in a resealable plastic bag the night before. Store oranges, avocado, nuts and dressing in separate bags or jars and add to the salad before serving.

Each spring, she chops, pre-measures and freezes rhubarb in the amounts needed for recipes like the pie. She labels the bag with the date and amount of rhubarb.

PICTURED AT LEFT: Ham with Cherry Sauce, Golden Scalloped Potatoes, Almond-Orange Tossed Salad and Double-Crust Rhubarb Pie (recipes are on the next page).

Golden Scalloped Potatoes

Prep: 20 min. **Bake:** 1 hour

1/4 cup butter
  3 tablespoons flour
  1 teaspoon salt
Dash pepper
  3 cups milk
  5 large Yukon gold potatoes, peeled and thinly sliced

In a large saucepan over medium heat, melt butter. Stir in the flour, salt and pepper until smooth. Gradually add milk. Bring to a boil; cook and stir for 2 minutes or until thickened and bubbly.

Place the potatoes in a greased 9-in. square baking dish. Add the sauce and stir gently to coat. Cover and bake at 325° for 30 minutes. Uncover; bake 30-40 minutes longer or until the potatoes are tender. **Yield:** 8 servings.

Almond-Orange Tossed Salad

Prep: 20 min. **Cook:** 15 min. + cooling

  2 tablespoons sugar
1/2 cup sliced almonds
  4 cups torn iceberg lettuce
  4 cups torn romaine
  1 can (11 ounces) mandarin oranges, drained

Ham with Cherry Sauce

Prep: 10 min. **Bake:** 1-3/4 hours

  1 fully cooked bone-in ham (6 to 8 pounds)
  1 cup packed brown sugar
  3 tablespoons maple syrup
  1 teaspoon ground mustard
1/2 cup sugar
  3 tablespoons cornstarch
  1 cup cold water
  1 can (16 ounces) pitted dark sweet cherries, undrained
  2 tablespoons lemon juice
  1 teaspoon almond extract

Place ham in a roasting pan. Score surface of ham with shallow diagonal cuts, making diamond shapes. Combine the brown sugar, syrup and mustard; rub over ham and press into cuts. Cover and bake at 325° for 1-3/4 to 2 hours or until a meat thermometer reads 140° and ham is heated through.

For cherry sauce, in a saucepan, combine the sugar, cornstarch and water until smooth. Add cherries. Bring to a boil; cook and stir for 2 minutes or until thickened. Remove from the heat; stir in lemon juice and extract. Serve with ham. **Yield:** 8-10 servings.

2 eggs
4 cups chopped fresh *or* frozen rhubarb
Pastry for double-crust pie (9 inches)
1 tablespoon butter

In a large bowl, combine the sugar, flour and cinnamon. Add eggs; whisk until smooth. Gently stir in rhubarb. Line a 9-in. pie plate with bottom pastry; add filling. Dot with butter.

Roll out remaining pastry to fit top of pie; place over filling. Trim, seal and flute edges. Cut slits in top. Bake at 400° for 45-50 minutes or until crust is golden brown and filling is bubbly. Cool on a wire rack. Store in the refrigerator. **Yield:** 8 servings.

Editor's Note: If using frozen rhubarb, measure rhubarb while still frozen, then thaw completely. Drain in a colander, but do not press liquid out.

Finishing Touches

To top off double-crust pies before baking, use a pastry brush to lightly and evenly apply one of the following washes to the top crust, avoiding the edges.

For a shine and light browning, brush with an egg white that was lightly beaten with 1 teaspoon of water.

For a slight shine, brush with half-and-half cream or heavy whipping cream.

For a crisp brown crust, brush with water.

1 large ripe avocado, peeled and cubed
1/2 cup diced celery
2 green onions, sliced
DRESSING:
1/4 cup vegetable oil
2 tablespoons sugar
2 tablespoons cider vinegar
2 teaspoons minced fresh parsley
1/4 teaspoon salt
1/4 teaspoon pepper

In a small skillet over medium-low heat, cook sugar, without stirring, for 12-14 minutes or until melted. Add almonds; stir quickly to coat. Remove from the heat; pour onto waxed paper to cool.

In a large serving bowl, combine the iceberg lettuce, romaine, mandarin oranges, avocado, celery, onions and almonds.

In a jar with a tight-fitting lid, combine the dressing ingredients; shake well. Drizzle over salad; toss gently to coat. **Yield:** 8 servings.

Double-Crust Rhubarb Pie

Prep: 20 min.   **Bake:** 45 min. + cooling

1 cup sugar
3 tablespoons all-purpose flour
1/2 teaspoon ground cinnamon

Super Southern Fare

This field editor fires up the grill for pork ribs along with other Southern-style fare.

By Katie Sloan, Charlotte, North Carolina

BORN in Massachusetts, I was raised on fresh seafood and traditional New England dinners. But when I moved to the South 12 years ago, I was introduced to different foods that have deliciously expanded my cooking style.

The menu I am sharing—Grilled Country Ribs, Triple-Cheese Macaroni, Sweet Potato Biscuits and Classic Red Velvet Cake—reflects this. Y'all gotta love it!

I couldn't move down south and not learn how to cook ribs. So I struggled through dry ribs, tough ribs and even salty ribs until I finally came up with this tasty finger-lickin' recipe.

Prebaking the ribs before grilling them is the secret to their tenderness. The meat just falls off the bone. And I'm proud to say that even my Southern friends have given my barbecue sauce their stamp of approval.

My Triple-Cheese Macaroni really wows my family, which believes "the more cheese, the better!" This rich and creamy casserole is popular for any party or holiday meal and is great to take to a covered-dish buffet or cookout.

Speaking of family, one of the greatest blessings that my move has brought me is my husband, Milton, and his family. I am stepmother to Milton II and twin brother and sister Lindsay and Alexandria.

They all like biscuits, which are a staple in the area. But plain biscuits can get a little boring after a while. So I started searching for something new and tasty to spice up Sunday dinner.

After tweaking the spices a bit, I finally came up with this version of Sweet Potato Biscuits. Everyone falls in love with their unique flavor. They are especially tasty with honey butter.

Classic Red Velvet Cake is my specialty dessert. This bright red cake has a mild chocolate flavor and sweet cream cheese icing. It's absolutely addictive!

I'd better not show up at a family event without bringing this eye-catching treat. In fact, I've been known to spend several days baking layer after layer to serve a crowd.

My mother and my grandmother took me under their wings and taught me all the basics of cooking. Even my father is excellent in the kitchen, making the best candy in town. He's been known to grill the most tender of steaks in the cold winter winds that blow off the Atlantic Ocean. So cooking comes second nature to me.

But as I mentioned earlier, I knew nothing about Southern cooking when I moved to North Carolina, and I had to adapt very quickly. I switched my Cream of Wheat for grits and spinach for collard greens. With fresh fish not as readily available, I learned how to fry chicken and make barbecue.

My mother-in-law, a great Southern cook, has shared some of her best recipes—like pound cake and carrot cake—which I treasure.

Now Milton and I enjoy the best of both worlds—great New England Clam Chowda' (when I'm feeling homesick) and the good ol' Southern meals that I've learned how to cook quite well. Hopefully, you and your family will enjoy the great Southern fare I've shared here as well.

Quick Tips from Katie

HERE'S A HANDFUL of helpful cooking tips Katie has learned over the years:

- When grilling meat, salt it after cooking. If you salt it before, the salt will draw out the meat's moisture and make it dry.
- To help cakes rise higher, have all the ingredients at room temperature.
- An easy way to butter corn on the cob is to use a slice of buttered bread.
- For lighter, fluffier pancakes made from a mix, substitute carbonated water for the water called for in the mix.
- Place a fresh lettuce leaf on the surface of soup to remove some of the fat; discard the leaf before serving soup. A raw potato added to salty soup will absorb some extra salt.

PICTURED AT LEFT: Grilled Country Ribs, Triple-Cheese Macaroni, Sweet Potato Biscuits and Classic Red Velvet Cake (recipes are on the next page).

Triple-Cheese Macaroni

(Also pictured on front cover)

Prep: 20 min.   **Bake:** 25 min.

- 1 **package (16 ounces) elbow macaroni**
- 2 **eggs**
- 1 **can (12 ounces) evaporated milk**
- 1/4 **cup butter, melted**
- 2 **tablespoons prepared mustard**
- 1 **teaspoon seasoned salt**
- 1 **teaspoon pepper**
- 8 **ounces process cheese (Velveeta), melted**
- 2 **cups (8 ounces) shredded mild cheddar cheese, *divided***
- 2 **cups (8 ounces) shredded sharp cheddar cheese, *divided***

Cook macaroni according to package directions. Meanwhile, in a large bowl, whisk the eggs, milk, butter, mustard, seasoned salt and pepper until combined. Stir in the process cheese and 1-1/2 cups of each cheddar cheese. Drain macaroni.

Stir into cheese mixture. Pour into greased 3-qt. baking dish. Top with remaining cheese. Bake, uncovered, at 350° for 25-30 minutes or until cheese is melted and edges are bubbly. **Yield:** 6 servings.

Grilled Country Ribs

Prep: 1-3/4 hours   **Grill:** 1 hour

- 4 **pounds bone-in country-style pork ribs**
- 1 **medium onion, chopped**
- 2 **garlic cloves, minced**
- 1/4 **cup vegetable oil**
- 1 **cup ketchup**
- 1/4 **cup packed brown sugar**
- 1/4 **cup cider vinegar**
- 1/4 **cup hot pepper sauce**
- 2 **tablespoons Worcestershire sauce**
- 2 **tablespoons prepared mustard**

Place ribs in a greased 13-in. x 9-in. x 2-in. baking dish. Cover and bake at 350° for 1-1/2 hours or until no longer pink.

Meanwhile, in a large saucepan, saute the onion and garlic in oil until tender. Stir in the remaining ingredients; bring to a boil. Reduce heat; simmer, uncovered, for 15 minutes, stirring occasionally. Set aside.

Drain ribs. Grill, covered, over indirect low heat for 45 minutes, turning once. Baste with barbecue sauce. Grill 15 minutes longer or until meat is tender, turning and basting frequently. **Yield:** 6 servings.

Sweet Potato Biscuits

Prep: 25 min.   **Bake:** 10 min.

☑ Uses less fat, sugar or salt. Includes Nutritional Analysis and Diabetic Exchanges.

- **2 cups self-rising flour**
- **1/4 cup packed brown sugar**
- **1 teaspoon ground cinnamon**
- **1 teaspoon ground ginger**
- **7 tablespoons cold butter,** *divided*
- **3 tablespoons shortening**
- **1 cup mashed sweet potatoes**
- **6 tablespoons milk**

In a bowl, combine the flour, brown sugar, cinnamon and ginger. Cut in 4 tablespoons butter and shortening until mixture resembles coarse crumbs. In another bowl, combine sweet potatoes and milk; stir into crumb mixture just until combined.

Turn onto a floured surface; knead 8-10 times. Roll to 1/2-in. thickness; cut with a 2-1/2-in. biscuit cutter. Place on ungreased baking sheets. Melt remaining butter; brush over dough. Bake at 425° for 10-12 minutes or until golden brown. Remove to wire racks. Serve warm. **Yield:** 1-1/2 dozen.

Nutritional Analysis: 1 biscuit equals 136 calories, 7 g fat (3 g saturated fat), 13 mg cholesterol, 211 mg sodium, 18 g carbohydrate, 1 g fiber, 2 g protein. **Diabetic Exchanges:** 1 starch, 1 fat.

Editor's Note: As a substitute for *each* cup of self-rising flour, place 1-1/2 teaspoons baking powder and 1/2 teaspoon salt in a measuring cup. Add all-purpose flour to measure 1 cup.

Classic Red Velvet Cake

Prep: 25 min.   **Bake:** 20 min. + cooling

- **1/2 cup shortening**
- **1-1/2 cups sugar**
- **2 eggs**
- **1 bottle (1 ounce) red food coloring**
- **3 teaspoons white vinegar**
- **1 teaspoon butter flavoring**
- **1 teaspoon vanilla extract**
- **2-1/2 cups cake flour**
- **1/4 cup baking cocoa**
- **1 teaspoon baking soda**
- **1 teaspoon salt**
- **1 cup buttermilk**

FROSTING:
- **1 package (8 ounces) cream cheese, softened**
- **1/2 cup butter, softened**
- **3-3/4 cups confectioners' sugar**
- **3 teaspoons vanilla extract**

In a large mixing bowl, cream shortening and sugar. Add eggs, one at a time, beating well after each addition. Beat in food coloring, vinegar, butter flavoring and vanilla. Combine the flour, cocoa, baking soda and salt; add to creamed mixture alternately with buttermilk.

Pour batter into three greased and floured 9-in. round baking pans. Bake at 350° for 20-25 minutes or until a toothpick inserted near the center comes out clean. Cool for 10 minutes before removing from pans to wire racks to cool completely.

In a large mixing bowl, combine frosting ingredients; beat until smooth and creamy. Spread between layers and over top and sides of cake. **Yield:** 12 servings.

Fun Pizza Party!

One of our 1,000 field editors shares a terrific pizza menu that's perfect in any season.

By Gaylene Anderson, Sandy, Utah

MY FAMILY loves homemade pizza. It makes dinnertime seem like a party! So when it came to sending my favorite meal to *Taste of Home* magazine, I didn't deliberate very long.

In the summertime—or anytime—a menu that has Homemade Pizza Supreme, Cream of Broccoli Soup, Parmesan Breadsticks and Buttermilk Cocoa Cake rates "high fives" from my husband, Russell, our children and their friends.

I found the pizza recipe in a community cookbook from the 1980s. Homemade Pizza Supreme has a great crust and colorful toppings. Even if you've never made pizza from scratch, I hope you'll try this recipe. It makes two pizzas, which is wonderful when our four children are all home.

Older son Paul and youngest daughter Janalyn live with us. Carli is finishing up her master's degree at Brigham Young University in Provo (my alma mater). Jeff and his wife, Karen, live nearby.

Cream of Broccoli Soup is super-easy to make and yet it tastes like you've worked for hours. I always make sure I have the ingredients on hand just in case I want to whip some up quickly.

I first tasted Parmesan Breadsticks when my neighbor brought them to a church social. I time it so the breadsticks are the last thing out of the oven just before we sit down to eat. They fill the kitchen with a tempting aroma when they are baking, and they're wonderful served warm. My family tells me I can't make them too often.

The old cookbook where I found the pizza recipe also yielded another treasure—Buttermilk Cocoa Cake. Actually, its title in the book is "Betty Brundage's Buttermilk Brownie Cake."

We've had fun with the name over the years, saying it with exaggerated emphasis on all those Bs! People who've tasted it remember "that marvelous cake we had—you know, the B-B-B one." We have no idea who Betty Brundage is but are extremely grateful to her for the now family-favorite cake!

I love to bake, as you can tell from my menu. I can trace my baking experience back to my childhood, when I was in charge of making dozens and dozens of cookies for our family Christmas Eve party. I would start weeks ahead baking and freezing each batch.

Today, I have four big baking sheets and use all four for making cookies: one baking in the oven; one ready to bake; one I'm filling up; and one with cookies cooling. I get done in no time! I slightly under-bake my cookies so they won't be hard when they cool. I always set my timer earlier than the recipe suggests.

Russell and I have been married for 32 years and live in a suburb of Salt Lake City. Just outside my front door, I see the beautiful Wasatch Range of the Rocky Mountains. Originally from Los Angeles, I love this view and still glory in real live snow and the four seasons.

During the "wedding season," I play *Here Comes the Bride* at weddings and background music at receptions. I also compose and arrange choral and piano music that's published nationally.

For me, every season is cooking season, and I hope you'll enjoy my favorite menu. Let's see...if we nickname it "Gaylene's Great Grub," maybe your family will start asking for "that pizza meal—you know, the G-G-G one!"

Pizza Possibilities

YOU CAN ADD your own pizzazz to Gaylene's recipe for Homemade Pizza Supreme. Just change the toppings to fit your family's preferences. Try Italian sausage in combination with another meat or on its own. Vary the veggies to your taste.

Let each family member or guest bake his own individual pizza. Just grease ovenproof dinner plates, divide up the pizza dough and let each person pat out the dough to cover the plate. Have the sauce and a choice of toppings available.

If you're in a hurry and don't want to roll out the dough, press it out on cookie sheets, add sauce and toppings and bake as directed.

PICTURED AT LEFT: Homemade Pizza Supreme, Cream of Broccoli Soup, Parmesan Breadsticks and Buttermilk Cocoa Cake (recipes are on the next page).

Homemade Pizza Supreme

Prep: 45 min. + rising   **Bake:** 30 min.

1 package (1/4 ounce) active dry yeast
2 cups warm water (110° to 115°)
3 tablespoons vegetable oil
1-1/2 teaspoons salt
4 to 6 cups all-purpose flour
SAUCE:
2 cans (8 ounces *each*) tomato sauce
1-1/2 teaspoons grated onion
1 teaspoon dried oregano
1/4 teaspoon salt
1/8 teaspoon pepper
TOPPINGS:
4 cups (16 ounces) shredded mozzarella
   cheese
4 ounces Canadian bacon, diced
1 package (3-1/2 ounces) sliced pepperoni
1 medium sweet red pepper, sliced
1 medium green pepper, sliced
1 can (2-1/4 ounces) sliced ripe olives,
   drained
1 cup chopped onion
1 cup grated Parmesan cheese
1/2 cup minced fresh basil

In a large mixing bowl, dissolve yeast in warm water. Add oil, salt and 2 cups flour. Beat on medium speed for 3 minutes. Stir in enough remaining flour to form a soft dough. Turn onto a floured surface; knead until smooth and elastic, about 6-8 minutes. Place in a greased bowl, turning once to grease top. Cover and

let rest in a warm place for 10 minutes.

Combine sauce ingredients; set aside. Divide dough in half. On a floured surface, roll each portion into a 13-in. circle. Transfer to two greased 12-in. pizza pans; build up edges slightly. Bake at 375° for 15 minutes or until lightly browned. Spread with sauce; sprinkle with toppings. Bake for 15-20 minutes or until cheese is melted. **Yield:** 2 pizzas (6 slices each).

Cream of Broccoli Soup

Prep/Total Time: 25 min.

2 cups water
4 teaspoons chicken bouillon granules
2 packages (10 ounces *each*) frozen
   chopped broccoli
2 tablespoons finely chopped onion
2 cans (10-3/4 ounces *each*) condensed
   cream of chicken soup, undiluted
2 cups evaporated milk
2 cups (16 ounces) sour cream
1 teaspoon dried parsley flakes
1/4 teaspoon pepper

In a large saucepan, combine the water and bouillon. Add broccoli and onion. Bring to a boil; reduce heat. Simmer for 10 minutes or until broccoli is crisp-tender. Combine soup, milk, sour cream, parsley and pepper; add to broccoli mixture. Cook and stir for 3-5 minutes or until heated through. **Yield:** 6-8 servings.

Parmesan Breadsticks

Prep: 40 min. + rising   **Bake:** 10 min.

2 packages (1/4 ounce *each*) active dry
  yeast
1-1/2 cups warm water (110° to 115°)
1/2 cup warm milk (110° to 115°)
3 tablespoons sugar
3 tablespoons plus 1/4 cup butter, softened,
  divided
1 teaspoon salt
4-1/2 to 5-1/2 cups all-purpose flour
1/4 cup grated Parmesan cheese
1/2 teaspoon garlic salt

In a large mixing bowl, dissolve yeast in warm water.
Add the milk, sugar, 3 tablespoons butter, salt and 2
cups flour. Beat until smooth. Stir in enough remaining flour to form a soft dough. Turn onto a floured surface; knead until smooth and elastic, about 6-8 minutes. Place in a greased bowl, turning once to grease
top. Cover and let rise in a warm place until doubled,
about 45 minutes.

Punch the dough down. Turn onto a floured surface;
divide into 36 pieces. Shape each piece into a 6-in.
rope. Place 2 in. apart on greased baking sheets.
Cover and let rise until doubled, about 25 minutes.

Melt remaining butter; brush over dough. Sprinkle
with Parmesan cheese and garlic salt. Bake at 400° for
8-10 minutes or until golden brown. Remove from pans
to wire racks. **Yield:** 3 dozen.

Buttermilk Cocoa Cake

Prep: 30 min.   **Bake:** 30 min. + cooling

1/4 cup baking cocoa
1 cup water
1/2 cup butter, cubed
2 cups all-purpose flour
2 cups sugar
1 teaspoon baking soda
2 eggs, lightly beaten
1/2 cup vegetable oil
1/2 cup buttermilk
BUTTERMILK FROSTING:
1/4 cup baking cocoa
1/2 cup butter, cubed
1/2 cup buttermilk
3-3/4 cups confectioners' sugar
1 teaspoon vanilla extract
1/2 cup chopped pecans, optional

In a large saucepan, combine the cocoa and water until smooth; add butter. Bring just to a boil. Remove from
the heat. In a large mixing bowl, combine the flour, sugar and baking soda; add cocoa mixture. Combine eggs,
oil and buttermilk; add to cocoa mixture and beat until
smooth. Pour into a greased 13-in. x 9-in. x 2-in. baking dish. Bake at 350° for 30-35 minutes or until a toothpick inserted near the center comes out clean.

In a large saucepan, bring the cocoa, butter and buttermilk to a boil. Remove from the heat. Whisk in the
confectioners' sugar and vanilla. Spread over the warm
cake. Sprinkle with pecans if desired. Cool on a wire
rack. **Yield:** 12-15 servings.

Lip-Smacking Chicken Menu

This popular supper is a family-pleasing favorite from one of our field editors.

By Norma Harder, Melfort, Saskatchewan

WHETHER served as patio fare in the summer or comfort food in the winter, we love this chicken dinner. So I'm delighted to share my recipes for Barbecued Chicken, Lemony Caesar Salad, Pillow-Soft Dinner Rolls and Almond Apple Cheesecake with fellow cooks.

Our three grown children were raised on flavorful Barbecued Chicken. I still have the original recipe card that a friend gave me 25 years ago—the stains on it attest to its frequent use! I bet I make this almost monthly, and nobody complains that's too often. The chicken turns out juicy and tender, and the sauce makes a tasty gravy.

Early in the day, make the sauce for the chicken and refrigerate it. This will save you time later when you're ready to brown the chicken and assemble the dish for the oven.

My Lemony Caesar Salad has the same fresh, classic flavor as one I used to order at a nearby steak house. Making it at home lets me adjust the garlic—if I want it zesty, I add two cloves.

I believe you can never have too much garlic! (To remove the smell of garlic, rub your fingers over a stainless steel spoon.) You can mix up the salad dressing ahead, but add it just before serving so the greens stay crisp.

The dough for Pillow-Soft Rolls has a nice texture and is simple to shape. I also use the dough to make cinnamon buns and braided wreaths at Christmas. The recipe for these easy rolls came from an old church cookbook my sister gave me.

When the fruit ripens on our trees, Almond Apple Cheesecake is a must. The flavorful apple-cinnamon-nut topping along with a raspberry jam layer make this dessert outstanding. Prepare the cheesecake a day ahead—it tastes even better after sitting.

I'm known for serving cheesecakes at parties. I place them on pedestal cake plates for a lovely presentation. I also take them to potlucks and give them as a gifts.

To me, cooking goes hand-in-hand with entertaining. My husband, John, and I enjoy hosting family and friends in our home and at our lake cottage.

My love of cooking came from my mother, who always encouraged me to make things on my own. She was a stay-at-home mom with four children, and we were often greeted with the aroma of freshly baked bread after school. I also recall her making pies, cakes, loaves, jams and jellies to enter in the local fair every year—and she always came home with ribbons.

I am currently employed part-time as a teacher's aide, working with mentally and physically challenged students at our local high school. It's a rewarding job that I truly love.

I can still find time for reading, gardening, sewing, knitting, folk art painting and, of course, cooking which I enjoy so much.

I hope you'll try my recipes. You'll likely receive compliments on them from your own family and guests, just as I have.

Party at the Harders!

PLANNING gatherings with good food is natural for Norma Harder, who loves to cook.

"At our lake cottage each summer, we invite the whole street down for a pancake and sausage breakfast," she says. "The turnout is terrific, and everyone has a good time. Of course, when our kids were teenagers, they always groaned about getting up early to help set up!"

Norma and John have also hosted theme dinners after trips abroad, like a recent visit to Spain. "We fell in love with the food there," she recalls. "So back at home, I served guests a Spanish meal complete with paella, roasted red pepper salad and sangria.

"I also planned a special dinner after a visit to Italy. It's a great way to share some of our memories and the great flavors of the country's cuisine."

PICTURED AT LEFT: Barbecued Chicken, Lemony Caesar Salad, Pillow-Soft Dinner Rolls and Almond Apple Cheesecake (recipes are on the next page).

Lemony Caesar Salad

Prep/Total Time: 10 min.

    1/2 cup olive oil
      2 tablespoons lemon juice
      1 garlic clove, peeled
    1/2 teaspoon salt
    1/2 teaspoon ground mustard
    1/2 teaspoon Worcestershire sauce
    1/8 teaspoon pepper
      4 to 6 cups torn romaine
      1 cup shredded Parmesan cheese

For dressing, combine the first seven ingredients in a blender; cover and process until the mixture is well blended.

  Place romaine in a salad bowl. Drizzle with desired amount of dressing; sprinkle with Parmesan cheese and toss to coat. Refrigerate any remaining dressing. **Yield:** 4-6 servings.

Pillow-Soft Dinner Rolls

Prep: 30 min. + rising **Bake:** 20 min.

✓ Uses less fat, sugar or salt. Includes Nutritional Analysis and Diabetic Exchanges.

  4-1/2 teaspoons active dry yeast
    1/2 cup warm water (110° to 115°)
      2 cups warm milk (110° to 115°)

Barbecued Chicken

Prep: 20 min. **Bake:** 55 min.

      1 broiler/fryer chicken (4 to 5 pounds),
        cut up
      1 tablespoon vegetable oil
    1/2 cup chicken broth
    1/2 cup ketchup
    1/4 cup cider vinegar
      1 tablespoon brown sugar
    1/2 teaspoon curry powder
    1/2 teaspoon paprika
    1/4 teaspoon salt
    1/4 teaspoon ground mustard
    1/8 teaspoon chili powder
Pinch pepper
      2 tablespoons onion soup mix

In a large skillet, brown the chicken on all sides in oil in batches; drain. Place the browned chicken in a greased 13-in. x 9-in. x 2-in. baking dish and in an 8-in. baking dish.

  Combine the broth, ketchup, vinegar, brown sugar, curry powder, paprika, salt, mustard, chili powder and pepper; pour over the top of the chicken. Sprinkle with the onion soup mix. Cover and bake at 350° for 55-65 minutes or until the chicken juices run clear. **Yield:** 4-6 servings.

FILLING:
  2 packages (8 ounces *each*) cream cheese, softened
1/2 cup sugar
  2 eggs, lightly beaten
  2 teaspoons vanilla extract
TOPPING:
1/3 cup sugar
1/2 teaspoon ground cinnamon
  3 cups thinly sliced peeled tart apples
1/2 cup sliced almonds

In a bowl, combine the flour and sugar; cut in butter until crumbly. Press onto the bottom and 1-1/2 in. up the sides of a greased 9-in. springform pan; prick with a fork. Place on a baking sheet. Bake at 350° for 10 minutes or until soft but set. Cool on a wire rack.

Carefully spread jam over crust. For filling, in a small mixing bowl, beat cream cheese and sugar until smooth. Add eggs and vanilla; beat just until blended. Spread over jam. For topping, combine the sugar and cinnamon in a bowl. Add apples and toss to coat. Spoon over filling. Sprinkle with almonds.

Bake at 350° for 55-60 minutes or until center is almost set. Cool on a wire rack for 10 minutes. Carefully run a knife around edge of pan to loosen; cool 1 hour longer. Chill overnight. Remove sides of pan. Refrigerate leftovers. **Yield:** 10 servings.

Editor's Note: When preparing a crust in a springform pan, use a flat-bottomed measuring cup or glass to firmly press the crumb mixture onto the bottom (and up the sides if the recipe directs).

  6 tablespoons shortening
  2 eggs
1/4 cup sugar
1-1/2 teaspoons salt
  7 to 7-1/2 cups all-purpose flour

In a large mixing bowl, dissolve yeast in warm water. Add the milk, shortening, eggs, sugar, salt and 3 cups flour; beat until smooth. Stir in enough remaining flour to form a soft dough.

Turn onto a floured surface; knead until smooth and elastic, about 6-8 minutes (dough will be sticky). Place in a greased bowl, turning once to grease top. Cover and let rise in a warm place until doubled, about 1 hour.

Punch dough down. Turn onto a lightly floured surface; divide into 24 pieces. Shape each into a roll. Place 2 in. apart on greased baking sheets. Cover and let rise until doubled, about 30 minutes. Bake at 350° for 20-25 minutes or until golden brown. Remove to wire racks. **Yield:** 2 dozen.

Nutritional Analysis: 1 roll (prepared with fat-free milk) equals 184 calories, 4 g fat (1 g saturated fat), 18 mg cholesterol, 164 mg sodium, 31 g carbohydrate, 1 g fiber, 5 g protein. **Diabetic Exchanges:** 2 starch, 1/2 fat.

Almond Apple Cheesecake

Prep: 20 min.   **Bake:** 55 min. + chilling

  1 cup all-purpose flour
1/3 cup sugar
1/2 cup cold butter
1/3 cup seedless raspberry jam

Savory Steak Dinner

Another of our 1,000 field editors shares some of her best recipes for a meat-and-potatoes meal.

By Kelly Ward Hartman, Cape Coral, Florida

A MOUTH-WATERING menu of mine that's especially welcome in autumn includes Garlic-Mushroom Rib Eyes, Rosemary Red Potatoes, Bacon Cauliflower Salad and Delicate Lemon Pound Cake.

Made up of some of my never-fail recipes, it's a meal my family thinks is terrific. And when we're expecting guests, I know I can count on all four of these dishes.

Garlic-Mushroom Rib Eyes are simple but delicious. My husband, Greg, especially loves the garlic and mushrooms that accompany the steak. I came across this recipe about 10 years ago and, after altering it just a little, added it to my recipe box as a "keeper."

Greg and I have three sons—Mick, Quinn and Cole. I work in Greg's chiropractic clinic as his office manager. One of his patients is a culinary instructor. During one of his visits to the clinic, I mentioned that I needed an easy side dish for that night's dinner…and he told me about Rosemary Red Potatoes.

I hurried back to my desk to write down the recipe. I sure was pleased with the results! I've also discovered that these potatoes are versatile enough to serve alongside chicken or pork, too.

My Aunt Lavern taught me how to make her Bacon Cauliflower Salad while I was still in high school, and I've been making it ever since. Lots of flavor and plenty of crunch seem to be the winning combination for this dish. It's definitely a "people-pleaser."

I do think this salad is best eaten the same day it's fixed to appreciate the fresh textures. Good thing there are seldom any leftovers—one serving is never enough!

I started cooking when I was about 10 years old. My first cookbook was a Betty Crocker cookbook for boys and girls—I still have it! Back then, I just made simple treats from sugar cookies to coffee cakes, but now I'm like a mad scientist and our kitchen is my laboratory!

Desserts have always been my favorite fare, and I treasure the collection of tried-and-true dessert recipes I've gathered over the years. I enjoy making them as much as eating them.

The recipe for Delicate Lemon Pound Cake was shared several years ago by a good friend who's an excellent cook. Slices of this cake on a pretty holiday plate make an impressive gift, which I often accompany with a nice box of herbal tea.

I truly delight in taking dishes to parties or sharing whatever my current cooking spree bounty produces with our neighbors.

I grew up in California but went to high school in Indiana. I've noticed my cooking style has been influenced by both regions. I love anything with avocado in it, but good old stick-to-your-ribs Midwest comfort food also has a place in my kitchen.

Since I became a field editor for *Taste of Home*, my love of cooking has grown and prompted me to seek out ways to improve my skills and knowledge. I've taken a cake decorating class and cooking classes at a local gourmet market. I just recently finished a night course at the culinary school near us.

Cooking gives me such joy and peace. I'm grateful to have discovered a way to spend time doing something that brings me so much happiness and can also be shared with others. I hope that's what you'll experience if you try any of my recipes!

Kelly's Quick Tips

HERE are a few cooking tips Kelly has learned from experimenting in the kitchen:

- Save small glass jars with screw-on lids for homemade salad dressings. She puts in all her ingredients and gives the jar a good shake, which blends the ingredients better than using a bowl and whisk.
- Before whipping cream, put your bowl (glass or stainless steel) and beaters into the freezer. She's always amazed by how much faster the cream thickens when she remembers to do this.
- Refrigerate a ripe cantaloupe overnight before cutting to bring out all of its sweetness. She learned this from a produce manager.

PICTURED AT LEFT: Garlic-Mushroom Rib Eyes, Rosemary Red Potatoes, Bacon Cauliflower Salad and Delicate Lemon Pound Cake (recipes are on the next page).

Rosemary Red Potatoes

Prep/Total Time: 30 min.

1-3/4 pounds small red potatoes, quartered
   1 small onion, quartered
  1/4 cup olive oil
1-1/2 teaspoons dried rosemary, crushed
   2 garlic cloves, minced
  1/4 teaspoon garlic salt

In a bowl, combine the potatoes, onion, oil, rosemary, garlic and garlic salt; toss to coat. Transfer to a foil-lined 15-in. x 10-in. x 1-in. baking pan. Bake, uncovered, at 425° for 25-30 minutes or until potatoes are tender and browned. **Yield:** 4 servings.

Bacon Cauliflower Salad

Prep: 20 min. + chilling

1 medium head cauliflower, broken into florets
1 pound sliced bacon, cooked and crumbled
1 cup cubed cheddar cheese
1 medium green pepper, chopped
1 medium onion, chopped

Garlic-Mushroom Rib Eyes

Prep/Total Time: 25 min.

4 boneless rib eye steaks (1 inch thick)
1/4 teaspoon pepper
1/8 teaspoon salt
4 tablespoons butter, *divided*
4 to 8 garlic cloves, peeled and sliced
1 pound sliced fresh mushrooms
3 tablespoons beef broth

Sprinkle steaks with pepper and salt. In a large skillet, melt 1 tablespoon butter. Cook the steaks for 2 minutes on each side or until meat reaches desired doneness (for medium-rare, a meat thermometer should read 145°; medium, 160°; well-done, 170°). Remove and keep warm.

  In the same skillet, cook the garlic in 1 tablespoon butter for 2 minutes. Remove garlic and set aside. Add mushrooms and remaining butter to skillet; saute for 5 minutes. Stir in the broth. Bring to a boil; cook and stir over high heat until liquid is absorbed. Add reserved garlic. Serve over steaks. **Yield:** 4 servings.

Pour into a greased and floured 10-in. fluted tube pan (pan will be full). Bake at 325° for 1-1/4 hours or until a toothpick inserted near the center comes out clean. Cool for 10-20 minutes before removing from pan to a wire rack to cool completely. Dust with confectioners' sugar. **Yield:** 12 servings.

Preparing a Cake Pan

For a tender golden crust, use aluminum pans with a dull finish rather than a shiny or dark finish. If using glass baking dishes, reduce the oven temperature 25°.

Grease and flour baking pans for cakes that will be removed from the pans. Grease the sides and bottom of the pan by spreading shortening with a paper towel over the interior of the pan. Sprinkle 1 to 2 tablespoons of flour into the greased pan; tilt the pan to coat bottom and sides. Turn pan over and tap to remove excess flour.

Cakes that will be served from the pans should be greased but not floured.

1 cup mayonnaise
2 to 4 teaspoons sugar

In a large salad bowl, combine the cauliflower, bacon, cheese, green pepper and onion. Combine the mayonnaise and sugar; spoon over cauliflower mixture and toss to coat. Cover and refrigerate for at least 4 hours before serving. **Yield:** 4 servings.

Delicate Lemon Pound Cake

Prep: 15 min. **Bake:** 1-1/4 hours + cooling

    1 cup butter, softened
  1/2 cup shortening
2-1/2 cups sugar
    5 eggs
    1 teaspoon lemon extract
    1 teaspoon vanilla extract
    3 cups all-purpose flour
  3/4 cup lemon-lime soda
Confectioners' sugar

In a large mixing bowl, cream the butter, shortening and sugar until light and fluffy, about 5 minutes. Add eggs, one at a time, beating well after each addition. Stir in extracts. Add flour alternately with soda, beating just until combined.

Meals in Minutes

Serve your family a hot, homemade meal in a matter of minutes
(30 or less to be exact). These 12 complete menus
let you deliciously and easily do just that!

SPEEDY MEALS. Clockwise from upper left: Cut Kitchen Time with Cube Steak Dinner (p. 260), Dinner for Four Looks Like You Fussed (p. 272), Treat Your Family to Italian-Style Supper (p. 262) and Down-Home Meal Made in a Hurry (p. 270).

Fix a Pork Chop Dinner in a Jiffy

TIME isn't always on your side when it comes to getting a decent dinner on the table for a hungry family. What you need is a meal that's fast, filling and tasty, too.

Our Test Kitchen home economists came up with the quick-to-fix meal here using favorite recipes from three great cooks. It's not only delicious...it's also ready to serve in just 30 minutes.

Janette Hutchings of Festus, Missouri covers her succulent Raspberry Pork Chops with a yummy glaze made with mustard, vinegar and jam. Fixed fast in a skillet, these tender chops are great for everyday or special occasions.

Corn Zucchini Saute makes a colorful accompaniment to the pork chops or to any Mexican-style meal. "I've loved this dish since I was a child," says Sylvia Sonnenburg of Ogden, Utah.

"I've found a fun way to serve cheesecake," Janice Greenhalgh from Florence, Kentucky says about her Cheesecake Waffle Cups. The crunchy store-bought "bowls" hold a smooth cream cheese filling that's layered with cherry pie filling. They're a snap to prepare and attractive, too. Blueberry pie filling would be a wonderful alternative.

Raspberry Pork Chops

Prep/Total Time: 20 min.

☑ **Uses less fat, sugar or salt. Includes Nutritional Analysis and Diabetic Exchanges.**

- 4 boneless pork loin chops (about 5 ounces *each*)
- 1 tablespoon canola oil
- 1/4 cup cider vinegar
- 1/4 cup seedless raspberry jam
- 1 tablespoon prepared mustard

In a large skillet over medium heat, brown pork chops in oil on both sides. Stir in the vinegar, jam and mustard. Reduce heat; cover and simmer for 10-15 minutes or until the meat juices run clear. Remove pork chops and keep warm.

Cook sauce over high heat until reduced by half, stirring occasionally. Spoon over pork chops. **Yield:** 4 servings.

Nutritional Analysis: 1 pork chop with 4-1/2 teaspoons sauce prepared with reduced-sugar jam equals 266 calories, 12 g fat (3 g saturated fat), 83 mg cholesterol, 111 mg sodium, 9 g carbohydrate, 1 g fiber, 29 g protein. **Diabetic Exchanges:** 3-1/2 lean meat, 1 fat, 1/2 fruit.

Corn Zucchini Saute

Prep/Total Time: 30 min.

- 3/4 cup chopped sweet onion
- 3 tablespoons olive oil
- 2 garlic cloves, minced
- 3 medium zucchini, quartered lengthwise and sliced
- 1 plum tomato, seeded and chopped
- 1 can (15-1/4 ounces) whole kernel corn, drained
- 1/4 cup water
- 1 tablespoon dried parsley flakes
- 1/4 teaspoon salt
- 1/4 teaspoon pepper
- 1/2 cup shredded cheddar cheese

In a large skillet, saute onion in oil until tender. Add garlic; saute for 1 minute. Add the zucchini and tomato. Cook for 5 minutes, stirring occasionally.

Stir in the corn, water, parsley, salt and pepper. Bring to a boil. Reduce heat; simmer, uncovered, for 10 minutes. Sprinkle with cheese. Cover and cook 2 minutes longer or until cheese is melted. **Yield:** 4 servings.

Cheesecake Waffle Cups

Prep/Total Time: 10 min.

- 1 package (8 ounces) cream cheese, softened
- 1 can (14 ounces) sweetened condensed milk
- 1/3 cup lemon juice
- 1 teaspoon vanilla extract
- 4 waffle bowls
- 1 cup cherry pie filling

In a small mixing bowl, beat cream cheese until smooth. Gradually beat in milk. Stir in lemon juice and vanilla. Spoon about 1/3 cup into each waffle bowl; top with 2 tablespoons pie filling. Repeat layers. **Yield:** 4 servings.

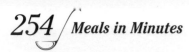

This Fast Fish Supper Tastes Great!

SOMETIMES speed is the most important ingredient in a recipe, but fast-to-fix dishes can be flavorful and filling, too.

Our Test Kitchen home economists concocted this inviting menu using favorite recipes from three *Taste of Home* readers. Together, these recipes make a satisfying meal that you can serve your family in just 30 minutes.

For a refreshing change of pace, serve Cod with Rhubarb Sauce from Sarah Bradley of Athens, Texas. The distinctive sweet-tart sauce complements any grilled fish nicely.

For her appealing Rice 'n' Spinach Salad, Josee Saint-Jean of Clair, New Brunswick combines rice and fresh spinach with raisins, mushrooms, red onion, celery and cashews, then tosses it all with a tasty soy sauce and oil dressing. "I love garlic, so I add extra to the dressing," Josee notes.

Few desserts are as quick and delicious as an ice cream sundae. To make hers special, Sharon Brereton of Vaudreuil, Quebec adds sliced bananas, a maraschino cherry and her homemade Chocolate Ice Cream Topping. Yum!

Cod with Rhubarb Sauce

Prep/Total Time: 25 min.

✓ **Uses less fat, sugar or salt. Includes Nutritional Analysis and Diabetic Exchanges.**

    1 teaspoon olive oil
    3 cups diced fresh *or* frozen rhubarb, thawed
  1/4 cup sugar
  1/2 cup chopped red onion
4-1/2 teaspoons Dijon mustard
    3 teaspoons minced fresh parsley
    1 teaspoon minced fresh basil
  1/4 teaspoon lime juice
Coarsely ground pepper to taste
    4 cod fillets (6 ounces *each*)

In a large saucepan, heat oil over medium heat. Add rhubarb and sugar; cook for 5-7 minutes or until rhubarb is tender. Remove from the heat; stir in the onion, mustard, parsley, basil, lime juice and pepper.

Coat grill rack with nonstick cooking spray before starting the grill. Grill cod, covered, over medium heat for 5-6 minutes on each side or until fish flakes easily with a fork. Serve with rhubarb sauce. **Yield:** 4 servings (2 cups sauce).

Nutritional Analysis: 1 fillet with 1/2 cup sauce equals 216 calories, 3 g fat (trace saturated fat), 65 mg cholesterol, 239 mg sodium, 19 g carbohydrate, 2 g fiber, 28 g protein. **Diabetic Exchanges:** 4-1/2 very lean meat, 1 fruit.

Rice 'n' Spinach Salad

Prep/Total Time: 20 min.

1-1/2 cups torn fresh spinach
    1 cup cooked rice
    2 celery ribs, thinly sliced
  1/2 cup sliced fresh mushrooms
  1/2 cup golden raisins
  1/2 cup salted cashew halves
  1/2 cup chopped red onion
1-1/2 teaspoons minced fresh parsley
    3 tablespoons vegetable oil
    3 tablespoons soy sauce
    1 garlic clove, minced
  1/2 cup chow mein noodles

In a bowl, combine the first eight ingredients. Combine the oil, soy sauce and garlic; pour over salad and toss to coat. Sprinkle with chow mein noodles. **Yield:** 4 servings.

Chocolate Ice Cream Topping

Prep/Total Time: 10 min.

1/3 cup water
1/4 cup sugar
  1 tablespoon butter
3/4 cup semisweet chocolate chips
1/2 teaspoon vanilla extract
Ice cream, sliced bananas and maraschino cherries

In a small saucepan, bring the water, sugar and butter to a boil. Boil for 2 minutes. Remove from the heat; add the chocolate chips and vanilla. Whisk until chips are melted and mixture is smooth. Serve warm over ice cream with bananas and a cherry. **Yield:** 1 cup.

Serve a Taste of Spring in No Time

WITH spring in the air, you'll likely be spending more time outdoors...and less time in the kitchen. So a fast menu that's appetizing, too, will allow you to hoe your garden and still feed your family a meal they'll enjoy.

Our Test Kitchen home economists combined three reader favorites into this inviting menu that can be table-ready in just 30 minutes.

Peachy Chicken is a sweet and refreshing main dish that's attractive enough to serve guests, too. Bill Brown of Haddonfield, New Jersey likes to serve this fruity stovetop entree over rice.

Bacon Onion Asparagus gets its tang from vinegar and its crunch from toasted sesame seeds. "This is a wonderful way to dress up that seasonal favorite," notes Sheila Elliott of Bear, Delaware.

"Golden Garlic Bread will enhance any meal, but especially Italian dishes," says Andrea Holcomb of Oxford, New York.

Peachy Chicken

Prep/Total Time: 25 min.

    4 boneless skinless chicken breast halves
      (4 ounces *each*)
    1 tablespoon vegetable oil
    1 tablespoon butter
    1 can (15-1/4 ounces) sliced peaches,
      undrained
  1/2 cup packed brown sugar
  1/2 cup orange juice
    1 envelope onion soup mix
Hot cooked rice, optional

In a large skillet over medium heat, brown chicken in oil and butter; remove and keep warm. Add peaches with juice, brown sugar, orange juice and soup mix to skillet; stir until combined. Bring to a boil; cook and stir for 2 minutes.

Reduce heat; return chicken to pan. Simmer, uncovered, for 15-20 minutes or until chicken juices run clear. Serve over rice if desired. **Yield:** 4 servings.

Bacon Onion Asparagus

Prep/Total Time: 25 min.

1-1/2 pounds fresh asparagus, trimmed
    2 tablespoons olive oil

  1/4 teaspoon salt, *divided*
  1/4 teaspoon pepper, *divided*
    6 bacon strips, diced
    1 medium onion, chopped
    2 tablespoons cider vinegar
    1 teaspoon sesame seeds, toasted

Place the asparagus in a 15-in. x 10-in. x 1-in. baking pan. Drizzle with oil; sprinkle with 1/8 teaspoon salt and 1/8 teaspoon pepper. Bake at 400° for 10-15 minutes or until lightly browned.

Meanwhile, in a small skillet, cook bacon over medium heat until crisp. Remove to paper towels; drain, reserving 2 teaspoons drippings. Saute onion in drippings until tender. Remove from the heat; stir in the vinegar, bacon and remaining salt and pepper.

Transfer the asparagus to a large shallow bowl; top with the warm bacon dressing and toss gently to coat. Sprinkle with the sesame seeds. **Yield:** 4 servings.

Golden Garlic Bread

Prep/Total Time: 20 min.

  3/4 cup butter, softened
  1/2 cup mayonnaise
    3 cups (12 ounces) shredded cheddar cheese
  1/2 cup grated Parmesan cheese
    3 green onions, chopped
    1 teaspoon Italian seasoning
    1 to 2 garlic cloves, minced
    1 loaf (1 pound) French bread, cut in half
      lengthwise

In a small mixing bowl, beat butter and mayonnaise until blended. Stir in the cheeses, onions, Italian seasoning and garlic. Spread over cut sides of bread.

Place on an ungreased baking sheet. Broil 4-6 in. from the heat for 3-5 minutes or until topping is lightly browned and bubbly. Cut into 2-in. slices. **Yield:** 4-6 servings.

Trimming Asparagus

To trim asparagus, simply cut or snap off the tough ends and discard.

Summer Menu Is Speedy And Scrumptious

SUMMER'S no time to be spending hours in the kitchen slaving over a hot stove. With gardens to tend, lawns to mow and vacations to plan, you need recipes that go together in a flash.

The three reader recipes here make up a delicious warm-weather menu that takes less than 30 minutes to prepare.

"My mother made Broiled Pizza Burgers when I was growing up. We like them for Sunday supper," says Ann Bailes of Anderson, South Carolina. "They're even faster to fix if you use pre-browned hamburger from the freezer. We sometimes substitute slices of cheddar for the process cheese."

Mary Lou Wayman of Salt Lake City, Utah sent in the recipe for Vegetable Trio with its pretty mix of garden-fresh green beans and carrots. It's a nice accompaniment to any meat.

Black Forest Parfaits are guaranteed to sweeten up a meal, whether you're dining indoors or out, assures Barbara Rudolph of Sevierville, Tennessee. With only five ingredients, you can whip them up in no time!

Broiled Pizza Burgers

Prep/Total Time: 25 min.

- 1 pound ground beef
- 1 tablespoon chopped onion
- 2 teaspoons cornstarch
- 1 can (14-1/2 ounces) diced tomatoes, undrained
- 1 teaspoon dried oregano
- 1/4 teaspoon salt
- 1/4 teaspoon onion salt
- 10 slices process American cheese, *divided*
- 4 hamburger buns, split

In a large skillet, cook beef and onion over medium heat until meat is no longer pink; drain. Sprinkle with cornstarch. Stir in the tomatoes, oregano, salt and onion salt. Cook, uncovered, for 5 minutes or until slightly thickened. Add six cheese slices; cook and stir until cheese is melted and blended.

Place hamburger buns cut side up on a baking sheet; spoon about 1/4 cup meat mixture onto each bun half. Cut remaining cheese slices in half diagonally; place over meat mixture. Broil 6-8 in. from the heat for 4 minutes or until the cheese is melted. **Yield:** 4 servings.

Vegetable Trio

Prep/Total Time: 25 min.

✓ Uses less fat, sugar or salt. Includes Nutritional Analysis and Diabetic Exchanges.

- 4 large carrots, julienned
- 1/2 pound fresh green beans, cut into 2-inch pieces
- 1-1/2 cups sliced fresh mushrooms
- 1 teaspoon salt
- 1/2 teaspoon dried thyme
- 2 tablespoons butter

In a skillet, cook and stir carrots, green beans, mushrooms, salt and thyme in butter over medium heat 15 minutes until beans are crisp-tender. **Yield:** 4 servings.

Nutritional Analysis: 3/4 cup (prepared with reduced-fat butter) equals 79 calories, 3 g fat (2 g saturated fat), 10 mg cholesterol, 654 mg sodium, 12 g carbohydrate, 4 g fiber, 3 g protein. **Diabetic Exchanges:** 2 vegetable, 1/2 fat.

Black Forest Parfaits

Prep/Total Time: 10 min.

- 2 cups cold milk
- 1 package (3.9 ounces) instant chocolate pudding mix
- 1 can (21 ounces) cherry pie filling, *divided*
- 2 cups whipped topping, *divided*
- 6 maraschino cherries with stems, optional

In a bowl, whisk milk and pudding mix for 2 minutes. Let stand for 2 minutes or until soft-set. Stir in 1 cup pie filling; gently fold in 1 cup whipped topping.

Spoon half of the pudding mixture into six tall glasses or cups. Top with remaining pie filling, pudding mixture and whipped topping. Garnish with cherries if desired. **Yield:** 6 servings.

Freezing Ground Beef

To get a head start on meals, cook several pounds of ground beef. Freeze in heavy-duty plastic bags or freezer containers up to 3 months.

Cut Kitchen Time with Cube Steak Dinner

ARE YOU ALWAYS in a rush to get weekday meals on the table? You don't have to rely on fast food or frozen dinners when you can make mouth-watering homemade meals like the one shown here in just 30 minutes or less.

Our Test Kitchen home economists chose three recipes from readers to put together this deliciously quick menu. Your family will be all smiles every time you serve it.

Fried Mustard Cube Steaks are a cinch to make, but they look and taste like you fussed, shares Lori Shepherd of Warsaw, Indiana. "Instead of Dijon, you can use regular mustard, hot-and-spicy mustard or your favorite variety."

Minted Zucchini Salad, from Carol Anderson of Salt Lake City, Utah, is a great way to use up some of the fresh crop from your backyard garden or from the farmers market. Lemon and mint accent the zucchini slices nicely.

Cheesy Pesto Bread is from Karen Grant of Tulare, California. "I was out of French bread one day and remembered I had a packaged, prebaked bread crust on hand," she recalls.

"I topped it with pesto, garlic salt and two kinds of cheese for dinner. Now it's expected whenever I make pasta and salad. It's great heated up for lunch the next day, too."

Fried Mustard Cube Steaks

Prep/Total Time: 30 min.

      1 jar (10 ounces) Dijon mustard
1-1/4 cups water
      6 beef cube steaks (about 2 pounds)
      2 cups all-purpose flour
  1/2 teaspoon salt
  1/8 teaspoon pepper
Oil for frying

In a large resealable bag, combine the mustard and water; add cube steaks. Seal the bag and turn to coat; let stand for 10 minutes. Drain and discard the marinade.

In a shallow bowl, combine the flour, salt and pepper. Dip steaks in flour mixture. In an electric skillet, heat 1/4 in. of oil to 375°. Fry steaks, two at a time, for 3-4 minutes on each side or until crisp and lightly browned. Remove and keep warm. Repeat with remaining steaks. **Yield:** 6 servings.

Minted Zucchini Salad

Prep/Total Time: 10 min.

✓ Uses less fat, sugar or salt. Includes Nutritional Analysis and Diabetic Exchanges.

  1/4 cup olive oil
      2 tablespoons lemon juice
      1 tablespoon minced fresh mint
  1/4 teaspoon salt
Dash cayenne pepper
1-1/2 pounds zucchini, thinly sliced

In a large bowl, whisk the olive oil, lemon juice, mint, salt and cayenne pepper until blended. Add the zucchini and toss to coat. Refrigerate until serving. **Yield:** 6 servings.

Nutritional Analysis: 3/4 cup equals 97 calories, 9 g fat (1 g saturated fat), 0 cholesterol, 102 mg sodium, 4 g carbohydrate, 1 g fiber, 1 g protein. **Diabetic Exchanges:** 1-1/2 fat, 1 vegetable.

Cheesy Pesto Bread

Prep/Total Time: 20 min.

      1 prebaked Italian bread shell crust
          (14 ounces)
      3 tablespoons prepared pesto
  1/8 teaspoon garlic salt
      1 cup (4 ounces) shredded mozzarella
          cheese
  1/2 cup shredded Parmesan cheese

Place crust on a pizza pan or baking sheet. Spread with pesto; sprinkle with garlic salt and cheeses. Bake at 300° for 15 minutes or until cheese is melted. Cut into wedges. **Yield:** 6-8 servings.

About Cube Steak

In some parts of the country, a cube steak may be called a minute steak. When purchasing the meat, look for brightly colored, red to deep red cuts. It can be stored in the coldest part of your refrigerator for 2 to 3 days.

Treat Your Family to Italian-Style Supper

ON EVENINGS when your family's ready for dinner but you're not, a quick solution is often frozen pizza or carry-out chicken.

This fast-to-fix meal, made up of three reader favorites, delivers from-scratch flavor in just 30 minutes. Try it out tonight!

Shrimp Scampi, from Lori Packer of Omaha, Nebraska, looks like you fussed but it's a snap to prepare. Lemon and herbs enhance the shrimp, and the bread crumbs lend a pleasing crunch. Served over angel hair pasta, this main dish is pretty enough for company.

"Garlic-Almond Green Beans is my family's favorite way to eat this popular vegetable," Genny Monchamp says from Redding, California. "The beans stay so tender and crisp. To speed things up even more, you could use frozen green beans instead of fresh."

Short and sweet, the recipe for yummy Granola Fudge Clusters uses only four ingredients. "I have overheard people say, 'You have to try one of these,' when I serve them at get-togethers," shares Loraine Meyer of Bend, Oregon. "I always double the batch because no one can eat just one."

Shrimp Scampi

Prep/Total Time: 20 min.

    3 to 4 garlic cloves, minced
1/4 cup butter, cubed
1/4 cup olive oil
    1 pound uncooked medium shrimp, peeled
       and deveined
1/4 cup lemon juice
1/2 teaspoon pepper
1/4 teaspoon dried oregano
1/2 cup grated Parmesan cheese
1/4 cup dry bread crumbs
1/4 cup minced fresh parsley
Hot cooked angel hair pasta

In a 10-in. ovenproof skillet, saute garlic in butter and oil until tender. Stir in the shrimp, lemon juice, pepper and oregano; cook and stir for 2-3 minutes or until shrimp turn pink.

Sprinkle with Parmesan cheese, bread crumbs and parsley. Broil 6 in. from the heat for 2-3 minutes or until topping is golden brown. Serve over pasta. **Yield:** 4 servings.

Garlic-Almond Green Beans

Prep/Total Time: 15 min.

✓ **Uses less fat, sugar or salt. Includes Nutritional Analysis and Diabetic Exchanges.**

    1 pound fresh green beans
    2 garlic cloves, minced
    1 tablespoon olive oil
1/4 cup slivered almonds, toasted
Pepper to taste

Place the beans in a large saucepan and cover with water. Bring to a boil; cook, uncovered, for 8-10 minutes or until crisp-tender. Meanwhile, in a large skillet, cook garlic in oil for 2-3 minutes. Drain beans. Add the beans, almonds and pepper to skillet; toss to coat. **Yield:** 4 servings.

Nutritional Analysis: 1 cup equals 102 calories, 7 g fat (1 g saturated fat), 0 cholesterol, 6 mg sodium, 9 g carbohydrate, 4 g fiber, 3 g protein. **Diabetic Exchanges:** 2 vegetable, 1 fat.

Granola Fudge Clusters

Prep/Total Time: 25 min.

       1 cup semisweet chocolate chips
       1 cup butterscotch chips
1-1/4 cups granola cereal without raisins
       1 cup chopped walnuts

In a microwave-safe bowl, melt the chocolate and butterscotch chips; stir until smooth. Stir in granola and walnuts. Drop by tablespoonfuls onto waxed paper-lined baking sheets. Refrigerate for 15 minutes or until firm. **Yield:** about 2-1/2 dozen.

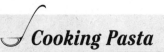

Cooking Pasta

To test pasta for doneness, remove a single piece from the boiling water with a fork; rinse under cold water and taste. Pasta should be cooked until "al dente," tender but still firm to the bite. Test pasta often while cooking to avoid overcooking, which can result in a soft or mushy texture.

Flavorful and Fuss-Free Fare for July Fourth

CELEBRATE the stars and stripes with this back-yard barbecue from our Test Kitchen staff. From start to finish, it takes less than a half hour to whip up!

Spicy Grilled Steaks will easily add spark to your menu. Meat lovers will be in their glory when they see—and smell—the steaks sizzling on the grill. Rubs, like the one used here, are a wonderful way to add flavor to meat when you don't have time to marinate.

Round out the meal with a colorful skillet side dish like Summer Vegetable Saute. Fresh vegetables need little more than sauteing in oil and tossing with basil to enhance their fresh flavor. Feel free to experiment with different vegetables.

For the grand finale, Strawberry Cookie Tarts are sure to earn oohs and aahs! For an even more festive touch on the Fourth of July, top half of the cookies with strawberries or raspberries and the other half with blueberries.

Spicy Grilled Steaks

 1 tablespoon paprika
 2 teaspoons dried thyme
 1 teaspoon onion powder
 1 teaspoon garlic powder
1/2 teaspoon rubbed sage
1/2 teaspoon salt
1/2 teaspoon pepper
1/2 teaspoon cayenne pepper
 4 boneless beef top loin steaks (about 12 ounces *each*)

In a small bowl, combine the first eight ingredients; mix well. Rub about 1 teaspoon of spice mixture over each side of steaks.

Grill, covered, over medium heat for 6-8 minutes on each side or until meat reaches desired doneness (for medium-rare, a meat thermometer should read 145°; medium, 160°; well-done, 170°). **Yield:** 4 servings.

Summer Vegetable Saute

 1 medium zucchini, cut into 1/4-inch slices
 1 medium yellow summer squash, cut into 1/4-inch slices
 1 medium sweet red, orange *or* yellow pepper, julienned

 1 tablespoon olive oil
1/2 cup seasoned bread crumbs
 3 tablespoons snipped fresh basil *or* 1-1/2 teaspoons dried basil

In a skillet, saute vegetables in oil for 6-8 minutes or until crisp-tender. Add crumbs and basil; toss to coat. **Yield:** 4 cups.

Strawberry Cookie Tarts

1/2 cup vanilla *or* white chips, melted and slightly cooled
 1 package (3 ounces) cream cheese, softened
1/2 cup whipped topping
1/4 cup confectioners' sugar
 1 teaspoon lemon juice
1/2 teaspoon vanilla extract
 12 sugar cookies (about 2-1/2 inches)
 4 to 5 fresh strawberries, sliced

In a small mixing bowl, beat melted chips, cream cheese, whipped topping, sugar, lemon juice and vanilla until smooth. Spread about 1 heaping tablespoon onto each cookie. Top with sliced strawberries. Refrigerate until serving. **Yield:** 1 dozen.

Editor's Note: We recommend using sturdy sugar cookies for this dessert.

Grilling Basics

To test the temperature of a charcoal grill, cautiously hold your hand 4 inches over the coals. Count the seconds you can hold your hand in place before the heat forces you to pull away.

For medium heat, the coals should be gray with a red under-glow; you shouldn't be able to hold your hand above them for more than 3 seconds.

For a gas grill, the temperature will read about 350°.

Cleanup will be easier if you coat the grill with nonstick cooking spray before beginning to cook. Don't spray the grill over the fire or you could have a flare-up.

Cool Combination Perfect For Hot Evenings

IF THE DOG DAYS of summer leave you with little desire to cook, a sandwich and salad combination will always satisfy, as this menu from our Test Kitchen deliciously proves. Even better, it will have you in and out of the kitchen in 30 minutes or less.

With their cool and zesty flavors, Roast Beef Tortilla Wraps and Tomato 'n' Red Onion Salad are perfect partners.

Cumin, chili powder and cayenne pepper give the cream cheese spread in the extraordinary sandwiches a deliciously mild Southwestern flavor. Feel free to add more of the seasonings if you like even more of a zip.

Ruby red tomatoes and pretty sliced onions in a tangy lime vinaigrette offer a nice change of pace from typical tossed green salads.

Refresh your spirits with Peppermint Fudge Sundaes. Ice cream is the perfect dessert choice, especially during summer.

You can use either homemade or store-bought brownies in this recipe, or vary the flavor of the ice cream.

Roast Beef Tortilla Wraps

    2 tablespoons cream cheese, softened
    2 tablespoons mayonnaise
1/2 teaspoon ground cumin
1/4 teaspoon salt
1/4 teaspoon chili powder
1/8 teaspoon cayenne pepper
    4 flour tortillas (10 inches)
    4 leaf lettuce leaves
1/2 pound thinly sliced deli roast beef
    8 thin slices tomato
    4 slices red onion, separated into rings

In a small mixing bowl, combine the cream cheese, mayonnaise, cumin, salt, chili powder and cayenne; beat until well combined.

Spread 1 tablespoon on one side of each tortilla; top with the lettuce, roast beef, tomato and onion; roll up tightly. Cut on a diagonal. **Yield:** 4 servings.

Tomato 'n' Red Onion Salad

    5 medium tomatoes, thinly sliced
    4 slices red onion, separated into rings

1/4 cup lime juice
    2 tablespoons olive oil
1/2 teaspoon sugar
1/4 teaspoon salt
1/4 cup minced fresh cilantro

Place the tomatoes and onions in a shallow serving bowl. In a jar with tight-fitting lid, combine the lime juice, oil, sugar, salt and cilantro; shake well. Pour over salad and toss gently to coat. Serve immediately. **Yield:** 4 servings.

Peppermint Fudge Sundaes

    1 cup crumbled brownies
    4 scoops chocolate chip mint ice cream
1/2 cup hot fudge ice cream topping
1/4 cup chopped mint Andes candies

Place brownies in individual dishes. Top with ice cream and hot fudge. Sprinkle with chopped mints. **Yield:** 4 servings.

Ice Cream Social

Make your own premium stir-in style of ice cream by adding 1/2 to 3/4 cup of any of the following to a softened pint of your favorite ice cream: Crushed cream-filled chocolate cookies; raisins or chopped, re-hydrated dried fruit; chopped nuts; chopped fresh fruit; chocolate chunks; miniature marshmallows; chopped chocolate-covered mints...the list is endless.

Next time you entertain, create an ice cream sundae dessert buffet. Provide bowls of various-flavored ice cream and sherbet balls, chopped fruit, sauces, chopped nuts and whipped cream. You'll get raves!

An electric knife makes easy work out of cutting blocks of commercial ice cream into slices. Or use nonstick cooking spray to thinly coat ice cream scoops to remove ice cream from the carton—the ice cream will slip right off.

Melted refrozen ice cream never tastes the same as the original. But don't throw it out—use it as a creamy topping for pudding, cake, pie...even hot breakfast cereal.

Fast-to-Fix Meal with Real Kid Appeal

RING IN the back-to-school season with this meal packed with undeniable kid appeal! Our *Taste of Home* Test Kitchen staff came up with the menu that can be hooked and landed on the table in 30 minutes or less.

Young and old alike will dive into comforting Seasoned Fish Sticks and Jazzy Mac 'n' Cheese.

Even families who turn a cold shoulder to frozen fish sticks will warm up to these sticks coated with a blend of slightly spicy seasonings.

Adding Parmesan and mozzarella to already-cheesy macaroni will have your clan clamoring for this tried-and-true pasta dish. Diced tomatoes and chilies add color and zip.

Chocolate-Dipped Waffles give fun flair to a traditional breakfast food. It's so simple to dip the waffle wedges in chocolate and to garnish with sprinkles that the kids can help you assemble them.

Seasoned Fish Sticks

  1 teaspoon paprika
  1 teaspoon chili powder
  1/2 teaspoon garlic powder
  1/2 teaspoon onion powder
  1/2 teaspoon ground cumin
  1/4 teaspoon cayenne pepper
  2 tablespoons vegetable oil, *divided*
  2 packages (8 ounces *each*) frozen breaded fish sticks

In a small bowl, combine the first six ingredients; mix well. Transfer half of the seasoning mix to a large resealable plastic bag; set aside.

Place 1 tablespoon oil in a large resealable plastic bag; add half of fish sticks and shake to coat. Transfer fish to resealable bag with seasonings and shake to coat.

Place in a single layer on an ungreased baking sheet. Repeat with remaining ingredients. Bake at 400° for 18-22 minutes or until golden brown. **Yield:** 4 servings.

Jazzy Mac 'n' Cheese

  1 package (7-1/4 ounces) macaroni and cheese dinner mix
  1 can (10 ounces) diced tomatoes and green chilies, undrained
  1/4 cup butter
  1/2 cup grated Parmesan cheese
  1/2 cup shredded mozzarella cheese

In a saucepan, bring 6 cups water to a boil. Add macaroni; set aside cheese packet. Reduce heat; simmer, uncovered, for 6-8 minutes or until pasta is tender.

Drain and return to saucepan. Add tomatoes and butter; mix until butter is melted. Add the reserved cheese packet; mix well. Remove from heat; add Parmesan and mozzarella cheese. **Yield:** 4 cups.

Chocolate-Dipped Waffles

  1/2 cup semisweet chocolate chips
  1/4 cup butterscotch chips
  1/2 teaspoon shortening
  4 frozen round waffles, crisply toasted
Colored sprinkles

In a small microwave-safe bowl, melt chips and shortening; stir until smooth. Cut each waffle into 4 wedges. Dip point of each into chocolate, covering about 1/2 in. on one side. Shake off excess chocolate. Place on a waxed paper-lined baking sheet and garnish with sprinkles. Refrigerate until set. **Yield:** 16 pieces.

Mac and Cheese Add-ins

Traditional macaroni and cheese has long been a favorite.

Thomas Jefferson brought a macaroni mold home from Paris and served a casserole version at a White House dinner in 1802. But according to food historians, its status as a culinary icon was assured after Kraft Foods introduced Kraft Dinner in 1937.

Today, there are all kinds of ways to prepare it. A more substantial macaroni and cheese might include chunks of cooked chicken or hamburger meat and even some cut-up hot dogs or sausage. Crispy bacon or diced ham are delicious additions, too.

For something a bit more upscale, you could add chunks of cooked lobster, shrimp or crabmeat.

Down-Home Meal Made in a Hurry

HARVEST A BUSHEL of compliments with this down-home dinner from our Test Kitchen staff. The meal looks like you fussed, but it only takes half an hour or less to prepare.

The aroma of Swedish Meatballs and Puffed Apple Pastries baking will remind you of Grandma's kitchen. Those recipes bake at the same temperature, giving you time to make Herbed Egg Noodles.

Nutmeg, allspice and cardamom lend to the traditional taste of the moist meatballs. The creamy sauce has a rich beef flavor with a touch of dill.

A seasoned butter sauce pleasantly coats the tender noodles, making them perfect alongside the meatballs or any other meaty entree.

For a little extra indulgence, serve the oven-fresh apple pastries with a scoop of creamy vanilla ice cream. Cherry pie filling can be substituted for the apple.

Swedish Meatballs

1/2 cup soft bread crumbs
1 medium onion, chopped
1 egg, lightly beaten
2 tablespoons heavy whipping cream
1/2 teaspoon salt
1/8 teaspoon ground nutmeg
1/8 teaspoon ground allspice
1/8 teaspoon ground cardamom
3/4 pound lean ground beef
1/2 pound ground pork
GRAVY:
2 tablespoons butter
2 tablespoons all-purpose flour
1 cup beef broth
1/2 cup heavy whipping cream
1/4 teaspoon dill weed
1/4 cup minced fresh parsley, optional

In a large bowl, combine the first eight ingredients. Crumble beef and pork over mixture and mix well. Shape into 1-1/2-in. meatballs. Line a 15-in. x 10-in. x 1-in. baking pan with foil and grease. Place meatballs 1 in. apart on prepared pan. Bake at 400° for 11-12 minutes or until no longer pink.

Meanwhile, in a saucepan, melt butter. Stir in flour until smooth; gradually add broth. Bring to a boil; cook and stir for 1-2 minutes or until thickened. Stir in cream and dill; simmer for 1 minute. Place meatballs in a serving dish; pour gravy over top. Garnish with parsley if desired. **Yield:** 4 servings.

Herbed Egg Noodles

8 ounces uncooked wide egg noodles
3 tablespoons butter
1 garlic clove, minced
1/4 teaspoon salt
1/4 teaspoon dill weed
1/4 teaspoon dried thyme

Cook the noodles according to package directions. Meanwhile, in a skillet, melt butter. Add the garlic, salt, dill and thyme; mix well. Drain noodles and add to butter mixture; toss to coat. Serve warm. **Yield:** 4 servings.

Puffed Apple Pastries

1 package (10 ounces) frozen pastry shells
1 can (21 ounces) apple pie filling
1/2 teaspoon ground cinnamon
1/4 teaspoon ground nutmeg

Prepare puff pastry according to package directions. Bake at 400° for 20-25 minutes or until golden brown.

Meanwhile, in a small saucepan, combine the apple pie filling, cinnamon and nutmeg; mix well. Cook and stir over medium-low heat for about 3-4 minutes or until heated through.

Remove the tops from the shells. Fill each shell with about 1/3 cup of filling. Serve warm. **Yield:** 6 servings.

Making Meatballs

When shaping meatballs, handle the mixture as little as possible to keep the final product light in texture. Combine all of the ingredients except for the meat. Then crumble the meat over the mixture and mix well.

The mixture for some meatballs can be very moist. If you're having a hard time shaping them, try wetting your hands.

You can use a 1-1/2- or 1-3/4-inch-diameter scoop to scoop the mixture into equal sized portions. Carefully roll each into a ball.

Dinner for Four Looks Like You Fussed

AFTER A LARGE Thanksgiving gathering, this dinner for four is a welcome sight. Our Test Kitchen staff pulled together the timely fare to be prepared in less than 30 minutes.

Chicken Cordon Bleu in Pastry is an elegant yet easy entree. Baking chicken breasts in a flaky dough makes them turn out moist and delicious every time. The fancy dish is nice to serve family as well as guests.

Convenience foods give Autumn Salad with Orange Vinaigrette and Pumpkin-Layered Angel Cake a head start. In the salad, a light orange dressing nicely accents sweet dried cranberries and crunchy almonds. If you prefer, you can use your favorite salad greens in place of the ready-to-serve package.

The eye-catching torte captures the taste of two favorite desserts—angel food cake and pumpkin pie. When you have time, prepare it earlier in the day and refrigerate until serving.

Chicken Cordon Bleu in Pastry

  1 tube (8 ounces) refrigerated crescent rolls
1/4 cup spreadable chive and onion cream cheese
  4 thin slices deli ham
  4 boneless skinless chicken breast halves (4 ounces *each*)
  4 slices Swiss cheese

On an ungreased baking sheet, separate dough into four rectangles; seal perforations. Spread 1 tablespoon cream cheese lengthwise down the center of each rectangle. Place ham widthwise over dough. Arrange chicken in center of each rectangle. Wrap ham around chicken. At each long end, pinch dough together around chicken, forming points.

Bake at 375° for 15 minutes. Top with Swiss cheese; baking 5 minutes longer or until cheese is melted and pastry is golden brown. **Yield:** 4 servings.

Autumn Salad with Orange Vinaigrette

  3 tablespoons olive oil
  1 tablespoon sugar
  1 tablespoon red wine vinegar
  2 teaspoons orange juice concentrate
1/8 teaspoon salt

Pinch coarsely ground pepper
  4 cups ready-to-serve salad greens
1/2 cup sliced almonds, toasted
1/4 cup dried cranberries
1/4 cup thinly sliced red onion

In a jar with a tight-fitting lid, combine the first six ingredients; shake well. In a large bowl, combine the salad greens, almonds, cranberries and onion. Add vinaigrette; toss to coat. **Yield:** 4 servings.

Pumpkin-Layered Angel Cake

1-1/2 cups canned pumpkin
1-1/4 cups heavy whipping cream
    1 package (5.1 ounces) instant vanilla pudding mix
    1 teaspoon ground cinnamon
  1/2 teaspoon ground allspice
    1 prepared angel food cake (16 ounces), split twice horizontally
  1/4 cup crushed gingersnaps (about 5 cookies)

In a mixing bowl, combine pumpkin and cream; mix well. Add pudding mix and spices; beat on low speed for 2 minutes or until thickened.

Place bottom layer of cake on a serving plate; spread with 3/4 cup pudding mixture. Repeat once. Top with remaining cake layer and spread with remaining pudding mixture. Sprinkle with crushed cookies. Refrigerate until serving. Store in the refrigerator. **Yield:** 12 servings.

Cake and Ice Cream

Angel food can also easily be made into an ice cream cake.

Simply split it horizontally and put the bottom half on a serving platter. Spread with softened ice cream. Replace the top half of the cake and finish with more ice cream. Place the cake in the freezer for about 2 hours or until the ice cream is firm.

If an ice cream cake has been frozen for so long that it's hard, remove it from the freezer 20 to 30 minutes before serving. Cut into squares or wedges and top with fresh berries or a chocolate or caramel sauce.

Present Family and Friends With Festive Fare

THERE'S NO BETTER present you can give your family than a hearty weekday meal. (Think of this half-hour fare as a gift to you from our Test Kitchen.)

Start with broiled Pecan Pork Chops and Mashed Winter Squash. A delicate butter and brown sugar glaze is a tasty topping for the chops. Frozen cooked squash and a microwave make quick work of assembling the colorful side dish. Each bite features the subtle blend of cinnamon, nutmeg and ginger.

Cranberry-Apple Biscuits provide the festive finishing touch. Tangy cranberries and sweet apples blend beautifully with tender biscuits in the pretty holiday dessert.

Pecan Pork Chops

    8 **boneless pork loin chops (3/4 inch thick)**
1/4 **cup packed brown sugar**
    2 **tablespoons cornstarch**
1/4 **teaspoon salt**
1/8 **teaspoon ground mustard**
    2 **tablespoons butter, softened**
    2 **teaspoons cider vinegar**
    3 **tablespoons chopped pecans**

Broil pork chops 3-4 in. from the heat for 6 minutes. Meanwhile, in a bowl, combine the sugar, cornstarch, salt and mustard. Stir in the butter and vinegar until blended. Turn chops over and broil for 4 minutes.

Spoon about 2 teaspoons sugar mixture over top of each chop. Broil 2 minutes longer. Top each chop with 1 teaspoon pecans. Broil 1 minute more or until pecans are toasted and meat juices run clear. Let stand for 1-2 minutes before serving. **Yield:** 8 servings.

Mashed Winter Squash

    4 **packages (12 ounces *each*) frozen cooked winter squash**
1/2 **cup packed brown sugar**
1/4 **cup butter**
    1 **teaspoon salt**
1/2 **teaspoon ground cinnamon**
1/4 **teaspoon ground nutmeg**
1/8 **teaspoon ground ginger**

Place squash in a microwave-safe bowl. Cover and microwave on high 10 minutes or until heated through, stirring after 5 minutes. Add sugar, butter, salt, cinnamon, nutmeg and ginger. Microwave, uncovered, 3-4 minutes longer until heated through. **Yield:** 8 servings.

Editor's Note: This recipe was tested in a 850-watt microwave.

Cranberry-Apple Biscuits

    2 **tablespoons butter, melted**
    2 **tablespoons sugar**
1/4 **teaspoon ground cinnamon**
1/4 **teaspoon ground ginger**
    1 **tube (17.3 ounces) large refrigerated biscuits**
SAUCE:
3/4 **cup sugar**
1/2 **teaspoon ground cinnamon**
1/2 **teaspoon ground ginger**
    3 **cups diced peeled tart apples**
    1 **cup fresh *or* frozen cranberries**
1/2 **cup water, *divided***
    1 **tablespoon lemon juice**
    2 **tablespoons cornstarch**

Place butter in a shallow bowl. In another shallow bowl, combine the sugar, cinnamon and ginger. Dip the top of each biscuit in butter, then in sugar mixture. Place sugar side up 2 in. apart on an ungreased baking sheet. Bake at 350° for 15-17 minutes or until golden brown. Remove to a wire rack.

For sauce, in a saucepan, combine sugar, cinnamon and ginger. Add the apples, cranberries, 1/4 cup water and lemon juice. Bring to a boil. Reduce heat; cover and simmer for 3-4 minutes, stirring occasionally.

Combine the cornstarch and remaining water until smooth. Stir into fruit mixture. Bring to a boil; cook and stir for 2 minutes or until thickened. Pour about 1/3 cup sauce over each biscuit. **Yield:** 8 servings.

Purchasing Pork

When buying pork, look for meat that's pale pink with a small amount of marbling and white fat. The darker pink the flesh, the older the animal.

If you want succulent pork chops, buy those that are 3/4 to 1 inch thick. Thinner chops have a tendency to dry out.

Meals on a Budget

Here, our Test Kitchen shows you how to save money making meals for your family without scrimping on flavor.

CENTSIBLE COOKING. Clockwise from upper left: Feed Your Family for $1.53 a Plate! (p. 284), Feed Your Family for $1.54 a Plate! (p. 282), Feed Your Family for $1.84 a Plate! (p. 286) and Feed Your Family for 99¢ a Plate! (p. 288).

Feed Your Family For $1.62 a Plate!

IS YOUR household budget feeling the pinch of the holidays? The good news is you can serve up family dinners that are flavorful and satisfying...without breaking the bank.

Our Test Kitchen home economists have combined three easy reader favorites into the hearty low-cost meal shown at left. You can prepare this tasty trio for just $1.62 per serving.

"Turkey Taco Bake is a great way to use up leftover turkey from Thanksgiving or Christmas," says Trudie Hagen from Roggen, Colorado. Trudie's hearty Mexican-style casserole is chock-full of popular south-of-the-border ingredients including corn chips, salsa, Monterey Jack cheese and refried beans. It's a guaranteed family-pleaser.

Lemon Vinaigrette on Greens gives this frugal menu a light, refreshing touch. "The vinaigrette also tastes good on spinach salad," writes Susan Garoutte of Georgetown, Texas. "It keeps well in the refrigerator in a container with a tight-fitting lid. Just shake and serve."

You can't go wrong with Butterscotch Fudge Bars for dessert. Everyone will savor these homemade treats from Edna Hoffman of Hebron, Indiana. The trick is to eat just one!

Turkey Taco Bake

Prep: 15 min.   **Bake:** 20 min.

- 2 cups coarsely crushed corn chips
- 1 can (16 ounces) refried beans
- 2 cups (8 ounces) shredded Monterey Jack cheese, *divided*
- 1 cup salsa
- 2 cups shredded cooked turkey
- 1 teaspoon Mexican *or* taco seasoning
- 1 green onion, sliced
- 1 medium tomato, chopped

Place corn chips in a greased shallow 2-1/2-qt. baking dish. Place the refried beans in a small saucepan; cook and stir over medium heat until heated through. Remove from the heat; stir in 1 cup cheese and salsa. Spread over chips.

Toss the turkey and Mexican seasoning; sprinkle over bean mixture. Top with remaining cheese. Sprinkle with onion. Bake, uncovered, at 400° for 20-25 minutes or until cheese is melted. Sprinkle with tomato. **Yield:** 4 servings.

Lemon Vinaigrette on Greens

Prep/Total Time: 10 min.

- 1/4 cup lemon juice
- 1/4 cup vegetable oil
- 1/4 cup olive oil
- 2 green onions, finely chopped
- 1 tablespoon minced fresh parsley
- 1-1/2 teaspoons sugar
- 1/2 teaspoon ground mustard
- 1/4 teaspoon salt
- 1/8 teaspoon pepper
- 4 cups torn romaine

In a jar with a tight-fitting lid, combine the first nine ingredients; shake well. Place romaine in a salad bowl. Drizzle with dressing; toss to coat. **Yield:** 4 servings.

Butterscotch Fudge Bars

Prep: 15 min.   **Bake:** 25 min. + cooling

- 1/2 cup butter
- 1 square (1 ounce) unsweetened chocolate
- 2/3 cup packed brown sugar
- 1 egg
- 1 teaspoon vanilla extract
- 1 cup all-purpose flour
- 1 teaspoon baking powder
- Dash salt
- 1 cup butterscotch chips

In a large saucepan over low heat, melt butter and chocolate. Remove from the heat; stir in brown sugar until dissolved. Cool to lukewarm. Add egg and vanilla; mix well. Combine the flour, baking powder and salt; stir into chocolate mixture until blended. Stir in chips.

Spread into a greased 9-in. square baking pan. Bake at 350° for 22-27 minutes or until a toothpick comes out with moist crumbs. Cool on a wire rack. Cut and serve. **Yield:** 1 dozen.

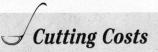

Cutting Costs

Cook from scratch when possible. It's usually less expensive than buying frozen meals or package mixes.

Feed Your Family For $1.74 a Plate!

JUST BECAUSE you're on a budget, that doesn't mean you have to scrimp on flavor when it comes to feeding your family. Our Test Kitchen home economists have combined recipes from three good cooks for this St. Patrick's Day menu…and it won't cost a pot o'gold to make. You can serve this festive meal for just $1.74 per plate.

But don't limit these delicious dishes to March 17. They'll please your family—and fit your budget—any time of the year.

"I have some Irish ancestry, so I started a family tradition on St. Patrick's Day. I came up with my own recipe for Corned Beef 'n' Cabbage," writes Jo Ann Honey from Longmont, Colorado. "The meat is tender, and the apple juice gives it a mellow flavor."

Ham, cheese and sour cream flavor Slow-Cooked Potato Soup, shared by Mary Jo O'Brien of Hastings, Minnesota. "I make this thick soup for our annual St. Patrick's Day party, and it's gone in no time," Mary Jo notes.

Relates Marge Nicol of Shannon, Illinois, "Each month, my 'lunch bunch ladies' group gets together to try new recipes. I hosted a St. Patrick's theme luncheon, and my Wearing O' the Green Cake was a hit. The sprinkles on top make it even more festive."

Corned Beef 'n' Cabbage

Prep: 5 min.   **Cook:** 8 hours

1 large onion, cut into wedges
1 cup apple juice
1 bay leaf
1 corned beef brisket with spice packet
  (2-1/2 to 3 pounds), cut in half
1 small head cabbage, cut into wedges

Place the onion in a 5-qt. slow cooker. Combine the apple juice, bay leaf and contents of spice packet; pour over onion. Top with brisket and cabbage. Cover and cook on low for 8-10 hours or until meat and vegetables are tender. Discard bay leaf. **Yield:** 6 servings.

Slow-Cooked Potato Soup

Prep: 30 min.   **Cook:** 5 hours

5-1/2 cups cubed peeled potatoes, *divided*
2-3/4 cups water
1/3 cup butter, cubed
1-1/3 cups cubed fully cooked ham

2 celery ribs, chopped
2/3 cup chopped onion
3/4 teaspoon garlic powder
3/4 teaspoon paprika
1/8 teaspoon pepper
1/2 pound process cheese (Velveeta), cubed
2/3 cup sour cream
Milk, optional

Place 4-1/2 cups of the potatoes in a saucepan; add water. Bring to a boil. Reduce heat; cover and cook for 15-20 minutes or until tender. Remove from the heat (do not drain). Mash potatoes; stir in butter.

In a 3-qt. slow cooker, combine the ham, celery, onion, garlic powder, paprika, pepper and remaining cubed potatoes. Stir in the mashed potatoes; top with cheese. Cover and cook on low for 5-6 hours or until potatoes and other vegetables are tender. Stir in the sour cream until blended. Thin soup with milk if desired. **Yield:** 6 servings.

Wearing O' the Green Cake

Prep: 25 min.   **Bake:** 30 min. + cooling

1 package (18-1/4 ounces) white cake mix
2 packages (3 ounces *each*) lime gelatin
1 cup boiling water
1/2 cup cold water
TOPPING:
1 cup cold milk
1 package (3.4 ounces) instant vanilla
  pudding mix
1 carton (8 ounces) frozen whipped topping,
  thawed
Green sprinkles

Prepare and bake the cake according to the package directions, using a greased 13-in. x 9-in. x 2-in. baking dish. Cool for 1 hour. In a small bowl, dissolve the gelatin in boiling water; stir in the cold water and set aside.

With a meat fork or wooden skewer, poke holes about 2 in. apart into cooled cake. Slowly pour gelatin over cake; refrigerate. In a bowl, whisk milk and pudding mix for 2 minutes; let stand for 2 minutes or until soft-set. Fold in whipped topping. Spread over cake. Decorate with sprinkles. Cover and refrigerate until serving. **Yield:** 12-15 servings.

Feed Your Family For $1.54 a Plate!

IF YOU'RE NOT an avid coupon-clipper, you might wonder how you can save more on your grocery bill. Our Test Kitchen shows you how by combining economical recipes from budget-minded readers into the meal shown above.

This low-cost menu makes a hearty brunch or even a light evening meal...and you can serve it for just $1.54 per plate.

The Vegetable Ham Quiche, from Betty Albee of Buhl, Idaho, is an easy egg dish filled with zucchini, bell pepper, ham and cheese. "With our garden produce, it's even more economical," Betty informs. "It's pretty enough to serve company, too."

"Breakfast Sausage Patties are a perfect accompaniment to any egg entree," says Carolyn Rose Sykora of Bloomer, Wisconsin. "Cayenne pepper gives the sausage just the right amount of zip."

Edna Hoffman of Hebron, Indiana shares her recipe for Orange Ginger Scones. A sprinkling of sugar tops off these tender treats with a touch of sweetness. "I like to serve them hot with butter and jam," Edna notes.

Vegetable Ham Quiche

Prep: 25 min.   **Bake:** 30 min.

    1 egg, beaten
    3 cups frozen shredded hash brown
      potatoes, thawed
  1/4 cup grated Parmesan cheese
FILLING:
1-1/2 cups thinly sliced zucchini
    1 small sweet red pepper, chopped
    1 tablespoon butter
  1/2 cup diced fully cooked ham
    1 tablespoon minced fresh basil
  1/4 teaspoon salt
  1/4 teaspoon pepper
    2 eggs
  1/4 cup milk
  3/4 cup shredded Colby-Monterey Jack cheese

In a large bowl, combine the egg, hash browns and Parmesan cheese. Press onto the bottom and up the sides of a greased 9-in. pie plate. Bake at 400° for 15 minutes or until crust is set and edges begin to brown.

Meanwhile, in a large skillet, saute zucchini and red pepper in butter for 5 minutes. Stir in the ham, basil, salt and pepper. Remove from the heat; cool slightly.

In a large bowl, beat eggs and milk; add zucchini mixture. Stir in cheese. Pour into crust. Bake for 15-20 minutes or until set. Let stand for 5 minutes before cutting. **Yield:** 4 servings.

Breakfast Sausage Patties

Prep/Total Time: 20 min.

    1 pound ground turkey
  3/4 teaspoon salt
  1/2 teaspoon rubbed sage
  1/2 teaspoon dried thyme
  1/2 teaspoon ground nutmeg
  1/8 teaspoon cayenne pepper
    2 teaspoons vegetable oil

In a large bowl, combine the turkey, salt, sage, thyme, nutmeg and cayenne. Shape into eight patties. In a large skillet, cook patties in oil over medium heat for 5 minutes on each side or until juices run clear. Drain on paper towels. **Yield:** 4 servings.

Orange Ginger Scones

Prep/Total Time: 30 min.

    2 cups all-purpose flour
    4 tablespoons sugar, *divided*
    2 teaspoons baking powder
    2 teaspoons ground ginger
  1/2 teaspoon salt
  1/4 teaspoon baking soda
  1/2 cup cold butter
    1 egg
  3/4 cup sour cream
1-1/2 teaspoons grated orange peel

In a bowl, combine the flour, 2 tablespoons sugar, baking powder, ginger, salt and baking soda. Cut in butter until mixture resembles coarse crumbs. Combine the egg, sour cream and orange peel; add to crumb mixture and stir until a soft dough forms.

Turn onto a floured surface; knead 5-6 times. Divide dough in half. Pat each portion into a 7-in. circle; cut each into six wedges. Separate wedges and place 1 in. apart on ungreased baking sheets. Sprinkle with remaining sugar. Bake at 400° for 10-12 minutes or until lightly browned. **Yield:** 1 dozen.

Feed Your Family For $1.53 a Plate!

EVERYONE wants to save money, but when it comes to meals, there's no one who wants to scrimp on flavor just to save a few dollars.

Our Test Kitchen has put together three inexpensive reader favorites to create this meal. At just $1.53 a plate, you'll cut back on cost but not on good taste.

"Spanish Rice Dinner has been a family favorite since I discovered it in our church cookbook," says Jeri Dobrowski of Beach, North Dakota. "I always have the ingredients on hand."

Soft, buttery Onion Crescent Rolls are a nice complement to the skillet supper. "They'll fill your home with that wonderful bread-baking aroma," Mary Maxeiner says from Lakewood, Colorado. "They're easy to make, too. I even serve them for special occasions like Easter and Christmas."

Lime Ice Cream, from Betsy Hedeman of Relay, Maryland, ends the meal with a burst of sweet-tart flavor. It's an inexpensive way to cool off on hot days or any time of the year.

Spanish Rice Dinner

Prep: 5 min. **Cook:** 50 min.

 1 pound ground beef
 1 can (14-1/2 ounces) stewed tomatoes
 1 can (14-1/2 ounces) cut green beans, drained
1/2 cup uncooked long grain rice
 1 tablespoon dried minced onion
 1 tablespoon sugar
 1 teaspoon salt
 1 teaspoon Worcestershire sauce
1/2 teaspoon ground mustard
1/4 teaspoon garlic powder
1/8 teaspoon pepper
1/8 teaspoon hot pepper sauce

In a large skillet, cook beef over medium heat until no longer pink; drain. Stir in the remaining ingredients. Bring to a boil. Reduce heat; cover and simmer for 40 minutes or until rice is tender. **Yield:** 4 servings.

Onion Crescent Rolls

Prep: 30 min. + rising **Bake:** 10 min.

1/2 cup plus 2 tablespoons butter, softened, *divided*
1/2 cup sugar

 2 eggs
 1 package (1/4 ounce) active dry yeast
 1 cup warm milk (110° to 115°)
 1 cup diced onion
1/2 teaspoon salt
3-1/2 to 4-1/2 cups all-purpose flour

In a large mixing bowl, cream 1/2 cup butter and sugar. Add the eggs, one at a time, beating well after each addition. Dissolve the yeast in warm milk; add to creamed mixture. Add the onion, salt and 1 cup flour; beat until blended. Stir in enough remaining flour to form a soft dough.

Turn onto a floured surface; knead until smooth and elastic, about 6-8 minutes. Place in a greased bowl, turning once to grease top. Cover and let rise in a warm place until doubled, about 1 hour.

Punch dough down. Turn onto a lightly floured surface; divide in half. Roll each portion into a 12-in. circle; cut each circle into 12 wedges. Roll up wedges from the wide end and place point side down 2 in. apart on greased baking sheets. Curve ends down to form crescents. Cover and let rise in a warm place until doubled, about 30 minutes.

Bake at 400° for 9-11 minutes or until lightly browned. Remove from the pans to wire racks. Melt the remaining butter and brush over the warm rolls. **Yield:** 2 dozen.

Lime Ice Cream

Prep: 20 min. + freezing

 2 cups milk
1-1/4 cups sugar
1/3 cup lime juice
1-1/2 teaspoons grated lime peel
 1 cup heavy whipping cream

In a saucepan, combine milk and sugar. Cook over medium heat until sugar is dissolved and mixture reaches 175°. Cool to room temperature. Stir in the lime juice and lime peel. Freeze in an ice cream freezer according to manufacturer's directions.

Transfer frozen lime mixture to a bowl; allow to soften slightly. In a small mixing bowl, beat whipping cream until stiff peaks form. Fold into softened lime mixture. Allow ice cream to firm up in your refrigerator freezer for 4 hours before serving. **Yield:** 4 servings (about 1 quart).

Feed Your Family For $1.84 a Plate!

WHO SAYS you can't eat well when you're keeping an eye on your checkbook balance? *Taste of Home* readers know how to make meals taste great without spending a fortune at the grocery store.

Try this satisfying meal combining three reader favorites and see for yourself. It costs just $1.84 per serving!

"My Greek neighbors made Garlic Clove Chicken frequently, and I couldn't get enough of it," states Denise Hollebeke of Penhold, Alberta. "If you like garlic, you'll love this chicken."

"All of my children love my Vinaigrette Veggie Salad," says Connie Small of Schoolcraft, Michigan. "It's easy to make and attractive, too. Sometimes I cut up the vegetables ahead of time so dinner preparation goes faster."

With its crisp crumb crust, cool ice cream filling and crunchy toffee topping, frozen Pistachio Cream Dessert is a refreshing way to top off any warm-weather meal. "I find the candy bars crush more easily when cold or frozen," says Hazel King from Nacogdoches, Texas, who shares the recipe for the frozen meal-ender.

Garlic Clove Chicken

Prep: 10 min.   **Bake:** 2-1/4 hours + standing

     1 roasting chicken (5 to 6 pounds)
     1 small onion, quartered
    40 garlic cloves, peeled
   1/4 cup vegetable oil
 1-1/2 teaspoons salt
     1 teaspoon dried parsley flakes
   1/2 teaspoon dried celery flakes
   1/2 teaspoon dried tarragon
   1/2 teaspoon dried thyme
   1/2 teaspoon dried rosemary, crushed
   1/4 teaspoon pepper

Place chicken, breast side up, on a rack in a shallow roasting pan. Place onion in chicken; tie drumsticks together. Arrange garlic cloves around chicken. In a small bowl, combine the remaining ingredients. Drizzle over chicken and garlic.

Cover and bake at 350° for 1-3/4 hours. Uncover and bake 30-45 minutes longer or until a meat thermometer reads 180°, basting occasionally with juices. Cover and let stand for 10 minutes before slicing. **Yield:** 6 servings.

Vinaigrette Veggie Salad

Prep/Total Time: 15 min.

✓ Uses less fat, sugar or salt. Includes Nutritional Analysis and Diabetic Exchanges.

   1 medium cucumber, sliced
   1 medium green pepper, cut into 1-inch strips
   1 cup halved cherry tomatoes
 1/4 teaspoon salt
 1/4 teaspoon celery seed
   2 tablespoons canola oil
   1 tablespoon white vinegar

In a serving or salad bowl, combine the cucumber, green pepper and tomatoes. Sprinkle with salt and celery seed.

In a small bowl, whisk the oil and vinegar; drizzle over salad and toss to coat. Serve immediately. **Yield:** 6 servings.

Nutritional Analysis: 2/3 cup equals 60 calories, 5 g fat (trace saturated fat), 0 cholesterol, 101 mg sodium, 4 g carbohydrate, 1 g fiber, 1 g protein. **Diabetic Exchanges:** 1 vegetable, 1 fat.

Pistachio Cream Dessert

Prep: 15 min. + freezing

   2 tablespoons butter
 3/4 cup butter-flavored cracker crumbs
 3/4 cup cold milk
   1 package (3.4 ounces) instant pistachio pudding mix
   2 cups vanilla ice cream, softened
   1 carton (8 ounces) frozen whipped topping, thawed
   2 Heath candy bars (1.4 ounces *each*), crushed

In a microwave-safe 8-in. square dish, melt butter. Stir in cracker crumbs; press mixture onto bottom of dish. In a bowl, whisk milk and pudding mix for 2 minutes. Whisk in the ice cream. Pour over crust. Cover and freeze for 2 hours.

Spread with whipped topping; sprinkle with crushed candy bars. Freeze for 1 hour or until firm. **Yield:** 8 servings.

Feed Your Family For 99¢ a Plate!

TRYING to stretch your dollars with the holidays just around the corner? You won't have to scrimp on flavor with this budget-friendly menu made up of three tried-and-true reader favorites.

Ground Beef Vegetable Soup is sure to chase the chill after a day of raking leaves or running errands. A variety of fresh veggies along with ground beef and macaroni make this a hearty main-dish soup. Raymonde Bourgeois of Swastika, Ontario shared the recipe.

The appetizing aroma of Honey-Oat Casserole Bread often fills Beverly Sterling's Gasport, New York kitchen. The round yeast loaf is tender and moist with a wonderful flavor.

Oatmeal Chip Cookies are a fun way to finish this meal. Susan Henry from Bullhead City, Arizona says, "My mom liked to add different spices to traditional recipes and create unexpected tastes. Molasses and cinnamon make these cookies stand out."

Ground Beef Vegetable Soup

Prep: 10 min.   **Cook:** 35 min.

  3/4 **pound ground beef**
    2 **cans (14-1/2 ounces** *each***) beef broth**
    2 **cups water**
    1 **can (28 ounces) diced tomatoes, undrained**
    3 **celery ribs, chopped**
    2 **large carrots, sliced**
    2 **medium onions, sliced**
    1 **medium potato, peeled and cubed**
1-1/2 **cups fresh cauliflowerets**
    2 **tablespoons minced fresh tarragon** *or* 2
       teaspoons dried tarragon
    1 **tablespoon garlic powder**
    1 **tablespoon minced fresh parsley**
  1/2 **teaspoon salt**
  1/8 **teaspoon pepper**
  3/4 **cup uncooked macaroni**

In a Dutch oven, cook the beef over medium heat until no longer pink; drain. Add the broth, water, tomatoes, celery, carrots, onions, potato, cauliflower, tarragon, garlic powder, parsley, salt and pepper. Bring to a boil. Reduce heat; cover and simmer for 30 minutes or until vegetables are tender, stirring occasionally.

Cook the macaroni according to package directions; drain. Stir into the soup and heat through. **Yield:** 8 servings.

Honey-Oat Casserole Bread

Prep: 20 min. + rising   **Bake:** 35 min. + cooling

    1 **package (1/4 ounce) active dry yeast**
  1/4 **cup warm water (110° to 115°)**
  1/4 **cup butter, softened**
  1/4 **cup honey**
    1 **cup boiling water**
    2 **eggs**
    1 **cup quick-cooking oats**
    1 **teaspoon salt**
3-1/2 **cups all-purpose flour**

In a large mixing bowl, dissolve yeast in warm water. Combine butter, honey and boiling water; stir until butter is melted. Cool to 110°-115°. Add eggs, oats, salt, butter mixture and 2 cups flour; beat on medium speed 2 minutes. Stir in enough flour to form a soft dough. Cover; let rise in a warm place until doubled, 55 minutes.

Punch dough down. Transfer to a greased 1-1/2-qt. round baking dish. Cover; let rise in a warm place until doubled, 30 minutes. Bake at 375° for 35-40 minutes or until golden. Cool for 10 minutes; remove from baking dish to a wire rack to cool. **Yield:** 1 loaf (12 wedges).

Oatmeal Chip Cookies

Prep: 20 min.   **Bake:** 10 min.

  1/2 **cup shortening**
    1 **cup sugar**
    1 **tablespoon molasses**
    1 **egg**
    1 **teaspoon vanilla extract**
    1 **cup all-purpose flour**
    1 **cup quick-cooking oats**
    1 **teaspoon baking soda**
    1 **teaspoon ground cinnamon**
  1/2 **teaspoon salt**
    1 **cup (6 ounces) semisweet chocolate chips**

In a large mixing bowl, cream shortening and sugar. Beat in the molasses, egg and vanilla. Combine the dry ingredients; add to creamed mixture. Stir in chips.

Roll into 1-1/2-in. balls. Place 2 in. apart on greased baking sheets. Bake at 350° for 8-10 minutes or until golden. Cool 5 minutes; remove from pans to wire racks. **Yield:** about 1-1/2 dozen.

Getting in the Theme of Things

Add a festive atmosphere to any special occasion with these themed menus featuring fun recipes and decorating ideas.

CAUSE TO CELEBRATE. Clockwise from upper left: Good Gobblin' for a Ghostly Night (p. 302), Luncheon Hams It Up (p. 300), Rack Up Points with Bowling Party (p. 296) and Tomatoes Top Off Buffet (p. 298).

Caroling Party's in Tune with Season

By Nella Parker, Hersey, Michigan

AS A FESTIVE way to celebrate Christmas Eve, I invited my four sisters and their families for a caroling theme dinner. Then we all bundled up for an evening of singing carols and delivering cookies to shut-ins and our local police and fire departments.

I had a jolly time thinking up the menu of Yuletide Brochettes, Fa-La-La Prosciutto Puffs, Noel Salmon Cheesecake and Merry Note Cookies.

Most of the preparations for the colorful Yuletide Brochettes can be done the day before. I precooked the sausage, marinated the chicken and cut up the zucchini and peppers so everything was ready to

skewer and simply broil on Christmas Eve.

Fa-La-La Prosciutto Puffs are light, tasty treats that practically melt in your mouth. Young and old alike said how much they enjoyed eating one...then another...and another!

During the holidays or any time you're expecting a crowd, Noel Salmon Cheesecake is sure to be a popular appetizer. The mild smoked salmon flavor is delicious.

Merry Note Cookies—made from a recipe similar to one my mom always used—were a fitting dessert before we set out for caroling.

After our evening of singing and spreading cheer throughout our community, we arrived back at my house to sit around the cozy fireplace. Why not plan a similar evening for your family? It could become a tradition they'll treasure!

Yuletide Brochettes

Prep: 15 min. + marinating   **Cook:** 15 min.

- 2-1/4 pounds boneless skinless chicken breasts
- 1/4 cup chicken broth
- 1/4 cup Dijon mustard
- 2 tablespoons olive oil
- 2 teaspoons Worcestershire sauce
- 1 garlic clove, minced
- 1/2 teaspoon dried thyme
- 1/4 teaspoon salt
- 1/8 teaspoon pepper
- 4 Italian sausage links
- 2 medium zucchini
- 2 medium sweet red peppers
- 2 medium sweet yellow peppers

Cut chicken into 32 cubes. In a large resealable plastic bag, combine the broth, mustard, olive oil, Worcestershire sauce, garlic, thyme, salt and pepper. Add chicken; seal bag and turn to coat. Refrigerate overnight.

In a large skillet, cook sausages over medium heat until juices run clear. Cut each sausage into eight slices. Cut each zucchini into 16 slices. Cut each pepper into 16 chunks. Drain and discard marinade.

On metal or soaked wooden skewers, thread chicken, sausage, zucchini and peppers. Broil 6 in. from the heat for 15-20 minutes or until chicken juices run clear and vegetables are tender, turning occasionally. **Yield:** 16 servings.

Fa-La-La Prosciutto Puffs

Prep: 15 min.   **Bake:** 20 min.

- 1 cup water
- 6 tablespoons butter
- 1/8 teaspoon pepper
- 1 cup all-purpose flour
- 5 eggs
- 3/4 cup finely chopped prosciutto *or* fully cooked ham
- 1/4 cup minced chives

In a large saucepan, bring the water, butter and pepper to a boil. Add flour all at once and stir until a smooth ball forms. Remove from the heat; let stand for 5 minutes. Add eggs, one at a time, beating well after each addition. Continue beating until mixture is smooth and shiny.

Stir in prosciutto and chives. Drop by heaping teaspoonfuls onto greased baking sheets. Bake at 425°

for 18-22 minutes or until golden brown. Remove to wire racks. Serve warm. Refrigerate leftovers. **Yield:** 4-1/2 dozen.

Noel Salmon Cheesecake

Prep: 15 min.   **Bake:** 45 min. + cooling

- 1/2 cup pumpernickel bread crumbs
- 4 packages (8 ounces *each*) cream cheese, softened
- 1/2 cup heavy whipping cream
- 1/8 teaspoon pepper
- 4 eggs, lightly beaten
- 8 ounces smoked salmon, chopped
- 1/3 cup chopped green onions
- Assorted crackers

Grease bottom and sides of a 9-in. springform pan. Sprinkle bread crumbs into pan, coating bottom and sides; set aside. In a bowl, beat cream cheese until fluffy. Beat in cream and pepper. Add eggs; beat on low speed just until combined. Fold in salmon and onions.

Wrap a double thickness of heavy-duty foil around bottom of prepared pan. Pour the salmon mixture into pan. Place in a large baking pan. Fill larger pan with hot water to a depth of 1-1/2 in. Bake at 325° for 45-55 minutes or until center is almost set. Cool on a wire rack for 1 hour (cheesecake may crack while cooling). Refrigerate overnight. Remove foil and sides of pan. Serve cheesecake with crackers. **Yield:** 16 servings.

Merry Note Cookies

Prep: 25 min. + chilling   **Bake:** 10 min.

- 1 cup butter, softened
- 1 package (3 ounces) cream cheese, softened
- 1 cup sugar
- 1 egg
- 1 teaspoon vanilla extract
- 2-1/2 cups all-purpose flour
- 1/4 teaspoon salt
- Red and green colored sugar

In a large mixing bowl, cream the butter, cream cheese and sugar. Beat in egg and vanilla. Combine the flour and salt; gradually beat into creamed mixture. Cover and refrigerate the dough for 2 hours.

On a lightly floured surface, roll out dough to 1/4-in. thickness. Cut with a 3-3/4-in. x 2-1/2-in. musical note cookie cutter dipped in flour. Place 2 in. apart on ungreased baking sheets. Sprinkle with colored sugar. Bake at 375° for 8-10 minutes or until the edges are golden brown. Remove to wire racks to cool. **Yield:** about 4 dozen.

A Winning Family Game Night

By Leslie Dumm, Cleveland Heights, Ohio

TO CELEBRATE all of our birthdays, which fall within 1 week, three friends and I planned a game night party for our families. It was a real winner!

We gathered favorite board, card and dice games to fill the evening with activities. Plus, food was a big part of the fun. A checkerboard of cheese and crackers, Par-Cheesy Pizza, I Spy Salad and High Roller Cake were popular items on the buffet.

When the gang arrived, we began by munching on the cheese-and-cracker checkerboard. To make this fun appetizer, simply alternate square and round crackers in eight rows of eight crackers each to form the checkerboard. Arrange cubes on cheddar and Swiss cheese on the crackers for edible checkers (see photo at far right).

Par-Cheesy Pizza has a hearty bread-like crust and toppings to resemble a Parcheesi game board. In each corner, there is a large slice of salami to mimic the game's starting circles. Strips of onions and red pepper form the paths around the board...and sliced olives serve as the pawns.

We also dug into I Spy Salad, named after a memory game we played with the kids. This colorful layered salad is chock-full of flavorful ingredients and garnished with cute hard-cooked egg-and-olive eyes on the top. Perky eyebrows are made with the sliced white portion of the eggs.

We were "on a roll" right through dessert! Our eye-catching High Roller Cake was shaped like a giant die with chocolate sandwich cookie spots. The level of difficulty for making this tender chocolate cube is "Easy"!

There's no need to wait until a birthday. If you're game for a gathering, just pick up on our theme—and put your own spin on it!

Par-Cheesy Pizza

Prep: 45 min.   **Bake:** 15 min.

1 **pound frozen bread dough**
4 **thin slices salami**
1 **to 2 medium onions**
1 **to 2 large sweet red peppers**
3/4 **cup pizza sauce**
1-1/2 **cups (6 ounces) shredded mozzarella cheese**
4 **to 6 stuffed olives, halved**

Thaw dough according to package directions. Cut the salami into 2-1/2-in. rounds. Cut onions and red peppers into 2-in. x 1/2-in. strips. On a lightly greased baking sheet, roll dough into a 12-in. square.

Spread with pizza sauce. Sprinkle with cheese. Arrange the salami, onions and peppers over top to resemble a Parcheesi board. Bake at 400° for 15-20 minutes or until crust is lightly browned and cheese is melted. Top with olives. **Yield:** 6 servings.

I Spy Salad

Prep/Total Time: 25 min.

2-1/2 **cups torn iceberg lettuce**
2-1/2 **cups torn romaine**
3 **green onions, sliced**
1 **cup chopped sweet red pepper**
1 **cup chopped green pepper**
1/2 **cup sliced fresh mushrooms**
2 **radishes, thinly sliced**
4 **bacon strips, cooked and crumbled**
1/4 **cup shredded cheddar cheese**
2 **medium tomatoes, halved and sliced**
1 **small cucumber, thinly sliced**
2 **hard-cooked eggs, halved lengthwise**
1 **ripe olive, halved**
Salad dressing of your choice

In a 2-qt. salad bowl, layer the first nine ingredients in the order given. Arrange tomatoes and cucumber around the edge. Place two egg halves in the middle of salad for eyes; top with olive halves for pupils.

Remove yolk from the remaining egg halves. For eyelashes, cut six thin slices from egg white; place above eyes (refrigerate leftover egg for another use). Serve the salad with dressing of your choice. **Yield:** 6 servings.

High Roller Cake

Prep: 45 min.   **Bake:** 30 min. + cooling

6 **cups all-purpose flour**
4 **cups sugar**
3/4 **cup baking cocoa**
4 **teaspoons baking soda**
2 **teaspoons salt**
4 **cups water**
1-1/2 **cups vegetable oil**
1/4 **cup white vinegar**
4 **teaspoons vanilla extract**
3 **cans (16 ounces *each*) vanilla frosting**
10 **cream-filled chocolate sandwich cookies**

In a large mixing bowl, combine flour, sugar, cocoa, baking soda and salt. Add the water, oil, vinegar and vanilla; mix well. Pour into two greased and floured 13-in. x 9-in. x 2-in. baking pans.

Bake at 350° for 28-33 minutes or until a toothpick inserted near the center comes out clean. Cool for 10 minutes before removing from pans to wire racks to cool completely.

Cut two 6-in. squares from each cake (save remaining cake for another use). Spread the frosting between layers and over top and sides of cake. Split sandwich cookies apart; arrange on the cake (filling side down) for die spots. **Yield:** 18 servings.

Rack Up Points with Bowling Party

By Lizz Loder, Fox Point, Wisconsin

AT THE END of the bowling season a few years ago, my friend Linda Tesch and I threw a Perfect Game Party for our team.

While we rarely scored more than 150 on any given game during the entire season, this gathering scored a perfect 300 for fun and fellowship!

We served Kingpin Cheese Spread, Spare-Rib Sandwiches, 7-10 Split Layered Salad and Roll-a-Strike Sundaes. Just about everything for this fun menu can be made ahead of time, so there was no last-minute rushing around. And that means more time to enjoy your guests!

With a warm-up of Kingpin Cheese Spread and crackers, we were off to a great start. The creamy spread holds its shape well and is easy to form.

As an alternative to the bowling pin, you could

make it look like half a bowling ball. Simply cover the ball with chopped black olives, leaving three circles open for the finger holes.

Spare-Rib Sandwiches scored high with everyone. The tender pulled barbecued pork has a pleasant hint of lemon that you don't expect.

And although bowlers tend to frown when they leave a split, the team was all smiles over 7-10 Split Layered Salad. This potato salad is so pretty layered in a glass bowl and is very tasty.

For a season-ending splurge, we made Roll-a-Strike Sundaes. These yummy banana splits are topped with a velvety chocolate sauce that's scrumptious...and easy to make!

Our teammates were bowled over by the party! And we're happy to share the idea, hoping others can "spare" the time to spend with friends at a fun-filled gathering like ours.

Kingpin Cheese Spread

Prep: 20 min. + chilling

- 3 **packages (8 ounces** *each***) cream cheese, softened**
- 1 **cup (4 ounces) shredded sharp cheddar cheese**
- 1 **envelope ranch salad dressing mix**
- 2 **sweet red pepper rings**
Assorted crackers

In a large mixing bowl, beat the cream cheese, cheddar cheese and dressing mix until combined. Cover and refrigerate overnight.

On a serving platter, form cheese spread into the shape of a bowling pin. Add pepper rings at the neck of pin for stripes, trimming to fit if necessary. Remove from the refrigerator 15 minutes before serving. Serve with crackers. **Yield:** 3 cups.

Spare-Rib Sandwiches

Prep: 15 min.   **Cook:** 2 hours

- 3 **pounds boneless country-style pork ribs**
- 1 **can (12 ounces) frozen lemonade concentrate, thawed**
- 1-1/2 **cups water**
- 3 **tablespoons chili sauce**
- 1 **tablespoon brown sugar**
- 1-1/2 **teaspoons cider vinegar**
- 2 **teaspoons cornstarch**
Sandwich buns, split

Place the pork ribs in a Dutch oven and cover with water. Bring to a boil. Reduce heat; cover and simmer for 1 hour.

Drain; return ribs to pan. In a small bowl, combine the lemonade concentrate, water, chili sauce, brown sugar and vinegar. Pour two-thirds of the sauce over ribs; set remaining sauce aside. Cover and cook over medium heat for 50-55 minutes or until pork is tender and sauce is thickened.

When cool enough to handle, shred meat with two forks. In a large saucepan, whisk cornstarch and reserved sauce. Bring to a boil; cook and stir for 2 minutes or until thickened. Add shredded pork; heat through. Serve on buns. **Yield:** 8 servings.

7-10 Split Layered Salad

Prep: 30 min. + chilling

- 3 **cups torn romaine**
- 1 **package (10 ounces) frozen peas, thawed**
- 6 **medium potatoes, cooked and diced**
- 1/2 **to 1 cup diced red onion**
- 1 **cup mayonnaise**
- 1 **cup (4 ounces) shredded cheddar cheese**
- 1 **pound sliced bacon, diced and cooked**

In a 3- or 4-qt. glass bowl, layer the romaine, peas, potatoes and onion. Carefully spread mayonnaise over the top. Sprinkle with the cheese and bacon. Cover and chill for at least 2 hours before serving. **Yield:** 8 servings.

Roll-a-Strike Sundaes

Prep/Total Time: 20 min.

- 2 **cups (12 ounces) semisweet chocolate chips**
- 2/3 **cup heavy whipping cream**
- 3/4 **teaspoon cherry extract**
- 6 **medium firm bananas, cut in half lengthwise**
- 6 **scoops** *each* **strawberry, vanilla and chocolate ice cream**
Whipped topping, chopped nuts and maraschino cherries with stems

In a small heavy saucepan, cook and stir the chocolate chips and cream over low heat until smooth and blended. Remove from the heat. Stir in extract and keep warm.

Place two banana pieces in each of six shallow serving dishes. Top each with a scoop of strawberry, vanilla and chocolate ice cream. Drizzle with the warm chocolate sauce. Garnish with whipped topping, nuts and a cherry. **Yield:** 6 servings.

Tomatoes Top Off Buffet

By Faye Wortman, Evansville, Indiana

MY GARDEN was in full tomato production when my turn came up to host our Seedlings Garden Club monthly meeting. The bumper crop inspired me to have a theme luncheon.

Planning the menu for 14 club members, I chose a lineup of tomato dishes including Italian Tomato Salad, Tomatoes with Herb Stuffing, Tomato Eggplant Bake and Tomato Onion Pie.

My guests were delighted with the colorful fresh-tasting Italian Tomato Salad. It has a wonderful dressing—made with fresh basil and parsley—to comple-

ment the juicy tomato slices.

Everyone agreed that Tomatoes with Herb Stuffing really showcased my theme. The recipe uses hollowed-out whole tomatoes as cups for savory bread stuffing.

They also dug into Tomato Eggplant Bake. Cheesy and delicious, this casserole features a crisp crumb topping. It's a good meatless entree for a summer-time meal.

Tomato Onion Pie offers a tempting mix of flavors. The quiche-like dish is attractive and easy to cut.

As favors, I prepared two little booklets. One included all the recipes I served, plus several other of

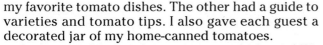

my favorite tomato dishes. The other had a guide to varieties and tomato tips. I also gave each guest a decorated jar of my home-canned tomatoes.

It was a red-letter day...tomato red, that is! We talked tomatoes, ate tomatoes and learned more about them. The idea could also be adapted for any type of produce party. How about it, gardeners?

Italian Tomato Salad

Prep/Total Time: 15 min.

     5 tablespoons olive oil
4-1/2 teaspoons red wine vinegar
     2 tablespoons minced fresh basil
     1 tablespoon minced fresh parsley
     1 garlic clove, peeled
   1/4 teaspoon salt
   1/8 teaspoon pepper
     4 medium tomatoes, sliced
     1 small red onion, thinly sliced and
         separated into rings

In a blender, combine the first seven ingredients; cover and process until smooth. Arrange the tomatoes in a shallow serving dish; top with onion and dressing. Refrigerate until serving. **Yield:** 6 servings.

Tomatoes with Herb Stuffing

Prep: 30 min.   **Bake:** 25 min.

     1 cup chopped celery
     1 cup chopped onion
   1/2 cup butter
     2 cups *each* cubed day-old white, whole
         wheat and rye bread
   1/4 cup minced fresh parsley
     2 teaspoons rubbed sage
     1 teaspoon dried thyme
   1/2 teaspoon salt
   1/2 teaspoon pepper
   1/4 cup condensed chicken broth, undiluted
     8 medium tomatoes

In a Dutch oven, saute celery and onion in butter until tender. Remove from the heat. Stir in the bread cubes, parsley, sage, thyme, salt and pepper. Add broth; toss to combine.

Cut a thin slice off the top of each tomato. Scoop out pulp, leaving 1/2-in. shells. Invert tomatoes onto paper towels to drain. Spoon about 1/3 cup stuffing into each tomato.

Place in a greased 11-in. x 7-in. x 2-in. baking dish. Place remaining stuffing around tomatoes. Bake, uncovered, at 350° for 25-30 minutes or until tomatoes are tender. **Yield:** 8 servings.

Tomato Eggplant Bake

Prep: 15 min. + standing   **Bake:** 30 min.

     1 medium eggplant (1 pound), peeled and
         cut into 1/2-inch slices
Salt to taste
     1 large tomato, sliced
     1 medium onion, sliced
     6 tablespoons butter, melted, *divided*
   1/2 teaspoon dried basil
   1/2 cup dry bread crumbs
     4 slices mozzarella cheese, cut into thirds
     2 tablespoons grated Parmesan cheese

Place eggplant slices in a colander over a plate. Sprinkle with salt; toss. Let stand 30 minutes. Rinse and drain well.

Layer the eggplant, tomato and onion in a lightly greased 13-in. x 9-in. x 2-in. baking dish. Drizzle with 4 tablespoons butter; sprinkle with basil. Cover and bake at 450° for 20 minutes.

Toss the bread crumbs and remaining butter. Arrange mozzarella cheese over the vegetables; sprinkle with crumb mixture and Parmesan cheese. Bake, uncovered, for 10 minutes or until the cheese is bubbly. **Yield:** 6 servings.

Tomato Onion Pie

Prep: 30 min.   **Bake:** 35 min. + standing

     8 cups thinly sliced sweet onions
     2 tablespoons butter
   12 bacon strips, cooked and drained
     2 cups soft bread crumbs
     3 to 4 medium tomatoes, thinly sliced
     2 cups (8 ounces) shredded cheddar cheese
     3 eggs
   1/4 teaspoon salt
   1/8 teaspoon pepper
Additional tomato slices, optional

In a large skillet, saute onions in butter until tender. Crumble nine bacon strips; set remaining strips aside. Place the bread crumbs in a greased 9-in. deep-dish pie plate. Layer with half of the tomatoes, onions, crumbled bacon and cheese. Top with the remaining tomatoes, onions and crumbled bacon.

In a bowl, beat the eggs, salt and pepper; pour over the top. Sprinkle with remaining cheese. Top with reserved bacon strips. Arrange additional tomato slices around the edge if desired.

Bake at 350° for 35-40 minutes or until a knife inserted near the center comes out clean. Let stand for 10 minutes before cutting. Refrigerate leftovers. **Yield:** 6 servings.

Luncheon Hams It Up

By Wilma Bland, Proctorville, Ohio

IT WAS my turn to host a group of relatives who meet for lunch once a month, and I wanted to do something novel.

At that time, my grandsons were raising pigs for their 4-H project for the fair, which gave me the idea to have a Pig-Out Party.

I began *pigstorming* and came up with a menu of

Sow-per Glazed Ham, Silk Purse Potatoes, Snortin' Good Salad and Little Piggy Sugar Cookies.

It was such a *sowpigsticated* event that I had to rise and *swine* early the day of the party, even though I didn't get an *oink* of sleep all night.

On the table, I used a red-and-white checked cloth, bandanna-print napkins and straw place mats for a country look. The centerpiece was a piggy bank on a bed of straw.

Our gang said they never *sausage* a lunch! Sow-per Glazed Ham was an easy choice for the entree. The flavorful glaze gets its pleasant tang from fruit juice and mustard. This recipe is one I frequently fix for holidays and other special occasions.

Always a crowd-pleaser, Silk Purse Potatoes (as in "Can't make a silk purse from a sow's ear") have a delicious, creamy cheese sauce. I've taken this dish to many a potluck.

Bacon crumbles, of course, are an important layer in the Snortin' Good Salad. In this make-ahead side dish, you can substitute ingredients to suit your taste or to showcase whatever fresh vegetables happen to be in season.

Dessert took shape with a platter of Little Piggy Sugar Cookies. The dough can be mixed in a flash and is easy to roll and cut.

I'm happy to share this theme, hoping some of you will get out your *pigtionary* and come up with many more ideas for a Pig-Out Party of your own!

Sow-per Glazed Ham

Prep: 10 min. **Bake:** 2-1/2 hours + standing

    1 fully cooked bone-in half ham (8 to 9
        pounds)
    3 tablespoons whole cloves
    2 cups packed brown sugar
  1/2 cup unsweetened apple juice *or* fruit juice
        of your choice
    2 teaspoons ground mustard

Place ham on a rack in a shallow roasting pan. Score the surface of the ham, making 1/2-in.-deep diamond shapes; insert a clove in each diamond. Bake, uncovered, at 325° for 2 hours.

For glaze, combine brown sugar, juice and mustard; spoon some over ham. Bake 30 minutes longer or until a meat thermometer reads 140°, basting occasionally with remaining glaze. Let stand for 15 minutes before slicing. **Yield:** 16 servings.

Silk Purse Potatoes

Prep: 15 min. **Bake:** 1-1/2 hours

  1/4 cup butter
  1/4 cup all-purpose flour
    1 teaspoon salt
  1/8 teaspoon pepper
    2 cups milk
    6 slices process American cheese, cut into
        pieces
    6 medium potatoes, peeled and thinly sliced
        (about 6 cups)
    2 tablespoons chopped onion

In a large saucepan, melt butter over low heat. Stir in the flour, salt and pepper until smooth. Gradually add milk. Bring to a boil; cook and stir for 2 minutes or until thickened. Remove from the heat; stir in the cheese until melted. Stir in the potatoes and onion.

Transfer to a greased shallow 2-qt. baking dish. Cover and bake at 325° for 1 hour. Uncover; bake 30-40 minutes longer or until potatoes are tender. **Yield:** 6-8 servings.

Snortin' Good Salad

Prep: 15 min. + chilling

    1 medium head iceberg lettuce, torn
    1 medium head cauliflower, cut into florets
    1 medium red onion, sliced and separated
        into rings
    1 package (10 ounces) frozen peas, thawed
  1/2 cup crumbled cooked bacon
    1 cup mayonnaise
  1/4 cup sugar

In a large glass salad bowl, layer the lettuce, cauliflower, onion, peas and bacon. Combine the mayonnaise and sugar; spoon over salad. Cover and refrigerate for 2 hours or overnight. Toss just before serving. **Yield:** 10-14 servings.

Little Piggy Sugar Cookies

Prep: 15 min. + chilling **Bake:** 20 min. + cooling

  3/4 cup butter, softened
    1 cup sugar
    2 eggs
    2 tablespoons milk
  1/2 teaspoon almond extract
3-1/4 cups all-purpose flour
    2 teaspoons baking powder
Tinted frosting

In a large mixing bowl, cream the butter and sugar. Beat in the eggs, milk and extract. Combine the flour and baking powder; gradually add to creamed mixture. Cover and refrigerate for 2-3 hours or until the dough is easy to handle.

On a lightly floured surface, roll out dough to 1/8-in. thickness. Cut out with a 3-in. pig-shaped cookie cutter dipped in flour. Place 1 in. apart on ungreased baking sheets.

Bake at 375° for 7-9 minutes or until edges begin to brown. Remove to wire racks to cool. Outline cutouts with tinted frosting. Put on two dots for nose if desired. **Yield:** about 4 dozen.

Good Gobblin' for a Ghostly Night

By Darla Webster, Meriden, Iowa

TRICK-OR-TREATING is difficult in our rural area, so I planned a Halloween party at our home for our son, Ward, and his friends.

Holiday snacks were a big part of the fun! As the young guests arrived, we joked about "finger food," then offered them Fingers of Fright. Their eyes widened at the sight of these chewy digits.

I made hearty Spooky Joes, served open-faced so everyone could see slices of cheese cut into Halloween shapes topping the beef. Halloween Caramel Apples, Spider Cupcakes and a Great Pumpkin Brownie rounded out the menu.

A chocolate drizzle sprinkled with crushed candy makes ordinary caramel apples extra yummy.

Spider Cupcakes are creepy—and easy! Make a cupcake into a spider by adding a half-marshmallow "body" under the frosting, licorice legs and mini M&M eyes. Add chocolate sprinkles for a "hairy" effect.

Our kids beg for a Great Pumpkin Brownie every year. To make this eye-catching treat, bake brownie batter in a pizza pan, spread with orange-tinted frosting and let the kids design a jack-o-lantern.

It wasn't very tricky to pull off this party. I'm happy to share the idea with other parents who may want to scare up some tasty Halloween fun.

Spooky Joes

Prep/Total Time: 20 min.

- **2 pounds ground beef**
- **2 cans (10-3/4 ounces *each*) condensed tomato soup, undiluted**
- **1 teaspoon onion salt**
- **2 cups (8 ounces) shredded cheddar cheese**
- **8 hamburger buns, split**
- **8 slices cheddar cheese**

In a large skillet, cook beef over medium heat until no longer pink; drain. Stir in soup and onion salt; heat through. Stir in shredded cheddar cheese until melted.

Spoon about 1/2 cup onto bottom of each bun. Cut cheese slices with 2-1/2-in. Halloween cookie cutters; place over beef mixture. Serve bun tops on the side.
Yield: 8 servings.

Halloween Caramel Apples

Prep: 15 min. + chilling

- 1 package (11-1/2 ounces) milk chocolate chips
- 2 tablespoons shortening
- 2 packages (14 ounces *each*) caramels
- 1/4 cup water
- 8 large tart apples, room temperature
- 8 Popsicle sticks
- 3 to 4 Butterfinger candy bars (2.1 ounces *each*), coarsely crushed

In a microwave-safe bowl, melt chocolate chips and shortening; set aside. In another microwave-safe bowl, microwave the caramels and water, uncovered, on high for 1 minute; stir. Heat 30-45 seconds longer or until caramels are melted.

Line a baking sheet with waxed paper and grease the paper; set aside. Wash and thoroughly dry apples. Insert a Popsicle stick into each; dip into caramel mixture, turning to coat. Place on prepared pan. Drizzle with melted chocolate. Sprinkle with crushed candy bars. Refrigerate until set. **Yield:** 8 servings.

Editor's Note: This recipe was tested in a 1,100-watt microwave.

Spider Cupcakes

Prep: 30 min.   **Bake:** 25 min. + cooling

- 1 package (18-1/4 ounces) chocolate cake mix
- 2 cups sugar
- 1/2 cup baking cocoa
- 1/2 cup butter, cubed
- 1/2 cup milk
- 2 teaspoons vanilla extract
- 12 large marshmallows
- Chocolate sprinkles
- 48 M&M miniature baking bits
- 192 pieces black licorice (3 inches)

Prepare cake batter according to package directions. Fill 24 greased or paper-lined muffin cups. Bake at 350° for 21-26 minutes or until a toothpick comes out clean. Cool for 5 minutes before removing from pans to wire racks to cool completely.

For frosting, combine sugar, cocoa, butter and milk in a small saucepan. Bring to a boil over medium heat, stirring constantly. Remove from heat; stir in vanilla. Cool to 110°. Beat with a wooden spoon until thickened and mixture begins to lose its gloss, about 8 minutes.

Cut marshmallows in half widthwise; place a half on each cupcake. Frost marshmallow and top of cupcake. Dip cupcakes in chocolate sprinkles. Place a dab of frosting on each baking bit and press on cupcakes for

eyes. For spider legs, use a metal or wooden skewer to poke four holes on opposite sides of cupcake; insert a piece of licorice into each hole. **Yield:** 2 dozen.

Great Pumpkin Brownie

Prep: 25 min.   **Bake:** 20 min. + cooling

- 1 package fudge brownie mix (13-inch x 9-inch pan size)
- 1 can (16 ounces) vanilla frosting
- Orange paste food coloring
- 16 green milk chocolate M&M's
- 22 yellow milk chocolate M&M's
- 13 orange milk chocolate M&M's
- 8 dark brown milk chocolate M&M's
- 20 pieces candy corn

Prepare brownie batter according to package directions for fudge-like brownies. Spread on a greased 12-in. pizza pan to within 1 in. of edges. Bake at 350° for 20-25 minutes or until a toothpick inserted near the center comes out clean. Cool on a wire rack.

Tint frosting orange; frost entire top of brownie. For stem, arrange green M&M's in a square pattern at top of pumpkin. For each eye, arrange 11 yellow M&M's in a triangle. For nose, arrange orange M&M's in a triangle. For mouth, place brown M&M's in a horizontal line; surround with candy corn, tips pointing out. Cut into squares to serve. **Yield:** 16-20 servings.

Fingers of Fright

Prep/Total Time: 10 min.

- 5 red, black *and/or* green jelly beans
- 10 circus peanut candies

Cut jelly beans in half lengthwise. Press each half into the end of a circus peanut. **Yield:** 10 servings.

Substitutions & Equivalents

Equivalent Measures

3 teaspoons	=	1 tablespoon	**16 tablespoons**	=	1 cup
4 tablespoons	=	1/4 cup	**2 cups**	=	1 pint
5-1/3 tablespoons	=	1/3 cup	**4 cups**	=	1 quart
8 tablespoons	=	1/2 cup	**4 quarts**	=	1 gallon

Food Equivalents

Grains

Macaroni	1 cup (3-1/2 ounces) uncooked	=	2-1/2 cups cooked
Noodles, Medium	3 cups (4 ounces) uncooked	=	4 cups cooked
Popcorn	1/3 to 1/2 cup unpopped	=	8 cups popped
Rice, Long Grain	1 cup uncooked	=	3 cups cooked
Rice, Quick-Cooking	1 cup uncooked	=	2 cups cooked
Spaghetti	8 ounces uncooked	=	4 cups cooked

Crumbs

Bread	1 slice	=	3/4 cup soft crumbs, 1/4 cup fine dry crumbs
Graham Crackers	7 squares	=	1/2 cup finely crushed
Buttery Round Crackers	12 crackers	=	1/2 cup finely crushed
Saltine Crackers	14 crackers	=	1/2 cup finely crushed

Fruits

Bananas	1 medium	=	1/3 cup mashed
Lemons	1 medium	=	3 tablespoons juice, 2 teaspoons grated peel
Limes	1 medium	=	2 tablespoons juice, 1-1/2 teaspoons grated peel
Oranges	1 medium	=	1/4 to 1/3 cup juice, 4 teaspoons grated peel

Vegetables

Cabbage	1 head	=	5 cups shredded	**Green Pepper**	1 large	=	1 cup chopped
Carrots	1 pound	=	3 cups shredded	**Mushrooms**	1/2 pound	=	3 cups sliced
Celery	1 rib	=	1/2 cup chopped	**Onions**	1 medium	=	1/2 cup chopped
Corn	1 ear fresh	=	2/3 cup kernels	**Potatoes**	3 medium	=	2 cups cubed

Nuts

Almonds	1 pound	=	3 cups chopped	**Pecan Halves**	1 pound	=	4-1/2 cups chopped
Ground Nuts	3-3/4 ounces	=	1 cup	**Walnuts**	1 pound	=	3-3/4 cups chopped

Easy Substitutions

When you need...		Use...
Baking Powder	1 teaspoon	1/2 teaspoon cream of tartar + 1/4 teaspoon baking soda
Buttermilk	1 cup	1 tablespoon lemon juice *or* vinegar + enough milk to measure 1 cup (let stand 5 minutes before using)
Cornstarch	1 tablespoon	2 tablespoons all-purpose flour
Honey	1 cup	1-1/4 cups sugar + 1/4 cup water
Half-and-Half Cream	1 cup	1 tablespoon melted butter + enough whole milk to measure 1 cup
Onion	1 small, chopped (1/3 cup)	1 teaspoon onion powder *or* 1 tablespoon dried minced onion
Tomato Juice	1 cup	1/2 cup tomato sauce + 1/2 cup water
Tomato Sauce	2 cups	3/4 cup tomato paste + 1 cup water
Unsweetened Chocolate	1 square (1 ounce)	3 tablespoons baking cocoa + 1 tablespoon shortening *or* oil
Whole Milk	1 cup	1/2 cup evaporated milk + 1/2 cup water

Cooking Terms

HERE'S a quick reference for some of the cooking terms used in *Taste of Home* recipes:

Baste—To moisten food with melted butter, pan drippings, marinades or other liquid to add more flavor and juiciness.

Beat—A rapid movement to combine ingredients using a fork, spoon, wire whisk or electric mixer.

Blend—To combine ingredients until *just* mixed.

Boil—To heat liquids until bubbles form that cannot be "stirred down". In the case of water, the temperature will reach 212°.

Bone—To remove all meat from the bone before cooking.

Cream—To beat ingredients together to a smooth consistency, usually in the case of butter and sugar for baking.

Dash—A small amount of seasoning, less than 1/8 teaspoon. If using a shaker, a dash would comprise a quick flip of the container.

Dredge—To coat foods with flour or other dry ingredients. Most often done with pot roasts and stew meat before browning.

Fold—To incorporate several ingredients by careful and gentle turning with a spatula. Used generally with beaten egg whites or whipped cream when mixing into the rest of the ingredients to keep the batter light.

Julienne—To cut foods into long thin strips much like matchsticks. Used most often for salads and stir-fry dishes.

Mince—To cut into very fine pieces. Used often for garlic or fresh herbs.

Parboil—To cook partially, usually used in the case of chicken, sausages and vegetables.

Partially set—Describes the consistency of gelatin after it has been chilled for a small amount of time. Mixture should resemble the consistency of egg whites.

Puree—To process foods to a smooth mixture. Can be prepared in an electric blender, food processor, food mill or sieve.

Saute—To fry quickly in a small amount of fat, stirring almost constantly. Most often done with onions, mushrooms and other chopped vegetables.

Score—To cut slits partway through the outer surface of foods. Often used with ham or flank steak.

Stir-Fry—To cook meats and/or vegetables with a constant stirring motion in a small amount of oil in a wok or skillet over high heat.

Guide to Cooking with Popular Herbs

HERB	APPETIZERS SALADS	BREADS/EGGS SAUCES/CHEESE	VEGETABLES PASTA	MEAT POULTRY	FISH SHELLFISH
BASIL	Green, Potato & Tomato Salads, Salad Dressings, Stewed Fruit	Breads, Fondue & Egg Dishes, Dips, Marinades, Sauces	Mushrooms, Tomatoes, Squash, Pasta, Bland Vegetables	Broiled, Roast Meat & Poultry Pies, Stews, Stuffing	Baked, Broiled & Poached Fish, Shellfish
BAY LEAF	Seafood Cocktail, Seafood Salad, Tomato Aspic, Stewed Fruit	Egg Dishes, Gravies, Marinades, Sauces	Dried Bean Dishes, Beets, Carrots, Onions, Potatoes, Rice, Squash	Corned Beef, Tongue Meat & Poultry Stews	Poached Fish, Shellfish, Fish Stews
CHIVES	Mixed Vegetable, Green, Potato & Tomato Salads, Salad Dressings	Egg & Cheese Dishes, Cream Cheese, Cottage Cheese, Gravies, Sauces	Hot Vegetables, Potatoes	Broiled Poultry, Poultry & Meat Pies, Stews, Casseroles	Baked Fish, Fish Casseroles, Fish Stews, Shellfish
DILL	Seafood Cocktail, Green, Potato & Tomato Salads, Salad Dressings	Breads, Egg & Cheese Dishes, Cream Cheese, Fish & Meat Sauces	Beans, Beets, Cabbage, Carrots, Cauliflower, Peas, Squash, Tomatoes	Beef, Veal Roasts, Lamb, Steaks, Chops, Stews, Roast & Creamed Poultry	Baked, Broiled, Poached & Stuffed Fish, Shellfish
GARLIC	All Salads, Salad Dressings	Fondue, Poultry Sauces, Fish & Meat Marinades	Beans, Eggplant, Potatoes, Rice, Tomatoes	Roast Meats, Meat & Poultry Pies, Hamburgers, Casseroles, Stews	Broiled Fish, Shellfish, Fish Stews, Casseroles
MARJORAM	Seafood Cocktail, Green, Poultry & Seafood Salads	Breads, Cheese Spreads, Egg & Cheese Dishes, Gravies, Sauces	Carrots, Eggplant, Peas, Onions, Potatoes, Dried Bean Dishes, Spinach	Roast Meats & Poultry, Meat & Poultry Pies, Stews & Casseroles	Baked, Broiled & Stuffed Fish, Shellfish
MUSTARD	Fresh Green Salads, Prepared Meat, Macaroni & Potato Salads, Salad Dressings	Biscuits, Egg & Cheese Dishes, Sauces	Baked Beans, Cabbage, Eggplant, Squash, Dried Beans, Mushrooms, Pasta	Chops, Steaks, Ham, Pork, Poultry, Cold Meats	Shellfish
OREGANO	Green, Poultry & Seafood Salads	Breads, Egg & Cheese Dishes, Meat, Poultry & Vegetable Sauces	Artichokes, Cabbage, Eggplant, Squash, Dried Beans, Mushrooms, Pasta	Broiled, Roast Meats, Meat & Poultry Pies, Stews, Casseroles	Baked, Broiled & Poached Fish, Shellfish
PARSLEY	Green, Potato, Seafood & Vegetable Salads	Biscuits, Breads, Egg & Cheese Dishes, Gravies, Sauces	Asparagus, Beets, Eggplant, Squash, Dried Beans, Mushrooms, Pasta	Meat Loaf, Meat & Poultry Pies, Stews & Casseroles, Stuffing	Fish Stews, Stuffed Fish
ROSEMARY	Fruit Cocktail, Fruit & Green Salads	Biscuits, Egg Dishes, Herb Butter, Cream Cheese, Marinades, Sauces	Beans, Broccoli, Peas, Cauliflower, Mushrooms, Baked Potatoes, Parsnips	Roast Meat, Poultry & Meat Pies, Stews & Casseroles, Stuffing	Stuffed Fish, Shellfish
SAGE		Breads, Fondue, Egg & Cheese Dishes, Spreads, Gravies, Sauces	Beans, Beets, Onions, Peas, Spinach, Squash, Tomatoes	Roast Meat, Poultry, Meat Loaf, Stews, Stuffing	Baked, Poached & Stuffed Fish
TARRAGON	Seafood Cocktail, Avocado Salads, Salad Dressings	Cheese Spreads, Marinades, Sauces, Egg Dishes	Asparagus, Beans, Beets, Carrots, Mushrooms, Peas, Squash, Spinach	Steaks, Poultry, Roast Meats, Casseroles & Stews	Baked, Broiled & Poached Fish, Shellfish
THYME	Seafood Cocktail, Green, Poultry, Seafood & Vegetable Salads	Biscuits, Breads, Egg & Cheese Dishes, Sauces, Spreads	Beets, Carrots, Mushrooms, Onions, Peas, Eggplant, Spinach, Potatoes	Roast Meat, Poultry & Meat Loaf, Meat & Poultry Pies, Stews & Casseroles	Baked, Broiled & Stuffed Fish, Shellfish, Fish Stews

General Recipe Index

This handy index lists every recipe by food category, major ingredient and/or cooking method, so you can easily locate recipes to suit your needs.

✓ Recipe includes Nutritional Analysis and Diabetic Exchanges.

✓ Recipe includes Nutritional Analysis and Diabetic Exchanges.

✓ *Recipe includes Nutritional Analysis and Diabetic Exchanges.*

✓ Recipe includes Nutritional Analysis and Diabetic Exchanges.

✓ Recipe includes Nutritional Analysis and Diabetic Exchanges.

✓ Recipe includes Nutritional Analysis and Diabetic Exchanges.

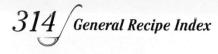

✓ Recipe includes Nutritional Analysis and Diabetic Exchanges.

✓ Recipe includes Nutritional Analysis and Diabetic Exchanges.

✓ *Recipe includes Nutritional Analysis and Diabetic Exchanges.*

Alphabetical Recipe Index

This handy index lists every recipe in alphabetical order so you can easily find your favorites.

✓ *Recipe includes Nutritional Analysis and Diabetic Exchanges.*

✓ Recipe includes Nutritional Analysis and Diabetic Exchanges.

✓ *Recipe includes Nutritional Analysis and Diabetic Exchanges.*

✓ Recipe includes Nutritional Analysis and Diabetic Exchanges.